生活即教育

社会即学校

教学做合一

MEXIC
peón de
plica el
México

# 陶 行 知 全 集

## 第 6 卷

英文著译

TREATISES, ESSAYS, ETC
论著（中译文）
LETTERS
书信（译文）
STORIES, FOLK TALES, FABLES, MYTHS AND JOKES
POEMS AND SONGS
译诗
译文

四川教育出版社
·成都·

**图书在版编目（CIP）数据**

陶行知全集．第6卷／方明主编．—2版．—成都：
四川教育出版社，2009.4
ISBN 978-7-5408-5050-0

Ⅰ.陶…　Ⅱ.方…　Ⅲ.陶行知（1891~1946）-全集
Ⅳ.G4-52

中国版本图书馆CIP数据核字（2009）第033523号

装帧设计　宁成春
责任编辑　顾　亚　李　炜
技术编辑　顾求实
责任校对　伍登富
责任印制　田东洋
出版发行　四川教育出版社
地　　址　四川省成都市锦江区三色路238号新华之星A座
邮政编码　610023
网　　址　www.chuanjiaoshe.com
印　　刷　成都市金雅迪彩色印刷有限公司
版　　次　2020年1月第3版
印　　次　2024年2月第2次印刷
成品规格　152 mm×228 mm
印　　张　50　　插页　4
字　　数　651千
全套定价　2200.00元

# 再版前言

1991年，张劲夫同志祝川版《陶行知全集》出版，在《人民日报》撰文，称这部巨著是一笔宝贵的精神财富。他在文章的结尾深情地写道："新版《陶行知全集》的出版，必将永育后人，光照千秋！"

陶行知是一位伟大的社会改革家，是中国20世纪推动现代化的先驱。他坚持以与时俱进的生活教育来推动川流不息的现代化。他热爱人民，躬亲实践，手脑并用，勇于创新，对祖国和人类所作出的贡献及取得的成果是多方面的。从《全集》中可以看出，他涉猎的领域很广，诸如对政治制度、经济发展、社会道德、国际交往、科学普及、民族团结、宗教信仰、新文字推广、环境保护、计划生育等等均有精辟的论述。陶行知又是伟大的人民诗人，其诗的大众化"独开风气之先"，《全集》中收入他的诗800余首，仍未搜齐。当然最突出的仍是他创立的生活教育理论。大家熟悉的"生活即教育"、"社会即学校"、"教学做合一"和他倡导的全民教育、终身教育、创造教育、民主教育以及他身体力行的崇高师德，是多么贴近我国的现实与未来的走向啊！

随着我国改革开放的不断深化，现代化进程的长足发展，人们对陶行知留下的这笔精神财富的借鉴意义也愈益有了更清晰的认识。近两年不少读者要求购书，有的省市成立了陶行知研究会，要求供应几十套上百套。而当年印制的新版《全集》8000套，早已罄尽。面对这日增的需求，中国陶行知研究会也希望能尽快再版。在此情势下，四川出版集团、四川教育出版社决定高质量地再版《陶行知全集》（十二卷本），并组成再版的编辑出版班子，对初版进行认真修订。《全集》约 800 万字，修订任务繁重，原来各卷的责任编辑年事已高，有的已经辞世（本套书第一版出版后辞世的编纂、出版人员未在《全集》编辑委员会和出版工作者委员会成员名单中注明）；最初使用的原稿，已交有关的博物馆和纪念馆保存，这更增添了校订的难度。出版社抽出十几位年富力强的编辑分担各卷的编务及协调工作，并请有关专家指导，两位老主编和张行可、吴琴南也全力投入，中国陶行知研究会又寄来陶行知自选集的影印本供校勘用。在共同努力下，终于按计划完成了再版的修订任务。

这次修订的主要情况如下：

一、原体例不变

开初有同志提出不论著作体例，统按时间顺序排列；有的主张前十卷不变，将最后两本补遗卷打散，分类按时序插入前面各卷。多数认为这样做不仅工作量过大，原有特色会消失，且不易查阅，故决定再版仍保持原状。

二、改错字及改正注释中的一些讹误

《全集》出版后，原来的编辑发现一些错处，特别是不少读者陆续来信指出发现的问题，这次都做了认真考证校订并逐一改正。此类改正达几百处，但仍有个别人名无从查考。这里特向来信的热心读者表示敬意和谢意。

三、几项调整

将各卷的人名索引合为一处，避免了重复，删去了该人名出现在书中的页码。人名索引刊在第九卷卷末，将原第九卷中1940年1至7月的书信移入第八卷。

抽去了两首重复的诗歌。另抽去第九卷附录中的《陶行知年表》，部分内容并入第十二卷《陶行知及其生活教育活动纪略》。抽去第十二卷附录中致陶行知的信57封，对《陶行知西旅长编》作了删节。另有少量附录因篇幅关系按时间顺序做了移动。

卷首的图片有小调整，第五卷和第三卷各换了一张照片，第四卷增加了一幅手迹。

最可喜的是增加了15篇最近得到的陶行知的佚作。一是1939年写给沈钧儒的信；二是1946年在中国人民救国会第五次大会上的报告记录；还有13篇是香港中文大学哲学博士何荣汉先生提供的英文稿：《一个金陵大学学生的自述》（1912年）、《陶文濬的伊利诺斯州立大学政治学博士入学申请表》（1914年）、《中国的道德和宗教教育》（1916年）、陶文濬致德芬道夫的4封信（1915~1917年）、《祈先生的新贡献》、《中国在转变中》、《中国的乡村教育运动》（1927年）、《生活即教育》（1932年）、《创造的教育》（1933年）、《小先生和识字运动》（1934年），这些均已翻译为中文编入第十二卷。这里，特向何荣汉先生致谢。

这次不仅认真校订内文，对书籍的开本、版式、封面等都提出了高要求，为此还请了北京的装帧设计家宁成春先生做装帧设计，力争出精品。

本书编辑中的不妥处，恳希读者指出，因为陶行知留下的这笔珍贵精神财富是属于我国人民和全世界人民的。

**编　者**

2004 年 12 月 1 日

# 《陶行知全集》
# 编辑委员会

**主　　编**　戴自俺

**副 主 编**　孙传华　苏辛涛　郭　笙　陶晓光

**分卷主编**　理论卷（第 1~4 卷）　孙传华　苏辛涛　洪　桥　祝德顺　周正章

教材卷（第 5 卷）　戴自俺　陶　城　陈贻鑫

英文著译卷（第 6 卷）　温致义

诗歌卷（第 7 卷）　聂大朋

书信卷（第 8、9 卷）　张邦民

衙备忘卷（第 10 卷）　庞曾漱

**编　　辑**　（按姓氏笔画为序）

王超英　刘有声　江长风　李　冬　陈　思　杨立义

张　颖　张德生　姚启安　鲁　风　裴未如　韩忠祥

程翊德　储朝晖

**审　　定**　陆静山（主任）吴树琴　楼化篷　徐明清

丁　丁　龚思雪　李能寿

**特邀主编**　胡晓风

新版

# 《陶行知全集》

## 出版工作委员会

# 编辑说明

一、陶行知（1891—1946）是我国伟大的人民教育家、伟大的共产主义战士。他为中国教育改造、普及人民教育、争取民族解放和建立人民民主的新中国奋斗了一生，留下了大量的著作。他的著作，散见于1913年到1946年的国内外报刊。生前曾以各种形式出版各种专集，流传甚广，影响深远。延安也曾出版《行知教育论文选集》。1946年，延安各界追悼陶行知筹备委员会倡议出版《陶行知全集》，但因限于当时条件，未能实现。1957年7月，张宗麟曾在《人民教育》发表文章，公开建议人民教育出版社编辑出版《陶行知全集》。1959年原中央教育部所拟定的《教育科学规划》曾有出版《陶行知全集》的项目，但因当时各种阻力尚未排除，终未实现。中国共产党第十一届三中全会以后，研究陶行知的活动又活跃起来。1981年，由邓颖超同志主持的陶行知诞辰90周年纪念大会在北京市全国政协礼堂召开。安徽、上海、江苏、四川、北京等地相继成立了陶行知研究会。1982年，华中师范学院（现华中师范大学）教育科学研究所和湖南教育出版社，在征得安徽、上海、江苏、四川、北京等省、市陶行知研究会赞同和陶行知先生亲属的大力支持下，组成《陶行知全集》编辑委员会，由华中师范学院教育科学研究所主编，湖南教育出版社于1985年出版了六卷本《陶行知全集》，在抢救我国民族文化遗产、促进我国教育改革、建设具有中国特色的社会主义教育体系等方面作出了有益的贡献。

二、1985年9月，中国陶行知研究会、中国陶行知基金会成立，对陶行知的研究开始了新的篇章。随之，中国陶行知研究会陆续收到了陶研工作者，陶行知生前友好、学生以及部分读者的许多宝贵建议，要求中国陶行知研究会争取时间，趁陶先生的一些老朋友和学生以及部分陶行知研究的老专家尚健在的时候，组织力量，在原有的基础上，重新编辑出版一部较完备的新版《陶行知全集》（以下简称《全集》），在1991年陶行知诞辰100周年时出版，以应时代及广大读者的需要。

三、本版《全集》的编辑工作，本着求“全”、求“真”的原则，增补了迄今为止收集到的佚文、佚诗、佚信等，并作了认真的校勘；在考订的基础上加了注释；对作者用外文所写著作均作了新的校译；各卷插图有了新的补充和调整。特别要指出的是，本版增补了作者自1936年4月至1946年7月所用的小笔记本55册，以作者所题《衔备忘》为名全部整理编入第十卷，约40万字，系首次发表，是研究陶行知最后十年战斗生涯的极为珍贵的史料。

四、本版《全集》按文章体裁分类，共成十卷。各卷保留了作者原有自编专集的原貌；专集外的文章，再按时间顺序排列。第一至四卷为论著卷（包括论文、演讲记录、谈话、提案等）；第五卷为教材卷（包括各类教材及编辑手稿、儿童科学读物、寓言、歌曲等）；第六卷为英文著译卷（包括英文著述、英文书信；著述中译、书信中译；中译英、英译中等）；第七卷为诗歌卷；第八、九卷为书信卷；第十卷为《衔备忘》。

五、本版《全集》的编辑原则为：（一）尽可能做到“全”；（二）保持陶行知著作的原貌；（三）所收文稿，均经慎重的考证、核查。

六、本版《全集》的注释要求是：（一）以具有中师毕业以上文化程度的广大教师及其他读者为对象；（二）注释条目的选择，以有助于理解原文为准；（三）文字力求简明扼要；（四）对人物、事件，介绍历史背景，力求客观真实，不带政治帽子；（五）人名索引根据其与原著及作者的关系而确定其详略。

七、本版《全集》的编辑和校勘，除充分利用中国陶行知研究会所珍藏的资料以外，并专门组织了力量，到江苏、上海、安徽陶行知纪念馆，中国第二历史档案馆以及华中师范大学近代历史研究所，浙江湘湖师范学校等单位查核大量原件，还尽量查阅手稿及各种版本的专集，多方比较、考证，以求臻于完善。凡有增删或改动者，均采用注释加以说明或以其他方式处理，以便对照。

八、本版《全集》的编辑工作是由中国陶行知研究会领导下组成的编辑委员会主持进行的；出版工作是由四川省党政领导及有关人士组成的出版工作委员会主持进行的，特别是中共四川省委宣传部在多方面给予了大力支持。

九、在编辑过程中，得到南京中国第二历史档案馆，北京中央档案馆，广东省档案馆，北京图书馆，华南师范大学图书馆，南京大学图书馆，南京图书馆，北京师范大学图书馆，上海图书馆，上海辞书出版社图书馆，中央教育科学研究所图书馆，安徽省图书馆，四川省图书馆，四川大学图书馆，广东省图书馆，广州中山大学图书馆，华中师范大学近代史研究所，江苏晓庄陶行知纪念馆，上海陶行知纪念馆，安徽陶行知纪念馆，四川教育学院，各省、市、自治区陶行知研究会以及陶行知先生生前友好、学生和亲属的赞助及支持，在此谨一一深表感谢!

十、由于水平及各种条件所限，本版《全集》疏漏、错误在所难免，敬请读者教正。

《陶行知全集》编辑委员会

1990年12月

# 凡 例

一、本全集编入迄今收集到的陶行知的全部文稿，有文章、诗歌、教材、书信、演讲、小说、谈话、章程、提案、文电、广告、备忘录等2530篇（其中教材13本、小说1部、备忘录55册）。凡有作者手稿，有作者个人署名，或虽未署名但有根据可确认为作者所著者，均收为正文；合署而非作者起草，或虽有个人署名但不能确认为作者所著的文稿，均与其他参考材料一起作为附录。附录共314篇（包括附在第九卷末的年表），一种为文末附，一种为卷末附录。

二、作者的自编集共17本（其中小说1部），大体上按出版的年代排在有关卷的前面，作为第一部分。自编集以外的集外文汇、集外诗汇、集外书信等均按写作或发表的时间逐年编入有关各卷，作为第二部分。有的诗文收入几种自编集内，此次只在一本集子中排印，其余均存目。第六卷英文著译卷，分类按年编排。第十卷《衞备忘》用手稿影印，一册为一篇，在篇末加少量的译文与注释。

三、除少数姓名和文言文中的个别字外，统用简化字，以国家语言文字工作委员会1986年重新发表的《简化字总表》为准。

四、陶行知原著中的纪年、数字、译名及章节标题的分层序码等均保持原貌。纪年多系民国纪年，如三年、廿一年、卅二年（即公元1914年、1932年、1943年）等。数字则汉字与阿拉伯字并存。翻译的人名、地名与通译不同的，在注释中注明通译的名称。编者所写的注释文字统用公元纪年，数字用法按国家语委等七部门公布的试行规定。

五、论著、诗歌、教材及儿童读物的标题用原题，个别有变动的在题注中说明。书信的标题，除作者自编集外，多系编者从信中摘取原话为题。

六、原著无标点的，由编者加添标点；原著用旧式标点或标点不规范的，重新标点。

七、改正了原稿中的错字，删除了衍文，漏字在〔　〕内添补，无法辨认的字用□号代替。通假字、古今字、异体字等，除文言文中的少数字外，均按有关规定处理。

八、编者的题注为脚注。书信及一些档案资料现存放何处，均不作注。

九、作者本人的署名，1934年7月16日前为“陶知行”，现一仍其旧。编者所写注释中则一律称“陶行知”。

十、第十卷和课本、小说不作人名索引，其余各卷正文中出现的人名，均按姓氏笔画作索引，附在卷末。附录不作人名索引和注释。

本卷为陶知行的英文著作和翻译作品，收入论著 14 篇，书信 48 封，故事、寓言 8 篇（中译英），诗歌 40 首（中译英），译诗 21 首（英译中），译文 15 篇，另有附录 16 篇共计 162 篇。

译诗《黑白之战》《打开眼睛看看》已收入《行知诗歌集》（1936 年生活书店版），《古歌》和《天要黑了》已收入《行知诗歌别集》。本卷不再收入。

译文中的人名、地名，仍依其旧，易产生误解的，注通译名。

论文和书信由温致义教授等翻译定稿。

1

No 16928 ORIGINAL.
THE UNITED STATES OF AMERICA
CERTIFICATE OF IDENTITY
ISSUED IN CONFORMITY WITH A REGULATION OF THE DEPARTMENT OF COMMERCE AND LABOR ADOPTED MARCH 19, [illegible]

This is to certify that the person named and described on the reverse side hereof has been regularly admitted to the United States as of the status indicated, whereof satisfactory proof has been submitted. This certificate is not transferable and is granted solely for the identification and protection of said Chinese person so long as his status remains unchanged, to insure the attainment of which object an accurate description of said person is written on the reverse side hereof, and his photograph likeness is attached, with his name written partly across, and the official seal of the United States Immigration officer signing this certificate, impressed partly over said photograph.

2

DESCRIPTION
Name: Tao Wen Tsung
Age: 21 Height: 5 ft. 5 1/4 in.
Occupation: Student Urbana, Ill.
Admitted as Section 6 Student #13173
[illegible] S.S. China September 7th 19[illegible]
Physical marks and peculiarities: [illegible] right corner of mouth
Issued at the port of San Francisco, Cal.
this 18 day of September 19[illegible]
Samuel W. Backus
Immigration Officer in Charge.

3

1 1937 年 9 月陶行知在墨西哥演讲,宣传抗日

2 1914 年秋，陶行知赴美留学。图为入境身份证

3 1914 年秋，陶行知赴美留学。图为入境身份证

1 W 54 N.Y. City 24
June 10 - 44

My dear Dr Tao – I have been happy to get news of you through your former associate Professor Chu. I am glad to know your health remains good and that your educational work goes on, even under the difficult conditions you experience. I am happy that the United States is doing at least a little for your distressed country and I look forward, as I am sure you do, to the time when it can do much more not only in a military way but in fundamental ways in behalf of a democratic society & democratic education. The world is so bound together now that unless democratic aims & methods are established everywhere throughout the world, I fear they will not long flourish in this country.

With regards & best wishes
Sincerely yours
John Dewey
(Professor Emeritus Columbia Univ).

To Dr W. T. Tao

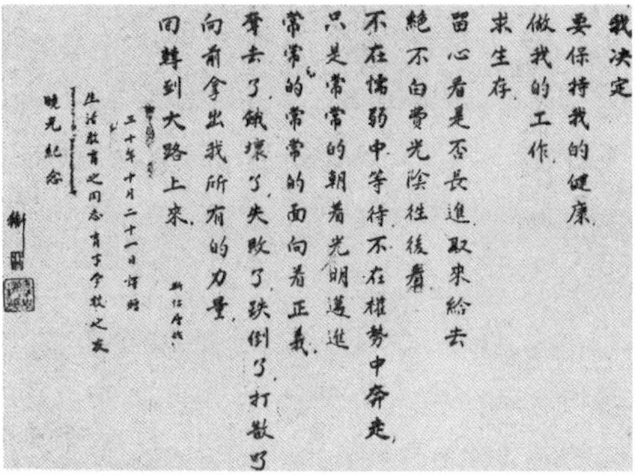

我決定
要保持我的健康，
做我的工作，
求生存，
留心看是否長進，取來給去
絕不白費光陰往後看，
不在懦弱中等待，不在權勢中奔走，
只是常常的朝着光明邁進
常常的常常的面向着正義，
拿去了，毁壞了，失敗了，跌倒了，打散了
向前拿出我所有的力量，
回轉到大路上來。

斯仁原作
三十年十月二十一日譯贈
生活教育之同志 育才今秋之友
曉光紀念

4　杜威致陶行知信手迹

5　陶行知将从国外募集的药品，交由在香港的宋庆龄转运到敌后抗日根据地

6　译诗《我决定》手迹

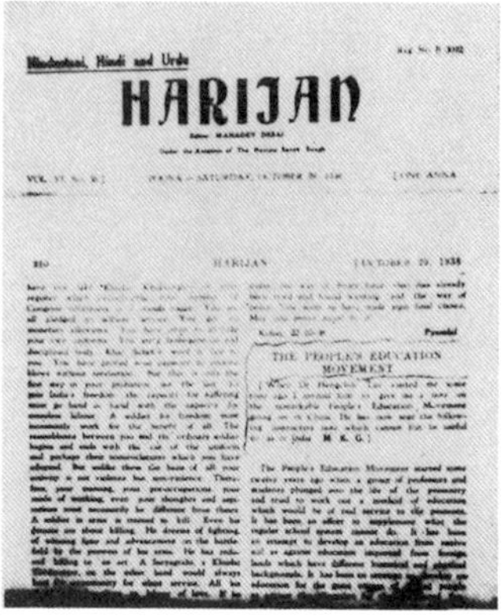
Hindustani, Hindi and Urdu
HARIJAN
HARIJAN
THE PEOPLE'S EDUCATION MOVEMENT

7

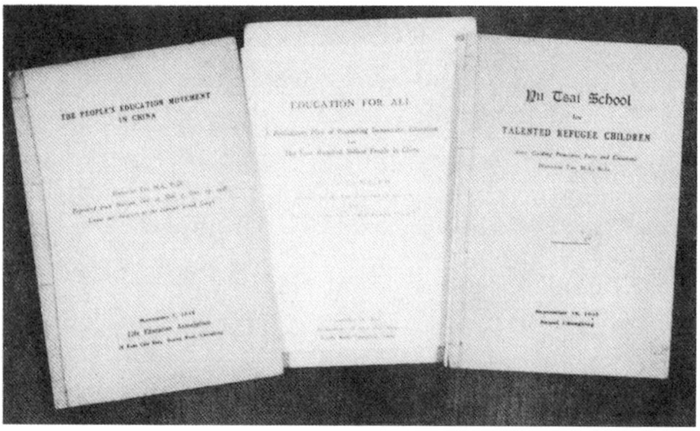
THE PEOPLE'S EDUCATION MOVEMENT IN CHINA
EDUCATION FOR ALL
Yu Tsai School
TALENTED REFUGEE CHILDREN

8

7　1938 年 10 月 29 日印度《民族旗帜》杂志刊载
陶行知著《大众教育运动》一文

8　陶行知英文著述版本，《中国的大众教育运动》
(左)《全民教育》(中)《育才手册》(右)

9　在埃及金字塔前骑骆驼留影。正中是陶行知

9

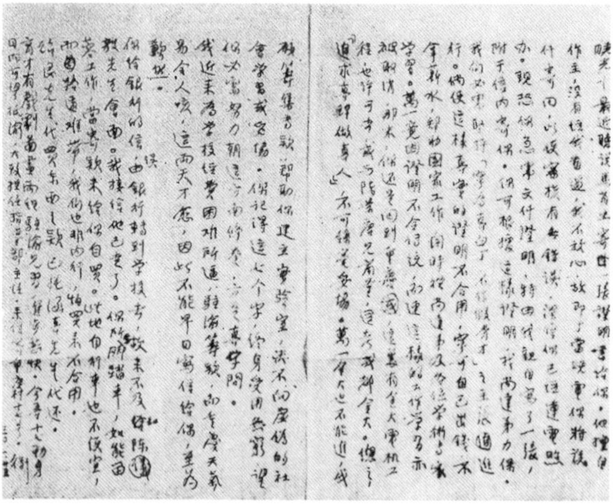

10

11

10　1941 年给陶晓光手迹

11　育才学校校门

# 目 录

## 论著（中译文） 189

## LETTERS 333

1942



1943



1944

1946



1916



1936



1937

## 1945



## 1946

## STORIES, FOLK TALES, FABLES, MYTHS AND JOKES



## POEMS AND SONGS

# TREATISES,
# ESSAYS, ETC

# Education In China 1924

## I. Introduction

China has been in the process of modernizing her education during the last two decades, but no greater progress has ever been made in any time of the period than in the last five or six years. Prior to 1919, roughly speaking, education in China was on a crossroads of foreign examples. At one time, she had to model after the Japanese system; at another, the German system; and at still another, the American system. The imported systems of education from foreign countries, however fruitful they might be on their own soils, could not blossom well when thus transplanted. It was not until very recently that an awakened realization began to set in in the minds of educators and people in general that they must thoroughly study and examine their own needs and problems before they can adequately work out a system of education which will be truly Chinese and of real service to China. But in order to understand fully the effects of this realization and of its subsequent deliberations and solutions as set down in the following pages, it will be well here to indicate the forces that have brought about this great change.

Perhaps the most profound influence is undoubtedly the so-called Chinese Renaissance. The Renaissance began in 1917 as a "Literary Revolution" when Dr. Hu Suh and his followers declared that the old classical language had outlived its usefulness and that Pai-hua, or the spoken language, should be its legitimate heir. The Literary Revolution met with astonishing success. In spite of strong opposition on the part of the conservative scholars, the younger generation received it with overwhelming enthusiasm. This rediscovery of a living language for the Chinese has enabled China to produce new literature fitted for the new age, has revolutionalized elementary school reading materials as well as methods of teaching them, and has made it possible for the mass education movement to go on with its program of eliminating illiteracy in the country.

But the influence of the Renaissance is more than this. It is a movement through which all the traditional values, including the educational, are judged from a new standpoint and with a new standard. Tradition is often thrown overboard, authority is cast aside, and old beliefs are being undermined. In the words of Dr. Hu, this "systematization of the national heritage is a revival or rebirth of that spirit of criticism and research which animated the works of the Han Hsueh scholars of the last three centuries." As has been said before, China in the former years followed her neighbors rather blindly. At first, she sacrificed everything old for the new. But now and only gradually, she has begun to realize that the old is not necessarily bad and the new is not necessarily good. Her reaction to new theories and practices is no longer imitative adoption, but question, examination, experimentation, and selection. This undoubtedly is a wholesome attitude, and the logical outcome of this attitude in the field of education is the creation of a new system which is best fitted for the need of New China by assimilating what is best in the old as well as in the new, in itself and from outside.

## II. Administration Of Education

### 1. Administrative Units

*a. Central Administration*

The administration of education in China is highly centralized in theory but decentralized in practicc. At the head of the educational system, there is the Ministry of Education which legally is the final authority over all the educational matters of the country. It has three bureaus, namely (1) the Bureau of General Education, (2) the Bureau of Higher Education, and (3) the Bureau of Social Education. The more important officers of the Ministry are the minister, the vice minister, three councilors, three directors of the Bureaus, four secretaries, and sixteen national inspectors of education. Important actions of the Ministry are generally brought to the consideration of the Ministry conferences, which are attended by the councilors, directors, secretaries and others who may be requested by the Ministry to be present from time to time. Such conferences are presided over by the minister. He is a member of the Cabinet and he chooses his subordinates subject to the approval of the Cabinet. Owing to the political instability of the country in recent years, the position of the Ministership changes hands frequently, sometimes as many as five times in a year. But the vice minister usually holds a longer time and the councilors, directors, and the secretariat remain in office for a still longer term. It is to them that the continual functioning of the Ministry is largely due.

However, in spite of the fact that the activities of the Ministry have often been resticted and held back by the frequent changes of its head, it still enjoys much of its old prestige. With the coming of a united country and the appointment of a right person at its head, the Ministry may still become a driving force in the advancement of education in the years to come, although it is likely that local initiative will be more encouraged and the ministry's former bureaucratic influence will be curtailed.

*b. Provincial Administration*

In the provinces, there are now three existing forms of educational administration, namely the bureau form, the department form, and the commission form. The province of Kwangtung has tried a fourth plan under the name of the Committee of Education, but it is now abandoned. In those provinces in the Southwest, the bureau of education has generally been adopted. Thus in Yunnan, Kweichow, and Hunan, the bureau form of education exists. The director of the bureau is appointed by the governor of Yunnan and Kweichow, but is elected in Hunan by the Provincial Assembly. The department form of education is found in the provinces of Kwangsi and Szechwan and is legally vested with less power than the bureau form of education. The rest of the provinces all have the commission form of educational administration at the head of which is the commissioner of education. He is appointed by the president of the Republic upon the recommendation of the minister of education, and is under the direct control of the Ministry. But in directing the educational affairs of the province and in supervising his subordinates in the management of local education, the commissioner of education is required to work under the governor of the province, being thus doubly responsible both to the minister and to the governor. As a consequence, the power of the commissioner varies with the different provinces, depending upon the will of the provincial governor. As he is farther away from the Ministry and nearer to the governor,there is every temptation for him to follow the dictates of the governor rather than his superior at Peking.

The Commission of Education has two or three departments for carrying out the main groups of educational affairs. Besides, there are generally from four to six inspectors of education for each province.

*c. Local Administration*

The local administration is divided into two units, the county unit and the school district. Below the province there is the county. There are two systems of county school administration. First, we have the Bureau for the Promotion of Education,whose function is to assist the magistrate in the educational administration and in supervising the school work of the self-governing district. The bureau has a superintendent and a few assistants. But besides the superintendent, there is under the magistrate an educational secretary and also a county inspector who is independent of the superintendent. These three men hardly agree with one another. This triangular administration of county education has proved very troublesome. It is now being gradually replaced by the new creation of the County Board of Education.

The County Board of Education was inaugurated in 1922. It attempts to unify the county school administration. Under this system, the inspectors are brought under the direction of the superintendent, who is appointed by the provincial commission of education upon the recommendation of the magistrate of the county. There is another attempt in this new scheme, that is, the granting of more powers to special cities for the independent management of their schools and making the county government take charge of the village education only. This principle, however, has not been vigorously applied, although the seeds have been widely sown.

The lowest unit of local administration is the school district. The county is divided into several school districts, each of which has a delegate of school affairs, sometimes with an assistant. The school districts in China are not vested with sufficient power to cope with their responsibility. It is most loosely and inefficiently organized. The province of Shansi alone has the best organization of the local unit. Every village in the county and every street in the city has responsible persons to take charge of the educational welfare and they are given much power to perform their duties. Reorganization of the lowest unit, therefore, is one of the most urgent problems today.

### 2. Inspection and Supervision

In China, there are three grades of inspection, namely the national, the provincial,and the county inspection.

According to the regulations of 1913, the whole conntry is to be divided into eight inspectional districts. Each district has two national inspectors. The regular school inspection generally begins in the latter part of August and ends in the first part of June. The inspection covers all phases of general and social education. Special inspection may be made by the special order of the minister. When the inspectors are not on their inspection tours, they are required to be present in the Ministry to attend to other duties that may be assigned to them. During the last few years, all these regulations appear in letters only, the national inspection of education being almost entirely absent.

The provincial inspectors of education are appointed by the commissioner of education. There are four inspectors for the smaller provinces and five or six for the larger ones. Below the province there are county school inspectors. Under the old system, they act as agents for the county magistrates for the school affairs. But with the adoption of the system of the Board of Education, the county inspecters are put under the direction of the county superintendent of education. The county inspectors visit the schools under their charge from once to three times a year.

The functions of the inspectors of education are enumerated in the educational code. There are seven duties for the national and provincial inspectors, and thirteen duties for the county inspectors. But in actual practice, the inspectors are simply visitors, reporters, and, worst of all, faultfinders. Most of them do not realize that their mission is to give inspiration, encouragement, and a helping hand to the principals and teachers in service. In recent years, there has been a tendency to protest against this negative inspection and to advocate in its place a system of constructive supervision. The province of Kiangsu has set up a noble example in this respect. Beginning with last year, the commissioner of education has invited experts from the National Southeastern University and other institutions to serve as supervisors of special subjects. Thus the supervision of vocational education, science teaching, physical training, and normal education was instituted. This year, the supervision of social sciences and national language has been introduced. It has thus opened in China a new era in school supervision and inspection.

### 3. Educational Finance

Roughly speaking, there are three grades of schools supported by three respective sources of funds. The higher education is mainly supported by the national funds, the secondary education by the provincial funds, and the elementary education by the county or local funds. There are exceptions, but in general, this statement holds true.

As the national revenue comes from the customs duties, salt tax, stamp tax, tobacco and liquor licenses, profit from telegraphs, railways, and postal service, land tax and the like, the national funds for national education are drawn from the complex of these sources. With the exception of a few institutions such as Tsing Hua College, the University of Communications, the Wuchang Normal University, which derive their respective support from special sources, others get their shares from the general appropriation. The national institutions located outside of Peking secure their appropriations from the national funds put under the custody of the provincial treasury. According to the budget of 1919, the only one accurately constructed, the appropriation for the national education of $5,028,836 was really less than one per cent of the total government appropriation for the year.

Although there are professional schools and colleges conducted by the provincial governments, the province is still mainly concerned with secondary education. There is a tendency for each province to maintain a full college, but so far very few provinces have succeeded in their realization. The main sources from which we draw funds for provincial schools are the surtaxes, especially the surtax on land. Kiangsu and Chekiang are now levying special taxes on tobacco for the specified use of provincial education. Two years ago, the province of Szechwan tried to devote its almost two million dollars of pork tax to education but without much result. The tax on transfer of deeds and ownership adopted in Honan yields an annual income of $1,000,000 for provincial support. In the face of financial distress, a number of new solutions have been proposed. They are still at the stage of trial and error. In order to give some idea of the extent of provincial support of education, we may mention as representatives of the extremes that Kiangsu is spending $2,800,000, Chekiang, $1,500,000 and Kiangsi, only $600,000 annually.

As a general rule, the county supports the elementary education by surtaxes on land, miscellaneous assessments, rent and interests from the academic properties handed down from the old dynasties, The Shansi system of supporting schools is, so far, the best that has been evolved in this country. In the cities, stores and houses are graded and assessed according to their standing for the support of the city elementary schools. In the villages, a land tax is levied according to its quality for the support of the village education.

On account of the political unrest and irregular expenses for military purposes, the schoolmen are confronted with the uncertainty of educational funds. The provinces that have been seriously short of funds are Kwangtung, Fukien, Kiangsi, Szechwan, Anhwei and Hunan. The provinces that are better off are Fengtien, Yunnan, Shansi, Shensi, Shantung, and Honan. But, in general, the teachers in China are serving the country at the greatest personal sacrifice.

The problems with which we are now chiefly concerned are: (1) How to insure regularity of payment of the educational fund by legal protection and economic devices, so that those who are in educational service can be free from financial anxieties and give their whole-hearted devotion to the educational cause; (2) how to reorganize the tax system so that the burden as well as opportunity for education can be equalized; (3) how to stimulate educational activities through a proper system of distribution and subsidies without curtailing local initiative; and (4) how to economize the use of the present fund so that the maximum of educational results can be achieved at the minimum cost.

# III. The New System Of Schools

## 1. The System

"China has had at least four systems of schools within the last twenty years." The newest one was adopted in 1922, as a result of three years' deliberation initiated by the Seventh Conference of the National Federation of Provincial Education Association in 1919. There is no space for us to discuss the historical development of the system. The issues that have been evolved in its make-up will be touched upon in connection with the discussions of the grades and types of schools which follow. Since 1922, committees have been organized and kept busy drawing up new courses of study in order to cover this skeleton with flesh. This year has witnessed the completion of all the new courses of study except a small part in vocational education. They were voted upon and approved by the Tenth Conference of the National Federation of Provincial Education Associations and were submitted to the Ministry of Education for promulgation.

On the next page is a diagrammatical representation of the new system of schools adopted by the Twenty-Third Ordinance of the Ministry of Education. It will be noted that the left column in the diagram represents the standard ages at which students should enter the different grades. In practice, however, these are to be determined according to intelligence, record, and other considerations.

## 2. The Divisions of Schools

*a. Pre-School and Kindergarten Education*

Kindergarten education has been given a place in the new system

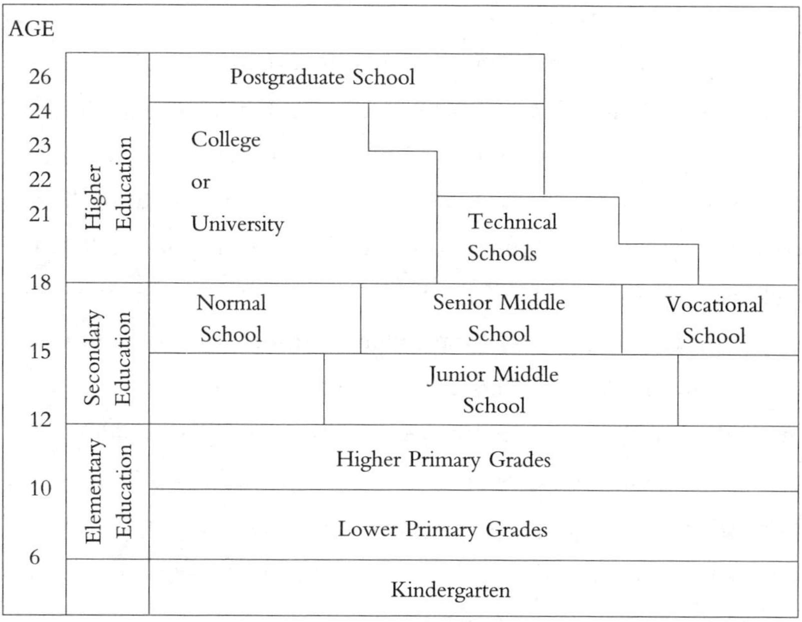


and admits children under six years of age. The practice schools of the normal schools, especially the normal schools for women, usually have kindergartens attached to them. There are also kinadergartens conducted by private persons and by the missions. But the total number of kindergartens is yet very small. As kindergarten training gives the children an opportunity for active self-expression and also for interaction between the child and the teacher, it is very necessary to have first the adequate institutions for the training of kindergarten teachers. The resolution for more trained kindergarteners passed in January, 1924, by the Kiangsu Conference of Educational Administrators is an indication of the need felt. The Hunan Education Association has also this year advocated the establishment of more kindergartens in cities and towns. The Kiangsu Compulsory Education Association has even recommeded the adoption of kindergarten methods in the lowest grade in the elementary schools. Another very encouraging and more significant fact is the experimet on kindergarten education conducted by Professor H. C. Chen of the National Southeastern University. Impressed by the fact that the subject matter and methods used in the kindergarten are borrowed from foreign countries and some of them may not be suitable for the Chinese children, he and his staff began in the fall of 1923 to experiment on the selfmade toys, Chinese Mother-Goose stories, and other materials. He is also trying to make the kindergarten a training center for mothers as well as a center for the education of young children. The Chinere National Association for the Advancement of Education and Professor Chen have agreed to cooperate in including in his plan an experiment on the least possible cost of conducting the kindergarten education so that it could be duplicated in the largest number of communities.

*b. Elementary Education*

According to the new system, attendance at the elementary school is limited to six years, but it may be extended to another year in order to suit local needs. The elementary school is to be divided into the lower primary and higher primary grades. The former consists of four years and may be establisned separately.

The courses of study drawn up by the Committee of Eighteen for elementary schools are as follows:

It is further recommended that there should be at least 1,080 minutes per week for the first two years, 1,260 minutes per week for the third and fourth years and 1,440 minutes for the two higher primary grades. The number of minutes are to be distributed into suitable periods for the six days' work. In village schools the subjects may be combined and simplified, but the time allotted to national

| Subjects | | Percentage of Time Devoted to Each Subject | |
|---|---|---|---|
| | | In Lower Primary Grades | In Higher Primary Grades |
| National Language | Conversation | 30% | 6% |
| | Reading | | 12% |
| | Composition | | 8% |
| | Penmanship | | 4% |
| Arithmetic | | 10% | |
| Social Science | Hygiene | 20% | 4% |
| | Citizenship | | 4% |
| | History | | 6% |
| | Geography | | 6% |
| Nature Study | | 12% | 8% |
| Gardening | | | 4% |
| Industrial Arts | | 7% | |
| Imagery Arts | | 5% | |
| Music | | 6% | |
| Physical Education | | 10% | |

language and arithmetic should by no means be reduced.

According to the new system, compulsory education is temporarily limited to four years. If local circumstances are favorable, the period may be extended. The school age for compulsory education is left to the determination of different provinces and special districts in accordance with their local situations.

Compulsory education has been contemplated by the central authority ever since the Tsing dynasty. It was not until 1920 that the Ministry of Education mapped out the definite steps for the enforcement of the same in different communities at specific times. The specifications are as follows:

1921, provincial capitals and open ports

1922, county seats and cities

1923, tows above five hundred families

1924, towns containing above three hundred families

1925 and 1926, towns containing above two hundred families

1927, villages containing above one hundred families

1928, villages containing below one hundred families

On account of the political disturbances in recent years, the above program has rarely been vigorously enforced. The province of Shansi alone, however, stands out most prominently in its achievements. The Shansi program has seven steps to be completed in seven half-years, from 1918 to 1921. Although complete success has yet to be achieved, the latest return of statistics shows that more than seventy-two per cent of the children at school age are now in schools. Illiterate adults below twenty-five years of age are also required to attend continuation schools to study common Chinese, arithmetic, and things which a citizen ought to know.

Another phase in connection with elementary education which may be mentioned here is the village school movement. As more than eighty per cent of the total population live in villages, it is of the greatest importance that village education should receive our closest attention. Recently, the Back-to-the-Country Movement has gathered much strength. The Chinese National Association for the Advancement of Education has created a special committee on rural education. The Tenth Conference of the National Federation of the Provincial Education Associations, which met in Kaifeng last October, has also devoted much deliberation to this important matter. The Kiangsu Compulsory Education Association, which met in Wusih in August, spent three days in drawing up seven practical suggestions for the development of the village schools. Beginnings of special investigations of typical village schools in typical communities have been conducted by the Kiangsu Compulsory Education Association and the Chinese National Association for the Advancement of Education. The reports, fragmentary as they are, have already stirred up great interest in and enthusiasm for the village education. As the average village generally cannot support an expensive education, the Chinese National Association for the Advancement of Education has selected a few village schools where the principals have shown ability in new village leadership to conduct experiments on the best possible village education with the lowest possible cost. It is hoped that in the course of a few years standards for village education can be developed for a nation-wide adoption.

The language problem has practically been settled after China has struggled through centuries against the diversity of dialects throughout the country. Dr. Hu Suh's Literary Revolution has exerted the most profound influence on the elementary schools. The vernacular language, or the "living language", is now welcomed by most of the elementary schools. The Fengtien authorities, however, have shown some reaction against the use of the vernacular language. Kwangtung is still hesitating to adopt this change. But in the long run, the living vernacular language is destined to prevail in all the elementary schools.

*c. Secondary Education*

In regard to secondary education, the new system has the following to say: "Attendance at the middle school is limited to six years, which are to be divided into two periods of three years each, the junior middle school and the senior middle school. The junior middle school offers general education, but it may give various vocational subjects according to local needs. The senior middle school is divided into the general, the agricultural, the technical, the commercial, and the normal course. These courses may be given independently or severally in one school at a time."

In the secondary schools, the credit system is adopted. A credit is defined as one hour of class work plus preparation. Subjects with no preparation will have a proportionate reduction in credits. The junior middle school requires the satisfactory completion of 180 credits for graduation, of which 164 credits are for required work. The required courses ,of study for the junior middle school as drawn up by the Committee of Twelve are as follows:

<table>
<tr><th colspan="2">Subjects</th><th>Credits</th></tr>
<tr><td rowspan="3">Social Sciences</td><td>Citizenship</td><td>6</td></tr>
<tr><td>History</td><td>8</td></tr>
<tr><td>Geography</td><td>8</td></tr>
<tr><td rowspan="2">Language and Literature</td><td>National Language</td><td>32</td></tr>
<tr><td>Foreign Language</td><td>36</td></tr>
<tr><td colspan="2">Mathematics</td><td>30</td></tr>
<tr><td colspan="2">Nature Study</td><td>16</td></tr>
<tr><td>Arts</td><td>Drawing<br>Manual Arts<br>Music</td><td>12</td></tr>
<tr><td>Physical Education</td><td>Physiology and Hygiene<br>Physical Exercises</td><td>4<br>12</td></tr>
<tr><td colspan="2">Total</td><td>164</td></tr>
</table>

The courses of study drawn up for the senior middle school by the Committee of Nine are composed of three years of study, namely: (1) General study required of all students should account for about forty-three per cent of the credits; (2) studies required of students who take the course of the special group vary with the course of the group; (3)pure elective studies should not exceed twenty percent of the credits. The vocational courses of study for the senior middle school have not been published yet. The liberal courses of study are of two groups, namely, that of the Arts and Social Science group and that of the Mathematics and Natural Science group. These two courses of study are as follows:

**A. Courses of Study for the Arts and Social Science Gruop**

| | | Subjects | Credits |
|---|---|---|---|
| I. General Requirements | | 1. National Language | 16 |
| | | 2. Foreign Language | 16 |
| | | 3. Philosophy of Life | 4 |
| | | 4. Social Problems | 6 |
| | | 5. History of Civilization | 6 |
| | | 6. General Principles of science | 6 |
| | | 7. Physical Education | 10 |
| II. Group Requirements | Prescribed | 1. Special Chinese Literature | 8 |
| | | 2. Beginner's Psychology | 3 |
| | | 3. Beginner's Logic | 3 |
| | | 4. One course of Social Science | 4 at least |
| | | 5. One course of Natural Science or Mathematics | 6 at least |
| | Electives | | 32 or more |
| III. Pure Electives | | | 30 or more |
| Total | | | 150 |

Secondary education, as pointed out by Dr. Paul Monroe after his general survey of Chinese education in 1921, is the weakest spot in the entire Chinese educational system. Since then, two national

**B. Courses of Study for Mathematics and Natural Science Group**

| | | Subjects | Credits |
|---|---|---|---|
| I. General Requirements | | 1. National Language | 16 |
| | | 2. Foreign Language | 16 |
| | | 3. Philosophy of Life | 4 |
| | | 4. Social Problems | 6 |
| | | 5. History of Civilization | 6 |
| | | 6. General Principles of Science | 6 |
| | | 7. Physical Education | 10 |
| II. Group Requirements | Prescribed | 1. Trigonometry | 3 |
| | | 2. Senior Geometry | 6 |
| | | 3. Senior Algebra | 6 |
| | | 4. Analytic Geometry | 3 |
| | | 5. Mechanical Drawing | 4 |
| | | 6. Physics, Chemistry, Biology (any two of the three subjects with six credits for each) | 15 at least |
| | Electives | | 23 |
| III. Pure Electives | | | 30 |
| Total | | | 150 |

organizations, the Chinese National Association for the Advancement of Education and the Chinese Federation of Secondary Education, have given much thought to the study of different phases of this grade of education. The attention of the administrators as well as of the secondary school teachers and officers has also been concentrated on this direction. Some of the more important problems and tendencies in regard to present-day Chinese secondary education may be briefly mentioned here.

First, the improvement of science teaching in secondary education occupies now a most important place in the minds of the students of education and also of secondary school officers and teachers. Of all the weak spots in secondary schools, the weakest is the teaching of science. Here science has been taught through lectures and textbooks with very little opportunity for the students actively to engage themselves in laboratory work. Science study that results in the function of an experimental attitude and in the acquisition of effective control of nature has been greatly neglected. In view of this fact, the Chinese National Association for the Advancement of Education sent an invitation through Dr. Paul Monroe to Professor G.R. Twiss of Ohio State University of America to make a special study of the science teaching in China and make recommendations for improvement. Professor Twiss, after a careful investigation of 187 schools in ten provinces, left with us a most comprehensive report with constructive recommendations, which is now already published under the title "Science and Education".

It is also very encouraging to mention that the Science Society is undertaking to include the improvement of science teaching as part of its regular work. The Society has among its members nearly all the prominent students of science in this country and will be able to exert great influence in the promotion of science education. Kiangsu province has been selected as a starting point for their investigation and experimentation.

The next subject that has received much attention in recent years is the teaching of the national language in the secondary schools. This important subject has been previously taught in a very unscientific and uninteresting way. The teachers without training in education and psychology have to rely on the pour-in and word-by-word methods. For the first time, national attention was called to the needed reform in teaching this subject when Dr. Hu Suh read his paper on the "Teaching of Chinese Language and Literature" at the Tsinan Conference of the National Federation of the Provincial Education Associations in 1922. Following Dr. Hu's address, there have been more than thirty articles written on the improvement of teaching Chinese, most of which have been published in the last two years. The discussions are now passing from that of a subjective and empirical nature to an objective and experimental basis. The place of the vernacular language in the secondary schools is different from that in elementary schools. The tendency is to have less and less vernacular language as the students go along and each decrease is made up by the classical language.

The second tendency is the increasing emphasis on school discipline in the secondary schools. Since the May Fourth Movement, there has been much relaxation in school discipline.Many principals and teachers have simply lost control over their students. A reaction, however, has set in during the last two years. On the one hand, there is a tendency towards negative control, prohibiting the students from participating in a number of activities in which they have hitherto taken an active part. On the other hand, the students are encouraged to organize themselves for self-control, naturally under the supervision of the school authority. Many ways have now been tried to substantiate these two tendencies, and there is every reason to believe that the students' conduct will be improved thereby.

The third tendency is a national feeling against the use of foreign languages as a required study in the junior middle schools. Although thirty-six credits have been put down as a requirement for foreign languages, yet in the presence of such vigorous attack, it is questionable whether it can maintain its present number of credits in the future.

The fourth tendency is the increasing emphasis on vocational training in the secondary schools. As shown by the Entrance Examination Statistics of the National University of Peking and the National Southeastern University at Nanking, less than ten per cent of the applicants could be admitted, and this ratio has remained for the last few years without much change. The vocational advocates feel that it is imperative that the preparatory nature of the secondary schools should be greatly reduced. The schools have answered this call by adopting more vocational courses. But just how these courses can suit the students in their work and furnish them with life positions is a question for which a satisfactory answer is yet to be sought.

The fifth tendency is the segregation of sexes in the secondary schools. Some middle schools have tried the coeducational system in recent years. But they are very limited in number. In spite of the fact that there is a favorable attitude toward coeducation in institutions of higher learning and in the elementary schools, there is a decidedly strong opposition to coeducation in the middle schools. Hunan, in March, and Shantung, in August, this year have actually prohibited the middle schools from becoming coeducational. Kiangsu takes a milder attitude. It authorizes the normal schools for men to take in women students and permits city middle schools to become coeducational on the condition that adequate provisions be made.

*d. Higher Education*

According to the new system of schools, "the institutions of higher learning may consist of several colleges or of one college. Attendance at the college or university is limited to four to six years". At the top, there is the postgraduate school, which is an institution of research for college and university graduates and students similarly prepared.

The following two tables will give some idea of the extent of higher education in China:

**A. Professional Distribution of Colleges**

| Kinds of Schools | Number of Schools |
|---|---|
| University | 35 |
| Teachers College | 8 |
| Agricultural College | 7 |
| Technical College | 13 |
| Commercial College | 8 |
| Medical College | 7 |
| Law College | 33 |
| Total | 111 |

**B. Distribution Of College According To Support**

| Source of Support | Number of Schools |
|---|---|
| National | 30 |
| Provincial | 48 |
| Private | 29 |
| Mission and Foreign | 18 |
| Total | 125 |

A few more universities have been added to the list this year and the more important among them are the Kwangtung Government University and the Northwestern University at Shensi.

As to the modern tendencies of Chinese university education, we may take Chancellor Tsai's statement as an indication of the first tendency in scientific research. He says: "The university is not merely intended to offer ready-made courses for students to attend at fixed hours, but primarily to be an institution for corporate work in scientific research. And by research, I mean not merely the introduction of European culture, but original contribution on the basis of what is already done in the West; nor merely the preservation of our national cultural heritage, but seeking by means of methods of scientific research to show what that heritage has actually been. ”

The second tendency which may be mentioned is the demand for academic freedom, for no scientific thought and research can ever be properly developed if exterior interference is too strong. Govervnment intervention has always been resented and repelled by the high institutions. This year, when the Ministry of Education announced the new university regulations, it met with severe opposition from the professors of the National University of Peking and it was finally compelled to lay them on the table for a while.

There is also tendency for closer co-operation on the part of the universities and colleges in the country. This last July, when the Chinese National Association for the Advancement of Education met in Nanking, the Chinese Federation of Universities was formally organized dealing with problems of common interest in regard to higher education. It is believed that such an organization, if it functions properly, will certainly raise the general standard of university work.

The fourth tendency is the extension of higher education to women. Most of the Chinese universities have opened their doors to women and have been made co-educational. The Peking Higher Normal College for Women has also been promoted to the university rank.

Finally, there is an abnormal increase of private colleges. In Peking alone, about ten private colleges came into existence this fall. A similar condition can be found in other big cities. The government, however, has refused to recognize those institutions, the purpose of whose existence is questionable.

*e. Trade and Vocational Education*

Vocational education has been given an important place in the new system of schools. "The curriculum of the elementary schools may include prevocational training... The junior middle school... may carry on various vocational courses... The senior middle school is divided into the general, the agricultural, the technical, the commercial, and the normal courses (domestic science being added later)...The year limit and the standing of the vocational schools may be determined in accordance with local need and situations."

On the basis of these provisions, the Committee on the Courses of Study for Vocational Education has spent three years in drawing up sixteen different courses of study. These are practically completed. Besides the prevocational course in elementary schools and special vocational courses in colleges, three steps of vocational education have been worked out, namely: (1) vocational courses for graduates, of four-year lower primary schools; (2) vocational courses for graduates of the six-year elementary schools; and (3) vocational courses for graduates of junior middle schools.

In regard to the distribution of time for practice and nonvocational studies, the Federation of Vocational Schools has made the following recommendations, which have been duly accepted. First, the time allotment for practice should not be less than that for class work which should have eighteen to twenty-four hours a week. Second, the subjects or study in vocational schools should be of three kinds, the vocational subjects as prerequisites to vocational and the nonvocational. The nonvocational subjects should account for at least twenty per cent of the total time allotment.

Among the important developments of vocational education in

recent years, we may mention the following: Szechwan, Kweichow, Kwangsi, Chekiang, and Fukien have promulgated plans for the reconstruction of vocational education according to the new system. Shansi has organized a provincial committee on vocational education and appointed one supervisor for each of the twenty educational districts to take charge of vocational education, compulsory education, and popular education. Yun-nan has set aside the tobacco tax for the development of vocational education. Hupeh has ordered all the counties to appropriate twenty per cent of the educational fund for the promotion of vocational training. The One Week Campaign for Vocational Guidance conducted in Shanghai, Nanking, Tsinan, and Wuchang has aroused much interest in this type of education. Lastly, the Ministry of Education has ordered all the girls' middle schools to offer practice opportunities for domestic science. There is also a special fund raised by the National Association of Vocational Education for the special purpose of promoting vocational education for girls.

## IV. The Training Of Teachers

In regard to the training of teachers, the new system of schools has the following provisions: "Attendance at the normal school is limited to six years. The normal school may be composed of only the last two or three years in order to admit the graduates of the junior middle schools... To supply the need of teachers for the lower grades of the primary schools, normal schools or normal institutes, varying in number of years, may be established." It is also provided that institutes for the training of vocational teachers may be opened in any suitable school. For the training of secondary school teachers, there is the normal college at which attendance is limited to four years. "In due time the higher normal schools established according to the old system should raise their standard in order to admit the graduates of the senior middle schools, with an attendance limited to four years; they shall then be known as Teachers Colleges." "To supply the teachers for the junior middle schools, a two-year normal course may be offered. It may be organized in the College of Education of a university, or in the Teachers College, or in the normal school, or in the senior middle school. It admits the graduates of the last two named institutions."

The courses of study for the normal schools are now completed by a special committee. Three sets of courses of study have been worked out.

The first set is for the three-year normal schools, corresponding to the senior middle school. Its general requirements are the same as the senior middle school with the addition of four credits of music, and have a total of sixty-eight credits. The profescsional requirements consist of Beginners' Psychology, two credits; Educational Psychology, three credits; General Methods, two credits; Methods of Teaching Special Subjects, six credits; Teaching Materials in Elementary Schools, six credits; Educational Statistics and Measurements, three credits; Elementary school Administration, three credits; Principles of Education, three credits; and Practice Teaching, twenty credits, making a total of forty-eight credits. The elective studies are of two kinds: (1) group electives and (2) pure electives. Group electives aim to meet the needs of three classes of prospective teachers, namely: (1) those with special inclination towards language, literature and social sciences; (2) those with special inclination towards mathematics and natural sciences, and (3) those with special inclination towards arts and physical education. Each group of students shall elect at least twenty credits from group studies. Besides, all students shall elect at least eight credits from the nine educational studies. Pure electives are left for the schools to determine.

The second set of cources of study is drawn for the six-year normal school corresponding to the six-year middle schools. In a general way, the junior middle school feature is preserved in this type of normal school, yet the whole course of study aims at a continuous process rather than at a break in the middle. It is much simpler and is recommended for adoption in the smaller schools, where, as a consequence, there is no group differentiation, and very few electives. Out of three hundred and thirty credits required for graduation, there are three hundred and nineteen credits for required studies and only eleven credits for electives.

The third set of courses of study is drawn for the training of teachers of the four lower grades of the primary schools. It has three forms, namely: the three-year course admits graduates of the six-year primary schools, the two-year course admits graduares from the old higher primary schools, and the one-year course admits graduates from the junior middle schools. All three forms have been very carefully worked out. Since space does not allow full presentation, they are given in tabular forms as follows:

| | **FORM Ⅰ** | **FORM Ⅱ** | **FORM Ⅲ** |
|---|---|---|---|
| | Three-Year Course | Two-Year Course | One-Year Course |
| Education | 36 Credits | 24 Credits | 14 Credits |
| National Language | 36 | 24 | 8 |
| Social Science | 26 | 18 | 8 |
| Mathematics | 25 | 16 | 8 |
| Nature Study, | | | |

| | | | |
|---|---|---|---|
| Gardening, and Agriculture | 33 | 22 | 8 |
| Arts | 15 | 10 | 8 |
| Physical Education | 9 | 6 | 6 |
| Total | 180 | 120 | 60 |

**Note.** The study of Elementary School Material and Methods of Teaching Elementary School Subjects are included under each subject taught. Practice Teaching is given eight credits in Forms Ⅰ and Ⅱ, and is incorporated in each subject in Form Ⅲ.

In the new courses of study for the normal schools, four important changes can be observed. In the first place, there is more flexibility and variety, which enable the normal school principals to adapt their schools to special conditions instead of having one standard course of study as was the case in former times. In the second place, there is more emphasis laid on the professional subjects. The newer developments of education which will make a better teacher are included. In the third place, more time has been given to practice teaching. In the fourth place, great emphasis has been put on teaching materials and methods of teaching subjects. Formerly, the needs of elementary schools had not been adequately felt and met, and most of the normal schools were run on the middle school basis. This emphasis on elementary subjects certainly indicates a new era in normal education.

In actual practice, the higher normal schools have been busy in transforming themselves into teachers colleges. The old normal schools are also taking steps to adopt the six-year course or the three-year course, according to their needs and conditions. Some senior middle schools have also opened new normal courses. Another very important move is found in the increasing emphasis on training the village teachers. Kiangsu has since last year established five village normal schools. The Chinese National Association for the Advancement of Education, the College of Education and College of Agriculture of National Southeastern University, the National Association of Vocational Education, the Kiangsu Compulsory Education Association, and the Kiangsu Commission of Education are cooperating in establishing an experimental normal school for training village teachers. Mr. C. T. Chao, professor of rural education of National Southeastern University and director of village education of the Chinese National Association for the Advancement of Education, has been selected to organize this school.

Students in most of the normal schools enjoy free tuition and board. There are students who are admitted on payment of half fees or whole fees, but these are very few. The regular normal students whose fees have been exempted are required to render service in the elementary schools or the secondary schools, as the case may be. A few years ago, an investigation made in Kiangsu province showed that more than eighty per cent of the normal graduates take up teaching after graduation. This rule of required compulsory service has been rather leniently enforced. The tendency is for a more strict enforcement, as is shown in the resolutions adopted at the Kaifeng Conference of the National Federation of Educational Associations. Kiangsu Province has this year prohibited graduates of the county normal institutes from taking more advanced education before the fulfillment of the compulsory service. Fengtien Province has even introduced the plan of withholding the diploma until the term of compulsory service has expired.

With the exception of the normal school graduates, all other elementary school teachers should apply for certification. The certification of teachers are of two kinds: (1) certification with examination and (2) certification without examination. Those who have studied in the secondary schools for two years or more, or have taught on the elementary schools for one year or more, or have graduated from normal institutes lasting six months or longer, or have a sufficient knowledge of educational principles and have studied the special subjects to be taught which are shown in the articles or essays written by the applicants, are qualified to teach by passing an examination in the subjects of the regular normal schools with due consideration to grade and sex variation. The examination for assistant teachers is much easier. Those who are certified without having to go through the examination on the subject are (1) middle school graduates who have been elementary school teachers for one year or more; (2) graduates of secondary industrial schools who have made good record in their studies; (3) graduates of professional schools whose special studies will qualify them to teach the subjects, and (4) elementary school teachers with three years' teaching experience and have made good record of service certified by the county superintendent of schools.

All the applicants for certification should produce school diplomas, and statements of good conduct by guarantors, and should go through a physical examination.

The certification of teachers in China is under the charge of the Provincial Committee on Certification. The results shall be reported annually by the governor of the province to the Ministry of Education at Peking.

In regard to the recompensation of the teachers in China, a brief survey was once made in the province of Kiangsu. The result is as follows:

**Annual Salary of Elementary School Teachers**

| | Higher Primary | Lower Primary |
|---|---|---|
| Maximum | $ 600 | $ 240 |
| Average | 200 | 120 |
| Minimum | 70 | 30 |

In 1921, another investigation conducted by Mr. Tai, covering six provinces, gives a medium annual salary of $160.25 Mex. for all elementary school teachers, and a medium annual salary of $125.10 Mex. for their first year's service. Making sufficient allowance for the very high purchasing power of money in China, we must still consider the present salary paid to the elementary school teachers as very low. The new tendency is for a higer pay on the basis of increase in teaching experience and professional preparation. The immediate problem, however, is how to make the pay more regular.

Besides the tendency for a higher salary, there are attempts at remuneration for encouraging longer service. The importance of the pension system has not yet been fully realized, yet a beginning has been well made. The Chekiang Conference of Educational Administrators has recommended a sabbatical year for elementary school teachers who have served for six years and an annual pension of a quarter of the last year's salary after twenty years of services, or, if made disabled, after ten years of service. It has also recommended a system of special grants from a quarter to the equivalent of the whole salary to be made to the families of the teachers. when the latter die. The Kiangsu Commission of Education has this year adopted a temporary system of pension. According to this system, an elementary school teacher shall be given annually one third of his last year's salary, if (1)he is disabled on account of sickness after a continuous tenure of service for eight years, or (2) he is disabled or seriously wounded in performing his official duties, or (3) he retires on account of old age after a continuous tenure of service for twenty years. Besides, one of his children may attend any government school in the province without paying the fees.

In regard to the tenure of elementary school teachers, very little investigation has been made. The contract of the teachers is, as a rule, on a half-year basis. The data on the tenure of service of teachers in thirteen schools in Kiangsu gathered a few years ago may give some idea of the situation. But it will be a mistake to take this meagre data as representative of the whole country.

| Years of Service | Percentage of Higher Primary Teachers | Percentage of Lower Primary Teachers |
|---|---|---|
| 1 | 6 | 26 |
| 2 | 10 | 12 |
| 3 | 23 | 20 |
| 4 | 17 | 18 |
| 5 | 44 | 24 |
| Total | 100% | 100% |

The need for teachers is imperative in China. Estimating on the basis of forty million children of school age for the four years elementary education, we shall need at least one million teachers for the four elementary grades. But according to the latest report we have only 223,279 teachers who are now serving in the lower primary schools. More than three times as many as the present number have to be added in order to enforce a nation-wide compulsory education. There are now 43,846 students in the normal schools and normal institutes, and no more than 10,000 teachers can be turned out every year as against the need for 770,000 teachers. The problem is both serious and urgent and will have to be solved only gradually.

## V. Some Recent Educational Activities And Developments

### 1. Educational Tests and Measurements

The educational test movement began in China four or five years ago when Professors Liao and Chen of Nanking, and Professors Lew and Chang of Peking started to give courses on scientific measurements in education and did some original work in the construction of tests. It was not until the coming of Professor William A. McCall of Teachers College, Columbia University, in 1922 that this movement began to start its great momentum. In cooperating with Chinese psychologists at different centers, Professor McCall succeeded in getting twenty tests constructed for the use of elementary and secondary schools. The tests added this year are as follows:

| | |
|---|---|
| 1. Comprehensive English Test | Andersen |
| 2. Geography Test | Young |
| 3. Arithmetic Practice Test | Yui |
| 4. Drawing Test | Yui |
| 5. Intelligence Test | Liu-Bradshaw |
| 6. Self-Survey Comprehensive Test | Terman |
| 7. Lower Primary Non-Verbal Intelligence | Test Chen |
| 8. Higher Primary Non-Verbal Intelligence Test | Chen |
| 9. Chinese Grammar Test for Higher Primary | Chen |
| 10. Composite Mathematics Test | Liao |
| 11. Composite Science Test | Liao |
| 12. Chinese Language and Literature Test | Liao |
| 13. Chinese Grammar Test | Liao |
| 14. History Test | Liao |

15. Geography Test Liao

There are two special features which are worth mentioning of the test movement in China. In the first place, all the tests are scaled according to a new uniform system, the T. B. C. F. system, so as to secure comparability of scores from test to test and thus facilitate the tabulation and interpretation of results, and all the direction books are modeled after one standard design so that the teacher will find it necessary to learn only one procedure. In the second place, all tests are published at one place, that is, the Chinese National Association for the Advancement of Education. This has saved the schoolmen much trouble in locating and securing the tests.

In the fall of 1923, Professor Terman of Yenching University at Peking, and Professor Cha of the Peking Normal Universiy were requested by the Chinese National Association to conduct a cooperative self-survey, using especially designed and self-administering tests. "The purpose of this survey is to acquaint educators with tests, to motivate teachers to make use of self-helps to be published by the Association, and to conduct a national contest among the pupils." This survey, in spite of its shortcomings, has accomplished its original purposes. The final report of its findings, known as the "Efficiency of Chinese Elementary Schools," by Terman, was published this spring.

**2. Medical and Social welfare of School Children**

The health and social welfare of students have received more attention in the elementary schools than in the secondary schools. The better schools, such as the Shian-Shan Children's Home, the practice schools of Southeastern University, of Peking Normal College for Men, and of Peking Normal College for Women, and the Tsu Yih School in Hunan, have given much opportunity for children to take active participation in social activities and have given much attention to the physical well-being of the pupils. The report that could be secured on this topic is that of the Practice School of the Peking Normal College for Women. It is a school of 590 pupils. The school physician was introduced in 1920. Medical inspection is conducted once every semester. Vaccination is a requirement and is done once every year. In extracurriculum activities, free play and athletics are emphasized. Chinese games as well as foreign games are introduced. Correction exercises are given by physical training, and general knowledge on health is given in a course on hygiene. Attention is also given to ventilation, lighting, seating, etc. School gardening furnishes another opportunity for healthful recreation. Out-of-door activities are encouraged. Excursions are arranged for each class at least once every semester. There are also student self-government, a literary society, class meetings, weekly mass meetings, the cooperative store, the children's club, the children's reading room, the savings society, and tens of other organizations which furnish ample opportunity for the development of the social life of the child.

Perhaps the most important thing that has been done this year is the enormous amount of research conducted by Professor C. H. McCloy under the joint auspices of the National Southeastern University and the Chinese National Association for the Advancement of Education. The following have been completed:

1. A series of studies in anthropometry and physical examination. Some of the results may be enumerated as follows:

a. A study of weight for body types has been completed. A new weight card has been prepared in which a new basis of calculating weight has been adopted.

b. A study of chest measurements has been made.

c. All measurements commonly taken have been intensively studied to determine whether or not they are really diagnostically useful. This has narrowed down the study to a few really important measurements and these have been studied as to how they can contribute to the welfare of the students.

d. The chest index as a basis of a test for hereditary stigmata of degeneration has been made and is nearly completed.

e. A study has been made of the vital measurements and school grades to see what the relation might be.

f. A new weighting for age-height-weight and athletic performance has been devised.

g. A careful statistical study of medical examination has been made and a new form devised to give results in graphic as well as numerical forms has been worked out.

2. A study has been made of a few athletic events to determine which of the quite similar events should be utilized. This has been done, for example, with three forms of the potato race and the best form has been statistically determined.

3. A careful study has been made of standard tests in athletics. A study of eleven events was made with three hundred primary school boys and a study of eighteen events with three hundred and thirty middle school boys. The best events for each standard test have been statistically determined.

4. A universal scoring table has been devised for over seventy events in track and field athletics. These give an approximately equivalent degree of difficulty for all events when the same point value is attained.

5. Methods have been evolved of determining the Motor Quotient of a boy or a girl in athletic events based on the standard

events and the above-mentioned age-height-weight weighting. This is quite accurate.

6. Studies of standard tests in football and basketball have been undertaken and the preliminary steps finished.

Some of the above material has been published, but some has yet to be published. When all ready, it will put physical education and physical examination in China at least ten years in advance.

### 3. Mass Education —A Movement to Remove Illiteracy

Mass illiteracy presents a unique problem in China. Deducting one hundred and twenty million children who are either below or in the school age, and eighty million who have spent on the average three years in the old schools, there are still about two hundred million, or fifty per cent of the whole population, who have never had any schooling. This is a gigantic problem for the advocates of popular education to solve. The National Y.M.C.A. several years ago started the new experiment on popular education. At the Second Annual Convention of the National Association for the Advancement of Education held at Tsing Hua College, 1923, the National Association for the Mass Education Movement with Mme S. L. Hsiung as its president was organized, and the movement immediately received nation-wide support and backing.

In substance, the so-called mass education utilizes four popular readers based on a vocabulary of about twelve hundred most common Chinese characters. An average illiterate can complete the four readers in four months by spending one hour a day. At the end of four months, he will be able to read newspapers, books, and correspondence based on the vocabulary and to express himself by using the same. As these four readers cost altogether only twelve cents

Mex., even the poorest can afford to buy. There are three ways in the teaching of illiterates. First, there is the People's School, which has a teacher who meets his classes regularly at definite periods of time. Second, there is the People's Reading Circle, which takes the home, the store, etc. as a unit, and encourages the literate people in the home or in the store to teach his own associates. Third, there is the People's Question Station where the illiterates may stop and ask questions on any point in the book which he does not understand. These stations are generally under the charge of shopkeepers who are willing to contribute their time to the work. with these means, the readers have been introduced into the homes, stores, factories, schools, churches, monasteries, *yamens*, steamships, prisons, and army camps. Within two years' time, the circulation of these readers has reached the two-million point. These readers are followed by a series of booklets on various branches of knowledge. It will not be long before we see a compulsory popular education in operation in China with its tax on ignorance. Friends of popular education have the ambition to achieve the miracle of eliminating two hundred million of the illiterates in a generation.

**4. The Development of Science Instruction**

For some time, there has been a growing dissatisfaction at the result of science instruction, especially in the secondary schools. The dissatisfaction was directed not only to the poor equipment, but largely to the methods employed. In 1922, Dr. Paul Monroe of the International Institute of Education, New York,visited China and his observation confirmed the opinion of many regarding science instruction. Upon his recommendation, the Chinese National Association for the Advancement of Education invited Dr. G. R.

Twiss of the Ohio State University to come to China to assist in the improvement of methods of instruction in the science subjects. He made very extensive trips throughout China. Though brief has been his sojourn and limited have been his recommendations, his visit has provided a great stimulus to the science teachers of the country. Another important fact that may be mentioned is the establishment of summer institutes for science teachers in which the teachers of science can pursue, under expert supervision, further studies during the summer months. Such institutes are to be held under the joint auspices of educational and scientific organizations. The first one was held in 1924 in Tsing Hua College, Peking, and the second one will be held in the National Southeastern University at Nanking.

### 5. The Library Movement

China has had libraries ever since the Chow Dynasty, several centuries before the Christian era. But they were only accessible to the few intellectual aristocrats and could hardly be reached by ordinary students, not to speak of the mass of the people. With the advent of new education, school libraries have gradually come into existence, until this year there are a dozen college libraries with the best modern equipment and quite a number of fairly equipped secondary school libraries in this country. This means more opportunities for the teachers and students to get at the sources of knowledge. In the meantime, the classical libraries in various educational centers, however hesitative they may be, are gradually opening their doors to more advanced readers.

Having realized the needs of modern methods for the management of modern libraries, institutions of higher learning have sent, from time to time, a number of students abroad to study library science. When the Chinese National Association for the Advancement of Education held its First Conference in Tsinan in 1922 there were already several Chinese librarians with modern training, who immediately set to work to organize a committee on library science under the auspices of the Association. Their aims are to promote more libraries, to have better methods of managing libraries, and to draw more people to use the libraries. In order to carry out these projects more effectively, they put through, at the Second Conference held in Tsing Hua College in 1923, a resolution for organizing local library associations. Thus, in 1924, eight such associations were formed. It was simply natural and spontaneous that when the Third Annual Conference was held at National Southeastern University in July, 1924, they looked forward to organizing a national library association of China to unify the efforts of individuals and institutions interested in this movement. This national organization is to take form in 1925. Thus, the cry for more books and better books, more libraries and better libraries, has become nation-wide. Our librarians are losing no time in making their unique contributions. At the same time, the cry for more people to use books and libraries is being answered by promoters of the Mass Education Movement. Miss Wood, one of the best friends of our library movement, and others are kept busy in securing portions of the American Boxer Indemnity Fund for founding model public libraries in this country. The Chinese National Association for the Advancement of Education has requested the American Library Association to send a library expert here to help make a systematic plan for such an undertaking.

## VI. Missionary Education

Acccording to the statement of Dr. Wallace, the associate general secretary of the China Christian Educational Association, it is probable that the total number of students in the Protestant missionary institutions at present is near three hundred thousand. It is still in the direction of increase. The college students have increased in the four years from 1920 to 1924 by seventy-six per cent. Archbishop Celso Costantini gives 253, 953 as the number of students under the training of the Catholic churches. Thus, out of every hundred students in China, there are eight in the missionary schools.

The outstanding event of the year in regard to the missionary education has been the organization of the China Association for Christian Higher Education. This Association has appointed a council to act as an interim body, also as the Council of Higher Education of the China Christian Education Association, thus linking up the higher education with other activities of the latter organization. Rev. E. C. Lobenstine, the Council's secretary, is now engaged in making a study of the institutions, particularly with reference to their financial position and the possibilities of coordinating their efforts. The chief purpose of the Council is to enable the Christian institutions of higher learning with their limited resources to make the most effective contribution to the needs of China.

Missionary education, in spite of its good record, has been attacked on three different grounds. First, it is generally attacked on the ground that the Christian institutions are entirely under foreign control. Even qualified Chinese Christians are rarely given opportunity for holding responsible positions. Secondly, it is criticized for teaching religion to young children who are not mature enough to make intelligent decision for themselves. Finally, there is serious suspicion on the part of the Chinese that the missions are organizing a system of Christian education parallel to the Chinese government system which might become in time an irreconcilable group within a larger group.

As a consequence of these facts, we have witnessed two successive attacks on the missionary education in the two National Educational Conferences held in July and October this year. The more conservative Chinese, however, think that, in this transitional stage, missionary education of the more liberal type does have a unique contribution to make by way of supplementing the government education in providing wider educational opportunities for the students and setting up a better example in school discipline. They also believe that missionary education should be more socialized, liberalized, and made more Chinese. Finally, they feel that the missions would be able to make a better contribution, if they should concentrate their efforts and resources on a few institutions of higher learning and not for the establishment of secondary and elementary schools of poorer grade. They believe that secondary and elementary schools of experimental nature might be opened by the missions as well as by other private agencies, and any attempts to multiply them and build a system out of them are bound to conflict sooner or later with the government system.

## VII. A Few Concluding Remarks

The Chinese schoolmen are working under overwhelming difficulties and adverse conditions. It is generally true that instead of being discouraged under such circumstances, they regard these as opportunities for effort and endeavor. China may be said to be a virgin soil for educatoinal service or as a social vacuum which absorbs any amount of energy that one is willing to put into it. In order to understand Chinese education today, therefore, we must see it in terms of the difficulties that are involved and the effort that has been put into it.

## Note

EDUCATION IN CHINA 1924, by Tao Tchi-Shin, General Director of Chinese National Association for the Advancement of Education, and C.P. Chen, Professor of Education in National Southeastern University, was first published in book form in June 1925 by the Commercial Press in Beijing.

# China





## Introduction

**General survey of the forces acting upon Chinese education.** — Education as a social institution and process is constantly influenced by the political, social, economic, and physical forces of the environment in which education is carried on. These forces may be favorable or unfavorable to the development of education. They may handicap the orderly working out of educational schemes as well as stimulate further educational activities. In order to secure a better understanding of Chinese education in this year, it is necessary to have before us a picture of the more important forces that have been acting and reacting upon educational thought and practice during the same period.

Politically the year opens with a nation-wide dissatisfaction over the election of Tsou Kun to the Presidency on October 10, 1923. It was felt that this election must inevitably breed internal war, although at that time no one could tell when such a war would come. It is the teachers of the land who worry most, because many of them have felt that the example of one election would be powerful enough to nullify the educational effort of ten years. The schoolman cannot but be stimulated to consider how through education the character of future representatives could be trained if representative government is a good thing for this country. Education for citizenship as a movement has here received its great momentum.

Following the election, the leaders of different political parties began to ally themselves in a united front against the Chihli Party. Dr. Sun Yat-sen, Marshals Tuan Chi-Shui and Chang Tso-ling, although differing on national policies, are one in their effort against Tsou Kun and Wu Pei-fu. In less than a year's time, we find the Chihli Party and the Anti-Chihli Parties meeting on the battlefield. The expenses involved in military operations on both sides are estimated at not less than twenty million dollars gold. If the loss of civilian property and the harvest is included, no less than seventy-five million dollars gold have been lost in this present war.

The year begins with a military force of one and one-half million soldiers. The preparation for hostilities on all sides nearly throughout the year has greatly increased the number of soldiers at public expense. The total expenditure for army purposes has been estimated to be about one hundred fifty million dollars gold. This is the burden of militarism on the Chinese people.

Militarism and the present war as its result have affected education in two ways. In the first place, they have drained away enormous resources which might have been turned into the development of education. In the second place, they serve to stimulate the introduction of vocational education into the armies. The educators had constantly in their minds the demobilization of soldiers as one of the fundamental ways of saving the country; but they also believed that many of the soldiers cannot be disbanded without giving them first a vocational training for independent living. Vocational training for the rehabilitation of disabled soldiers is a direct outcome of the present war.

**Foreign affairs.** —In international relations, there are three phases which need special mention. The treaties hitherto made between foreign countries and China on unequal terms have been attacked this year more ardently than at any time before. These have humiliated the Chinese people and caused the assumption of a superior air on the part of not a few foreigners. A Chinese writer has remarked, "As foreigners love us, we love them in turn; but as foreigners despise us, we hate them." These treaties have occasioned the recent development of a strong nationalistic tendency which has even found expression in educational conferences held this year. The present attack on missionary education in China, aside from religious reasons, is partly due to the indirect influence of this nation-wide opposition to unequal treaties, cancellation of which by mutual consent will benefit all parties concerned. It is believed that such a cancellation by mutual consent will not only enable China to occupy a more appropriate place in the family of nations but will make our foreign friends feel much more at home in China.

The next thing which should be considered is the restoration of diplomatic relationship with Russia. Through the cancellation of all treaties made between Old Russia and the Tsing Dynasty, Russia has won a warm friendship from the Chinese people. This was shown in the honor accorded to Lenin, on January 26, and in the parade for demanding the recognition of Russia. The good feeling entertained by the Chinese toward New Russia is not so much for Russia's Bolshevism as for Russia's stand for international justice and equality, not in words but in action. It is yet too early to forecast the influences of this new friend upon our education. However, one thing we are pretty sure of is that contact with New Russia will make Chinese education less favorable for further realization of imperialism and capitalism.

**Cancellation of Boxer indemnities.** —The Japanese and British Governments have already adopted a policy of using the indemnities which in their present forms are not acceptable to the Chinese people. The French indemnity is still hanging on the gold franc question. These three sources, if the methods of administration of the fund are changed, will be partly devoted to educational and cultural purposes. The American portion of indemnity, a sum of $12, 545, 438.67 gold, was cancelled by the American Congress on May 21, and is to be used for educational and cultural purposes. Dr. Paul Monroe's visit to this country in August resulted in the formation of a foundation called "The China Foundation for the Promotion of Education and Culture", composed of ten Chinese and five Americans, to direct the use of this fund. The Russian portion of indemnity available for educational use amounts to about $ 45,000,000 gold and is intrusted to a committee of two Chinese and one Russian for its management. These funds will give stimulation to new educational and cultural activities. Many projects have been proposed. But the promotion of science and village education seem to have received the largest amount of approval.

**Public opinion in China.** —A word must be said about the influence of public opinion in China before closing the discussion of the action of political forces upon education. Public opinion is a more important political and social force in this country than we have usually thought. Its influence is latent but continuously present. It acts slowly but very steadily and surely. Political and social movements rise or fall according to whether they are backed up or knocked down by this invisible force. It can be shown that public opinion was one of the most decisive factors in the founding of the Republic, the defeat of the Second Revolution, the downfall of Yen Shi-kai, the failure of the restoration of the Manchu Monarchy, the fall of the Anfuit Party, and the present fall of the Chihli Party. The public opinion of China today stands for an honest and efficient government in internal affairs, and for just and friendly relations in external affairs. Nothing short of these ideals could satisfy the intelligent public opinion of the day. How to make opinion more public and more intelligent is the problem of popular education which has on its program the transformation of two hundred million illiterates into intelligent and responsible citizens in ten years' time!

**China, an agricultural nation.** —More than 80 per cent of the Chinese population live in farming villages. An understanding of the conditions of the farmer is therefore necessary to an appreciation of the economic and educational problems involved. The Chinese farmers are contented and conservative people. They have contributed to the stability and persistence of Chinese civilization. In spite of all difficulties they have been very successful in growing food and in maintaining fertility of the soil. Small farms which produce barely enough for the support of their families prevail all over the country. In the absence of any rural credit system the best the farmer can do when in need of financial assistance is to pawn his personal effects. The interest reaches as high a rate as 36 per cent per annum. Other factors which handicap our farmers are many, but the more important are poor transportation facilities, absence of cooperative buying and selling, lack of rudimentary knowledge of the written language which is the key to the many new knowledges needed for the improvement of farming, and the lack of sanitary control which is undermining the health of the farmers and of their children. These facts call forth the economic and educational attack of the village problem. A village education effective enough to regenerate the social and economic life of the farmers is considered the most important issue of the day. Hand in hand with village education, the conditions of the farmers have stimulated higher agricultural education, which in time will help the farmers in scientific farming.

**Industrial development and the labor problem.** —In spite of this dominant agricultural influence, new industries have gradually and steadily sprung up and are rapidly increasing in extent and influence. There are now more than 100 flour mills and 70 oil mills in operation. Cement is being manufactured in Shanghai and Nanking, and very soon Shantung, Honan, and Manchuria will enter this field. We now refine our own sugar and salt, wash with home-made soap, light with home-made matches. More than two hundred cities are now lighted with electricity. There are more that a dozen prosperous companies owned and operated by the Chinese with an aggregate capital of sixty million dollars and a capacity of producing eight million of the fourteen million tons produced by all the modern mines in China. This roughly represents an increase of 400 per cent in the space of thirteen years.[①] During 1918-1919 the cotton industry in China suddenly rose into prominence; after 1921 it began to decline. The total number of spindles in 1924 was 2,160,406 as against 2,221,486 in 1923. [②] While Chinese spindles decreased from 64 per cent in 1923 to 56 per cent in 1924, the Japanese spindles in China increased from 25 per cent to 34 per cent in a year's time. Hewerer, the number of looms is on the increase; 7,817 were in operation in 1923, while in 1924 the number rose to 9,481. These figures represent prewar conditions; the present war must have seriously checked the natural growth of industries.

Along with the development of industries there comes the problem of labor and class wars. "Hundreds of labor unions of one description or another have sprung up with Canton as the most active centre. Strikes have kept pace with the growth of labor organization. Though poorly led and at times exploited by would-be labor leaders, the workers have had a taste of their own strength··· The workers are now becoming conscious of their misery, their rights, and their power." ③ Especially has the labor of women and children in China been the least protected and worst exploited. Most of the laborers are illiterates.

Such being the industrial conditions that are found in China today, the educators are confronted with problems of bringing the human element into industrialism, cultivating a right attitude toward labor as well as capital, making industries capable of meeting the needs of the nation and the world with a minimum sacrifice of the higher life. Education and legislation must join hands in securing the fullest benefit from industrialism and in reducing to the lowest limit the calamities that have accompanied the introduction of industrialism in the West.

**Commercial development.** —"In spite of political disturbances, foreign trade has advanced steadily every year during the past twenty years, each succeeding year's return being in advance of its predecessor. "[4] "The foreign trade of China in 1923 was at Hk. Tls. 1,676,320,303, which represents an increase of Hk. Tls. 76,378,720 over the preceding year's total. The value of imports declined by about twenty-two million taels, but exports increased by nearly one hundred million taels. " [5] Much allowance should be made for price fluctuations. Our tea and silk trade with America has declined, partly owing to our neglect to improve the quality to conform with American standards, and partly due to the severe competition of Japan. These failures have stimulated scientific studies in sericulture and tea manufacturing. The increase in private endowment funds for educational purposes during recent years can be explained partly by the steady increase in commercial prosperity. This year business has been greatly disturbed on account of the war, and has deprived education of much of its potential support from the commercial world. As Mr. Arnold says, "When China has the same per capita foreign trade as Australia in its aggregate, it will amount to about $60,000,000,000 instead of its present $1,000,000,000." A proper system of commercial education hand in hand with the improvements in agriculture and industry must be relied upon to make China's trade sixty times the present size.

**Flood and famine.** —Other forces which visit China at intervals of time are flood and famine. The floods that occurred in July and August of this year, notably in Chihli, Hunan, Kiangsi, and in the far South have been a terrible calamity. It is not possible to obtain figures of the total loss. In Kalgan, Hunan, and Fukien alone, the estimates of damages amount to $45,000,000 gold. According to the report of the International Famine Relief Commission, it would take at least ten million dollars gold in order to relieve the ten million people who have been affected by this disaster. The direct effects of this flood are: first, the call upon all possible financial resources for relief work, leaving practically no room for new educational activities; second, the need for a systematic program of reforestation together with hydraulic engineering works is widely recognized; and the third, the use of the relief fund for preventive work through a system of practical education is insisted upon. The promoters of popular education have also tried to take this opportunity to educate the illiterate refugees during the leisure hours.

**The status of communications.** —Education as a general rule follows improvements in communication. The extent of new education corresponds very closely to the extent of railway and steamship communication. Although China is larger in area than the United States, Mexico, and Central America combined, and has four times the population of the United States, she has less than 7,000 miles of railways compared to 265,000 miles in the United States. As a consequence six sevenths of China's population is concentrated in about one third of its territory. Railways will open up nearly 2,000,000 square miles now unsettled and undeveloped. They will assist in a better distribution of the population, in the unification of the country, and in the eradication of brigandage and famine. Railways and good roads are indispensable to the spread of education, for universal education is dependent upon universal communication.

**The Chinese Renaissance.** —Of all the forces that are now acting upon Chinese education the Chinese Renaissance⑥ has exerted the most profound influence. The movement began in 1917 as a "Literary Revolution" when Dr. Hu-suh and Mr. Chan Tu Siu, the leaders of the movement, declared that the classical language had outlived its usefulness and that *Pei hua*, the spoken language, was its legitimate heir. As the *Pei hua* is the most widely spoken language in the country, the culmination of over twenty centuries of linguistic evolution, and the language in which the nation's most favored literatures were produced, the Literary Revolution met with astonishing success. In spite of strong opposition on the part of conservative scholars, the younger generation received it with overwhelming joy. This rediscovery of a living language for Chinese has enabled China to produce new literatures fitted for the new age, revolutionized elementary school reading materials as well as methods of teaching them, and made it possible for the popular education movement to go on with its program of eliminating illiteracy.

The second phase of the Renaissance has to do with higher education. During the later years of the movement scholars have been seeking to apply the modern scientific methods of research to the work of systematizing the old learning of China. In the words of Dr. Hu, this "systematization of the national heritage is a revival or rebirth of that spirit of criticism and research which animated the works of the Han Hsueh scholars of the last three centuries".

But the influence of the Renaissance is wider than this. It is a movement through which "all traditional values are judged from a new standpoint and with new standards. Tradition is often thrown overboard, authority is cast aside,old beliefs are being undermined". This explains why the Renaissance movement is so permeating and far-reaching and its effects are spreading over the whole fabric of national life.

**Visits of world scholars.** —Since 1918, a number of eminent scholars like John Dewey, Bertrand Russell, Paul Monroe, Von Driesch, Rabindranath Tagore, and others have visited this country. All of them, through their lectures and contact with our intellectual leaders and students, have exerted much influence upon Chinese thought and life. Special mention should be made of Dr. Dewey's and Dr. Monroe's visits because of their unique significance for the reconstruction of Chinese education. Besides his influence upon advanced students, Dr. Dewey's pragmatic philosophy of education has been one of the guiding principles in the reforms of our elementary education. Since his visit a number of experiments have been conducted in elementary education. His philosophy has stimulated several students of education to work out techniques and methods for its realization. Education as an application instead of acquisition of ideas has been emphasized by Dr. Monroe. His recommendations, resulting from careful investigations in 1921, have aroused serious deliberation on various educational problems and stimulated especially reforms in secondary education and science teaching.

**The critical attitude of Chinese schoolmen.** —So far we have only mentioned the more important forces and the effects which they have exerted upon Chinese education. These are sufficient to show that in China problems are many and perplexing. Solutions are sought in her own past civilization as well as in contemporary examples. Thus China has tried to learn from one country after another, until today she has quite a cosmopolitan group of tutors from which to select. Japan, Germany, America, England, the Philippines, India, and Russia are the more important countries whose edcuational theories and practices have had influence upon Chinese education. China has in the past followed her teachers rather blindly but as yet no one has succeeded in offering her a satisfactory solution for her problems. Each is helpul to her in some ways but wholesale adoption of any one system has led her astray. At first she sacrificed everything old for the new. Gradually she came to a realization that the old is not necessarily bad and the new is not necessarily good. Thus our schoolmen have become much more critical than in former years. Their reaction now toward new theories and practices is no longer imitative adoption, but questioning, examination, experimentation, and selection. The logical outcome of this attitude tends to work out an education that is best fitted for the need of New China by assimilating what is best in the old and the new, both at home and in other countries. Experiences in the past and in the outside world must be assimilated before they can contribute to the nation's vitality and well-being. The critical and experimental attitude is creative. It is only with such an attitude that a real Chinese education adapted to Chinese life is possible. Such a creation has begun.

## Administration Of Education

**Central authority.** —At the head of the educational system is the Ministry of Education, which, under the direction of the President, is in charge of education, arts, science, and astronomical observation. It has three bureaus: (1) the Bureau of General Education, (2) the Bureau of Higher Education, and (3) the Bureau of Social Education. The more important officers of the Ministry are the Minister, the Vice-Minister, three councilors, three directors of the bureaus, four secretaries, and sixteen national inspectors of education. ⑦ Important actions of the Ministry are brought to the consideration of the Ministry conferences which are attended by the councilors, directors, secretaries, and others invited by the Minister to be present. Such conferences are presided over by the Minister. The Minister of Education is a member of the Cabinet and has the general direction of the Ministry. He chooses his subordinates, including the Vice-Minister, subject to the approval of the Cabinet. Three years ago the Minister was changed about twice a year. In the last two or three years the position has become more unstable. This year the Minister has been changed five times. However, the Vice-Minister usually holds office for a longer term but only about twice as long as the Minister. Councilors, directors, and their subordinate staff remain in office for a much longer time; it is to them that the continuous functioning of the Ministry is due. On account of political dissension in the country and the lack of financial support for education, the activities of the Ministry have been so restricted and held back that the office is often spoken of as the Ministry of Pekin schools, and worse still as the Ministry of the Ministry, for the Ministry has even lost control of the Pekin schools and has been sometimes dictated to by them. However, in spite of the absence of constructive activities for the provinces, the Ministry still enjoys much of its old prestige. With the coming of a united country and the appointment of the right person to be its head, the Ministry may still become a driving force in the advancement of education in the years to come, although it is likely that local initiative will be more encouraged and its former bureaucratic influence will be curtailed.

**Provincial administration of education.** —In the provinces there are now three existing forms of educational administration; namely, the bureau of education, the department of education, and the commission of education. Kwangtung tried a fourth plan, the committee of education, which has now been abandoned. In those provinces that have declared their independence, it is the bureau of education or department of education that has been adopted. Thus in Yunnan, Kweichow, and Hunan, the bureau form of educational administration exists. The director of the bureau is appointed by the governor in Yunnan and Kweichow and is elected in Hunan by the Provincial Assembly. In both Yunnan and Kweichow the bureau is supplemented by a committee of educational administration which passes upon important educational policies and plans. The department of education is found in Kwangsi and Szechuen and is vested with less power than the bureau of education. The rest of the provinces have the commission form of educational administration at the head of which is the commissioner of education, appointed by the President of the Republic upon the recommendation of the Minister of Education. The commission of education is under the direct control of the Ministry. But in directing educational activities in the province and in supervising his staff and the magistrates for the management of local education, thc commissioner of education is required to work under the governor of the province. Thus the commissioner of education though theoretically responsible to the Ministry is practically serving under two masters, the Minister and the governor. As a consequence the power of the commissioner varies in different provinces, depending upon the will of the provincial governor. As he is farther from the Minister and nearer to the governor, there is every temptation for him to follow the dictation of the governor.

The commission of education has two or three departments for carrying out the main group of educational activities, and there are four to six inspectors of education for each province.

**County educational administration.** —Below the province is the county. There are two systems of county school administration: first, the bureau for the promotion of education whose function is to assist the magistrate in educational administration and in supervising the educational work of the self-governing districts. The bureau has a superintendent and a few educational promoters. Besides the superintendent, there is under the magistrate an educational secretary and also a county inspector of education who is independent of the superintendent. This type of administration of county education has proved to be very troublesome, and it is now being gradually replaced by a second system, the county board of education.

The county board of education was inaugurated in 1922, and attempts to unify county school administration.Under this system, the inspectors are brought under the direction of the superintendent, who is appointed by the provincial commissioner of education upon the recommendation of the magistrate. Another effort in this new scheme is to grant more powers to special cities for the independent management of their schools and to place village education under the control of the county government. This principle, however, has not been applied vigorously although the seeds have been sown. This year has seen more places, especially Kirin, adopting the board system for county school administration.

**Local units of educational administration.** —The lowest unit of local educational administration is the school district. The county or *hsien* is subdivided into several school districts, each of which has a delegate for school affairs, sometimes with an assistant. The school districts in China are not vested with sufficient power to cope with their responsibility. It is most loosely and inefficiently organized.

Reorganization of the lowest units so that they can be held responsible for the educational progress of the district is one of the most urgent needs of today. Shansi alone has the best organization of the local units. Every village in the county or every street in the city has responsible persons to take charge of the educational welfare and is given more power to perform its duties.

## Educational Finance

Roughly speaking, there are three grades of education supported by three sets of funds. Higher education is mainly supported by the national fund, secondary education by the provincial fund, and elementary education by the county or local fund. There are exceptions, but in general this practice is uniform.

As national revenue comes from customs duties, salt tax, stamp tax, tobacco and liquor licenses, revenue from telegraphs, railways, postal service, land tax, likin, etc., the national fund for nationai education is drawn from the complex of these sources. With the exception of a few institutions such as Tsing Hua, the University of Communications, the Wu Chang Normal University, which draw their respective funds from a special source, others get their shares from this general appropriation. The national institutions located outside of Pekin secure their appropriations from the national fund placed under the custody of the provincial commissioner of finance. According to the budget of 1919, the only budget to which we can refer, the appropriation for national education, $5,028,836 Mex., was less than 1 per cent of the total appropriation for the year.

Although there are professional schools conducted by the provincial government, yet the province is still mainly concerned with secondary education. There is a tendency for each province to maintain a full college, but so far very few provinces have succeeded in its realization. The main sources from which funds for provincial education are derived are surtaxes, especially the surtax on land. Kiangsu and Chekiang are now levying a special tax on tobacco for the use of provincial education. Szechuen tried in 1922 to devote its pork tax to education but without much result. The tax on the transfer of deeds and ownership adopted in Honan yields an annual income of $1,000,000 Mex. for provincial education. In the face of financial distress a number of solutions have been proposed. In order to give some idea of the extent of provincial support of education, we may mention that Kiangsu is spending $ 2, 800,000 Mex., Chekiang $1,500,000 Mex., and Kiangsi $ 600,000 Mex. annually.

As a general rule the county supports elementary education by surtax on land, miscellaneous assessment, rent, and interest from the academy properties handed down from the Tsing Dynasty. ⑧ The Shensi method of supporting elementary education is so far the best that has been evolved in this country. In the cities, stores and houses are graded and assessed according to their standing for the support of city elementary education. In the villages a land surtax is levied according to qualities for the support of village education. ⑨

On account of political unrest and the irregular expenses for military purposes, the schools are confronted with the uncertainty of educational funds. The provinces that have suffered a serious shortage of funds are Kuangtung, Fukien, Kiangsi, Szechuen, Anhuei, Kiangsu, Pekin District, and Hunan. Salaries of teachers have been held back two months, three months, and even as long as ten months. The teachers of China today are serving the country at greatest personal sacrifice. The provinces which are better off are Fengtien, Yunnan, and Shensi. Shantung and Hunan before the outbreak of the war were paying the teachers regularly.

The problems that are of chief concern are: (1) How to insure the regularity of the payment of educational appropriations by legal protection and economic devices, so that those who are in educational service can be free from financial anxieties and give their whole-hearted devotion to the cause of education; (2) how to reorganize the tax system so that the burden as well as the opportunity for education can be equalized; (3) how to stimulate educational activities through a proper system of distribution and subsidy without curtailing local initiative; (4) how to economize the use of the present fund so that the maximum of educational results can be achieved at minimum cost.

## Inspection And Supervision

In China there are three grades of inspection, national, provincial, and county. According to the 1913 regulation, the whole country is divided into eight inspection districts. Each district has two national inspectors of education. School inspection is to begin from the latter part of August and end with the first part of June. The inspectors are required to inspect all phases in the general and social eduation. Special inspection shall be made by special order of the Minister. When the inspectors are not on inspection tours, they are required to be present in the Ministry. During the last few years this has been a dead letter, and national inspection of education has been almost entirely absent.

Provincial inspectors of education are appointed by the commissioner of education. There are four inspectors for smaller provinces and five or six for larger provinces. Below the province there are county school inspectors. Under the old system they act as agents for the magistrate in inspecting the schools ,but with the adoption of the system of a board of education the county inspectors of education are under the direction of the county superintendent of education. The county inspectors visit the schools under their charge one to three times a year.

The functions of inspectors of education are enumerated in the Educational Code. There are seven duties for the national and provincial inspectors and thirteen duties for the county inspectors to perform. But in actual practice the inspectors are simply visitors, reporters, and, worst of all, faultfinders. Most of them do not realize that their mission is to give inspiration, encouragement, and a helping hand to the principals and the teachers in service. In recent years there has been a tendency to protest against this negative inspection, or inspection for the sake of inspection, and advocate in its place a system of constructive supervision. The province of Kiangsu has set up a noble example in this respect. Beginning with the last year the commissioner of education has invited experts in Southeastern University and other places to serve as supervisors for special subjects. Thus the supervision of vocational education, science teaching, physical training, and normal education was instituted; this year supervision of social sciences and national language has been introduced. This practice has opened in China a new era in school supervision.

## The New System Of Education

"China has had at least four systems of education within the last twenty years." ⑩ The newest one was adopted in 1922 as a result of three years' deliberation, initiated by the Conference of Provincial Educational Associations in 1919.

The issues that have been involved in this system will be touched upon in connection with the discussion of the grades and types of education. Since 1922 committees have been kept busy in drawing up courses of study and curricula in order to fill out the general framework. This year has witnessed the completion of all the courses of study except a small part in vocational education. It was voted by

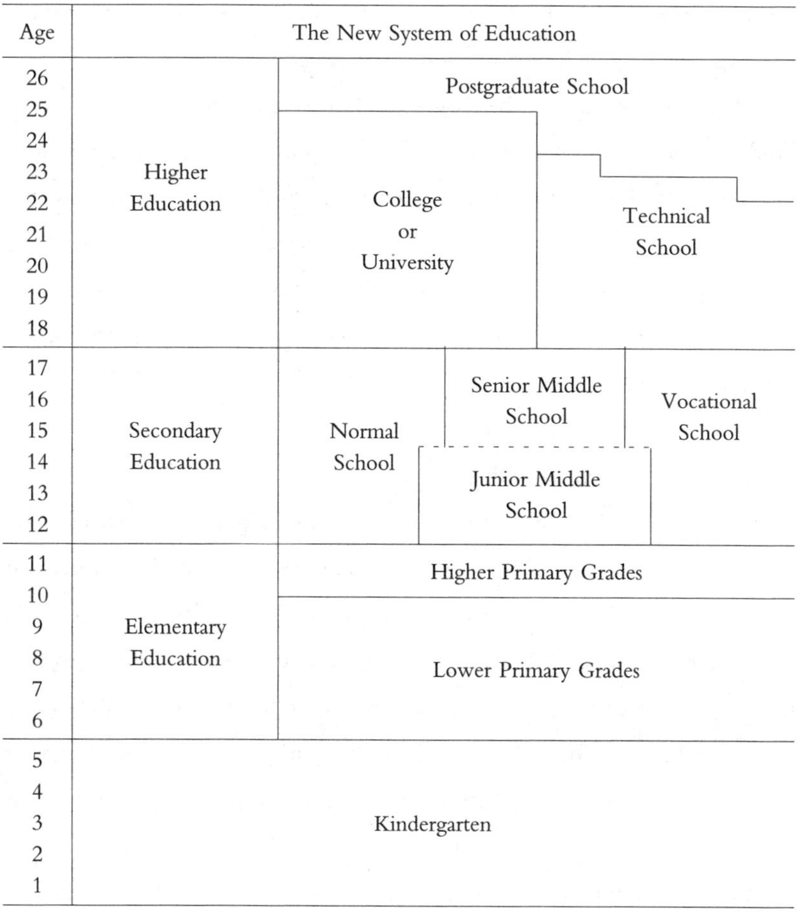

the October Conference of the Provincial Educational Associations to submit them to the Ministry of Education for promulgation. On the next page is the diagrammatic representation of the new system, adopted by the twenty-third Ordinance of the Ministry of Education.

## Preschool And Kindergarten Education

Kindergarten education has been given a place in the new system and "admits children under six years of age". The practice schools of normal schools, especially normal schools for women in cities, have a kindergarten. There are also kindergartens conducted by the missions. But the combined number of kindergartens is still very small. As kindergarten training gives the child an opportunity for active self-expression and also for the interaction between the child and the teacher, this type of education is very much needed. In order to have more kindergartens, it is very necessary to have first adequate institutions for training kindergarteners. The resolution for more trained kindergarteners passed in January, 1924, by the Kiangsu Conference of Educational. Administrators, is an indication of the need felt. The Hunan Educational Association has also this year advocated the establishment of kindergartens in cities and towns. The Kiangsu Compulsory Education Association has even recommended the adoption of kindergarten methods in the lowest grade in elementary schools. [11] Another very encouraging and more important fact is the experiment in kindergarten education conducted by Professor H. C. Chen. Impressed by the fact that the subject matter and methods used in the kindergartens are borrowed from foreign countries, some of them unsuited to Chinese children, he and his staff began in October, 1923, to experiment with selfmade toys, Chinese

Mother Goose stories, and other materials. He is also trying to use the kindergarten as a center for training mothers as well as for the education of young children. The National Association for the Advancement of Education and Professor Chen have agreed to cooperate in including in his plan an experiment on the least possible cost for kindergarten education, so that it can be duplicated in the largest number of communities.

## Elementary Education

According to the new system, "attendance at the elementary School is limited to six years; temporarily it may be extended another year in order to fit into local situations. The elementary school may be divided into the lower primary and higher primary grades. The former consists of four years and may be established separately".

The subjects of instruction and the percentage of time allotments as drawn up by the Committee of Eighteen for elementary schools are given in Table (1)(on the next page [12])

It is further recommended that the school week should be at lesat 1,080 minutes in length for the first two years, 1,260 minutes per week for the third and fourth years, and 1,440 minutes for the two higher primary grades. The number of minutes are to be distributed into suitable periods for six days' work. In village schools the subjects may be combined and simplified, but the time allotted to national language and arithmetic should never be reduced.

According to the new system, "compulsory education is temporarily limited to four years". Under adequate circumstances this may be extended to meet local requirements. The school age for compulsory education is left to be determined by the different

**Table 1**

<table>
<tr><th rowspan="2">Subjects</th><th colspan="2">Percentage of Time Devoted to Each Subject in</th></tr>
<tr><th>Lower Primary Grades</th><th>Higher Primary Grades</th></tr>
<tr><td>National Language</td><td></td><td></td></tr>
<tr><td>Conversation</td><td rowspan="4">30</td><td>6</td></tr>
<tr><td>Reading</td><td>12</td></tr>
<tr><td>Composition</td><td>8</td></tr>
<tr><td>Penmanship</td><td>4</td></tr>
<tr><td>Arithmetic</td><td>10</td><td></td></tr>
<tr><td>Social Sciences</td><td></td><td></td></tr>
<tr><td>Hygiene</td><td rowspan="4">20</td><td>4</td></tr>
<tr><td>Citizenship</td><td>4</td></tr>
<tr><td>History</td><td>6</td></tr>
<tr><td>Geography</td><td>6</td></tr>
<tr><td>Nature Study</td><td rowspan="2">12</td><td>8</td></tr>
<tr><td>Gardening</td><td>4</td></tr>
<tr><td>Industrial Arts</td><td colspan="2">7</td></tr>
<tr><td>Imagery Arts</td><td colspan="2">5</td></tr>
<tr><td>Music</td><td colspan="2">6</td></tr>
<tr><td>Physical Education</td><td colspan="2">10</td></tr>
</table>

provinces and special districts, according to local situations.

The introduction of compulsory education has been contemplated by the central authorities ever since the Tsing Dynasty. It was not until 1920 that the Ministry of Education mapped out definite steps for the enforcement of compulsory education in different communities at specified times. The specifications are as follows:

1921 —provincial capitals and open ports

1922 —county seats and cities

1923 —towns containing above five hundred families

1924 —towns containing above three hundred families

1925 and 1626 —towns containing above two hundred families

1927 —villages containing above one hundred families

1928 —villages containing below one hundred families

On account of political disturbances, the above provisions have rarely been put into practice. Shansi, under the governorship of Yen Hsih-shan, has, however, enforced a most effective program of compulsory education. The Shansi program had seven steps, to be completed in seven half-years, from 1918 to 1921. Although complete success has not been achieved, yet the latest return of statistics shows that 72 per cent of children of school age has been reached in Shansi. Coeducated adults below 25 years of age are now required to attend continuation schools to study Chinese, arithmetic, and citizenship.

Next to Shansi, the effort of the Kiangsu Compulsory Education Association, under the leadership of Mr. Yuan Shi-tao, to equalize educational opportunities,should be mentioned. Here the emphasis is put on the training of teachers as the initial step to compulsory education. This year fifty of the sixty counties in Kiangsu have conducted county institutes for the training of teachers. Yunnan province has also in this year achieved admirable results in compulsory education. In Quenming city, the capital of Yunnan, under the leadership of Mr. Tong Yu-chuan, the commissioner of education for the province, [13] a fine of at least $1 Mex. is imposed on parents or guardians who are deliberately opposed to sending their children to school. Kweichow province has also taken vigorous measures in enforcing compulsory education. [14] Employers are prohibited from preventing children from attending schools. A fine of from $1 Mex. to $5 Mex. is imposed on guardians of children below ten years of age, and an additional $2 is charged for each additional year of age above ten. Those who are opposed to the payment of the compulsory education assessment are also to be fined a sum not exceeding $80 Mex. At the close of the year it was announced that Kwangsi has also adopted a very comprehensive plan for enforcing compulsory education in that province.

Another phase in connection with elementary education should be mentioned—the village education movement. As more than 80 per cent of the Chinese population live in villages, it is of the greatest importance that village education should receive the closest attention. Recently, especially this year, the back-to-the-country movement has gathered much strength. The National Association for the Advancement of Education has created a special committee on village education. The Ninth Conference of the Provincial Educational Associations met in Kaifen this last October and also devoted much thought to this important problem, The Kiangsu Compulsory Education Association, which met in August in Wu-sih, spent three days in drawing up seven practical suggestions for the improvement of village schools. ⑮ Special investigation of village schools in typical communities has been conducted by the Kiangsu Compulsory Education Association and the National Association for the Advancement of Education. The reports, though fragmentary, have stirred up great interest in and enthusiasm for village education. As the average village cannot support an expensive education, the National Association for the Advancement of Education has selected a few village schools where the principals have shown genius in new village leadership, to conduct experiments on the best possible village education at the lowest possible cost. It is hoped that in the course of a few years types or standards for village education can be developed for nation-wide adoption.

The language problem has practically been settled. Dr. Hu-suh's Literary Revolution has exerted the most profound influence in the elementary schools. The vernacular language, or the "living

**Table 2**

*Percentage of Elementary Students to Estimated Number of Children of School Age for Four Years of Elementary Education*

| Province | Percentage |
| --- | --- |
| Shansi | 72.0 |
| Shantung | 25.5 |
| Chihli | 24.2 |
| Shensi | 23.1 |
| Pekin District | 22.1 |
| Three Eastern Provinces | 22.1 |
| Yunnan | 20.6 |
| Kansu | 18.8 |
| Chekiang | 18.4 |
| Kwangsi | 17.0 |
| Kiangsu | 11.9 |
| Kwangtung | 11.4 |
| Hunan | 10.9 |
| Fukien | 10.3 |
| Szechuen | 9.1 |
| Honan | 8.9 |
| Kiangsi | 8.7 |
| Hupeh | 7.6 |
| Kweichow | 5.8 |
| Anhwei | 4.9 |
| Sinkiang | 2.1 |

language," is now welcomed by most of the elementary schools. The Fengtien authorities have this year been reactionary in prohibiting the use of the vernacular language in elementary schools; and Kwangtung still shows some hesitation in welcoming this change. As a means of ready expression, however, the living language is destined to prevail in elementary schools.

Another tendency that is noticeable is the increasing interest in making studies on subject matter and in methods of teaching in elementary schools. The scientific tendency in elementary education is gaining ground,and has been enhanced by the introduction of measurements and tests which will be discussed later.

## Secondary Education

The new system gives the following statements on secondary education:

Attendance at the middle school is limited to six years, which are to be divided into two periods of three years each, the junior middle school and the senior middle school... The junior middle school offers general education, but it may carry on various vocational courses, according to local needs. The senior middle school is divided into the

**Table 3**

| Subjects | Credits |
|---|---|
| Social Sciences | |
| Citizenship | 6 |
| History | 8 |
| Geography | 8 |
| Languages and Literature | |
| National Language | 32 |
| Foreign Language | 36 |
| Mathematics | 30 |
| Nature Study | 16 |
| Arts | |
| Drawing<br>Manual Arts<br>Music | 12 |
| Physical Education | |
| Physiology and Hygiene | 4 |
| Physical Exercise | 12 |
| Total | 164 |

general, the agricultural, the technical, the commercial, and the normal courses. In accordance with local situations only one course may be offered or several courses together.

In secondary schools the credit system has been adopted. A credit is defined as one hour of class work plus preparation. Subjects with no preparation will have a proportionate discount on their credits. The junior middle school requires the satisfactory completion of 180 credits for graduation, of which 164 credits are for required work. The subjects and credits for the junior middle school as drawn up by the Committee of Twelve are shown in Table (3). [16]

The curricula for the senior middle school drawn-up by the Committee of Nine are composed of three types of studies, namely:

**Table 4**

*Arts and Social Sciences Group*

| Subjects | Credits |
|---|---|
| General Requirements | |
| National Language | 16 |
| Foreign Language | 16 |
| Philosophy of Life | 4 |
| Social Problems | 6 |
| History of Civilization | 6 |
| General Principles of Science | 6 |
| Physical Education | 10 |
| Group Requirements | |
| Prescribed | |
| Special Chinese Literature | 8 |
| Beginner's Psychology | 3 |
| Beginner's Logic | 3 |
| One course of Social Science | 4 (at least) |
| One course of Natural Science or Mathematics | 6 (at least) |
| Electives | 32 (or more) |
| Pure Electives | 30 (or more) |
| Total | 150 |

**Table 5**

*Mathematics and Natural Sciences Group*

| Subjects | Credits |
|---|---|
| General Requirements | |
| National Language | 16 |
| Foreign Language | 16 |
| Philosophy of Life | 4 |
| Social Problems | 6 |
| History of Civilization | 6 |
| General Principles of Science | 6 |
| Physical Education | 10 |
| Group Requirements | |
| Prescribed | |
| Trigonometry | 3 |
| Senior Geometry | 6 |
| Senior Algebra | 6 |
| Analytic Geometry | 3 |
| Mechanical Drawing | 4 |
| Physics, Chemistry, Biology (any two of the three subjects with six credits for each) | 12 (at least) |
| Electives | 22 |
| Pure Electives | 30 |
| Total | 150 |

(1) General studies required of all students and granted about 43 per cent of the eredits; (2) required studies prescribed according to the special course pursued; and (3) pure elective studies not exceeding 20 per cent of the credits. The vocational courses of study for the senior middle school have not been published. The general courses of study are of two groups; namely, the arts and social sciences group, and the mathematics and natural sciences group. These two courses are given in Table (4) and Table (5). [17]

**Tendencies.** —Secondary education, as pointed out by Dr. Paul Monroe after his general survey of Chinese education in 1921, is the weakest spot in the Chinese educational system. Since then two organizations, the Chinese National Association for the Advancement of Education and the Chinese Federation of Secondary Education, have given much thought to studying the different phases of secondary education. The attention of the administrative authorities as well as of secondary school officers and teachers has been concentrated on improving this phase of education. Some of the more important problems and tendencies in regard to present-day Chinese secondary education may be here briefly discussed.

**Curriculum.** —First of all, the scientific study of secondary education has occupied a most important place in the minds of students of education and secondary school officers and teachers. This is a very hopeful sign for progress. The subject matter and methods of teaching secondary school subjects, school organization and administration are all now under examination, criticism, experimentation, and reformulation.

Of all the weak spots in secondary education, the weakest is the teaching of science. Here science has been taught through lectures and textbooks with very little opportunity for the students themselves to engage actively in laboratory work. Science study that result in the formation of an experimental attitude and in the acquisition of effective control of nature has been greatly neglected. In view of this fact, the National Association for the Advancement of Education invited Professor G. R. Twiss to undertake a special study of science teaching in China and to make recommendations for improvement. Professor Twiss, after a careful investigation of 187 schools in ten provinces, prepared a most comprehensive report with constructive recommendations, which will be published shortly. The Chinese Science Society is undertaking to include the improvement of science teaching as a phase of its regular work. This society, which has among its members nearly all of the prominent scientists in this country, will be able to exert great influence on the advancement of science education. Kiangsu Province has been selected as a starting point for their field of investigation and experimentation.

The next subject that has received much attention in recent years is the teaching of the national language in secondary schools. This important and vital subject in the hands of the old literati was taught in a very dry and uninteresting way, China is rich in masterpieces of national literature, but in practice poor selections are made. The teachers without training in education and psychology have to rely on the pouring-in and word-by-word explanation methods. For the first time, national attention was called to the reform needed in teaching this subject when Dr. Hu-suh read his paper on the Teaching of Chinese Language and Literature at the Tsinan conference of the National Association for the advancement of Education in 1922. Following Dr. Hu's speech, more than thirty articles have been written on the improvement of teaching Chinese; most of these are published in this and last year's periodicals. Mr. Liang Chi-chao, Dr. Husuh, Mr. H. C. Meng, and Mr. King Chu are the chief exponents of this movement. The discussions are now passing from that of a subjective and empirical nature to an objective and experimental basis. The place of the vernacular language in secondary schools is different from that in elementary schools. The tendency is to have less and less vernacular language as the students go along and each decrease is taken up by the classical language.

**Discipline.** —The second tendency observed is the increasing emphasis on school discipline in secondary schools. Since the May Fourth movement of 1919 there has been much relaxation of school discipline. Many principals and teachers have simply lost control over the students. A reaction has set in during the last year or two. On the one hand there is a tendency to negative control, prohibiting the students from a number of activities in which they have hitherto enjoyed freedom. Anhwei furnishes a good example of this negative reaction which attempts to secure discipline at the expense of educative extracurriculum activities. The Hunan method takes a milder form, allowing sufficient opportunities for student activities while enforcing school discipline. The last method that has been tried in some schools for securing discipline is through personal example of the principal and teachers, and their common sharing of school life with the students. The results that have so far been attained with this method in the Nanking Anhwei Academy show much promise.

**Nationalism.** —The third is the nationalistic tendency that has found expression in a very strong opposition to foreign languages as required studies in junior middle schools. Although thirty-six credits have been assigned for foreign languages, yet in the presence of such vigorous attack it is questionable whether in the future they can maintain their present position.

**Vocational training.** —The fourth tendency is the increasing emphasis on vocational training in secondary education. As shown by the entrance-examination statistics of the National University of Pekin and the National Southeastern University, less than 10 per cent of the applicants could be admitted, and this ratio has remained for the last few years without much change. The vocational educationalists think it imperative that the preparatory nature of the secondary schools should be greatly reduced. The schools have answered this call by adopting vocational courses, although it is not yet clear how these courses can really fit students for work and equip them for a lifelong career.

**Coeducation.** —The fifth tendency is segregation of the sexes in secondary schools. Some city middle schools, limited in number, have in recent years tried coeducation. In spite of a favorable attitude toward coeducation in institutions of higher learning and in elementary schools, there is decidedly a strong opposition to coeducation in middle schools. Hunan in March and Shantung in August of this year prohibited the middle schools from becoming coeducational. Kiangsu takes a milder attitude; it authorizes normal schools for men to take in women and permits city middle schools to become coeducational on condition that adequate provision is made for them.

**Economy and efficiency.** —The sixth tendency is economy and effieiency. With the limited resources at the disposal of the middle schools, they have to make every cent count, or they must be contented to give the students an education not fitted for life. The tendency to give the best possible education at the lowest possible cost is also finding increasing expression in China's secondary education. Except in normal schools, tuition fees are charged. There is now a secondary school population of 182, 804, which is less than 3 per cent of the elementary school population. Secondary education in China, in spite of its open door to all who are fit for it, is highly selective.

## Vocational Education

Vocational education has been given a very important place in the new system of education:

The curriculum of the elementary school may include prevocational training... The junior middle school ... may carry on various vocational courses ... The senior middle school is divided into general, agricultural, technical, commercial, and normal courses ( domestic science added later ) ... The year limit and the standing of the vocational schools may be determined in accordance with local needs and situations.

The secondary and elementary industrial schools established according to the old system are to be reorganized according to the new system.

On the basis of these provisions the Committee on Courses of Study for Vocational Education has spent three years in drawing up sixteen different courses of study, which are practically completed. Besides the prevocational course in elementary schools and special vocational courses in colleges, three stages of vocational education have been worked out: (1) vocational courses for graduates of the four-year lower primary school, (2) vocational courses for graduates of the six-year elementary school, and (3) vocational courses for graduates of the junior middle school.

On the distribution of time for practical work and nonvocational studies, the Federation of the Vocational Schools has made the following recommendations which have been duly accepted. First, the time allotment for practical work should not be less than that for classwork, which should have 18 to 24 hours per week. Second, the subjects for study in vocational schools should be of three kinds: (1) vocational subjects, (2)subjects as prerequisites to vocational studies, and (3) nonvocational subjects. The nonvoeational subjects should occupy at least 20 per cent of the total time allotment.

Among other important developments of vocational education during the year are the following: Szechuen, Kweichow, Kwangsi, Chekiang and Fukien have promulgated plans for the reconstruction of vocational education according to the new system. [18] Shensi has organized a Provincial Committee on Vcational Education, and appointed one supervisor for each of the twenty educatioual districts to take charge of vocational education, compulsory education, and popular education. [19] Yunnan has set aside the tobacco tax for the development of vocational education. Hupeh has ordered all the counties to appropriate 20 per cent of the educational fund for the promotion of vocational education. The One Week Campaign of Vocational Guidance in Shanghai, Nanking, Tsinan, and Wuchang has aroused much interest in this movement. Vocational guidance has been introduced into Tsing Hwa College, University Middle School of Southeastern University, and Pu-tong Middle School. The Ministry of Education has ordered all girls' middle schools to offer practical work in domestic science. A special fund has been raised by the National Association of Vocational Education for the special purpose of promoting vocational education for girls. Vocational schools for girls have been established in eight provinces.

## Teachers

**Preparation of teachers.** —In regard to the training of teachers, the new system of education has these provisions:

Attendance at the normal school is limited to six years. The normal school may be composed only of the last two or three years in order to admit the graduates of the junior middle schools. ... To supply the need of teachers for the lower grades of the primary schools, normal schools or normal institutes, covering a varying number of years, may be established after due consideration.

It is also provided that institutes for the training of vocational teachers may be opened in any adequate school. For the training of secondary school teachers, there is the normal college at which attendance is limited to four years:

In due time, the higher normal schools established according to the old system should raise their standard in order to admit the graduates of the senior middle schools, with an attendance limited to four years. They shall then be known as teachers colleges ... To supply the need of teachers for the junior middle school, a two-year normal course may be offered. It may be organized in the college of education of a university, in the teachers colleges, or in the normal or the senior middle school. It admits the graduates of the lastnamed institutions.

**Curriculum.** —The courses of study for normal schools are practically completed. Three sets of courses of study have been worked out. The first set is for the three-year normal school, corresponding to the senior middle school. Its general requirements are the same as for the senior middle school with the addition of 4 credits in music, with a total of 68 credits. The professional requirements consist of beginners' psychology (2 credits), educational psychology (3 credits), general methods (2 credits), methods of teaching special subjects (6 credits),teaching materials in elementary schools (6 credits), educational statistics and measurement (3 credits), elementary school, administration (3 credits), principles of education (3 credits), and practice teaching (20 credits), with a total of 48 credits. The elective studies are of two kinds, group electives and pure electives. Group electives aim to meet the needs of three classes of prospective teachers: (1) those with special inclination toward language, literature, and social sciences; (2) those with special inclination toward mathematics. and natural sciences; and (3) those with special inclination toward arts and physical education. Each class of students must elect at least 20 credits from group studies. All students must in addition elect at least 8 credits from the nine educational studies. Pure electives are left for the schools to determine.

The second set of courses of study is drawn up for the six-year normal schools corresponding to the six-year middle school. In a general way the junior middle school feature is preserved in the first stage of this type of normal school, yet all the courses of study aim at a continuous process rather than at a break in the middle. It is much simpler and is recommended for adoption by the smaller schools. As a consequence there is no group differentiation, and there are very few electives. Out of the three hundred and thirty credits required for graduation, three hundred, and nineteen credits are for required studies and only eleven credits for electives.

The third set of courses of study is for the training of teachers of the four lower grades. It has three forms: (1)the three-year course admitting graduates of the six-year primary schools; (2)the two-year course admitting graduates from the old higher primary schools, and (3) the one-year course admitting graduates from the junior middle school. All three forms have been very carefully worked out. Since space does not allow for full presentation, they are given in a condensed form as follows:

**Table 6**

*Normal School Courses*

| Subject | Form I, Three-Year Course (Credits) | From II, Two-Year Course (Credits) | Form III, One-Year Course (Credits) |
|---|---|---|---|
| Education | 36 | 24 | 14 |
| National Language | 36 | 24 | 8 |
| Social Sciences | 26 | 18 | 8 |
| Mathematics | 25 | 16 | 8 |
| Nature Study, Gardening, and Agriculture | 33 | 22 | 8 |
| Arts | 15 | 10 | 8 |
| Physical Education | 9 | 6 | 6 |
| Total | 180 | 120 | 60 |

**Notes.** —The study of elementay school materials and methods of teaching elementary school subjects are included under each subject taught. Practice teaching is given eight credits in Forms I and II, and is incorporated in each subject in Form III.

In the new courses of study for normal schools four important changes can be observed. In the first place there is more flexibility and variety which enable normal school principals to adapt their schools to special conditions instead of having one standard course of study, as was the case in former times.There are a number of courses of study adapted to different conditions. In the second place more emphasis is laid on educational subjects and the newer developments of education which will make a better teacher. Third, more time has been given to practice teaching so that the students may acquire the technique of teaching through doing. In the fourth place great emphasis has been laid on teaching materials and methods of teaching elementary school subjects. Formerly the needs of elementary schools were not adequately felt and met, and most of the normal schools were run as middle schools. The emphasis on elementary subjects thus indicates a new era in normal education.

In actual practice the higher normal schools have been engaged this year in transforming themselves into teachers colleges. The old normal schools are also taking steps to adopt the six-year course or three-year course according to their conditions. Some senior middle schools have also opened normal courses. Another very important move is found in the increasing emphasis on training village teachers. Kiangsu has since last year opened five village normal schools. The National Association for the Advancement of Education, the College of Education and the College of Agriculture of Southeastern University, the National Association of Vocational Education, the Kiangsu Compulsory Education Association, and Kiangsu Commission of Education are cooperating in establishing an experimental normal school for training village teachers. Mr. C. T. Chao, Professor of Village Education in Southeastern University and Director of Village Education of the National Association for the Advancement of Education, has been appointed organizer of this school.

Students in most normal schools enjoy free tuition and board. A few students are admitted on payment of half fees or whole fees. The regular normal students whose fees have been remitted are required to render service in schools for seven years. A few years ago an investigation made in Kiangsu shows that more than 80 per cent of the normal graduates do take up teaching after graduation. This rule of required service has not yet been strictly enforced. The tendency is for stricter enforcement, as is indicated in the resolution of the Kaifen

Conference. Kiangsu has this year prohibited graduates from county normal institutes from taking more advanced education before the completion of compulsory service. Fengtien Province has even conceived the idea of withholding the diploma until the term of compulsory service has expired.

**Certification of teachers.** —With the exception of normal school graduates, all other elementary school teachers must apply for certification. The certification of elementary school teachers is of two kinds: (1) certification by examination, and (2) certification without examination. Those who have studied in secondary schools for two years or more, or have been taught in elementary schools for one or more years, or have graduated from normal institutes lasting six months or longer, or have a sufficient knowledge of educational principles and have studied the special subjects to be taught, as proved by articles or essays written by the applicants, are qualified to teach by passing an examination in the subjects of the regular normal schools with due consideration to grade and sex variations. The examinations for assistant teachers are easier. Those who are certified without examination in subject matter are: (1) middle school graduates who have been elementary school teachers for one year or more; (2) graduates of secondary industrial schools who have made good records in their studies; (3) graduates of professional schools whose special studies really qualify them to teach the subjects; and (4) elementary school teachers with three years teaching experience and a good record of service certified by the county superintendent of schools. All the applicants for certification, however, must produce a school diploma if they have one, a statement of good conduct by a guarantor, and must undergo a physical examination.

The certification of elementary school teachers in China is directed by a provincial Committee on Certification. The results must be reported annually to the Minister of Education by the Governor of the Province. The merits and defects of a centralized and uniform system of certification find no exception in this country.

**Salaries**. —A few years ago a brief survey of the salary situation in Kiangsu showed the following results:

In 1921 another investigation conducted by Mr. Tai, covering six provinces, gives a median annual salary of $160.25 Mex. for all the elementary school teachers he has studied, and a median annual salary of $125.10 Mex. for their first year's service. Even if sufficient allowance is made for the very high purchasing power of money in China, the present salary of the elementary school teachers must be considered as very low. The Ministry of Education announced a salary schedule in 1917 and required the schools to pay teachers salaries not lower than the minimum amount.

There is a tendency to pay higher salaries on the basis of teaching experience and professional knowledge. The immediate problem, however, is how to make the pay more regular.

Attempts are also being made to encourage longer service by

**Table 7**

*Annual Salaries of Elementary School Teachers in Kiangsu*

| | Higher Primary $ Mex. | Lower Primary $ Mex. |
|---|---|---|
| Maximum | 600 | 240 |
| Average | 200 | 102 |
| Minimum | 70 | 30 |

**Table 8**

*Salary Schedule for Primary School Teachers*

| Classes | Special $ Mex. | 1 | 2 | 3 | 4 | 5 | 6 | 7 | 8 | 9 | 10 | 11 | 12 | 13 | 14 |
|---|---|---|---|---|---|---|---|---|---|---|---|---|---|---|---|
| Principal and Head Teachers | 960 | 720 | 660 | 600 | 540 | 480 | 420 | 360 | 312 | 264 | 216 | 180 | 144 | 120 | 90 |
| Special Teachers | 720 | 480 | 420 | 360 | 312 | 264 | 216 | 180 | 144 | 120 | 98 | 72 | | | |
| Assistant Teachers | 360 | 264 | 216 | 180 | 144 | 120 | 98 | 72 | 48 | | | | | | |

increased remuneration. Although the importance of a pension system has not yet been fully realized, beginnings have been made and there is a movement in this direction. The Chekiang Conference of Educational Administrators has recommended a sabbatical year for teachers who have served for six years, and an annual pension of one fourth of salary after twenty years of service or incases of disability after ten years of service. A system of special grants from one fourth to full salary are recommended to the family of a teacher in case of death. The Kiangsu Commission of Education has this year adopted a temporary system of pension according to which an elementary school teacher shall be given annually one third of his last year's salary (1) if he is disabled on account of sickness after continuous service for eight years, or (2) if he is disabled or seriously wounded in performing his official duties, or (3) if he retires on account of old age after continuous, service for twenty years; in addition one of his children may attend a government school in the province without paying tuition fees.

**Tenure.** —Very little investigation has been made on the tenure of elementary school teachers. The contract is as a usual rule on a half-year basis. The data on the tenure of service of teachers in thirteen schools in Kiangsu, gathered by the writer a few years ago, may give some idea about the situation, but it would be a mistake to consider these meager data as representative of the country as a whole.

**Table 9**

*Tenure of Teachers*

| Years of Service | Percentage of | |
|---|---|---|
| | Higher Primary School Teachers | Lower Primary School Teachers |
| 1 | 6 | 26 |
| 2 | 10 | 12 |
| 3 | 23 | 20 |
| 4 | 17 | 18 |
| 5 | 44 | 24 |

The need for teachers is imperative in China. Estimating on the basis of forty million children of school age for four years elementary education, at least one million teachers will be needed for the four elementary grades. According to latest returns there area only 223, 279 teachers who are serving in the lower elementary schools. More than three times as many as the present number have to be added in order to enforce a nation-wide system of compulsory education. There are now 43,846 students in normal schools and institutes, which cannot turn out more than 10,000 teachers every year as against the need for 770,000 teachers. The problem is a serious one.

# Educational Tests And Measurements

The test movement began in China four or five years ago when Doctor Liao and Professor Chen in Nanking and Doctor Liu and Professor Chang in Pekin gave courses on scientific measurement in education and made some start in the construction of tests. It was not until the coming of Professor William A. McCall of Teachers College, Columbia University, in 1922, that this movement gathered its great momentum. In cooperation with the Chinese psychologists at different centers Professor McCall succeeded in having twenty tests constructed for the use of elementary and secondary schools. The tests added this year are as follows:

| | |
|---|---|
| Comprehensive English Test | Andersen |
| Geography Test | Young |
| Arithmetic Practice Test | Yue |
| Drawing Test | Yue |
| Intelligence Test | Liu-Bradshaw |
| Self-survey Comprehensive Test | Terman |
| Lower Primary Nonverbal Intelligence Test | Chen |
| Higher Primary Nonverbal Intelligence Test | Chen |
| Chinese Grammar Test for Higher Primary Schools | Chen |
| Composite Mathematics Test | Liao |
| Composite Science Test | Liao |
| Chinese Language and Literature Test | Liao |
| Chinese Grammar Test | Liao |
| History Test | Liao |
| Geography Test | Liao |

Two special features may be mentioned about the test movement in China. In the first place, all the tests are scaled according to a uniform system, the T-B-C-F system, so as to secure comparability of scores from test to test and thus facilitate the tabulation and interpretation of results, and all direction booklets are modeled after a standard design, so that teachers will find it necessary to learn Just one procedure. In the second place, all the tests are published under the auspices of one body, the National Association for the Advancement of Education, a practice which has saved schoolmen much trouble in locating and securing the tests.

In the fall of 1923 Professor Terman of Yenching University and Professor Cha of the Pekin Normal College were invited by the National Association to conduct a cooperative self-survey, using specially designed and self-administering tests. "The purpose of this survey is to acquaint educators with tests, to motivate teachers to make use of self-helps to be published by the Association, and to conduct a national contest among pupils." The final report of its findings, known as the *Efficiency of Chinese Elementary Schools*, by Professor Terman, was published this spring.

The test movement has been well received. A number of schools have used these tests to take the place of the conventional examination and several schools have included tests as part of the examination.

## Medical And Social Welfare

The health and social welfare of students have received more attention in elementary schools than in secondary schools. The better schools such as the Shan-shan Children's Home, the practice schools of Southeastern University, Pekin Normal College for Men, Pekin Normal College for Women, Kiangsu First and Third Normal Schools for Men, Kiangsu First and Second Normal Schools for Girls, the Tsu Yih School in Hunan, have provided much opportunity for children to take active part in social activities and have given much attention to the physical wellbeing of the students. The best report that has been secured on this topic is that of the Practice School of Pekin Normal College for Women [20] a school of 590 students. Medical inspection, introduced in 1922, is conducted once every semester. Vaccination is a requirement, and is done once annually. This year 226 of the 590 students were vaccinated. In extracurriculum activities, free play and athletics are emphasized. Chinese games as well as foreign games are introduced. Corrective exercises are given as part of physical training and general knowledge on health is included in a course of hygiene. Attention is also given to ventilation, lighting, seating, etc. School gardening furnishes another opportunity for healthful recreation. Out-of-door activities are encouraged and excursions are arranged for each class at least once for every semester. Provision is also made for students' self-government, a literary society, class meetings, a weekly mass convention, a cooperative store, a children's club, a children's reading room, a thrift society, and numerous other organizations which furnish ample opportunities for the development of the social self. Such is the picture of a better school, or a representative of the better schools.

Appalling ignorance and indifference to hygienic control of school life are noticed in a large number of schools, especially in the village or town school in the interior where the gospel of health is most needed. Here children are nearest to nature and yet are farthest from it. Socially the children are under the rule of a despotic teacher who denies the children all freedom of social activity on the ground that it lowers the dignity of the school and the prestige of the teacher.

A considerable number of investigations have been conducted this year in physical education by Professor McCloy under the joint auspices of the National Southeastern University and the National Association for the Advancement of Education. The following have been completed:

(1) A series of studies in anthropometry and physical measurements. Some of the results are as follows: (a) A study of weight for the body types has been completed. A new weight chart has been prepared and is now about to be issued for all ages. A new basis of calculating weight has been found. (b)A study of chest measurements has been made and their practicability developed. This has opened a new field for research as well, but one which will be difficult to follow out. (c)All measurements commonly taken have been intensively studied to determine whether or not they were really diagnostically useful. This has narrowed down the study to a few really important measurements, and these have been studied to discover how they can really contribute to the welfare of students. (d)The chest index as a basis of a test for hereditary stigmata of degeneration has been studied, and is nearly completed. Enough has been found to make it clear that this index is of significance, (e)A study has been made of the vital measurements and school grades to see what the relation between the two might be. (f) A new weighting for age-height-weight and athletic performance has been devised. (g)A thorough study of the history records of the physical examination has been made as a basis for revision of the card at present in use. (h)A careful statistical study of medical examinations has been made and a new report sheet devised that gives results in a

graphic form and also in a numerical form.

(2) A study has been made of a few athletic events to determine which of quite similar events should be utilized. This has been done, for example, with three forms of the potato race, and the best form has been statistically determined.

(3) A careful study has been made of standard tests in athletics. A study of eleven events was made with 300 primary school boys, and a study of eighteen events with 330 middle school boys. The best events for such standard tests have been statistically determined.

(4) A universal scoring table has been devised for over 70 events in track and field athletics. These given, an approximately equivalent degree of difficulty for all events with the same point value is attained.

(5) Methods have been evolved for determining the motor quotient of a boy or girl based on the standard events mentioned in the age-height-weight weighting.

(6) Studies of standard tests in football and in basketball have been undertaken and the preliminary studies finished. These are as yet only in the beginning stages, but the studies are very suggestive and determine the line of future research. It will probably be about another year before these can be finished.

Of the above studies some have been published, others will be ready in a few months. When ready, they will mean an advance of about ten years in physical education and physical examinations in China.

## Higher Education

According to the new system of education, the "institution of higher learning may consist of several colleges or only one college.

Attendance at the college or university is limited to four to six years." At the top there is a post-graduate school which is a school of research for college and university graduates and others with similar preparation.

The two following tables will give some idea as to the present status of higher education in China:

**Table 10**

*Professional Distribution of Colleges*

| Type of Institution | Number of Schools | Number of Students |
|---|---|---|
| University | 35 | 13,098 |
| Teachers College | 8 | 3,093 |
| Agricultural College | 7 | 1,271 |
| Technical College | 13 | 2,026 |
| Commercial College | 8 | 1,890 |
| Medical College | 7 | 832 |
| Law College | 33 | 10,864 |
| Others | 14 | 1,806 |
| Total | 125 | 34,880 |

**Table 11**

*Distribution of Colleges according to Sources of Support*

| Sources of Support | Number of Schools | Number of Students |
|---|---|---|
| National | 30 | 10,535 |
| Provincial | 48 | 9,801 |
| Private | 29 | 10,524 |
| Mission and Foreign | 18 | 4,020 |
| Total | 125 | 34,880 |

A few universities have been added this year; the more important ones are (1)Kwangtung University and (2)Northwestern University.

The present tendency in higher education has thus been summarized by Chancellor Tsai:

The University is not merely intended to offer ready-made courses for students to attend at fixed hours, but primarily to be an institution for corporate work in scientific research. And by research I mean not merely the introduction of European culture, but original contributions on the basis of what is already done in the West; nor merely the preservation of our national-culture heritage, but seeking by means of methods of scientific research to show what that heritage has actually been.[21]

As original research can never be properly developed if outside interference, is dominant, So the second tendency is a demand for academic freedom. Government interference has been repeatedly resented and repelled. This year when the Minister of Education announced the University Regulations, he met with the greatest opposition from the professors of the National University of Pekin and he was finally compelled to withdraw them.

There is also a tendency for closer cooperation on the part of the universities and colleges. In July when the National Association for the Advancement of Education met in Nanking, a Chinese Federation of Universities was organized dealing with problems of common interest in regard to university education. It is believed that such an organization if properly administered will raise the general standard of university education.

A fourth tendency is the extension of higher educational opportunities to women. Most of the Chinese universities have opened their doors to women and have been made co-educational.

The Pekin Higher Normal School for Women was this fall promoted to the standing of a Teachers College.

Finally there is an abnormal increase of private colleges. In Pekin alone about ten private colleges came into existence this year. The situation is similar in Shanghai and other large cities. It is alleged that in order to be a big man in China one must have three things: a newspaper, a bank, and a university. The government, however, has refused to recognize any one of these institutions whose existence is invariably due to ulterior motives.

## Missionary Education

According to the statement of Mr. Wallace, Associate General Secretary of the China Christian Educational Association, it is probable that the total number of students in Protestant missionary institutions at present is near 300,000, and is still increasing. There has been an increase of 76 per cent in the number of college students in the four years between 1920 and 1924. Archbishop Celso Costantini gives 258,953 as the number of students under the training of the Catholic Church. Out of every hundred students eight are in missionary schools.

The outstanding event of the year in regard to missionary education has been the organization of the China Association for Christian Higher Education, which has appointed a Council to act as an *ad interim* body. It also acts as the Council of Higher Education of the China Christian Educational Association, thus linking up higher education with the other activities of the latter organization. Rev. E. C. Lobenstine, the Council's secretary, is engaged in making a study of the institutions, particularly with reference to their financial position and the possibilities of coordinating their efforts. The chief purpose of this council is to enable the Christian institutions of higher education with their limited resources to make the most effective contribution to the needs of China.

Another event of great importance is the Conference on Agriculture and Rural Education. As a result of this conference, three colleges, twenty middle schools and higher primary schools, and eighty-three agricultural workers have joined hands in carrying on projects of rural education.

Among other important things done this year may be mentioned the very practical program of school health passed by the Conference on School Health, and the new emphasis on the teaching of Chinese language and citizenship in Christian schools and colleges.

Missionary institutions, in spite of their good record, have been attacked on three grounds. Hitherto these institutions have been under foreign control. Even qualified Chinese Christians are rarely given an opportunity of holding responsible positions. Another criticism is that they are giving religion to young children who are not mature enough to make intelligent decision for themselves. Finally there is serious suspicion on the part of the Chinese that the missions are organizing a system of Christian education parallel to the government system which might in time become an irreconcilable group within the group. As a consequence of these factors this year has witnessed two successive attacks on missionary education in the two National Educational Conferences held in July and October. The more conservative Chinese, however, think that in this transitional state, missionary education of the more liberal type does have a unique contribution to make by way of supplementing the government activities in providing wider educational opportunities for the students and setting up better examples in school discipline. They also believe that missionary education should be more socialized, liberalized, and made more Chinese. Finally, they feel that the missions may be able to make a better contribution if they could concentrate their effort and resources in a few institutions of higher learning and make them first-class institutions, instead of scattering their resources in establishing secondary and elementary schools of poorer grade.They believe that secondary schools and elementary schools of an experimental nature might be opened by the missions as well as other private agencies, and any attempts to multiply them and build a system out of them are bound to conflict sooner or later with the government system.

## Popular Adult Education

**A movement to eliminate illiteracy.** —Mass illiteracy presents a unique ppoblem in China. Deducting 120 million children, who are either below school age or fall within the scope of compulsory education, and 80 million who have spent on the average three years in the old-fashioned Chinese schools, from the total population, there are about 200 million illiterates, a problem for popular education to solve. The Y.M.C.A. under the leadership of Mr. James Yen has started experiments on this type of education. At the second Annual Conference of the National Association for the Advancement of Education held at Tsing Hua in 1923, a National Association for the Promotion of Popular Education with Mime Hsung as its president, was organized and the movement immediately received nation-wide support.

In substance it offers four readers, composed by Professor King

Chu and the present writer, based on a vocabulary of about 1,200 most common Chinese characters. An average illiterate can complete the four readers in four months by spending one hour a day. At the end of four months he will be able to read newspapers, pamphlets, books, and correspondence based on this vocabulary and he will be able to express himself by using the same. The four readers cost 0.12 Mex.,so that even the poorest can afford to buy them. The books are used in a number of ways and types of institutions: first, in the People's School, which has a teacher who meets his class regularly at definite periods of time; second, in the People's Reading Circle, which takes the home, the store, etc., as a unit and encourages the literate in the home and in the store to teach the other members; third, in the People's Question Station, where the illiterates can stop and ask questions on any points in the books which they do not understand. The readers have in this way been introduced into homes, stores, factories, schools, churches, monasteries, yamens, steamships, prisons, and armies. Within a year's time, in spite of flood, famine, and war, the circulation of these readers and other series has reached the million mark.

The readers are followed by series of booklets on various branches of knowledge. It will not be long before a system of compulsory education is in operation in this country with its tax on ignorance. Friends of popular education have the ambition to achieve the miracle of eliminating illiteracy among 200 million people in ten years.

Chinese educators are working under overwhelming difficulties. Some of them succumb; others take these as a matter of course and instead of being discouraged they regard them as opportunities for effort and endeavor. China is virgin soil for educational service. She is a social vacuum that absorbs any amount of energy one is willing to put into it. In order to understand Chinese education today, It must be thought of in terms of the difficulties involved and the efforts made.

## Bibliography


**Books by the Commercial Press**

Andersen —*Comprehensive English Test* (Translated into Chinese); C. N. A. A. E. Series.

—*Teacher's Manual for Comprehensive English Test* (Translated into Chinese); C. N. A. A. E. Series.

Chao and Others —*The Practice of the Project Method.*

Chen — *A Study of Children's Library.*

—*Primary School Curriculum;* C. N. A. A. E. Series.

Chien and Others —*Fundamental Principles of Learning.*

Hwa —*Silent Reading Test in Chinese Spoken Language.*

—*The Outlines of Education Measurements.*

Liao —*Secondary Education.*

McMurry, C. A. and F.M. —*Guide to the British and American Educational Publications* (Translated into Chinese).

*Statistical Summaries of Chinese Education;* C. N. A. A. E. Series.

Terman, E.L. —*Comprehensive Self-Survey Educational Tests for Senior Middle Schools;* C. N. A. A. E. Series .

—*The Efficiency of Elementary Schools in China* (Translated into Chinese); C. N. A. A. E. Series.

Twiss —*A National Movement for the Improvement of Science Education*; C. N. A. A. E. Series.

— *Science and Education in China*; C. N. A. A. E. Series.

—*Suggestions for Organizing Science Teachers Clubs*; C. N. A. A. E. Series.

Yue —*Manual of Composite Arithmetic Tests for Ele mentary Schools*; C. N. A. A. E. Series.

—*Statistical Computation and Tes-tmaking.*

Yueh —*Primary School Administration.*

—*Teaching by Projects.*

**Books by various publishers in 1924**

Ching —*How to Organize Boy Scouts.*

Chow and Ao —*Illustrations for Chinese Written Language Test.*

Hsu —*A Treatise on the Dalton Plan.*

—*Studies in the Dalton Plan.*

Liu —*Educational Psychology.*

Shih —*The Methods of Educational Survey.*

*Standard Courses of Study for the New System of Instruction;* Kiangsu Provincial Educational Association.

Tong —*The Method of Teaching in Primary School Civics.*

Wong —*Vocational Guidance for Young Men.*

Yueh —*The Gary School System.*

**Educational journals**

*Compulsory Education*; Kiangsu Compulsory Education Association.

*Democracy and Education*; Normal University, Pekin.

*Educational Miscellany*; The Commercial Press.

*Elementary Education*; The Commercial Press.

*Physical Education Quarterly*; The Commercial Press.

*Secondary Education*; The Commercial Press.

*The Chung Hwa Educational Review*; Chung Hwa Book Co.

*The Educational Quarterly*; The Commercial Press.

*The Educational Review*; The Commercial Press.

*The New Education*; National Association for the Advancement of Education.

In addition to these magazines, which are national in scope, each province has its own journal as a rule.

**Author's Note:**

1. *North China Daily News*, Sixtieth Anniversary Number, p. 2.

2. *China weekly Review*, September 27, 1924, p. 110.

3. *North China Daily News*, Sixtieth Anniversary Number, p. 33.

4. *China Weekly Review*, March 22,1924, p. 115.

5. *Ibid*., July 12, 1924, p. 180.

6. *The Chinese Renaissance*, Bulletin 6, Vol. II, 1923. Chinese National Association for the Advancement of Education, abbreviated as C.N.A.A.E.

7. *Educational Laws and Regulations*, p. 4.

8. *Chung Hwa Educational Review*, "Problem of Supporting Elementary Education,"p. 1.

9. *Chung Hwa Educational Review*, "Problem of Supporting Elementary Education,"and Sin Wen Pao, July 13, 1924, p. 3.

10. *China's New System of Instruction*, C.N.A. A.E. ,Bulletin 8, Vol. II, 1923, p. 17.

11. *Kiangsu Educational Gazette*, No. 1, 1924.

12. *Standard Courses of Study for the New System of Instruction*, p. 7.

13. *Compulsory Education*, No. 26, p. 15.

14. *Kweichow Educational Gazette*, March, 1924.

15. "*Education and Life*", Shun Pao, p. 600.

16. *Standard Courses of Study for the New System of Instruction*, pp.

1—7.

17. *Standard Courses of Instruction for the New System of Instruction. Senior Middle School Section*, pp. 1—7.

18. *Vocation and Education*, No. 52, p. 81, No. 17, p. 425, No. 19, p. 549.

19. *Vocation and Education*, No. 57, p. 425.

20. *Chung Hwa Educational Review*, September, 1924.

21. *North China Daily News*, Sixtieth Anniversary
Number, p. 49.

## Note

(1) CHINA, by W. Tchishin Tao, M. A., General Director of Chinese National Association for the Advancement, of Education, was first published in the EDUCATIONAL YEARBOOK OF THE INTERNATIONAL INSTITUTE OF TEACHERS COLLEGE, Columbia University, 1924.

(2) W. Tchishin Tao: Tao Heng-Chih (or Heng-Chih Tao, or H. C.Tao) was originally named Tao Wen Tsing (or Wen Tsing Tao, or W. T. Tao) and later Tchishin Tao. (See A BRIEF BIOGRAPHY OF TAO HENG-CHIH.) What the initial "W" stood for remains unknown.

# The New Mass Education Movement

A cultural revolution against an edueational system as old as China itself is taking place in China today. This system made the Chinese language so dififcult that it condemned 80% of the people to illiteracy. Requiring years of study, it was possible only for the privileged few to master the tens of thousands of Chinese characters necessary to read and write. The students and intellectuals, who call themselves "cultural workers", have taken upon themselves the task of romanizing the intricate alphabet and teaching it to the masses. This romanized alphabet, containing 28 letters, is known as *Latin Hua*.

In order to bring the new education to the people, a system of workers' and peasants' schools was created. These schools have no paid teachers.The students and intellectuals give one or two hours a day to training the masses, and after a time the masses develop teachers of their own.In nearly every class there are four or five persons, who have a natural aptitude for teaching and who, after a training of some months, can lead a class or a group on their own initiative. Thus you find peasants teaching peasants in the rural districts, and in the cities workers' schools which are taught by the workers themselves.

The principle of the Mass Education Movement is that everyone who knows a little, even though he has attended school only a few months, should teach what he knows to others. This is the basis of the "Little Teacher" system. Even little children can be found playing the role of these "Little Teachers", —the more able ones leading classes and others teaching groups of three or four. It is not uncommon to find girls and boys of five or six years teaching their parents, grandparents, servants, etc., to read and write.

A new psychology underlies this new mass education movement. Changes in life mean changes in education. This education need not and sometimes can not be accomplished in an ordinary school. Therefore our education is not confined to the school form. Any place where the people live or congregate is essentially a mass school, since real education comes from the contact of life with life. Thus our schools are held in courtyards, in corridors, in the streets, in the shops, in the village temples and in the army camps. The whole society becomes our school and all of life our curriculum.

Cultural workers are organizing this system of mass education throughout China. Similar organizations of musicians and cinema workers carry on the same activity, and propaganda for the new education is embodied in the tales told in the tea-houses. Thus the idea is spread far and wide.

New textbooks have been written and periodicals published in the Latin Hua. The Peiping and Shanghai alphabetical systems have been completed, and we are now working on the Fukien and Canton alphabets, since each of these provinces has its own dialect. It is estimated that an illiterate man or woman can learn to read and write with this new alphabet in one month. Thus after a very short period of training, the people can continue their education by themselves.

The new mass education movement, which was initiated in

Shanghai, should not be confused with that type of education advocated by Mr. James Yen at Ting Hsien. In the Chinese language the Ting Hsien type of education is called "*ping ming giao yü*", meaning the common people's education, while the New Mass Education is called Dazhung Giao Yü, meaning the education of the great masses. The difference in terminology implies fundamental differences in essentials. Ting Hsien advocates mass education, but in practice it results in an education of the few, while the new mass education aims at a real education of the mass, by the mass and for the mass.

This movement is entirely self-supporting. The Association for National Liberation Education is supported by a ten cent membership fee, and while contributions from sympathizers of the movement are always welcomed, the main activities of the society do not depend on these contributions, but upon the people themselves.

It is quite natural that this cultural revolution should be inextricably connected with the movement for national liberation. Mass education cultivates mass consciousness, and the movement aims not only to teach the people to read and write, but also to teach them the problems of today, and to guide them so that they will understand how to meet these problems. The test of the validity of any educational system is whether or not it can stand the test of reality. The masses need an education that will help them face life. The educational system that evades reality implies an intrinsic weakness which unfits it to perform its function.

Although the Mass Education Movement teaches national liberation, it must not be understood that it advocates a narrow nationalism. In spite of our national crisis, we have not forgotten to cultivate international-mindedness. International-mindedness is, needless to say, the foundation of world peace. The teachers of the masses in China dare not forget this important principle.

With the possible exception of India, there is no other country in the world where education has been so much a privilege of wealth as China. This new movement, developed and continued over a period of years, will make it possible to abolish the appalling illiteracy in China, to bring culture to the people, and to enable them to defend their national culture against foreign cultural aggressions.

## Note

THE NEW MASS EDUCATION MOVEMENT, written "by Professor Tao Xing-zhi" (spelt according to a new alphabetical system of written Chinese), was first published on March 15, 1936, in VOICE OF CHINA, Shanghai (No. 1, Vol. 1).

# China's New Language

For the past seventy years efforts have been made to create a new written language for the Chinese people. This article will not attempt to deal with the history of these efforts, but will only explain the last and most significant step which is being taken at the present moment. A written language has been perfected, which is certain to revolutionize the whole fabric of Chinese culture.

The Chinese New Language Research Institute, which was established in December, 1935, has worked out and adopted alphabetical systems for both the Northern and the Shanghai dialects. The Northern New Language contains 28 letters, *and that of the Shanghai dialect 31 letters. The Research Institute is now directing its efforts toward an alphabetical system for the Fukien and Canton dialects, which will be completed in the course of the next two months.

This new language, formerly called *Latin-hua*, has three characteristics which distinguish it from its predecessors.

1. In contrast with the Chinese characters (*xanz*) it is phonetic and not ideographic.

2. In contrast with the national phonetic script (*gyjinzmu*) it is an independent language, and not an appendage of *xanz*.

3. In contrast with the romanization of the national language, it is adaptable to the local dialects, so that the various districts may have their own variations of the written language, adapted to their own dialects.

Since it is obviously impossible for the masses of the people in the various localities to study both the Peking dialect and the romanized script, the authority of the Peking dialect as the only national language shall be abolished. In addition the New Language has another virtue superior to both the national phonetic script and the romanization of the National Language, i.e. it has done away with the symbols recording to the tonic variations. This simplification makes it possible for the masses to learn the language with very little difficulty.

The New Language for the Northern Dialect was adopted four years ago. During these four years very slow progress was made in bringing this language to the masses. However, as the National Liberation Movement gains momentum, the New Language appears like a rising sun in the discussions of mass language and literature for the people. Readers, magazines, pamphlets made their appearance in great numbers, and the final result was the inauguration of the National New Language Research Institute, which now has charge of the whole movement.

It is significant that this new language and its ready acceptance by the masses has met with severe opposition. Following the suppression of the "Life of the Masses", the authorities in Shanghai and elsewhere have confiscated all periodicals and books published in the New Language. Two reasons are given for this drastic measure. First, they say that this New Language has its origin in the Soviet Union, and therefore, anyone who promotes it is tinged with "red". Second, they state that it will break the unity of the Chinese Republic.

It is obvious that these reasons are falacious. First, it is true that the original system of the New Language for the Northern Dialect originated in Vladivostock, but it was the work of the Overseas Chinese in that city. And now the systems for the Shanghai, Fukien and Canton dialects are all worked out by Chinese scholars on Chinese soil. As to the alleged destruction of national unity, it is our opinion that the speedy adoption of the New Language will help to bring to China an ever-increasing national unity that has heretofore been unknown.

The *xanz* (ideographic system) has held merely a nominal unity in the written language for a very few scholars. The masses have neither the time nor the money to learn *xanz*, and therefore must remain without a written language. It is obvious therefore that the means of creating unity was lacking, since reliance had to be placed upon the spoken word, or upon the mingling of the people. Since each locality has its own dialect, even the spoken word has great limitations. But with the adoption of the new language, the masses within each district can easily learn to read and write their own dialect and since it is not a difficult task for the intelligentsia to master the various languages, the peoples of the various districts can have access not only to newspapers, but also to the literature of the nation and that of the world. Their present isolation will be broken, and they will become in reality citizens of China, instead of,at present, isolated peoples of provinces, separated from each other by the barrier of the spoken word.

After a short time, there need be no dependence upon the so-called "scholars", since these can be recruited from the people themselves. This will certainly help China to cultivate a new unity which can never be achieved through the present ideographic language.

The fact that the latinization of the 182 different languages of the various peoples of Soviet Russia has enabled that country to establish a really unified state is an indication of the possibilities of the New Language Movement in China.

Despite the severe persecutions, the Shanghai New Language Movement is increasing in strength and popularity. New battalions, consisting of thousands of peasants, clerks, workers and children, have learned to read and write in less than a month. A manifesto signed by more than a thousand adherents has been issued in support of the struggle of the New Language for victory over the ancient feudal ideography.

The prerequisite of any educational movement in China is its ability to stand the test of economy of time and cost. An average peasant can learn the fundamentals of reading and writing in less than a month. The foundation reader costs only one cent. With an additional pencil and exercise book, the poor peasant will be able to complete his first course at a cost of three cents. Even a rickshaw puller can pay for his own education. He will no longer be dependent upon charity for his learning. With this new tool, an education of the mass, by the mass and for the mass is made possible.

The New Language therefore, represents a great advance, not only in Chinese culture, but it will soon remold the whole life of the Chinese people:

***Alphabet of Northern Dialect**

Vowels

| | |
|---|---|
| a [ah] as in pap*a* | o [o] as in h*o*me |
| e [eh] as in aft*e*r | u [oo] as in f*oo*d |

| | |
|---|---|
| i [i] as in *i*s | y [ü] like German ü |

Consonants

| | |
|---|---|
| b [beh] as in *B*erlin | p [peh] as in *p*art |
| c [ts] as in *Tsits*ihar | r [r] as in *r*un |
| ch [ch] as in *ch*ild | rh as in *ear*, pronounced with tongue drawn back |
| d [deh] as in won*d*er | |
| f [feh] as in *f*or | sh [sh] as in *sh*e |
| g [geh] as in *g*irl | t [teh] as in *t*ea |
| j [i] as in *y*es | w [oo] as in *w*ood |
| k [keh] as in *k*ind | x [heh] like English *h* |
| l [leh] as in *l*et | z [ds] pronounced *tz* |
| m [meh] as in *m*an | zh-ch with tongue drawn back and concavely pressed on upper roof |
| n [neh] as in *n*ame | |
| ng [ngeh] as in ki*ng* | |

**Note**

CHINA'S NEW LANGUAGE, written by "Professor Tao Xing-zhi" was first published on May 1, 1936, in VOICE OF CHINA, Shanghai (No. 1, Vol. 4). (spelt according to a new alphabetical system of written Chinese.)

# China: The Mass Education Movement



China is predominantly an agricultural country and a poor one at that, so that it cannot afford the expense of educating its whole people along Western lines. If China is to make its population literate in the next few years it must develop a technique of its own. This is now doing through the Mass Education Movement, which began twelve years ago but has entered upon a new stage during the last two years. The Movement has set itself to solve three of the most pressing problems that face education in China today. In the first place there is the expense of erecting new schools. Instead of putting money into buildings, the organizers of the movement conceived of the whole of society as a school. Temples, theatres, parlours and attics of private houses, and even outhouses, have been utilised as schools for the masses, and thus money surely needed for other projects has been saved.

A second problem has also been solved in a new way. Chinese peasants and workers have no money to buy knowledge and pay teachers. So the organizers of the movement laid it down that anyone who possesses knowledge has the responsibility of sharing it with others. The thirty or forty farmers who join an evening class, or come for instruction either before or after harvest when they have more leisure, are not only students but also teachers. They are encouraged to go home, even after the first lesson, and teach their wives and daughters what they have just learnt. Children, too, are acting successfully as teachers. A grandmother of fifty-seven is taught to read and write by her grandson of six. Teachers in the elementary and middle schools are therefore encouraged and helped to train their children to become"little teachers".

The term "little teachers" may sound curious, but in China these little teachers have acquired a great prestige. They have been able to deal more effectively than adults with one of China's special problems. Most Chinese women are illiterate and women teachers are very rare. But it is not convenient for a man to teach girls of sixteen or seventeen. So children, who are in school in the day time, become little teachers in the evening and teach the women and girls in their neighbourhood. This system has been extraordinarily successful, and wherever it has been adopted the literacy of the men and the women is nearly equal.

Certain dangers have of course to be guarded against. The system must be kept a voluntary one. But the children are enthusiastic, and as soon as they hear of it most of them want to become teachers and thus do a service to the nation. Another danger is that they may do too much teaching and thus injure their health. Care must be taken to prevent this happening. It might be supposed that the knowledge they pass on is very faulty. In practice, however, it is found that they are very conseiencious and by teaching what they have learnt make the subject-matter clearer to themselves.

The Mass Education Movement has tackled another problem, that of a simple Chinese script. Chinese characters, one picture for each word, are very hard to learn. A new latinised script has been worked out for the Chinese language which has been tried in Canton, Shanghai, and the Northern Provinces. It can be understood by three-fourths of the whole nation, and a farmer can learn to read and write by means of it in one month.

With the solution of these three problems an instrument has been forged which will enable the masses to educate themselves without waiting for the industrialization of China. If she had to wait so long, it would be too late; without mass education China would be a ruin, losing her integrity and freedom. For, to be frank, Chinese education has now one aim—national liberation. if education fails to help China to make herself a free and independent nation, education is meaningless.

But when national liberation is emphasised, this does not mean narrow nationalism. A free and independent China will help world peace, for China has not the least idea of adopting an imperialistic policy. It seeks to cultivate in its youth the spirit of national liberation in relation to China and of international understanding in relation to the world as a whole.

## Note

*CHINA*: *The Mass Education Movement* was a report made by Dr. Heng-Chih Tao at the Seventh World Conference of the New Education Fellowship held at Cheltenham, England, in August 1936. Dr. Tao was one of the two representatives from China attending the conference, his report appeared later in the year 1936 in THE FREEDOM WE SEEK edited by Mr. Wyatt Rawecn.

# Outline Of Speech At Canadian Congress

Nov. 19, 1937, Canadian Congress, 8 p.m. Victoria Theatre.

(1) Greetings.

(2) Peace and Democracy in China.

(3) We want peace, so we want democracy.

1) Want peace, peace with you. War forced upon us.

2) What kind of peace we want. We want peace with liberty. We want peace with justice. We want peace on equal footing; life and death struggle *vs* liberty and slavery struggle.

3) How to secure peace?

A. Peace must be sought. It does not rain from heaven. It can't be puffed out from the cigar. We must pay price for peace.

B. Peace must be sought through cooperation.

C. Who should cooperate in seeking for peace? Democracies unite!

a. Unified resistance of the invaded.

b. Noncooperation of the democratic forces of the invading countries.

c. Water bridge of the world democratic forces.

d. East and West meet in two ways.

e. World in one.

a) War breeds war;

b) Aggression encourages aggression;

c) Liberty of all men in all lands;

d) Aware of helping enemy of democracy and peace.

## Note

The manuscript of this OUTLINE is in the custody of the Tao Heng-Chih Museum at Xiao Zhuang Normal School in Nanjing.

# Outline Of Chinese People's Education

1. By people, of people and for people.

2. A family experiment: Hsiao Tao teaches his grandmother.

3. Disastrous failure in imitating Western education, conscious of.

4. Back to country: develop an education from Chinese soil, 1925.

5. Goodwill scholars with big head look dwindled. Learning from farmers.

6. The Morning Village:

   a. cottages;

   b. no walls;

   c. live the simple life among farmers;

   d. village kindergarten, defense league, Gate of peace well — Village as school;

   e. Life as education;

   f. Reflective acting, learning and teaching.

7. Trip to Japan, Japanese invasion: Need for national awakening.

8. Shan Hai Labor Science Union:

   1)Labor to support life;

   2)Science to understand life;

   3)Union to protect life;

4) All come all served;

5) A medical box, a Victrola, a few balls;

6) Study of a watch;

7) Cotton Labor Science Union;

8) The little teacher movements;

9) Deliver education as milk;

10) Handwriting and copying text books;

11) Each student raises a few hens to support school;

12) Free admission to cinema and reading ticket;

13) Shan Hai Experiment and the family incident synthesized;

14) Little teachers as a solution for female education;

15) Little teachers serving as live wires connecting school and villages;

16) Little teachers awaken the vision and enthusiasm of the regular teachers;

17) Little teachers learn more;

18) Little teachers and relay teachers;

19) Warnings: little teachers' imitation of regular teachers;

20) Self guard against blind propaganda-free criticism, searching for truth;

21) Little teachers touring through China;

22) Little teachers for national liberation.

23) Threefold principle of the little teachers;

a) Qualification, b) duty and c) joy.

24) Content: labor, science, union, songs, stories, problems, activities;

25) The magnificent auditorium;

26) The new scripts;

27) Government attitude: Laissez faire-close watch-adoption;

28)Turn stone into bread;
29)Periodical;
30)Regular teachers;
31)Training center;
32)Research center;
33)Travelling directors;
34)Full use of radio and reel;
35)The ability of little teachers correcting my poems;
36)The seven dwarfs;
37)Mr. Carpenter;
38)College students come to country;
39)Little nurses;
40)Little teachers and peace;
41)Little teachers in occupied areas: non-co-operation and non-literary transmission;
42)Education as sunshine, air and water;
43)Cold storage of knowledge;
44)Education racing with calamity;
45)Poor people give room;
46)triple defense: a) regular and mobile army; b)regular and mobile industry and c)regular and mobile education;
47)The self-moving school;
48)The husband-wife school;
49)Simple health: a) vaccination;b) midwifery; c)health rules;
50)Kid of Ong Chia-shan teaches his grand. mother;
51)The scholar ghost;
52)Hands and brain unites;
53)Education as an ornament, a toy vs a means for emancipation;

54)Will to be free and equal;

55)Miss Chu Pin Ru's teaching;

56)Ma's teaching;

57)West bridge;

58)Lavatory school;

59)Amateur writers union;

60)Reform marriage;

61)Reform funeral;

62)Little workers;

63)Little scientists;

64)Cooperatives.

**Note**

The manuscript of this OUTLINE is in the custody of the Tao Heng-Chih Museum at Xiao Zhuang Normal School in Nanjing.

# War In China Struggle For Liberty Or Slavery

*—Speech made in Canada, 1938*

China is struggling for ideals that it holds in common with Canada, ideals of peace, freedom, justice and democracy.

Peace with equality, enough to eat, liberty and justice are what the Chinese people want.

Democracy is an old tradition in China. A great Chinese once said, 'Heaven sees through the eyes and hears through the ears of the people. 'This is a cardinal principle of the Republic of China.

Japan's eyes are bigger than her stomach. While you are listening to me, every minute of the time, five human beings are being killed or wounded in China. Yet it will take Japan 400 years to wipe out China at that rate.

The Chinese people have made up their minds to stop the march of Japan. We have achieved unity in our country through our determination to resist the oppressor.

Dealing with the Japanese allegations of the cause of the struggle, there are five chief ones, and none of them valid. To each we gave the following objections:

1. Japan must expand because of overpopulation—China formerly admitted Japanese without even demanding passports. While the Japanese declared their country overpopulated, they have encouraged

a high birthrate instead of controlling it.

2. Japan is fighting for the friendship and co-operation of China—an odd way to get it.

3. Japan wishes to increase trade with China—they have destroyed that great trade.

4. Japan wishes to civilize China—all the civilization of Japan and much of that of the world as a whole has been derived from China.

5. Japan is trying to stop the spread of Communism — it would be more sensible to attack even England on this score, for China is a highly individualistic nation, and England, on the other hand, harbored Karl Marx while he wrote "Das Kapital ", and the " Red Flag"was written by a man from Tipperary.

Real reason of the Japanese attack is the desire to monopolize the raw materials of China, and to secure more cheap labor.

One of China's main sources of arms supply is Japan. Our mobile army gets behind the Japanese forces and captures large supplies of material.

It is not correct to say the Chinese are conducting guerilla warfare, for they do not fight as civilians, but as authorized, uniformed troops. The mobile forces merely fight without a base and on a highly mobile system.

The war in China is not only a life or death struggle, it is liberty or slavery. For us, liberty is dearer than our lives.

## Note

WAR IN CHINA STRUGGLE FOR LIBERTY OR SLAVERY: A speech made by Dr. Heng-Chih Tao in Vancouver, Canada, in April 1938. The report of the speech was published in the Vancouver newspaper *Sun* on April 20, 1938.

# The People's Education Movement In China

The People's Education Movement started some twelve years ago when a group of professors and students plunged into the life of the peasantry and tried to work out a method of education which would be of real service to the peasants. It has been an effort to supplement what the regular school system cannot do. It has been an attempt to develop an education from native soil as against education imported from foreign lands which have different historical and physical backgrounds. It has been an attempt to develop an education for the great masses of toiling people as against the education for the privileged few. It has been an attempt to develop an education for the whole life as against the education for an abnormal intellect. In order to achieve these objectives we have laid down four conditions to guarantee its success:

1. The experimenters must live among the masses and learn from them;

2. The methods must be based on reflective acting instead of academic thinking;

3. The cost of education must be reduced to a minimum both in money and time;

4. A will to free ourselves from the bias and prejudices of the

teaching profession.

These are some of the things that show a partial picture of the Morning Village Experiment (Shao Chuang). The chief results of this experiment are the formulation of the theories of Life as Education, Society as School, and the Unity in Teaching, Learning and Reflective Acting. The Shan Hai Labour Science Union and the Little Teachers came to answer the challenge of the Invasion of 1931 and 1932. When the Invasion penetrated into North China and the Peking students rose to call for its protection, our movement took the form of the Society of National Crisis Education and co-operated hand in hand with the All-China National Salvation Association. Ever since December, 1935, the aims of this movement have been:

1. United defence of Chinese democracy;
2. World peace through international co-operation;
3. Self-uplifting of the people;
4. Free education for all.

It is only the last aim and the methods for attaining it that will receive detailed discussion here. Even here it is not linguistic literacy alone that is looked for, but also political and economic literacy. All the while we are trying our utmost to discover the simplest technique that will make it possible for an education of the people, by the people and for the people to be worked out so that our people will be qualified more and more for participating in the great struggle for a free China among the family of free nations.

## The Scholar Ghost

A wrong conception of education with centuries' tradition behind it is in our way. Education in the old sense has been identified with book-reading. A scholar is called 'dushurhen' which means one who reads books. When you ask a professor what his profession is, in a very usual manner he would answer, "I am teaching books in Peking University." In the same way a student would answer, "wo zai Beida dushu ",meaning that he is reading books in Peking University. While we value books as an important means of enlightening ourselves in past and comtemporary civilization, we doubt whether reading books alone can lead us to freedom and doubt whether one has done justice to books by merely reading them. In more progressive circles such scholars are nicknamed as 'bookworms'. My friend, Dr. P. C. Chang, calls them 'scholar ghosts'. Here is a little poem of mine which gives a picture of such scholars:

What is a scholar ghost?
He lives along the Pacific Coast.
He has bookish knowledge to boast.
He has his eyes on the official post.
He likes delicious food,
And makes the half-starved farmers to be his hosts.
When jobless, he teaches children,
And makes all of them little scholar ghosts.

## Hands And Brains Unite

Traditional education in China seems to have created two types of strange human beings. In the schools the students are fed with knowledge to swell their heads and are provided with little opportunity for the use of their hands. Servants are doing many things for them that should be done by themselves. The making of mud pie and the opening of a watch for examination are punished alike. From the development of the human race we know it was our hands that helped to make the brain. As our hands were set free by the erected position we began to work, and as we were working we made noises that were gradually selected to serve as our spoken languages. The written languages and tools are all the creation of our hands. The discouragement of the use of hands in the older schools has really defeated their own purposes of developing the brain. With this abnormal training the students have acquired a store of undigested and unrelated knowledges without being able to identify them with realities. They seem to have a big head which cannot think accurately in terms of the objective world. Therefore those who have had the opportunity of schooling come out with a big head and a pair of small hands, and in figurative speech, look somewhat like a kangaroo, having only the strength to pick up a pen and write a few lines. On the other hand the great masses of our people, doing the great bulk of work for the nation, are left without school education. While they are paying taxes for schools to run, they and their children have been deprived of every leisure hour for cultural growth. They have been forced to exist with the appearance of a small head and a pair of big hands. The Life Education Movement aims at the restoration of these strange human beings to normal life. We want to awaken the scholars to pull out their hands to work and awaken the great masses of people to blow something into their heads in order to think. The bringing into contact of the scholars with the peasants has achieved almost miracles. Both the scholars and the peasants have rediscovered something they had forgotten. The scholars, seeing the splendid productive work done by the peasants, cannot but cry out, "Don't we have hands too? Why don't we work?" In a similar way the peasants have rediscovered their brain: "We have head, sure, we have head, let us think ! " Indeed real education must help to produce person who can think and build. What we need is an education for brain-directed hands and hands-motorised brain. This new conception of education is pictured by a poem, entitled"Brain and Hands Unite":

Two treasures with us lifelong remain:
A pair of free hands and a great brain.
He who does not use his hand
Belongs to the dethroned king's band.
He who does not use his brain
Has to endure hunger and pain.
He who uses both his brain and hand
Can create a new world on exploited land.

## Labour Science Union

From the principle of the Unity of Brain and Hands we have evolved the idea of Labour Science Union. This seemed to be a very awkward term, but it tells the contents, methods and organization of our new education: labour to nourish life; science to understand life; union to protect life. This gives the whole content of education. Further, the methods of labour, science and union determine the methods of education which will no longer be purely academic. Finally, the term shows the nature of the organization. It is a richer term than school, because a school in the traditional sense may excel in science but offers very little opportunity for the students to work and co-operate. It is even a better term than a cooperative society which does not give enough attention to other phases of human life besides the immediate economic needs.

In practice the Labour Science Union takes three forms. First, those which apply the new principle in the strict sense and take the name of Labour Science Union, such as the Cotton Growers' Labour Science Union in Paoshan, and the News-Boys' Labour Science Union in Shanghai. In the former case, cotton-growing is labour, the seeking of a better way of growing cotton and a better understanding of life as a whole is science, and the organizing of the peasants engaged in growing cotton in such a way as to be able to protect their fruits of labour from exploitation as well as to participate in the greater protection of the nation and mankind against aggression constitutes the real meaning of a union. The improvement of the quality of cotton through a better selection of seeds has enabled a small community to reap an increase of 2, 000 dollars averaging at $6 per acre. One-tenth of this extra income has enabled them to start a Children's Labour Science Union in the same village, aiming to give a better education to their children.

The News-boys' Labour Science Union on Bubbling Well Road, Shanghai, was founded in a very interesting way. One day it was noticed that these boys could not read the newspapers they were selling. We offered the service of a young man to teach them. This was accepted by the boys with gladness. Then they met with the difficulty to find a classroom. The boys were charged with the mission to find a place by themselves. Finally, the mother of Lukungyi, one of the boys, was generous enough to offer her only room for the free use of these boys. They spent one hour a day with the voluntary teacher there. The newspapers became their text-books. Headlines were their first lessons. They were given education free, but in turn they had the duty to share what they learned with their neighbours. The boys were self-supporting. Selling newspapers began to be regarded as a very honourable labour. Once united the boys became strong. They had a better chance to deal with the news dealers. Some of them had even won respect from enlightened police.

The second form of Labour Science Union is worked out under the name of schools. They have enriched their programme by incorporating some productive and socializing activities, but still keep the name of a school.

The third form consists of vitalizing the co-operatives with cultural and defensive features while strengthening the productive phase. They are Labour Science Union in reality but keep the name of cooperative societies. This movement will render its timely service to the millions of refugees.

## The Little Teachers

The little teachers are the children who share education with others. During the earlier stage of development the most prevailing type of little teachers is school children who volunteer to help their home folks and neighbours to acquire the elements of knowledge. As time goes on even children of the street pass on whatever they have learned to their friends. The first hint of the possibility of the little teacher was suggested by an incident some fourteen years ago when my mother, then fifty-seven years of age, got interested in learning. She wanted to read my letters sent home and wanted to know something of what was going on in the world. The only teacher available for her was my second boy who was then six years old and happened to have finished the first reader. The grandma and the grandson played, and studied. In one month my mother finished the first book. This happy incident did not arouse much enthusiasm beyond my family circle at the time. But the fact that a six-year-old boy, without a diploma from a normal school or a certificate from a superintendent of education, succeeded in teaching a fifty-seven-year-old grandma to finish the first reader, had made upon my mind a very deep impression which was one of the determining factors in discovering "the little teacher".

When Manchuria was invaded and Shanghai attacked in 1931 and 1932, we began to be convinced that the nation could not be saved without national unity through a general awakening of the whole population. This calls for a free education for all at the lowest cost and within the shortest period of time. Young man and young ladies with progressive ideas flooded into the villages in order to help the peasants to understand the national crisis. Some of them came to me for a word of guidance. My advice was simple: all come all served. But as the peasants became increasingly aware of the importance of education to themselves and their children, they and their youngsters began to flood the small schools with attendance. Not a few teachers were doubting how long they could keep it going on this principle. Frankly saying, some teachers were considering how to reduce the attendance by charging fees or by having an entrance examination. If this was allowed the whole purpose of people's education would have been defeated, for it meant a return to the education for the few. We tried our best to urge them to face reality and devise new ways to meet the situation. Under the pressure of necessity, they naturally delegated some able pupils to take charge of the surplus attendance. One day, in November of 1932, I visited the Shan Hai Labour Science Union and was amazed to watch a twelve-year-old boy Lu Peng handling a class of more than forty children. Every little soul was in his palm! In a flash the incident of the grandson teaching his grandma emerged from my subconsciousness. A meeting of the staff was called at once and I told them that they themselves had already found a way to save the school and the nation. That is "the little teachers." With the rise of the little teachers we have been enabled not only to keep the guiding principle 'all come all served', but in addition we have a new slogan, "they who cannot come will receive education on delivery without cash. "Since then we have witnessed the little friends delivering education to housewives and cowboys who cannot possibly attend regular classes without breaking their rice bowls. This feature of delivering education and home teaching has made the little teacher system unique and differentiated it from the Lancastrian pupil-teacher. Another difference is found in the fact that sooner or later even the cowboys and housewives begin to share their education with others.

The little teachers are rendering one unique service to China, that is to help grown-up girls and women to acquire some education. Men teachers find it difficult to teach grown-up girls in the villages where old customs prevail. A young man daring to do so will run the risk of gossip and the girls will be scared a way and he will have to teach benches and chairs! Women teachers are very few. The problem of extending education to women has puzzled us for many years. But when the little teachers come up this problem just melts like snow before sunshine They can penetrate into the chamber of a bride and give her a lesson. The little ones are much more accommodating than the regular teachers. As a little teacher is delivering education to a peasant's home, if the housewife has not finished dish-washing, she can ask the little friend to wait for a while. The little friend will be glad to do so and take the opportunity to play a little while on the yard. In this way the little teachers have helped to promote women education. In the One Hundred Dukes Village,

Kwangtung, there were in 1934 two hundred school children who volunteered to teach two thousand villagers of whom fifteen hundred were girls and women.

The little teachers are very clever in convincing the older generation for further progress. A story may be of interest to all. Near the West Lake there is the Cave of Clouds and above the Cave there is a little tea growing community, called Wung Cha Hill, which has a school in a temple. This school has about one hundrde 'little teachers'. Once a little teacher just twelve years old told me a very interesting story of how he converted his grandma to take lessons from him. He approached his grandma with a beautiful book. "Grandma, if you like to study this book, I will be glad to help you." The old lady answered, "My good boy, your grandma is too old to study. I am about leaving this world. What is the use of learning to me? " This was quite a stiff problem for the little boy to solve. But after having puzzled for a little while, he returned to Grandma. "On leaving the world, where are you planning to go? " "Well, I am a good woman, and am entitled to enter Heaven. "The boy said, "Congratulations! But suppose the Angels at the Gate of Heaven should require you to sign your own name before you are admitted, what are you going to do? " Grandma seemed to be thoroughly convinced and immediately asked him to teach her how to write her name. "Bring me a pencil. Give me a piece of paper." She began to practice writing her name. A more interesting thing happened at midnight. In our country the grandma usually takes charge of the surplus children of the family. This boy was sleeping with grandma. At midnight he suddenly woke up and suspected that some insects were crawling up his legs! When he stretched his hand and felt, to his surprise, it was not insects, but the fingers of his grandma, making crosses, circles and strokes. When she was asked why she did it the grandma answered, "Well, I am practising writing my name."

From our experience, the little teachers are very enthusiastic. A song gives a better picture of the little teacher's enthusiasm:

I am a little teacher, you know,
My heart is like a little volcano.
I am not afraid of frost and snow;
I melt ignorance wherever I go.

The little teachers are sometimes called 'mosquito teachers'. I presume most of us do not like mosquitoes. But there is one thing I can defend for them. When you have gangsters around you, the mosquitoes will keep you awake all night. Indeed, the little teachers today have gone far beyond the teaching of reading and writing. They are constantly bringing to the people songs, stories, news, knowledge and problems for discussion. The Sin An little teachers have even gone a step further by organising themselves into a touring corps, carrying with them radio sets, news reels, records, and dramatic equipment. They have travelled through nearly all the northern provinces and visited many villages along the highways and army camps behind the battle fields. Wherever they go they give performances, shows and lectures, and start reading circles or discussion groups in order to keep the national struggle alive in the minds of our people.

The principle derived from the little teachers is very simple. Any one who has learned a simple truth has the qualification to teach it and has the duty to share it with others.

Speaking from our experience the little teacher movement has shown the following merits:

1. The children learn more by teaching others. He who keeps his

knowledge in the cold storage of his head learns the least.

2. Knowledge is no longer a commodity for sale. Education becomes a free gift for all. It is like the air which everybody can breathe, like water which everybody can drink, and like sunshine which everybody can enjoy.

3. The older generation and youths make progress together. The constant contact between adults and children in intellectual growth tends to make the old people younger.

4. It helps to solve the insurmountable difficulties of women's education and makes it possible for us to extend an essential education to half of our population which can be hardly reached by other means.

5. A new change in the school itself coincided with the arrival of the little teachers. Formerly the village school was a lonely thing in the country. Now with the little teachers as live-wires connecting the village school with every home, the whole village becomes the school, and the light of education radiates everywhere while the school is in turn vitalised by the stream of problems calling for solution. The lonely teacher in a ruined temple, joined suddenly with tens of little comrades, connot but see a new vision in his profession and feel elevated for the historic mission that he is to fulfill. Mr. Tsao Dai-kiang, a teacher in the Temple of Emperor Shun, was about to resign because he found it difficult to keep his family alive with the meagre salary at a Shansi village school. When on the point of resignation he came across the methods of the little teachers from a magazine called Life Education. He gave it a trial and sent out a message that has inspired many village teachers to stick to their posts. He said, "With the little teachers and the little workers as my comrades, I am confident that we can rebuild the village life in a few

years. I feel as if the destiny of the whole nation is in the hands of teachers. "In conclusion he wrote that he would not resign even if he should be offered a salary ten times higher.

The little teacher movement is not without its dangers. I may mention two. Firstly, the little teachers, under the control of over-enthusiastic leadership, are apt to be overworked. This will do harm to the child's health and retard the cause. As a rule we do not advise the little teachers to teach more than half an hour a day. Secondly, some politicians and dogmatic ministers have availed themselves to use these children as little propagandists. This is against our principle. A teacher is one who teaches truth and nothing but truth. In order to teach truth he has to seek truth. Free criticism is absolutely necessary. In order to prevent the abuse of children for propaganda, we must inject the anti-toxin of free criticism.

## Relay Teachers

Another type of voluntary teachers, modelled on the same principles that govern the little teachers, are called relay teachers. The difference is found in age. The little teachers are below sixteen while the relay teachers are above sixteen years of age. The term 'relay teacher' is derived from relay race, passing the banner to the succeeding runner. The best way to show the working of the relay teaching is to invite an audience to imagine themselves as the farmers of China attending an evening class in the village and the speaker as a country school teacher. The mission of the evening school teacher is not teaching the farmers as students but to help them to become relay teachers, who are supposed to go out to teach others not after four or five years' graduation; they are supposed to teach others right after the class is dismissed. After the class is dismissed, every student becomes a teacher and every home becomes a centre of learning. It is quite surprising to find that one tenth of our farmers have the ability to lead independent classes. The rest can teach at least two friends, one on the lefthand side and the other on the righthand side, If the two friends are too poor to buy books, the relay teacher's own book can be shared by three. The relay teacher has got his lesson fresh from the evening class and he has to review it. In reviewing his own lesson he has taught his two friends. And in teaching his friends he learns more, more clearly and more profoundly. The moment one wishes to share his knowledge with others his own knowledge will have a high jump. 'Pass the truth on to your neighbour' has been the motto for the relay teachers. It is very gratifying to see so many of our farmers and workers who have come to serve as relay teachers of their fellow men.

## Relay Teaching Applied By Women Workers

Miss Chu Ping-yu, a woman worker in a tobacco company, Yangtsepoo, Shanghai, has done most excellent work in extending relay aching to women workers. She works in Shanghai and lives in Pootung, about five miles distant. In Pootung, near her home, there is an evening school for the training of relay teachers, conducted under the auspices of the Shanghai Y.W.C.A., Miss Chu takes one hour lesson there every evening except Sunday. Before daybreak she crosses the Hwangpoo River and walks about two miles in order to enter the factory in time. At noon, the factory has one hour recess, releasing all the workers to take their lunch in the street. The factory is then closed and will not open until a few minutes before 1 p.m. The simple meal in the street lasts ten minutes. Miss Chu has a plan in her mind to help her sister workers to acquire some education by utilising the rest of the time. First, she calls for her comrades to meet in an open place. However, the men workers crowd into the same place in order to watch what the women are doing. They are curious about these women because never before did they see this wonder-women gathering in the open-air with books in hands and maps posted. The men are amazed to witness these women reading, discussing and singing songs. The presence of men has proved to be a great unisance to the sisters. Miss Chu is finally forced to seek for a shelter. This she has secured when an elementary school principal has been finally induced to let her have one classroom for holding the recitation since his school children do not return until one o'clock. Since then the enrolment of sister workers increases by leaps and bounds and in a few days Miss Chu has to choose an able student from her class to be relay teacher of a second group. In a month she has to occupy all the rooms at the disposal of the good principal in order to meet the increasing demand. After all the rooms have been crowded new groups are formed in the homes of the sisters and capable relay teachers are selected by each group for the evening instruction. Thus the classes started by Miss Chu and her associates have become the training centre of relay teachers for women workers in that district and the light of education radiates therefrom to every home that has come in contact with them. As time goes on, workers of other districts have caught the wind of what has been going here. Some of them have been inspired to carry on similar projects. Even those men workers who have caused some trouble to Miss Chu's class at the beginning begin to see the importance of this education and decide to start men's classes, applying similar principle.

# A New Script

The People's Education Movement is also interested in promoting a new script for the Chinese spoken language. The attempt of inventing a phonetic script for the Chinese spoken language started more than seventy years ago but the last attempt has proved to be the best and most fruitful. The scripts for the Northern, Shanghai, Canton, Amoy and a few other dialects have been worked out. The new script treats the Chinese spoken language as a polysyllabic language and has succeeded in eliminating the troublesome minute symbols for the different tones. It is this great merit that makes it surpass all the previous inventions. With the new scripts for the various dialects the peasants in different localities can learn to read and write letters in their own dialects in one or two months by spending one hour a day. How great is the amount of time saved!

The greatest and most urgent need of China today is to rally all the people around the central thought and action in resisting Japanese aggression. We must not hesitate in mobilizing all the vehicles of communication for achieving this unity. The New Scripts are some of the best vehicles at our disposal and must be used to their best advantage in spite of all the difficulties in the way.

For want of space I shall present only the New Script for the Northern Dialect. The six vowels are: **a** as **a** in pap**a**, **e** as **e** in aft**er**, **i** as **i** in **i**s, **o** as **o** in h**o**me, **u** as **oo** in f**oo**d, **y** as the German **ü**. The twelve consonants are: **b** as **be** in **Be**rlin, **c** as **ts** in **Tsits**ihar, **ch** as **ch** in **ch**ild, **d** as **de** in won**der**, **p** as **p** in **p**art, **r** as **r** in **r**un, **rh** as **r** with tongue drawn back and concavely pressed upon the jaw, **f** as **f** in **f**or, **g** as **g** in **g**irl, **j** as **y** in **y**es, **k** as **k** in **k**ind, **l** as **le** in **le**t, **m** as **me** in **men**, **n** as **ne** in Bren**ne**n, **ng** as **ng** in ki**ng**, **s** as **s** in **s**ee, **sh** as **sh** in **sh**e, **t** as **te** in **Te**rman, **w** as **woo** in **woo**d, **x** as **he** in **He**rman, **z** as **z** in **z**inc, **zh** as **ch** with tongue drawn back and concavely pressed on the upper jaw. The fifteen compound vowels are: **ai** as **i** in h**i**gh, **ao** as **ou** in **ou**t, **ei** as **a** in f**a**te, **ie** as first **i** in leg**i**timate, **ou** as **eu** in past**eu**r, with the low jaw extended out, **ia** as **ya** in **ya**rd, **iao** equals **i** plus **ao**, **iou** equals **i** plus **ou**, **iu** as **eu** in **Eu**rope, **uo** equals **u** plus **o**, **ua** equals **u** plus **a**, **uai** equals **u** plus **al**, **ui** equals **u** plus **i**, **ye** equals **ü** plus **e**, **yo** equals **ü** plus **o**. The fifteen nasal vowels are: an, ang, en, eng, ian, iang, in, ing, uan, uang, un, ung, yan, yn, yng. The three variable consonants are: g, k, x, which change into soft sounds when they appear before i and y. These complete the New Script for the Northern Dialect. The Northern Dialect can be understood by three fourths of the whole population. If the New Script of the Northern Dialect could command a universal adoption, three fourths of our illiteracy could be wiped out in two or three years. The New Script has received great momentum during the last year. In one city alone 300,000 have learned the new script and can read publications published in it. It is hoped that the government will see the importance of its adoption at least as one of the alternatives and use its prestige and influence to spread it among the less fortunate of the population who have neither time nor money to learn the thousands of Chinese characters which will take years to master.

## Society As School

Another conception is to regard the community as our school, utilising all the available resources for the uplifting of the people. An application of this idea is to utilise temples, tea houses and every possible vacant place for reading-circles, discussion groups, etc. Our policy is to spend as little as possible on buildings. Wherever a room will not be available, the shade of a tree will do. Bigger meeting is always held in the open air. The nature-made auditorium is indeed magnificent. With the blue sky as our roof, mother earth as our floor, the constellations as our walls, the moon there as our lamp, our farmers are holding their mass meetings and forums. It is in such an auditorium that the peasants of China are singing their songs, telling their stories, learning their simple truth, and discussing national and international problems.

## Birth Of A New Peasantry

Under all these forces operating in the villages, taking command of them and marshalling them, a new peasantry is rising in the East. The farmer in Good Earth trying all the time to get more and more land for his own family in order to become richer than his fellow farmers is no longer an example for others to follow. The present-day progressive farmers in China want to have land enough for every farmer to lead a decent life. It is for this reason that they take so great and heroic a part in the struggle against Japanese aggression. It is also for the same reason that they want to unite all the people in action in order to insure the final victory. Here is a picture of this New Peasantry:

**Dancing of the Hoe**

Take up your hoe.
Take up your hoe.
Cut off the weeds,

The crops will grow.
Drive off your foe!
Sons of the Ancient Country.
Under the hoe,
There is liberty.
Hail Revolution!
The hoe must defend.
Long live the hoe!
Fight to the end.
When fighting alone
The hoe cannot stand long.
Machines and hoes unite,
A new world is in sight.





**Note**

(1)THE PEOPLE'S EDUCATION MOVEMENT IN CHINA, by Heng-Chih Tao, M.A., Sc.D. , was reprinted in book form from the Indian magazine *Harijan*, Oct. 29, Nov. 5, Nov. 19, 1938, by Life Education Association, Chungking, Nov. 7, 1945.

(2)When the first part of this article was published in *Harijan*, Oct. 29, 1937, the great leader of the Indian people Mahatma Gandhi prefixed a short note to it, which reads as follows: "When Dr. Heng-Chih Tao visited me some time ago I invited him to give me a note on the remarkable People's Education Movement going on in China. He has now sent the following instructive note which cannot but be useful to us in India. —M. K. Gandhi. "

# China

## Conditions Of Rural Life

**The Chinese village.** —It has been estimated that China has a million villages with an average of four hundred persons for every village. The villages differ very widely in their composition and manner of living as may be seen along the Amur, the Yangtze, the Yellow, and the Pearl Rivers, or on the plateaus of the Northwest and the plains of North China. Some of the villages consist of families descended from the same ancestor, have an ancestral hall, and are ruled more or less by the elder of the clan. Others are of a mixed composition. A scholar or a retired official may serve as a liaison between the magistrate and the villagers, and often he has the final word in local affairs. The more progressive villages have a more democratic rule and are administered by elected officers. In many villages a tea-house serves as a center for public opinion. An occasional grocery store supplies salt, vegetable oil, sugar, paper, gasoline, and, other, necessities to the villagers. With the exception of a few landlords,most of the villagers live by farming. Commonly speaking, each peasant family has five or six members, and lives on 3.5 acres in the rice region or six acres in the wheat region, scattered in four or five places. Even this little piece of land in most cases does not belong to the farmer entirely or at all. The family is lucky if it has an ox or a donkey to help in the work. It usually has a pig or a sheep, two or three hens, a few trees,and a corner garden. Studies of land utilization by the University of Nanking reported that 15 per cent of the farm net income came from supplementary industries and services. These include weaving, milling, oil pressing, and the native industries of silk, tea, sugar, paper, utensils of wood, bamboo, and straw. Around industrial cities the villagers look for odd jobs in the free seasons. They also engage in peddling fruits, grains, or vegetables.

**Population.** —According to expert estimates 12 per cent of the total population live in towns of 10,000 or more. It is safe to say that 80 per cent of the 450,000,000 are in the villages. Out of the yearly increase of 4,000,000 people an increase of at least 3000,000 may be expected in the villages. This surplus population formerly sought its outlet in northeastern emigration into Manchuria, southern emigration into foreign countries, and with the growth of industries into the cities. Since the world depression of 1929 from 200,000 to 250,000 Chinese laborers abroad have been compelled to return to their homeland. There has been an annual peasant emigration of 150,000 to 180,000 toward the provinces north and northeast of the Great Wall, but this has been greatly checked by the Japanese occupation of Manchuria. The slow development of Chinese national industries, handicapped by foreign competition and without any protection by means of tariff, has not been an adequate outlet for the surplus peasant population.

**Land problem and land policy.** —The land problem is most

serious. The unequal distribution of land, the small size of farms, the share rent, and the increase of the landless have combined to precipitate the agrarian revolution in recent years. The seriousness of the situation can be seen from the tabulation given below:

**Unequal Distribution of Land Property**

| | Haves | | Have-Nots | |
|---|---|---|---|---|
| Locality | Per Cent of Families | Per Cent of Land Owned | Per Cent of Families | Per Cent of Land Owned |
| Ting Hsien (Hopei) ... | 2.3 | 19.1 | 71.5 | 29.4 |
| Wusih (Kiangsu) ... | 5.7 | 47.3 | 68.9 | 14.2 |
| Lingan (Chekiang) ... | 4.7 | 52.1 | 88.9 | 21.8 |
| Nanyang (Honan) ... | 4.2 | 30.5 | 88.9 | 7.2 |
| Kwangtung ... | 6.0 | 66.0 | 74.0 | 19.0 |

An investiation of 58,569,000 farms in twenty-five provinces covering 1,148,874,000 *mow* of land showed the following results (one *mow* is equal to 0.164 acre):

**Land Condition in 25 Provinces**

| Region | Percentage of Irrigation | Average Number of *Mow* per Family |
|---|---|---|
| Northeast .......................... | 2.0 | 52 |
| Southeast .......................... | 62.0 | 12 |
| Northwest .......................... | 8.8 | 29 |
| North Plain .......................... | 5. 7 | 20 |
| Lower Yangtze Valley ....... | 46.1 | 15 |
| Southwest .......................... | 43.6 | 17 |
| 25 Provinces ...................... | 24.0 | 19 |

**Land Rent in 22 Provinces**

| | Rent Practices in 22 Provinces | Rent in 700 *Hsien* (counties) Expressed in Per Cent of the Land Value |
|---|---|---|
| Cash rent ....... | 21.2 per cent | 11.0 per cent |
| Crop rent ...... | 50.7 | 12.7 |
| Share rent ...... | 28.1 | 15.2 |

**Increase of the Landless**

| | Owner Farmer | | Part Owner | | Tenant Farmer | |
|---|---|---|---|---|---|---|
| Province | 1912 | 1930 | 1912 | 1930 | 1912 | 1930 |
| Yunnan ......... | 45 | 28 | 26 | 31 | 29 | 41 |
| Kweichow ..... | 43 | 32 | 24 | 25 | 33 | 43 |
| Szechuan ........ | 30 | 20 | 19 | 27 | 51 | 58 |

Realizing the seriousness of the situation, the National Government in 1930 enacted the Land Law, which provided that, if the landlord is absent from the locality where his land is situated, the tenant may proceed to own the land under certain legal conditions after he has operated it for ten years. Rent shall not be more than 37.5 per cent of the main produce from the land. The farmers individually or collectively shall have the free use of the cultivated public land but they are not allowed to own it. The rate of taxation on improved farm land shall be one per cent of its value; that on unimproved land shall be 1.5 to 10 per cent of its value. The tenant is free to make any improvement he wishes on the land and will be compensated by the landlord. The tenant cannot be evicted unless he is two years in arrears in the payment of rent or has not operated the land for an entire year without proper reason.

The land policy of Soviet China, now incorporated as a Special

District, may be cited in contrast. Here a survey conducted in 1926 by the Peasants' Committee of the Kuomintang showed that 10 per cent of the rural population owned 70 per cent of the cultivable land in China; 15 per cent was owned by middle-class peasants; and only from 10 to 15 per cent of the arable land was owned by 65 per cent of the rural population—peasants, tenant farmers, and farm laborers. According to Edgar Snow the North-west Soviet Government promulgated a land law in 1935 which provided for the confiscation of land not cultivated by the owners themselves, and the distribution of such land, waste land, and land of absentee owners among poor peasants. The term landlord included any farmer, the major part of whose income was derived from land rented out to others. The aim of the law was to guarantee the basis of a decent livelihood for every peasant family by providing sufficient land and abolishing tax exploitation.

**Usury and cooperatives.** —In 1933 an investigation conducted by the University of Nanking into the indebtedness of the farmers of 850 counties in twenty-two provinces showed that 50 per cent of the farmers are in debt and 48 per cent of them borrow grain for food. On more than 90 per cent of the loans the interest was higher than 20 per cent per annum; on nearly 24 per cent of the loans the annual interest was over 40 per cent. Of the loans 95 per cent are borrowed from feudalistic sources (pawnshops, native banks, village stores, landlords, rich farmers, and merchants)and only 5 per cent from banks and cooperatives.

In order to check usury and to help relieve the peasants the cooperative movement was originated in connection with the student movement in 1918. From 1918 to 1927 the movement was primarily social and philanthropic in aim. Since 1927 political motives have been injected in its promotion. The Chinese banks since 1934 have invested more and more of their funds in the cooperatives. Beginning with one cooperative in 1918 the number grew to 37,318 in 1936 with 1,643,670 members and a share capital of CN $ 5,139,795 (Note—At the present rate of exchange the Chinese dollar is worth 25 cents.)

On account of the lack of popular control, the requirement of property guarantee, and a rate of interest ranging from 12 to 18 per cent per annum—more than the prevailing agricultural income—the cooperatives have not on the whole proved to be of advantage to the poor peasants. Dr. Chen, after studying the cooperative movement, reached the following conclusion: "In brief, the original sponsorship of the cooperative movement in China came from intellectuals and leaders sincerely desirous of bettering the lot of the country's millions. But in the course of development and expansion, it has fallen a victim to all the social ills inherent in China's economy ... For individual usury is substituted collective usury."

Soviet China also placed great emphasis on the cooperatives which have been continued under the present administration in order, among other things given in detail by Edgar Snow, "to raise the economic-political level of the masses" and "to encourage the participation of the lowest strata of society".

**Diseases and health centers.** —The rural population has suffered much more from diseases than the urban. The most prevailing diseases in the villages are malaria, consumption, and eye, teeth, and skin troubles. Casualties due to childbirth and infantile mortality are also high in the country because of lack of medical care and health information. Contagious diseases, such as smallpox, often levy a high toll upon the village people.

In recent years much work has been done, by way of experimentation and demonstration, in trying to improve the health conditions of the farming population. An independent National Health Administration was established in 1935. Consolidation of the work of the health services had been systematically developed in the seven provinces of Kiangsi, Hunan, Kansu, Ninghsia, Chinghai, Shensi, and Chekiang. Each provincial center has an administrative office,a hygiene laboratory, and a hospital. The work is furthered by *hsien* health centers, health stations, and health sub-stations or clinics in the towns and villages. Altogether 74 *hsien* health centers and 144 stations and clinics have been established. Demonstration centers have been established in Kiangning, Tinghsien Lanchi, and Chowping, which on account of the war have been moved to Central China. These village centers have attempted under the direction of the medical staff, to use village health workers who are laymen recruited in the villages and given only a short period of training in simple procedures such as smallpox vaccination, reporting of communicable diseases, births, and deaths, the use of a few simple drugs,first aid,and treatment of common skin diseases and simple surgical wounds. Throughout the country there are 27 medical schools, 217 schools of nursing, and 38 midwifery schools which are far from being sufficient for the overwhelming demands. A good beginning has been made, however, and the work is moving in the right direction.

**Famine and the control of nature**. —Famine is a frequent visitor to China, and it is the farmers who suffer most from it. Among the causes of famine may be mentioned deforestation, lack of irrigation, inadequacy of river control, primitive methods of farming, the decline of agricultural production as a result of the increase of large landholdings, and the diminution of the size of cultivation which combine to produce the flood and drought that have often reduced the people to starvation. Further, owing to lack of means of communication it is difficult to transport food from one region to another.

In recent years there has been a great movement for reforestation. Students, civil officers, and peasants are encouraged at the Tsingmin Festival to plant trees. The Relief Commission has devoted its attention to building dams in order to provide better irrigation for the Northwest. For the year 1936—1937, $5,000, 000 (Chinese) was appropriated for irrigation work and about $9,000,000 (Chinese) was used for conservation work on Hwai River, Hupeh Dyke, and the Haiho and Yunting Rivers. In scientific agriculture much has been done in the selection of seeds, especially cotton; the Central Bureau of Cotton Cultivation has increased the distribution of improved seeds in Kiangsu, Honan, Shensi, and Hopei from 570,000 *mow* in 1934 to 3,000,000 *mow* in 1936. Attention has also been given to the improvement of animal husbandry in the Northwest and to the Chimen tea. Finally,motor roads have increased from 1,185 km. in 1921 to 66,111 km. in 1931 and 96, 345 km. in 1935.

**External aggression and united resistance.** —The century-old aggression from outside has reduced China to a semi-colonial state. The recent aggression by Japan is threatening national existence. Here again the peasants are the ones who suffer most. First, foreign goods have destroyed the village handicrafts. Second, since China did not win her tariff autonomy until 1929, the development of Chinese national industry was handicapped and the peasants were unable to find sufficient employment in the cities. Third, the Japanese occupation of Manchuria closed a most important outlet for peasant emigration and made their life in North China much harder. Fourth, the smuggling of Japanese goods into the Chinese market without paying tariff duties since August, 1935, has been a most serious blow at Chinese industries and has been one of the main causes of unemployment as well as of loss of revenue to the National Government, amounting to $100,000,000 (Chinese)a year. Fifth, in the occupied areas the peasants are forced to sell their best land at a nominal price almost amounting to confiscation.

Since "divide and conquer" has been the policy of Japanese aggression, the only way to liberty for the Chinese is to "unite and resist". The peasants in China have cast in their lot to fight for national liberation. It is they who have formed the mass base for the Chinese Invisible Army that is now making it difficult or rather impossible for the invaders to secure permanent occupation of the country. Indeed, Chinese unity has been increasingly achieved. All armies are now fighting under the unified command of Generalissimo Chiang Kai-shek, and the Chinese peasants will play a decisive role in this historic struggle for freedom.

## Educational Conditions

**Illiteracy and education.** —By illiteracy is ordinarily meant the inability to read and write. In this sense China has about 120,000,000 people who can be classified as literate and the rest, numbering about 330,000,000 can be called illiterate. The percentage of this kind of illiteracy is much higher in the villages than in the cities. But literacy takes a broader definition as education widens its scope. Should life itself be considered as education, then there is social, economic, and political literacy as well as school literacy. In this sense the peasants of some parts of China may have a higher degree of literacy than some scholars or farmers of the West. Yet academic literacy being such an important means to further one's own education, mass illiteracy among the Chinese peasants must be solved in order to help them to achieve greater progress. At the same time, in discussing this phase of the problem, it must not be forgotten that a real education of the peasantry must include an understanding of all the vital problems in relation to village life, an appreciation of all the forces that are affecting the farmers, and positive efforts to help them or guide them to help themselves to solve these problems and achieve a decent standard of living.

**Elementary education.** —There are various types of elementary schools. First, there is the six-year elementary school comprising the four-year lower primary and the two-year higher primary courses. This type of school is usually located in the capital of the *hsien*, and is rarely found in the villages. Second, there is the four-year lower primary schools, most of which type exist in small towns and cities with a small percentage in the villages. Third, there is the one-year course which is primarily intended to reach village children. Fourth, there is the old-fashioned private school which is still the prevailing type in the villages.

The National Government has made a special attempt to spread the one-year course and to reform the old-fashioned private schools, which are induced to conform more or less to the standard of the one-year course. The subjects to be taught in the one-year primary schools are national language, composition, penmanship, arithmetic, citizenship, and physical training, distributed over thirty-six periods with 1,080 minutes per week.

The increase in the enrollment of pupils in these schools has been remarkable during the last two decades, and reached a total of 16,588,000 in 1935−1936. To this should be added another 7,000,000 pupils who are enrolled in the old-fashioned private schools, which, as a rule, are not yet registered.

The elementary schools are usually of small size and even in the cities they average around three classes per school. Very few schools have as many as ten or twenty classes. In the villages and small towns there is as a rule only one class per school. It is very interesting to notice the differences in per-pupil cost in the city and village schools. In the cities the per-pupil cost reaches as high as $28.71 (Chinese), while in the province of Kansu, where the population is mainly rural, the perpupil cost is $4.77 (Chinese). It has been said that the Chinese peasants are generous in giving the children of the landlords a rich education, their own children a poor education, and themselves no education.

The number of elementary schools increased from 86,318 in 1912 to 293,000 in 1935−1936; the enrollment in the same period increased from 2,795,475 to 16,588,000 pupils, and the expenditure from $ 19,334,480 (Chinese)to $106,594, 685 (Chinese).

**Adult education**. —Since the Literary Renaissance emphasis has been placed upon adult education to which a fresh momentum was given by the Mass Education Movement. A new demand for adult education was created by the Revolution of 1925−1927. Since that time the Government has undertaken to promote the movement. Its growth has been from 6,708 schools with 206,201 students in 1928 to

38,000 schools with 1,3000,000 students in 1934 –1935; the expenditure in the same period advanced from $466,562 (Chinese) to $1,900,000 (Chinese). The total expenditure for all types of adult education was $3,632,466 (Chinese) in 1928 and $16,900,000 (Chinese) in 1934–1935.

**Compulsory education.** —In 1930 a twenty-year plan for universalizing education in China was adopted by the Second Conference of Education called by the Ministry. In 1935 the Provisional Outline for Enforcing Compulsory Education was promulgated, and provided that between August, 1935, and July, 1940, all illiterate adults and children of school age must attend the one-year primary school; between August, 1940, and July, 1944, the two-year course; and from August, 1944 on, the four-year course. Every primary school district must have one one-year primary school. For every five to ten primary school districts there must be one four-year school. The school age for children was fixed as from eight to twelve. Adults between sixteen and thirty are to be given preference in the schools. Parents or guardians are liable to a fine of from $1 to $5 (Chinese) for failing to send their children to the appointed schools.

The most notable feature of the Law of 1936 was that adult education was to be made universal within six years. The Ministry of Education in 1937 alone distributed 5,500,000 copies of textbooks for adults. Large numbers of radios were also distributed to enrich the educational program. A special fund to promote compulsory education was provided by the Ministry and the provincial governments amounting to $15,847,000 (Chinese) in addition to the regular educational expenditures for 1936–1937. Through these efforts there was an increase of 33,000 one-year and four-year primary schools with an increased enrollment of 3,400,000 pupils in 1935−1936. The forecast for 1936−1937 was an additional increase of 46,000 one-year primary schools and 3,000 four-year primary schools with another increase of 6,000, 000 pupils. The Minister was optimistic enough to say that in two years (by the end of 1937) China would have 23,000,000 pupils.

**Training of village teachers.** —The movement to give special training to village teachers was originated in the Morning Village Experiment in 1927. The promoters of this movement advocated that village teachers should be trained in a village environment. The prospective teachers should spend some time in living among the peasants, learning from them, and sharing their sorrows as well as their joys. Since 1932 private experiments have been discontinued and all normal schools have become government institutions.

There are now several ways of training village teachers: First, the normal schools admitting students with junior middle school graduation and offering a course of three years; second, the special normal course, admitting senior middle school graduates to a one-year course; third, the short-course normal schools admitting higher primary school graduates and offering a four-year course; fourth, the short-course normal classes attached to normal or middle schools admitting junior middle school graduates to a one-year course.

In 1932 there were 50,150 students in 477 village normal schools, and 18,712 students in short-course village normal schools; the number of students in the 141 village normal courses attached to middle and vocational schools was not reported.

The subjects of instruction in the village normal schools include citizenship, physical training, military training for boys, military nursing and domestic science for girls, hygiene, Chinese, mathematics, geography, history, biology, chemistry, physics, logic, manual and fine arts, music, agricultural theory and practice, village economy and cooperatives, irrigation, introduction to education, educational psychology, primary school subjects, methods and administration, tests and statistics, village education, practice teaching, extra-curricular athletics, and private study. The program calls for 60 hours a week, 36 hours for classwork and practice teaching and 24 hours for athletics and private study.

**Experiments in village education.** —During the last fifteen years a number of experiments have been carried on in China in the field of village education; of these the following are outstanding.

(1) *The Association for Mass Education*, founded in 1923 by Mr. James Yen, has four objectives-health, vocation, citizenship, and culture. All work in educating the village people is carried on through three agencies, namely, the school, the home, and the social group. The Association advocated a reduced vocabulary for the peasants, usually known as the 1,000-character readers, and has a Training Institute for Rural Reconstruction consisting of four research departments in education, rural economics, agriculture, and public health.

(2) *The Shantung Institute of Rural Reconstruction*, founded by Mr. Liang Shou-ming, undertook an experiment in two *hsien* selected by the civil administration. Each *hsien* was divided into a number of districts which were further divided into a number of villages. The basic principle underlying this experiment is "government and education in one". Accordingly, the administrative power of the district is vested in the district school; that of the village in the village

school. The personnel making up a village school is composed of four divisions. (a) trustees, the village gentry who take charge of public affairs; (b) the principal, an elder who is supposed to teach the village people by example and precepts; (c) the teachers and supervisors; and (d) the pupils, the whole population of the village, men, women, and children. The emphasis in the economic reconstruction of the village is put on various forms of cooperatives. Village defense is emphasized for self-protection and discipline. A Research Department and a Training Department were also established.

(3) *Kiangsu College of Education*, founded in 1928 by Dr. Chao Tsungding, trains village teachers and administrators who prosecute research and experiment in rural education. A social survey has been conducted and studies have been made in psychology, adult reading materials, and educational literature. The college maintains four units of experiments, two of which are devoted to rural life and problems, with the three-fold purpose of bettering the economic conditions, raising the civic competency, and spreading the education of the people. Other experiments have been directed to (a) utilizing the village houses and village teaching personnel for educational activities; (b) economizing time in school courses; (c) combining classes for children and adults and (d) organizing the village people for village reform.

Because of the present war, all these experiments have been moved to Hunan where, as reported, there exists closer cooperation than before. More detailed information about these experiments may be found in an article by Mrs. Chindon Yui Tang, on "Adult Education and the Chinese Village".

**Peasant education in Soviet China.** —The story of Chinese peasant education is not complete without an account of the educational activities in Soviet China. According to Edgar Snow, the Communists, as they passed through provinces populated by more than 200,000,000, held great mass meetings, gave theatrical performances, taxed the rich heavily, freed many slaves, and preached liberty, equality, and democracy. The aims of the agrarian revolution and of the anti-Japanese policy were explained. Education was provided to disseminate literacy, to train for the army, and to spread political theory. Mass organizations were formed for self-study groups under Communists or literati as leaders with propaganda material for texts.





**The People's Education Movement.** —This movement, sometimes called the New Mass Education Movement, refers to an organization of education of the people, by the people, for the people. It was started about eleven years ago when a group of professors and students undertook to develop a method of education which would be of real service to the peasants. The aims of the movement, as defined in 1935, are to promote (1)the united defense of Chinese democracy; (2)world peace through international cooperation; (3)the uplift of the people by their own efforts; and (4)free education for all.

*Relay teachers.* —For the present discussion the last of these movements is important. Because of the simplicity of, its technique the peasants of China have been enabled to educate and qualify themselves more and more to participate in the great struggle for freedom. A system of relay teachers has been worked out; after a class is dismissed each pupil himself becomes a teacher and every home a center of learning. It has been found that one-tenth of the Chinese famers are born teachers, capable of handling large classes with the added advantage that they speak the farmer's language and understand his problems.

*Little teachers.* —In addition to the relay teachers, a system of "little teachers" has been established, school children who at the end of the school day return to their homes and teach their relatives and neighbours. Grandparents and grandchildren play and teach and learn together. Hundreds of thousands of "little teachers" are helping to disseminate education in China, with the special advantage that they can help women to acquire some education in a social situation where women teachers are few in number and custom frowns on men teachers for girls and women.

For some years progressive village schools have been guided by the principle "All come, all served". With the increasing attendance at school of peasants and their children, the little teachers have helped to save the situation and have added to the principle the slogan "Those who cannot come will receive attention on delivery without charge"; to those who cannot come to the school, the little teachers deliver education in their homes. In this way the isolation of the school is broken down, the whole village becomes the school, and the light of education radiates everywhere. The lonely teacher in a ruined temple joined suddenly by tens of little comrades cannot fail to see a new vision of his profession and to feel uplifted to the historic mission that he is to fulfill.

*The new script.* —The People's Education Movement is also interested in promoting a new script for the Chinese spoken language. The scripts for the Northern, Shanghai, Canton, and a few other dialects have been worked out. They treat the Chinese spoken language as a polysyllabic language and in so doing have succeeded in eliminating the minute symbols for the different tones. With the new script peasants in different localities can, by devoting an hour a day to it, learn to read and write letters in their dialect in one month.

*Use of public places for education.* —Since money is not available for special buildings people willingly offer the only rooms they have for educational purposes. Not only are temples, tea-houses, and vacant rooms utilized in this way, but a shady tree or a nature-made open-air auditorium for larger meetings are sufficiently adequate places for mass meetings, the singing of songs, telling stories, learning simple truths, and discussing national and international problems.

**Conclusion.** —With relay teachers, little teachers, the new script, and society as the school, peasants are enabled to provide an education by and for themselves. Education itself has changed; it is no longer a luxury for the few; it is like the sunshine for all to enjoy, like the air for all to breathe, like water for all to drink. A new peasantry is emerging in China with the help of all the forces that are cooperating in the villages. The farmer in Pearl Buck's *The Good Earth* striving to get more and more land for his own family in order to become richer than his fellow farmers is no longer an example for others to follow. Progressive farmers in China today desire to have land enough for each to live a decent life. A picture of the new Chinese peasantry is reflected in the following poem.

**The Dancing of the Hoe**

Take up your hoe!
Take up your hoe!
Cat off the weeds,
The crops will grow.

Drive off the foe,
Sons of the Ancient Country!
Under the hoe
There is Liberty.

Hail, Revolution !
The hoe must defend.
Long live the hoe!
Fight to the end.

When fighting alone,
The hoe can't stand long.
Machines and hoes unite!
A new world is in sight.

## Bibliography


Ministry of Education. *Chinese Educational Year Book*, 1934 (in Chinese). Shanghai.

—*Monthly Gazette*, Vol. VII, Nos. 33 and 34, 1935. Shanghai. *China Year Book* (English edition), 1936–1937, 1937–1938. Shanghai. Han-seng, Chen. "Cooperatives as a Panacea for Chinese Ills."

*Far Eastern Survey*, Vol. VI, No. 7. New York, March 31, 1937.

—*The Present Agrarian Problems in China*. Shanghai, 1933. Snow, Edgar. *Red Star Over China*. New York, 1938.


## Note

CHINA, by H. C. Tao , Ph.D., Director of National Liberation Education Association, was first published in the EDUCATIONAL YEAR BOOK OF THE INTERNATIONAL INSTITUTE OF TEACHERS COLLEGE, Columbia University, 1938.

# Yu Tsai School For Talented Refugee Children

## I. The Founding Of Yu Tsai School

In order to have a better understanding of Yu Tsai school it is necessary to give some explanation of how Yu Tsai has come into existence and how the school has proceeded to discover and nourish especially the scientific talents when they are very young. Among the influences that have given an impetus to my founding of a school like Yu Tsai, three persons stand out as beacon lights: Faraday, Thomas Alva Edison and Sanderson of Oundle.

Faraday spent his boyhood in serving as an apprentice in a book-binding store owned by Mr. Ribeau. He was slow in his work. Other apprentices made complaints to Ribeau about his slowness. But Ribeau remarked sympathetically that while Faraday was binding his book, he was eating it too, He told them that anyone who was as studious as Faraday would have his tolerance. Once Faraday came to a topic on electricity when he was binding an Encyclopedia and found only two pages on so interesting a topic which of course could not satisfy his appetite. Having read it with a hungry mind, he made the decision: "Some day I shall write a book on Electricity."This he succeeded in after he had found his way into Humphry Davy's Laboratory through the help of a customer who offered tickets to Faraday for attending his lectures.

As school education has not become universal in China, it is reasonable to estimate that a great many talents are imbedded under the rock of apprenticeship. Here is a rich mine of genius for modern educators to explore. And Ribeau's sympathy, understanding and tolerance are worthy examples not only for heads of stores and captains of industry but also for school masters to follow.

The childhood of Thomas Alva Edison and the sympathetical care of his mother, Mrs. S. Narcy Edison, have given a geat impetus to my founding of Yu Tsai. As you know, Edison, when a boy, was fond of playing with chemicals. Being dissatisfied with by his old-fashioned teacher, he was dismissed after only three months schooling. His mother had a better understanding of her boy and allowed him to continue his experiments in the cellar and taught him history and geography herself. It was under the care of such a kind mother and the push of his own genius that Edison made so many contributions to science and to the welfare of mankind. Two things impressed me: for one who is gifted with scientific aptitude the study of science should begin early and teachers of gifted children should learn more from the attitude of Edison's mother.

By the end of 1931, just before the outbreak of the First Shanghai War, I had completed the translation of "Sanderson of Oundle" for the Commercial Press but unfortunately the whole manuscript was burnt away by Japanese fire and the book never published. Ever since, Mr. Sanderson's idea has become my best friend and guide. His emphasis on the spacious and the bountiful has found its realization in Yu Tsai; the fact that visitors often get the impression of Yu Tsai as a "Children's University" can be explained partly by the constant presence of Sanderson's idea. Then his idea of personified and socialized science appears to me most important. To lead a scientific world and manage it according to scientific principles is Sanderson's best contribution and advice to mankind and all posterity. We have been struggling to put these important ideas into practice against age-long prejudices, anti-scientific habits and traditions.

## II. Threefold Criteria Of Yu Tsai School

**1. Absorbing:**

On the basis of the child's being continually absorbed in certain specific activities, and through special provision of environment and nourishment, we aim to nurse and guide the young talent to full growth, penetrating into the field of the Unknown.

**2. Understanding:**

On the basis of the child's general intelligence and through a liberal education, we aim to nurse and guide the young talent to attain a deeper understanding of his own line as well as a broader understanding of the relationships of different phases of life and the historical development of the universe and human society.

**Toward Creative Life**

**3. Loving:**

On the basis of the child's readiness to help others and through community life, we aim to nurse and guide the young talent to develop a higher love for mankind. 」

## III. The Guiding Principles Of Yu Tsai School

1. One Great Brain.

2. Two Strong Hands.

3. Three Circles. —The school badge is represented by three circles. The circle is symbolic of open mindedness, ceaseless endeavor, and unity in purpose and action. One circle represents Unity of the School; another one represents Unity of the Chinese Nation and the third represents Unity of the Democratic and Progressive World.

4. Four Keys to Cultural Treasures: —1) Chinese language, 2) One foreign language, 3) Mathematics, and 4) Scientific methods.

5. Five Roads to Truth: —1) Acting, 2) Learning from books, 3)Learning from teachers, 4)Learning from friends, and 5) Reflecting.

6. Six Groups of Studies: —Yu Tsai School has six groups of special studies: 1) Music, 2) Drawing, 3) Dramatics, 4) Literature, 5)Natural Sciences and 6) Social Sciences.

7. Seven Days of Collective, Creative Living.

8. Eight Advisers: —1)What? 2)Why? 3)Who? 4)When? 5)Where? 6)How? 7)What number? 8) What direction? The first six advisers need no explanation, 7) and 8) are newly added to cultivate a conception of accuracy and a dynamic outlook.

9. Nine Times Nine Difficulties: —Hsuan Chuang of Tang Dynasty, as a legend told us, passed through eighty-one difficulties before he could get the Buddhistic Scriptures from the Western Paradise. We must take it as a matter of fact the rubs and worries of life.

10. Tenth power of strength with a pure heart to win the battle

of life.

## IV. Facts About Yu Tsai School

**Aim**: Education for gifted refugee children.

**Grade**: Primary School and Middle School. Preparations are being made for founding a professional school.

**Curriculum**: The school is running all year round. 3/4 of time for general education, following the Ministry Standard and 1/4 of time for special studies in accordance with pupil's own interest and aptitude.

**Special Studies**: They consist of elective courses in Music, Dramatics, Painting, Ballet, Literature, Natural Sciences, and Social Sciences. Two more elective courses, Agriculture and Industrial Arts will be opened as soon as preparations are completed.

**Staff**: Teachers holding academic degree from abroad, 9; teachers of college graduation standing, 33; teachers and officers of high school graduation standing, 19; total number of staff members, 61. Family members of staff, 17.

**Students**: Regular students, 320; field students, 19; students in village reading circles, including farmers, coal miners, women, poor children, 1,500; students receiving lessons in Music Clubs, 140; total number of persons receiving Yu Tsai education, 1,960. Among the 320 regular students, there are 191 boys and 129 girls; 198 refugee and very poor children and 122 selfpaid children from 17 provinces and 2 foreign countries.

**Workers**: School and farm workers, 40.

**Equipment**: Books, 22,000; Pianos, 4; Violins, 6; Cello, 1; Scientific apparatus, more than 1,000 pieces; Land, 55 *mow*, owned by school; 300 *mow*, rented.

**Financial Status**: Funds for the new refugee children are provided for by UCR and other friends, including an allowance for offsetting, to some extent, rising prices due to inflation. But for the maintenance of the refugee and poor children formerly admitted, funds are far from being sufficient. The month of January began with a budget of expenditure of $590,000, and due to high jump in prices, the budget for August has increased to more than 400% amounting to CN $2,400,000. Against this sum UCR will grant $1,400,000, British Aid to China will give $17,000 (2,000,000 ÷12), the Middle School Relief Committee will give $160,000, the National Relief Commission will give $15,000, plus CN $468,000 to be supplied by friends of Yu Tsai and other sources, making a total of CN $2,213,000. Thus the school has a deficit of $187,000 for August.

**Urgent Needs**:

1) Reenforcement of scientific apparatus $5,000,000

2) Raising teachers salary from $8,500–15,000, 60 teachers totaling $ 390,000 a month — 4,680,000

3) Improving nutrition, $1,000 × 316 totaling $ 316,000 per month — 3,792,000

4) Balancing the budget for 12 months ($187,000 × 12) — 2,244,000

5) Capital Outlay for reenforcing the Research Institute of Life Education — 5,000,000

6) Capital Outlay for founding the Agriculture Department — 3,000,000

7) Capital Outlay for founding the

| | |
|---|---|
| Industrial Arts Department | 7,000,000 |
| 8) Scholarships for 50 more poor & talented children ($ 8,000 a month per child, amounting to about $100,000 for a year) | 5,000,000 |
| Total | $ 35,716,000 |



## V. Hands And Brain Unite

**(School Song of Yu Tsai)**

Two treasures with us life long remain:
A pair of free hands and a great brain.
He who doesn't use his hand,
Belongs to the dethroned King's band.
He who doesn't use his brain,
Has to endure hunger and pain.
He who uses both brain and hand,
Can set up Heaven's Kingdom on Satan's Land.

**Note**

"YU TSAI SCHOOL for Talented Refugee Children", by Heng-Chih Tao, M. A., Sc. D., was first published in book form on September 18,1945, by "Yu Tsai School, Beipei, Chungking".

# Education For All

**Ⅰ. Name of Project** —A Preliminary Plan Of Promoting Democratic Education For 450 Million People In China.

**Ⅱ. Auspices** —Life Education Association and Yu Tsai School.

**Ⅲ. Guiding Principles**:

1. Democracy First. To learn democracy by living a democratic life. Fundamental reconstruction of the schools and the school system according to democratic ideals needed in order that an education of the people, by the people and for the people may flourish in China. Democracy is not only penicillin for China's illness but also blood transfusion giving the Chinese people new vitality to create a better country.

2. Education for all. Equality of opportunity for boys and girls, men and women, adults and children, irrespective of differences in religion, race, wealth and class to which they belong.

3. An all round education. Heart, head, hands unite. Unity in political, economic and cultural literacy. Health, science, labor, art, and democracy will be woven into a harmony of life.

4. Education for the whole life. To cultivate an appetite for learning. Learn to live; live to learn. Learn as long as we live. Once

the habit of learning is established, a life long progress of the individual is insured.

5. The foundation of democratic education should be laid on as early as babyhood. Perhaps at the present,the best and most economical way to approach the problem is to teach the babies through teaching the parents and brothers and sisters, especially through teaching the mother, sisters, and women servants.

6. Recognizing China is still an agricultural country and is bound to be very poor, we must offer to the people wholesome cultural food at the lowest cost. By utilizing the handwriting class of 12,000,000 ordinary school pupils for copying people's readers, in a month we can have 12,000,000 books for the people to use. Daylight classes are preferred in order to save oil. Chopsticks can be applied with water on table to practice writing. Sign boards on the street can serve as a lesson if text books are not ready. High cost education means no education or education for the very few.

7. Society as school. Mobilizing all possible forces, institutions and personnel already existing in society to render this great service to the people. Temples, tea houses, prisons, army camps, shops, factories, disabled soldiers hospitals and vacant houses and rooms of ordinary schools should be utilized as reading circles or training centers. The 80 million adult literates with a period of reeducation can serve as teachers helping their family members and neighbors to make progress.

8. Cultivate a sense of responsibility, a feeling of honor and an inner urge to share learning with others. One who has learned a truth carries with him the duty and the privilege to transmit that truth. One who has learned a word has the qualification to teach that word and also has the duty to teach that word; after he has acquired the appetite

for intellectual sharing, he will consider it a pleasure to do so.

9. Under the principle of common sharing of truth with our fellow men we have developed the little teachers as vanguards of free education. Since the first little teacher came to our consciousness some twenty three years ago, it has come to acquire certain merits which are essential to the spread of education in such a country as China.

a) The little teacher system has been found to be the most effective weapon in solving the difficulties of women education.

b) Adults taking lessons from children can not help being reborn as children and catch the spirit of youth.

c) Knowledge in the hand of the little teacher is no longer a commodity for sale but a free gift for all.

d) The little teacher learns the subject matter more clearly and thoroughly from teaching it and learns many important things from the people whom he teaches.

e) The enrollment has changed its character. All come, all served; those who cannot come can receive education on delivery without cash.

f) The school itself has changed, and magnified many times. The community has become the school and the so called "School" has become one of the classrooms, or more realistically, a powerhouse, sending light, heat and power through the little teachers as live wires to the homes of the community so that all members can enjoy all that is generated. Then the little teachers bring in turn from the little dynamoes of the homes everything that makes the central power house more powerful in rendering its service to the people.

g) The lonely teacher in the country school has also changed. He is no longer teaching, living, cooking, struggling alone. In a stroke he has become a captain of fifty or a hundred little comrades, who are no longer little bookworms,but all active little teachers, little workers, little fighters and above all little builders of China's Democracy.

10. The principle of common sharing of truth not only gives rise to the little teachers but also gives birth to the relay teachers. The ablest teachers of the people I have ever seen have come out from the great masses of the people, from the peasants, the workers, the artisans, and the shop apprentices. They begin to help others in an informal way as soon as they themselves have had only a few lessons. In other words they have become relay teachers. At this stage, they are most enthusiastic, and the able ones can be developed as the best relay teachers of the people.

11. The greatest emphasis is to be put on the education of the people in villages and recovered territories.

12. Encouraging the people to study with a job in hand. Never throw away the rice bowl for a school diploma.

13. U sing Romanized (Latinized) scripts when ever and wherever it is necessary and possible.

14. Fullest utilization of the radio, cinema, airplanes, railways and steamships to convey ideas, personnel and materials of "democratic education" to the farthest corner of the country so that the most backward part of the country can be democratized at the earliest possible date.

15. Encouraging people's initiative and subsidizing local experiments.

16. Discovering and selecting talents from the masses and recommend them to Yu Tsai School or other suitable institutions for special and advanced learning.

17. The project confines itself in researching, experimenting,

training, publishing, demonstrating, promoting, motivating activites and making recommendations to the government and other agencies for reference and nationwide adoption.

18. Exchange of information and experience with other nations in regard to the progress of democratization of education.

**IV. Possibilities of realization**

In applying the principles stated above a dozen years ago, the Shan Hai Labor Science Union achieved universal and free education in 25 villages in half a year without costing the government a cent. The movement under the leadership of Life Education Association spread over 23 provinces in 9 months and continued to spread until thought control set in and since then it has dwindled with the retreat of Democracy, except of course in the 17 liberated areas where the little teachers have been most flourishing and are still multiplying themselves for the service of the 100 million people living there. Recently with the return of the democratic tide, one school, the Yu Tsai School alone, has extended educational opportunities to 4,500 adults and children in its vicinity. If the 113 colleges, 2, 278 middle schools, 218,758 elementary schools and 79,550 social education organizations under the control of the Ministry of Education should do the same thing with the same principles at the same rate, they might, in their combined effort, carry the 350,000,000 people with them in continuous learning and progress. Of course, the uneven distribution of these schools should make a big discount. But under the inspiration of Democracy, with the government power back of it, readers and materials ready for use, and nation-wide voluntary promotion and competition flourishing, the 300,699 institutions armed with the little teachers and relay teachers can hardly have any doubt to reach 100,000,000 people in a year; with the assistance of the reeducation of the 80 million literate adults, they could accomplish the whole job in four years, and making allowances for all unforeseen obstacles in the way they could accomplish complete success at most in ten years. Once the habit of learning and the habit to share learning with others have been formed they will march on with their own momentum, and continual progress toward Democracy is likely insured.

**V. First Year's Budget For Starting The Movement**

(October 1, 1945—September 30, 1946):

**a**) Research Institute $140,000 gold

In the light of democraey, studying the problems, difficulties and methods in regard to

1) Education of the peasants.

2) Education of the workers.

3) Education of shopemployees and apprentices.

4) Education of disabled soldiers.

5) Education of women.

6) Education adapted to Mongolian life.

7) Education adapted to Tibetan life.

8) Education adapted to Miao life.

9) Education adapted to the life of the Chinese Turkistan.

10) Education of abnormal children.

11) Education of prisoners.

12) Health education.

13) Science education.

14) Handicrafts, agricultural and industrial arts education.

15) Drama as a means of people's education.

16) Music as a means of people's education.

17) Painting as a means of people's education.

18) Further studies into the little teacher system.

19) Reconstruction of the existing educational system and army education.

20) Reeducation of the literates and leaders.

| | |
|---|---|
| Research Professors 40 at $1,000 | $40,000 |
| Research Assistants 80 at $500 | $40,000 |
| Travelling Expenses | $10,000 |
| Library | $20,000 |
| Building | $10,000 |
| Equipment | $16, 000 |
| Letters and Telegrams | $2,000 |
| Miscellaneous | $2, 000 |
| Total | $140,000 |

| | |
|---|---|
| **b**) Administrative Expenses | $60,000 gold |
| Director's Secretariat | |
| Secretaries 20 at $ 500 | $10,000 |
| Field Directors 30 at $1,000 | $30,000 |
| Travelling Expenses | $5,000 |
| Building | $1,000 |
| Equipment | $12,000 |
| Letters and telegrams | $1,000 |
| Miscellaneous | $1,000 |
| Total | $60,000 |

**c**) Institutes For Training the Promoting and Demonstrating Staff at 10 strategic centers in recovered areas and ordinary

| | |
|---|---|
| districts | $600,000 gold |
| Professors 100 at $1,000 | $100,000 |
| Promoting and Demonstrating Staff: 25,000 members to receive training from one month to three months | |
| 1) Partial subsidy for travel | $150,000 |
| 2) Partial subsidy for food | $150,000 |
| 3) Building 10 | $10,000 |
| 4) 10 sets of School Equipment and 100 sets of Radio, Cinema, Dramatic, Musical, and Medical Outfits | $150,000 |
| 5) Printed Materials For 25,000 Members | $30,000 |
| 6) Miscellaneous | $10,000 |
| Total | $600,000 |

**d**) 100 Demonstration Centers:

| | |
|---|---|
| 100 in recovered areas and ordinary districts | $100,000 gold |
| Superintendents 100 at $500 | $50,000 |
| Assistants 100 at $400 | $40,000 |
| Reading Materials for 1,000,000 people furnished by the printing office without cost | |
| Demonstration Outfits to be relayed by the Training Centers Without charge | |
| Miscellaneous | $10,000 |
| Total | $100,000 |

**e**) Subsidies for 5,000 local organizations:

Local schools or organizations which wish to extend democratic education to the people may apply for books, publications, technical training, and demonstration on the condition that the local agency agrees to bear part of the expenses (from 1/10 to 1/2) according to the financial condition of the applicant. Books and publications within the limit of 5,000,000 to 9,000,000 sets will be supplied by the printing office without extra charge to the budget.

Technical training and demonstration will be given partial subsidies for food and travel by the training centers and incur no additional expenses.

**f**) An Editorial Board and a Printing Office which are capable of keeping 10,000,000 people in constant supply of cultural food and capable of further development. In the first year we hope to produce four People's Readers, 10,000,000 copies; The First Shelve Of The People's Library consists of 100 books, one set for each Reading Circle of 10 persons, so we need 1,000,000 sets, totaling 100,000,000 separate books; then monographs of research, periodicals, and materials for 25,000 members in the ten Training Institutes, 100 Demonstration Centers, and guide books for 1,000,000 little teachers; finally a weekly Magazine for each of the 1,000,000 Reading Circles.

$1,100,000 gold

| | |
|---|---|
| Administrative Expenses | $20,000 |
| Editors 20 at $700 | $14,000 |
| Printers 12 at $700 | $14,000 |
| Printing Machines and Complete Outfits | $46,000 |
| Ink | $6,000 |
| Paper | $1,000,000 |

| | |
|---|---|
| Total | $1, 100,000 |
| Grand Total | $2,000,000 gold |

**Ⅵ. Financial Campaign:** It is our plan to raise the equivalent of $1,000,000 gold, from friends in China and to raise $1,000,000 gold from our allied friends who are interested in China's progress. The Chinese Campaign has been started since September 18. We hope to enlist the interest of 100,000 Chinese friends who will give contributions to match the allied donation.

**Ⅶ. Results Expected:** If conditions should prove to be favorable, with this fund of $ 2,000,000 gold we could introduce in the first year 6 million to 10 million people to the elements of democratic culture and turn all of them into fishermen who will fish people for Democracy; this will give great momentum and stimulus to the next and next year's movement and it will not be too ambitious to expect that within a decade the 450 million people of China with both individual and collective appetite for learning and to share learning will become the indestructible pillars and invincible defenders of Chinese and World Democracy.

## Note

EDUCATION FOR ALL, by Heng-Chih Tao, M. A., Sc. D., "Director of the Life Education Association and Yu Tsai School for Talented Refugee Children", is the reprint of the pamphlet "EDUCATION FOR ALL —A Preliminary Plan of Promoting Democratic Education for the Four Hundred Million People in China" published by "Life Education Association, Chungking, September 18, 1945." Some slight alterations, however, have been made according to the author's manuscript.

# War Clique Blamed For Nanking Attack

*—Accusations made at Press Conference*

We feel sure that the well-organized attack on the peace delegates at Nanking was made by a clique in the Central Government, men who want war because only through war can they remain in power, for a democratic movement or a peace movement is directly opposed to their ambitions.

This attack is one of a series, similar to attacks on students and the people which took place in Kunming, Chungking, Chengtu and other places. These forces of reaction are diliberately turning the Three Principles of the People into a fabric of fascism, and the C. C. clique cannot wash its hands of this affair.

The Federation was inaugurated on May 5 and has 54 units. Primarily it was organized for democratic progress, for the people of China cannot achieve progress without democracy. The national peace campaign was started in May and was formally inaugurated at a mass meeting held on June 23. It has a membership of 100,000, and about 50,000 were present at the meeting.

The Federation sent eleven delegates to make an appeal for peace in Nanking. As soon as they reached Chinkiang, men disguised as refugees tried, unsucessfully, to make an attack on them. When the delegates reached Nanking they were surrounded by so-called refugees.

Some gendarmes and policemen tried to take four of the delegates into one room and the rest into another room. While the police were there the mob made no attack but as soon as they withdrew the attack began.

## Authors Of Attack

There are three reasons why the attack could not have been made by refugees. One is that they could not have got news about the delegation and organize an attack so promptly. The second is that there is do headquarters to receive refugees in Nanking. Thirdly, our aim is to stop war, and this is beneficial to refugees, for as soon as peace is signed they can go back to their homes. Thus, our aims are the same.

Our association wants real peace and democracy. We want peace with democracy, peace with justice. That is our chief aim. In spite of the attack, we shall keep on struggling until peace comes to China and democracy rules. We are fighting for democracy because if there is no democracy there can be no peace.

Replying to questions, Dr. Tao said: "There is a political clique in the Central Government which likes to promote war; it is a fascist group. The C. C. clique cannot wash its hands of this affair."

As our great aim is to promote peace and democrecy, Dr. Tao said, the leaders have decided not to prosecute the assailants, but leave the affair to the judgment of public opinion.

## Anti-U.S. Posters

Asked about the anti-American posters in English found

plastering the walls of the city, such as "G. I.'s leave China," Dr. Tao admitted that his association was responsible and explained its action by saying that so long as the U. S. army remained in China more trouble would occur.

We are grateful to the United States for the support given to China against the Japanese invasion. But as regards the stay of the U. S. forces, such as the Marines in China after the Japs have surrendered, we wish that some measure be adopted so that this assistance to the government might be postponed until such time as a united and democratic government has been formed in China. We do not want the war clique to be encouraged to carry on internal war, for we believe that if they had not been so encouraged the war could have been stopped a long time ago. This is our convicition.

## The Communists

Queried whether the withdrawal of U. S. forces would not bring in the Communists, Dr. Tao replied that if the Communists have a platform for peace and democracy he would welcome them, and if the National Government had a similar platform it would be all the better.

Replying to another questioner, Dr. Tao said: there were no communist members in the association.

Asked whether U.S. withdrawal would not constitute indirect aid to the Communists, Dr. Tao said that if the U. S. forces were withdrawn the chances for peace would be greater. The association does not encourage the Communists to fight, he said, nor does it encourage the Government to fight. Two sides equally balanced in regard to power or strength will come to terms. But if one side felt that it: had the backing of a strong World Power it would not tend to discuss peace.

If the Communists took advantage of the withdrawal, the people would move against them, he said.

## Delegation's Mission

Asked when the peace delegation would return to Shanghai, Dr. Tao replied: "They went to make an appeal for peace. They were given orders by the mass meeting that they must succeed and must not fail. They cannot return until they have won peace. If they should fail, some of them may come back, but other delegates will be sent to take their places, until we get permanent peace."

Replying to a question as to whether Gen. Chiang Kai-shek desired peace, Dr. Tao said: "Gen. Chiang has a psychological complex, a complex which causes him to believe that anyone who wants peace or democracy is a Communist, but, as I have already said, not a single member of our organization is a Communist."

Dr. Tao here informed a questioner that six Chinese newspapers were in sympathy with the peace movement of his association.

In conclusion, Dr. Tao said he would, in the course of the next few days, issue a copy of an appeal which his organization was sending to the American people, in which the American people are asked not to do anything to contribute to an outbreak of civil war in China.

The appeal also accuses the forces of reaction in China of sabotaging the work of General Marshall and with having turned the Three Principles of the People into a fabric for fascism.

The appeal will point out that China needs aid for reconstruction, but not aid for destruction. Continued support of the government by the U.S. would only encourage fascism to promote civil war, the appeal asserts. It asks the American people to help in the relentless fight for the destruction of fascism in China.

## Note

(1) War Clique Blamed for Nanking Attack was a report of the accusations made by Dr. H. C. Tao, as a leader of peace movement in Shanghai, at a Press conference held on the afternoon of June 25, 1946, at the Park Hotel for a number of foreign correspondents and newspapermen. The report was published on June 26, 1946, on the front page of the North China Daily News, a British daily in English in Shanghai, one of the most influential foreign newspapers in old China.

(2) an appeal to the American people: On July 2, 1946, Dr. H. C. Tao formally announced this appeal at a Press conference in Shanghai. (See the full text of this appeal as an ANNEX to the above N. C. D. N. report.)

## Annex—An Appeal To The American People

**To the American people:**

You can decide whether China will suffer a devastating civil war. Shooting has already started. Whether it continues depends almost entirely upon you. If it does, you will be a participant.

This civil war will be fought in China, the country of your faithful and admiring ally. It will be the Chinese people who will be killed, Chinese towns and farms which will be destroyed and Chinese ideals and hopes which will be suppressed.

International trade will suffer, while economic development will be discouraged. Under such conditions, there will be no market for American goods. The world trade union movement will be deprived of a strong, united Chinese labour movement. Science, culture and education will be stifled. In other words, China will not be a desirable ally for the United States.

We understand that the United States intends to aid and assist the Chinese people for the recovery and reconstruction of their country. We learned that the United States is prepared to take the following steps:

1. grant extensive loans to China.
2. continue lend-lease.
3. sell surplus war properties.
4. maintain the United States Marines and Navy in China.
5. support the American Military Mission to China.

Naturally we are grateful for the generosity of the American people. But to extend such aid and assistance at this time arouses our greatest fears. We wonder if the American people really share our fears.

You are hardly responsible for the causes of civil war in China. The Chinese people are fully aware of their responsibilities. They are not ignorant of the consequences of their own history. They realize that they cannot achieve political and economic democracy without a strong and concerted effort. Vested interests of reaction are not easily uprooted, nor are the roots of personal liberties and individual economic opportunities deeply planted without a struggle. The Chinese people have learned many lessons from the American, French, British and other peoples in their fight for freedom and democracy.

But, on the other hand, the Chinese people cannot accept responsibility for the American contributions to the civil war in China. The Chinese people have looked and will still continue to look to the American people for guidance and understanding. They have received General Marshall with respect and friendliness. They accept his recommendations with hope and anticipation. They appreciate the fact that his efforts last January brought China closer to peace and democracy than anyone could have expected at that time.

However, in the past six months, General Marshall's excellent contributions have been deliberately and systematically sabotaged by the forces of reaction. These people do not care whether they plunge the Chinese people into the civil war as long as they can continue to terrorize and exploit the Chinese people. They are monsters who would rather destroy their country than abide by the wishes of the people. These forces of reaction are against democracy not only in China but also in the United States and the Soviet Union.

These forces of reaction now hold positions of prominence and leadership in the National Government. Already they have abandened Dr. Sun Yatsen's "Three People's Principles" in favour of fascist activities. Today they ban newspapers and arrest students. They are leading private business into bankruptcy.

The United States apparently intends to issue this aid and assistance to the Chinese people through the National Government which is permeated with the forces of reaction. Under such circumstances, we can hardly welcome this aid and assistance, for we know that it will be used to continue and enlarge the civil war. China needs aids for reconstruction, but any aid given to the National Government at this time will be aid for destruction. We feel that your contributions, intended to promote peace and democracy, will merely encourage fascism and war.

In other words, your lend-lease, loans, surplus property, marines and military mission will lead China into a prolonged state of civil war, for the Chinese people will relentlessly fight for the termination of fascism in their country. Although the odds will be against the Chinese people, they will remember that the odds were against the Americans in their own fight for independence and democracy. From these events in American history, the Chinese people will acquire the very inspiration necessary to fight for their ideals which American arms and money will help the forces of reaction to resist.

The forces of reaction cannot wage war without outside assistance. Lacking this assistance, they will be defeated. Hence, they have turned to the United States for contributions to their war chest. They have manufactured myths to deceive the American people into extending aid to China.

We believe in the sovereignty of the people. This explains why we address our appeal directly to the American people. The American Government will not do what you forbid. We ask you to prohibit your Government from destroying our chances for peace and democracy and for maintaining cordial and useful diplomatic, economic, and cultural relations with you.

June 29, 1946

# Chinese Peace Organizations Congratulate American People On Independence Day

(*Message drafted out by Dr. H. C. Tao*)

July 4, 1646

**To the American People:**

We, the undersigned organizations of the Chinese people, take special pleasure in extending our congratulations to you on your National Independence Day. Those who have been struggling in China for 60 years to found a democratic republic wish to acknowledge the inspiration we have received, both from your "Declaration of Independence", with its great emphasis on the basic rights of man, and from the noble interpretation of its deepest meanings given by President Abraham Lincoln.

Since Pearl Harbour our two peoples have been joined in a common struggle against the antidemocratic forces of imperialism. Victory has crowned our united effort, giving us a new opportunity for peace, progress and international cooperation. We look forward to the continued friendship and mutual helpfulness of our two peoples so that the scourge of war may be banished from Asia and that government of the people, by the people and for the people shall be well and truly founded in both our lands.

Executive Committee

Federation of Shanghai People's

Organizations

Promoting Committee

National Peace Campaign

## Note

This message was drafted out by Dr. H. C. Tao for the Executive Committee of the Federation of Shanghai People's Organizations and the Promoting Committee of the National Peace Campaign, which jointly sent the message addressed to the American People, Representatives of the United States Government, the Shanghai American Community, the U. S. Armed Forces in China, and to Gen. George C. Marshall through "American Embassy in Nanking". Furthermore, according to a report published on July 4, 1946, in the North China Daily News in Shanghai, the two committees also jointly sent the message addressed to Mr. Monnet Davis, U. S. Consul General, Gen. Alvin C. Gillem, Mr. J. Fairbanks, of the USIS, and Mr. W. Painter, President of American Chamber of Commerce. (USIS=U. S. Information Service)

# 论 著
（中译文）

# 民国十三年中国教育状况*

## 一 引 言

近二十年来，中国正处在使其教育现代化的过程中。但只是在最近五六年内，这项工作才取得较大进展。概略地说，在1919年以前，中国教育还处在模仿外国的十字路口。它时而模仿日本制度，时而模仿德国制度，时而模仿美国制度。这种从外国搬来的教育制度，不论它们在本国多么富有成效，经这样照搬过来，是不会结出成功之果的。直到最近，中国的教育界人士和一般人才开始清醒地认识到：他们只有透彻地研究自己的需要和问题，才能确有把握地制定出一套真正适合中国国情并为中国服务的教育制度来。然而，为了充分地理解产生这种认识的影响，认识下文中将要阐述的种种设想和实现这些设想的途径，有必要在这里简要地说明这种巨大的变化原因。

最深刻的影响，无疑是所谓的“中国的文艺复兴”。“中国

* 本篇是陶行知为出席“万国教育会议”以中华教育改进社主任干事身份与东南大学教授程其保共同署名的英文报告，题为EDUCATION IN CHINA1924，曾于1925年6月由商务印书馆初版发行。本文后经陶行知作了较多、较重要的修订并增加了长篇“导言”，更名为CHINA（《中国》），发表在美国哥伦比亚大学师范学院国际研究所的《1924年教育年鉴》（EDUCATIONAL YEARBOOK1924）上，仍以中华教育改进社主任干事的身份署名“陶知行硕士”（W. TchishinTao, M.A.）。

的文艺复兴”[①]运动始于1917年的“文学革命”。那时，胡适博士及其追随者们提出：文言文已经过时，理所当然地必须代之以白话文或语体文。“文学革命”[②]取得了惊人的成功，尽管遭到了一些守旧学者的激烈反对，却为年轻一代人所热烈拥护。对中国人民来说，这种活的语言的重新被发现，就使与新时期相适应的新文学的产生成为可能，也使小学的教材和教法得到了彻底改革，同时还使以扫除文盲为内容的平民教育运动能够继续进行其计划。

但是，“中国的文艺复兴”的影响远不止此。这是一场用新观点、新标准对包括教育方面的传统价值观念在内的所有传统价值观念进行批判的运动。旧传统被抛弃了，权威受到了冲击，旧信仰的基础破坏了。用胡适博士的话来说，就是：“整理国故是最近三百年中激励了汉学家的那种批评与研究精神的复兴和再生。”[③]如前所述，在这之前，中国有点盲目地模仿外国。最初，为了学习新的，就抛弃了一切旧的。现在，中国已经逐渐认识到，旧的未必一定就坏，新的也并非必定就好。它对于一切新理论、新方法的反应不再是生搬硬套，而是先存疑、考察、实验，然后才加以选择。毫无疑问，这是一种理智的态度，这种态度在教育领域产生的逻辑结果，就是新学制的诞生。这种新制度吸收了旧的和新的，国内的和国外的精华，因而是非常适合于新中国需要的。

## 二　教育行政

### （一）教育行政单位

1. 中央教育行政

中国的教育行政在理论上是高度集中的，但在实际上却是地方分权的。教育系统的最高行政机关是教育部，它在法律上全权主管全国的教育事宜。教育部辖三个司：普通教育司，高等教育司，社会教育司。教育部最重要的官员有总长、次长、三名参事、三名司长、四名秘书、十六名全国视学。教育部的重要事情都在部务会议上研究。出席部务会议的有参事、司长、秘书以及有时被教育部邀请出席的其他人士。部务会议由总长主持。总长是内阁成员，他的僚属由他挑选，提交内阁批准。近几年来因国内政局不稳，总长更换频繁，有时一年之内竟达五次之多。但是次长的在职期是比较长的，参事、司长、秘书的在职期更长。教育部的工作能够持续不断，应归功于他们。

虽然教育部的活动因总长更换频繁而受到阻碍，它仍然享有很高的威信。随着国家的统一，总长人选合适，教育部在未来的年月里仍然能成为促进教育的动力，尽管地方的积极性很可能会受到更多的鼓励，教育部以前的官僚政治的影响很可能被削弱。

2. 省教育行政

中国现存的省一级教育行政组织有三种形式，即教育司、教育科、教育厅。广东省曾试图实行第四种形式，即教育委员会，但现在又废除了。西南各省一般采用教育司的形式，如云南、贵州、湖南皆是。云南、贵州两省的教育司长由省长任命，湖南则由省议会选举产生。广西、四川的省一级教育行政组织称为教育科。在法律上，教育科的权力没有教育司大。其他各省都实行教育厅的体制，其主要负责人称为教育厅长。教育厅长经教育总长推荐，由中华民国总统任命，在教育部直接领导下进行工作；但是在指导本省教育事务，督促其下级管理当地教育方面，又得受省长领导。所以教育厅长是对教育总长和省长双重负责的。这样一来，不同的省份，教育厅长的权力也就不一样，这主要取决于省长的意志。因为教育厅长离教育部远而离省长近，对他来说，执行省长的命令比执行在北京的上级的命令更为实惠。

省教育厅长辖二至三个科来处理大量的教育事务。此外，每省还有四至六名教育视学。

3. 地方教育行政

地方教育行政分为县和学区两级。省下面是县。县级教育行政内有两种体系：首先是劝学所[4]，它的职责是协助县知事进行工作并监督自治区域内的学校工作。劝学所有一名所长和几名劝学员。但是，除所长外，在县知事下面还有一名教育秘书以及一名不受劝学所长管辖的县视学。这三人的意见很难统一，业已证明这种三足鼎立式的管理体制是常出毛病的，现正逐渐被新产生的教育局所代替。

县教育局这种体制创立于1922年，它试图统一县级教育行政。在这种新体制中，县视学划归教育局长领导，教育局长原由县知事推荐，由省教育厅长委任。对这种新体制，还有另一种尝试，即给特别城市以更多的权力，让其独立管理自己的学校，而让县政府只管理乡村教育。虽然这个原则已广为人们所知，但实际上并没有得到积极的实施。

最低的一级教育行政组织是学区。一个县划分成好几个学区，每个学区有一名管理学校事务的教育委员，有时还附设一名助手。在中国，并没有授予学区管理教育的足够权力。因此它是一个约束力很小，效率很低的组织。唯独山西一省的地方教育行政组织最好，县内农村的每一个乡村，城里的每一条街道，都有负责人主管教育福利事业，并且他们都有职有权。所以，改革基层教育机构是我们今天所面临的最迫切的任务之一。

### （二）视察与监督

中国教育的视察分为国家、省、县三级。

据1913年颁布的条例，全国划分为八个视察区，每区有全国视学两名。对学校的正常视察时间一般始于每年八月下半月，结束于第二年六月上半月。视察内容包括普通教育和社会教育的各个方面。特别视察则依据教育总长的特别命令进行。视学不外出视察时，则留在教育部里执行其他任务。最近几年来，这些规定只剩一纸空文。全国视察活动几乎完全停止。

省视学由省教育厅长任命，较小省份有四名视学，较大的省份则有五六名。省以下是县视学。根据旧体制，县视学是代表县知事视察学校的。采用县教育局这个新体制后，县视学划归教育局长领导，每年视察他们所负责的学校一至三次。

教育法规中有详细的条款规定视学的职责，全国视学和省视学的职责有七条，县视学有十三条。但是实际上，这些视学只是参观者、报告者，更坏的成了吹毛求疵者。他们大都不明白视学的使命是给在职的校长及教员以启发、鼓励和帮助。近年来，已经出现了一种倾向，即抗议这种消极的视察，而主张用一种建设性的监督制度来取代。江苏省教育厅长邀请国立东南大学和另外几所大学的几位专家来担任专科监督。这样一来，职业教育、自然科学教学、体育训练、师范教育等几方面的监督都设立了。今年，社会科学、国语的监督也产生了。这就使得中国的视察和监督制度开创了一个新时代。

### （三）教育经费

粗略地说，中国有三级学校，其经费来源各不相同。高等教育经费主要靠国家拨款，中等教育经费靠省拨款，初等教育经费则靠县及地方拨款。虽有例外，但一般来说，这种说法是可靠的。

由于国家岁收来自关税、盐税、印花税、烟酒专卖证，电报、铁路、邮电等事业的利润，以及土地税和厘金等，所以用于国民教育的国家经费，是从这个综合来源中提取的。除了清华学校、交通大学，武昌师范大学等少数几所学府的经费各有其特殊来源外，其他国立学校的办学经费，均从总的国家拨款中获得份额。校址不在北京的国立学校的经费，从各省金库所保管的国家经费中提取。据1919年的预算（这是唯一准确地制定的预算），政府用于国民教育的拨款为5,028,836元，占该年政府总拨款的百分之一弱。

虽然各省都有自己办的专科院校，但省主要关心的仍然是中等教育。目前有这样一种趋势，即各省都办一所学科齐全的高等学校，但至今成功的极少。省教育经费主要来自附加税，尤其是土地附加税。江苏和浙江正在征收一项烟草特别税，专门用作省教育经费。四川在1922年试图把生猪税用于教育，但无多大结果。河南省采取对契约转让和所有权转让征税的办法，每年约有一百万元的收入可用作教育经费。人们虽然提出了许多新的办法来解决当前教育经费缺乏的困难，但都还处于试验和摸索阶段。为了使人们大致了解各省究竟支出多少教育经费，可以举出几个极不相同的代表省份的数额来。江苏每年2,800,000元，浙江1,500,000元，江西仅600,000元。

县用于初等教育的经费，通常来自土地附加税、杂捐、租金以及从历代留传下来的校产所得的收益。到现在为止，山西省资助小学经费的制度是全国最完善的。他们的办法是：在城镇按商店房屋的地位来划分等级并确定征税金额，税款用来资助城镇教育；在乡村，则按照土地质量征土地税，用以资助乡村教育。

由于政局动荡，军费开支无常，办学人员面临着教育经费毫无保障的局面。经费已经严重短缺的省份有广东、福建、江西、四川、安徽和湖南；稍好一些的有奉天、云南、山西、陕西、山东、河南。总之，中国的教员是忍受着个人的最大牺牲来为国家服务的。

我们现在主要关心的问题有：（1）如何通过法律保障和经济措施来保证教育经费支付的经常化，使办学人员免受经济拮据的困扰而能一心一意献身于教育事业；（2）如何改革税收制度，以求对教育的负担和受教育的机会得以均等；（3）如何建立一项适当的分配和补贴制度来鼓励教学活动而又不削弱地方积极性，（4）如何节约使用现有经费，从而能以最小之开支换取最大之成果。

# 三　新学制

## （一）学制

在过去的二十年中，中国至少存在着四种学制。最新的一种是1922年开始采用的。它是由全国教育会联合会在1919年所召开的第七次会议上倡导，经过三年酝酿的结果。关于学制的历史演变过程我们没有篇幅在这里讨论，下面在讨论各级各类学校时将对学制构成中逐步形成的各种问题有所涉及。1922年以来，成立了各种委员会，它们忙于拟定新的课程，以便充实新学制的内容。今年除了职业教育的一小部分课程外，各级各类学校的新课程均已制定就绪，并已由全国教育会联合会第十次会议表决批准，然后提交教育部公布。

下图是教育部第二十三号指令所采用的新学制图解。

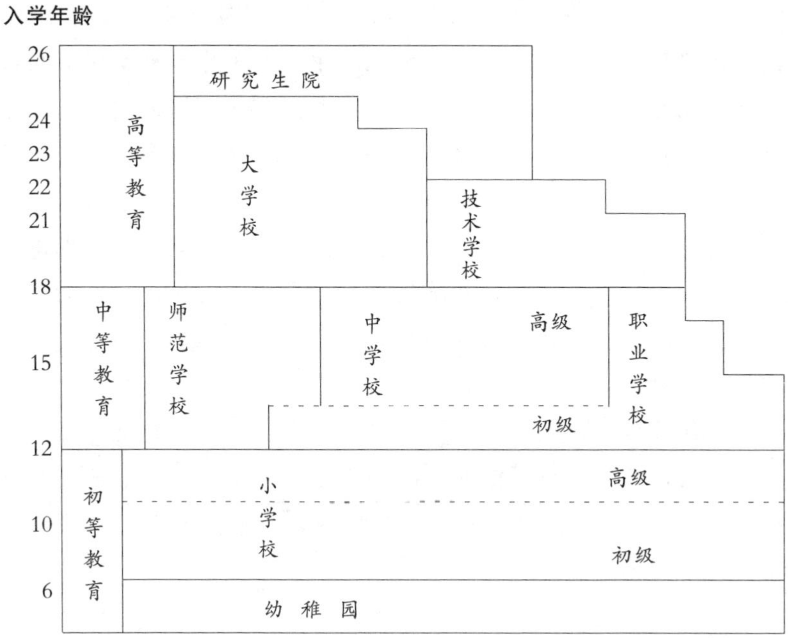

应该提醒读者注意的是，图中左边一栏是指各级学校学生入学的标准年龄，但实际上招收学生是根据其智力、成绩和其他考虑来确定的。

### (二) 各级学校

1. 学龄前教育和幼稚园教育

在新学制中，幼稚园教育占有一定地位。幼稚园主要招收六岁以下的孩子。师范学校，尤其是女子师范学校的实习学校，一般都附设幼稚园，也有私人和教会办的幼稚园。但幼稚园的数目仍相当少。幼稚园给孩子们提供了一个积极的自我表现以及孩子和教员相互了解的机会，所以，目前迫切需要有足够多的学校来培养幼教师资。江苏省于1924年1月召开的省教育行政会议，通过了一项加强培训幼教师资的决议，这是人们认识到了这种必要性的一种迹象。湖南教育会今年也倡导在城镇创办更多的幼稚园。江苏义务教育期成会还建议在小学低年级采用幼稚园教育方法。另外，国立东南大学陈鹤琴教授所指导的幼稚园教育实验，也是意义重大又令人鼓舞的。他和他手下的工作人员有感于目前在幼稚园教育中所使用的一些教材和教法都是照搬外国的，其中有一些不符合中国儿童的实际，所以在1923年秋季开始用自制的玩具，中国的儿歌、童话以及其他的教材在幼稚园中进行实验。他还打算使幼稚园不仅成为幼童教育的中心，而且成为培训母亲的中心。中华教育改进社和陈教授已同意通力合作，在他的计划中列入一项最经济实惠的幼教实验，以便尽可能多的各界民众能够照样举办。

2. 初等教育

根据新学制，小学修业期限为六年，但也可根据当地需要延长一年。小学分为初级小学和高级小学，前者的修业期限为四年，并可单独办。

由小学十八人委员会起草的小学各科课程如下表：

<table>
<tr><th colspan="2" rowspan="2">科　目</th><th colspan="2">每一科目所占时间的百分比（%）</th></tr>
<tr><th>初小各年级</th><th>高小各年级</th></tr>
<tr><td rowspan="4">国语</td><td>会话</td><td rowspan="4">30</td><td>6</td></tr>
<tr><td>阅读</td><td>12</td></tr>
<tr><td>作文</td><td>8</td></tr>
<tr><td>写字</td><td>4</td></tr>
<tr><td colspan="2">算术</td><td>10</td><td></td></tr>
<tr><td rowspan="4">社会科学</td><td>卫生</td><td rowspan="4">20</td><td>4</td></tr>
<tr><td>公民</td><td>4</td></tr>
<tr><td>历史</td><td>6</td></tr>
<tr><td>地理</td><td>6</td></tr>
<tr><td colspan="2">自然</td><td rowspan="2">12</td><td>8</td></tr>
<tr><td colspan="2">园艺</td><td>4</td></tr>
<tr><td colspan="2">工艺</td><td colspan="2">7</td></tr>
<tr><td colspan="2">美术</td><td colspan="2">5</td></tr>
<tr><td colspan="2">音乐</td><td colspan="2">6</td></tr>
<tr><td colspan="2">体育</td><td colspan="2">10</td></tr>
</table>

委员会建议，小学一二年级每周授课时间不得少于1080分钟，三四年级不得少于1260分钟，高级小学不得少于1440分钟。上述时数按每周六天分成若干节课。乡村小学的课程可以合并和简化，但国语和算术讲授时间一分钟也不能减少。

根据新学制规定，义务教育暂定为四年。有条件的地方，期限亦可延长。义务教育的入学年龄由各省或者特别区域根据各自情况自行规定。

自清朝以来，中央当局就一直打算实行义务教育，但只是到了1920年才由教育部制定出明确的在特定时间内各地实行义务教育的步骤。其详细规定如下；

1921年，省城及通商口岸。

1922年，县城及市镇。

1923年，五百户以上的乡镇。

1924年，三百户以上的乡镇。

1925—1926年，二百户以上的乡镇。

1927年，一百户以上的村庄。

1928年，不足百户的村庄。

由于近年来的政治动乱，上述计划很少得到积极实施，唯独山西一省取得了异常引人注目的成绩。山西计划在1918—1921年期间用七个半年完成上述七步计划。虽然还不能说取得了圆满的成功，但最近的统计表明，现在该省已有百分之七十二以上的学龄儿童入校就读。此外，还规定了二十五岁以下的成人文盲须上成人业余补习学校，学习常用汉字、算术和公民常识。

此处值得一提的是与初等教育有关的另一个方面，即乡村教育运动。中国百分之八十以上的人口居住在农村。因此，密切注意乡村教育，意义十分重大。最近，“回到农村去”的运动已积聚了很大的力量。中华教育改进社已经建立了乡村教育特别委员会。全国教育会联合会今年十月在开封召开的第十次会议，着重商讨了这一重要问题。江苏义务教育期成会八月在无锡召开的会议，花了三天时间草拟出了发展乡村学校的七条切实可行的提案。江苏义务教育期成会和中华教育改进社已开始对具有代表性的地区的典型乡村学校进行专门调查。尽管他们所报导的尚不全面，但已引起了人们对于乡村教育的极大兴趣和很高的热情。由于一般的乡村大都拿不出很多的钱来办教育，中华教育改进社选择了几个其校长已显露出新乡村领导才能的乡村学校，进行以最低廉的费用，创办出最优质的乡村教育的实验。但愿在今后的几年内，乡村教育能够在全国范围内普及和提高。

在对全国各种不同的方言进行了若干世纪的斗争以后，中国实际上已经解决了语言问题。胡适博士的“文学革命”已在初等学校产生了深远的影响。白话，或称之为“活的语言”，现在已受到绝大多数初等学校的欢迎。然而奉天当局却表示反对采用白话文。对于此种改变，广东省也仍持犹豫的态度。但是，生动活泼的白话文最终必将在所有的初等学校普及。

3. 中等教育

关于中等教育，新学制规定："中等学校修业期限为六年，分为初中、高中两级，各为三年。……初级中学为普通教育，但是根据地方的需要，亦可以兼设各种职业课程。高中分为普通、农业、技术、商业，以及师范等科。一所学校可单设一科或同时设数科。"

| | 学科 | 学分 |
|---|---|---|
| 社会科学 | 公民<br>历史<br>地理 | 6<br>8<br>8 |
| 语言文学 | 国语<br>外国语 | 32<br>36 |
| 数学 | | 30 |
| 自然科学 | | 16 |
| 艺术 | 图画<br>手工<br>音乐 | 12 |
| 体育 | 生理卫生<br>体育 | 4<br>12 |
| 合计 | | 164 |

中等学校实行学分制⑤。一个学分就是指上一小时课再加课外预习。无须预习的课程，应按一定的比例减少学分。初中毕业要求学完180个学分，其中164个学分为必修的。由十二人委员会起草的初级中学必修课程如下（图表见上页）。由九人委员会起草的高级中学的课程由三个学年构成，即：（1）所有的学生必修的公共课的学分大约占总学分的百分之四十三；（2）专业必修课随各专业而异；（3）纯选修课不得超过学分的百分之二十。高中的职业课程，尚未公布。文理科课目分为两组，即：艺术、社会科学组和数学、自然科学组。这两类所设置的课程如下：

(1) 艺术及社会科学组

| | 科目 | 学分 |
|---|---|---|
| 1. 公共必修课 | 1. 国语<br>2. 外国语<br>3. 人生哲学<br>4. 社会问题<br>5. 文明史<br>6. 科学概论<br>7. 体育 | 16<br>16<br>4<br>6<br>6<br>6<br>10 |
| 2. 分科必修课 | 规定:<br>1. 特设中国文学<br>2. 心理学初步<br>3. 伦理学初步<br>4. 社会科学之一种<br>5. 自然科学或数学之一种 | <br>8<br>3<br>3<br>4 (至少)<br>6 (至少) |
| | 选修科 | 32或以上 |
| 3. 纯选修科目 | | 30或以上 |
| 合计 | | 150 |

正如孟禄(Paul Monroe)博士于1921年对中国教育作了全面调查之后所指出的那样，中等教育是整个中国教育体制中最为薄弱的一环。自那时以来，中华教育改进社和全国中等教育联合会两个全国性教育团体，认真研究了这一阶段教育的各个不同方面。行政管理人员和中学教职员同样把注意力集中到了这一方面。在这里，不妨扼要地叙述一下当前中国中等教育几个比较重要的问题及发展倾向。

第一种倾向是改进中学的理科教学现已在学者和中学教职员的头脑中占据了极为重要的位置。中学里最为薄弱的环节就是理科教学。中学的理科教学只是通过讲课及课本来进行的，而很少让学生自己有机会到实验室进行实验。通过实验操作增长才干以及通过有效地控制自然以获得知识的理科学习，一直被严重地忽视了。鉴于这一事实，中华教育改进社通过孟禄博士邀请俄亥俄

(2) 数学及自然科学组

| | 科目 | 学分 |
|---|---|---|
| 1. 公共必修课 | 1. 国语 | 16 |
| | 2. 外国语 | 16 |
| | 3. 人生哲学 | 4 |
| | 4. 社会问题 | 6 |
| | 5. 文明史 | 6 |
| | 6. 科学概论 | 6 |
| | 7. 体育 | 10 |
| 2. 分科必修科目 | 规定： | |
| | 1. 三角 | 3 |
| | 2. 高等几何 | 6 |
| | 3. 高等代数 | 6 |
| | 4. 解析几何 | 3 |
| | 5. 机械制图 | 4（至少） |
| | 6. 物理、化学、生物（三项任选两项，每项六个学分） | 15（至少） |
| | 选修科 | 23 |
| 3. 纯选修科目 | | 30 |
| 合计 | | 150 |

州立大学推士（G. R. Twiss）教授，专门研究中国的理科教学并提出改进的意见。推士教授在对中国10省187所学校进行周密细致的调查之后，给我们留下了一份内容极为丰富和富有建设性的报告。这份调查报告已经以《科学与教育》为名出版了。

令人欢欣鼓舞、值得一提的另一件事，是科学社正在着手把改进理科教学作为他们的日常工作之一。在这个科学社的成员中，几乎包括了全国所有优秀的科学家。所以，该社必定能够在促进理科教育方面发挥巨大的作用。该社已选定江苏省为进行调查研究和实验的开始地点。

近几年来，引起人们很大关注的第二个问题是中等学校的国语教学。以前，这门重要的课程竟是用不科学的枯燥无味的方法教授的。教师们由于缺乏教育学及心理学的培训，所以不得不依靠灌输式和按字面逐字讲授的教学法。当胡适博士在全国教育会联合会于1922年在济南召开的会议上宣读他的论文《中国语言和文学的教学》时，首次引起人们注意到语文教学需要改革。继胡博士的讲话之后，又有三十多篇关于改进中国语文教学的文章，其中大多数已在最近两年内发表了。目前，讨论正在从主观的，经验主义的性质转到客观的，实验的基础上来，白话文在中学和小学所处的地位各不相同，趋势是年级愈高，白话文愈少，减少的部分由古文取代。

第二种倾向是中学愈来愈强调纪律。自"五四"运动以来，学校的纪律大为松弛。许多校长和教员简直无法管理学生。然而近两年出现了一种反响：一方面是对学生加以消极防范，即禁止学生参加迄今为止他们一直积极参加的一些活动；另一方面是在学校当局的监督之下，鼓励组织学生自治。现已用各种方法来证明这两种趋势的可靠性，所以，有充分理由相信，学生的操行将因此而有所改观。

第三种倾向是反对将外语作为初中必修课的民族感情。尽管规定的外语36学分已经减少，然而，在强烈的反对面前今后是否能继续保持这么多学分，还是一个问题。

第四种倾向是不断加强中学职业训练。正如《北京大学、南京东南大学入学考试统计》所示，能够录取的考生不到百分之十。这种比率在近几年并没有发生多大变化。职业教育倡导者认为中等学校的预科性质必须大大削弱。很多学校以增加职业课程对此类号召作出了积极响应。但是，这些课程怎样才能满足学生参加工作的需要，并使他们能找到终身职业，还没有令人满意的答案。

第五种倾向是中等学校男女隔离。近几年来，有些中学已试行男女同学，但是为数极少。虽然人们赞成在高等学校和小学实行男女同学，但中学男女同学却遭到极其强烈的反对。湖南在今年三月和山东在今年八月实际禁止中学男女同学。江苏采取了比较温和的态度，规定男子师范学校可以招收女生，城市中学在作好充分准备的情况下，可以男女同学。

4. 高等教育

根据新学制，“高等学府可由一个或几个学院组成。入校学生修业期限定为四至六年。”再上面是研究生院，它是为学院和大学毕业生及同等学力的学生设立的一个研究机构。

从下面两个表中可以看到中国高等教育的一些情况。

**A. 按专业分类的学院数**

| 学校类别 | 学校数量 |
|---|---|
| 综合大学 | 35 |
| 师范学院 | 8 |
| 农学院 | 7 |
| 工学院 | 13 |
| 商学院 | 8 |
| 医学院 | 7 |
| 法学院 | 33 |
| 总计 | 111 |

**B. 按经费来源分类的学院数**

| 经费来源 | 学校数量 |
|---|---|
| 国立 | 30 |
| 省立 | 48 |
| 私立 | 29 |
| 教会及外国 | 18 |
| 总计 | 125 |

今年这个名单中增加了几所大学，其中较重要的是广东公立大学及设于陕西的西北大学。

至于中国大学教育的近代发展趋势，我们可援引蔡校长[⑥]的一段言论，以说明科学研究的第一个趋势。他说，“所谓大学者，非仅为多数学生按时授课，造成一毕业生之资格而已也，实以为是为共同研究学术之机关。研究也者，非徒输入欧化，而必于欧化之中为更进之发明；非徒保存国粹，而必以科学方法，揭国粹之真相。”

值得一提的第二个趋势是要求学术自由。因为，如果外部的干涉太多，则任何一种科学思想及研究都不可能顺利发展。政府的干预总是激起高等学府的忿恨并拒绝。今年，当教育部公布新的大学管理规程时，遇到了国立北京大学教授们的强烈反对，最终不得不将此规程暂时予以搁置。

还有一个趋势是全国各大学及学院更密切的合作。今年七月，中华教育改进社在南京开会时，中国大学联合会正式组织起来，以处理有关高等教育中共同利益攸关的问题。可以相信，这样的一个机构如果正常发挥作用，必定可以提高大学工作的一般水准。

第四个趋势是高等教育扩展到女子。绝大多数中国大学已为女子敞开大门，并实行了男女同学。北京女子高师也已跻身于大学的行列。

最后一个趋势是，私立学院有了异乎寻常的增长。仅北京一地，今年秋天即有约十所私立学院成立。在其他的大城市，也可见到类似的情况。然而，政府拒绝承认那些办学目的可疑的学校。

5. 职业教育

在新学制中，职业教育占有一个重要地位。“小学课程可以包括预备职业训练，……初中可继续设置各种职业课程，……高中可分为普通科、农科、工科、商科及师范科（后来还增加了家政学科）。……职业学校的年限及地位可根据地方的需要及情况而定。”

根据这些规定，职业教育课程委员会花了三年时间编写16种不同课程的教材，这个工作实际上已经完成了。除了小学的预备职业课程和学院的专门职业课程外，已拟定三级职业教育，即：（1）为四年制初小毕业生开设的职业课程；（2）为六年制小学毕业生开设的职业课程；（3）为初中毕业生开设的职业课程。

关于实习时间及普通课程的安排，职业学校联合会提出了下列建议，它们已被适时地采纳了。第一，实习时间的安排不应少于课堂教育的时数，即每周不少于18至24小时。其次，职业学校的课程应分为三类，即职业课、职业基础课及普通课。普通课的学习时数至少应占学习总数的百分之二十。

近年来职业教育的重要发展可列举如下：四川、贵州、广西、浙江以及福建诸省已根据新学制颁布了重建职业教育的计划。山西已成立了一个省级的职业教育委员会，并为该省20个教育分区中的每一分区任命了一位监督，负责管理职业教育、义务教育及平民教育。云南已将烟草税专用于发展职业教育。湖北则下令各县调拨教育经费的百分之二十，用于发展职业训练。在上海、南京、济南及武昌等地出现的一周职业指导运动，唤起了人们对此种教育形式的极大兴趣。最后，教育部已命令所有女中提供家政学的实习机会。中华职业教育社也提供了一笔特别经费，专用于促进女子职业教育。

## 四 师资培训

关于师资培训，新学制有以下规定："在师范学校的修业期限为六年。师范学校亦可仅由最高的两三个年级组成，以便接纳初中毕业生就读。……为了满足对小学低年级教师的需要，可设立年限不等的师范学校或师范讲习所。"新学制还规定，培训职业教育教员的讲习所可在任何合适的学校举办。中等学校教师由四年制师范学院培养。"在合适的时候，根据旧学制建立的高等师范学校应提高它们的水准，以便招收高中毕业生，修业期限为四年，那时它们将称为师范学院。”“为了提供初中教员，可推行两年制师范课程。这类课程可在大学教育学院、师范学院、师范学校或高中予以筹办。它的招生对象是师范学校或高中的毕业生。”

师范学校的课程已由一个特别委员会制订完毕。有三组课程已拟定出来。

第一套课程是为相当于高级中学的三年制师范学校拟定的。它的普通必修课和高中是一样的，只是增加了音乐的4学分，总共有68学分。专业必修课由以下科目组成：心理学常识2学分，教育心理学3学分，普通教学法2学分，分科教学法6学分，小学教材6学分，教育统计与测验3学分，小学行政3学分，教育原理3学分，教学实习20学分。总计为48学分。选修科目有两种：（1）分组选修科，（2）纯选修科。分组选修科的目的是满足对三种未来教师的需要，即：（1）对语言、文学及社会科学有特殊爱好者，（2）对数学及自然科学有特殊爱好者，（3）对艺术及体育有特殊爱好者。每组学生将从一组选修科中至少选择20学分的课程。此外，全体学生将从九种教育课程中至少选修8学分。纯选修课由各校自行决定。

第二套课程是为相当于六年制中学的六年制师范学校拟定的。一般来说，在这种师范学校中保留了初级中学的特点，然而，整个课程的目标是继续提高，而不是中途停留。这种课程很简单，被推荐为较小的学校采用。因此，在这种学校里没有分组的差别。而且几乎没有什么选修课。在毕业须得到的330学分中，必修课程为319学分，选修课仅为11学分。

第三套课程是为培训初小四个低年级的教员而拟定的。它有三种形式，即：三年制课程接受六年制小学毕业生，二年制课程接受旧高小毕业生及一年制课程接受初中毕业生。所有这三种形式，课程内容都非常仔细地拟定了。由于篇幅所限，此处不能一一列举，简单列表如下（见下页）。

| | 第一种形式（三年制课程） | 第二种形式（二年制课程） | 第三种形式（一年制课程） |
|---|---|---|---|
| 教育学 | 36学分 | 24学分 | 14学分 |
| 国　语 | 36 | 24 | 8 |
| 社会科学 | 26 | 18 | 8 |
| 数　学 | 25 | 16 | 8 |
| 自然科学 | | | |
| 园艺及农业 | 33 | 22 | 8 |
| 艺　术 | 15 | 10 | 8 |
| 体　育 | 9 | 6 | 6 |
| 总　计 | 180 | 120 | 60 |

说明：小学各种教材教法包括在所教的各门课程中。在第一和第二种形式的课程中，教学实习各为8学分；在第三种形式的课程中，教学实习则和各门课程的教学结合进行。

从师范学校这些新课程中，可以看出四个重要变化：第一，它们更灵活多样了，这就使得师范学校的校长能够使他们的学校适应特殊的条件，不是像过去那样只有一种课程标准。第二，它们更强调专业课程，利用了教育的较新发展成果，以便培养更优秀的教员。第三，为教学实习安排了更多的时间。第四，极其重视教材及各科教学法。以前，对于小学的需求未予充分考虑与满足，绝大多数师范学校因袭中学的模式。这种对初等教育各科的强调，肯定标志着师范教育的新纪元。

实际上，高等师范学校一直在忙于使自身升级为师范学院。旧的师范学校也正在根据其自身需要及条件，采取步骤，以便采用六年制或三年制课程。部分高中也开设了新的师范课程。另一个很重要的动向是：正在愈来愈强调培训乡村教员。从去年开始，江苏已创办了五所乡村师范、中华教育改进社、国立东南大学教育学院及农学院、中华职业教育社，江苏义务教育期成会及江苏教育会正在进行协作，以创立一所培训乡村教员的实验师范学校。国立东南大学乡村教育教授，中华教育改进社乡村教育部主任赵叔愚先生已被推选来组织这所学校。

绝大多数师范学校学生食宿学杂免费，也招收半费生或全费生，但为数很少。免费的正式师范生毕业后尽可能到小学或中学执教。几年前在江苏省的一个调查表明，百分之八十以上的师范毕业生毕业后都从事教学工作。要求强制服务的这条规定执行得相当宽容。在全国教育会联合会开封会议所通过的决议中，显示了要求更严格地执行这一规定的趋势。今年江苏省已禁止县师范讲习所毕业生在服务期满以前升学。奉天省甚至提出了在强制服务期满前扣发文凭的计划。

除了师范毕业生以外，所有其他小学教员都要申请资格证明。教员资格证明有两种：（1）通过考试的资格证明；（2）不通过考试的资格证明。凡在中学学习过二年或二年以上，或在小学执教一年或一年以上，或在半年或半年以上师范讲习所毕业，或有足够的教育原理知识，学习过要教的学科，并能在申请者所写的文章或论文中反映出来者，按照不同的等级和性别，通过正规师范学校课程的考试，即可取得教员资格。助理教员的考试要容易得多。无须通过有关科目考试即可获得资格证明的人员是：（1）有一年或一年以上教龄的中学毕业生；（2）学习成绩良好的中等实业学校毕业生；（3）能胜任专科教学的职业学校毕业生；（4）有三年的教龄，由县劝学所所长证明其服务成绩优良的小学教员。

凡申请资格证明者，都应提交学校文凭和保证人保证其品行端正的保单，并须通过体检。

在中国，教员资格证明是由省资格证明委员会管辖的。其情况由省长每年向北京教育部报告。

至于中国教员的酬劳，江苏省曾作过一次简单的调查，其结果如下：

**小学教员年薪**

| | 高小 | 初小 |
|---|---|---|
| 最高额 | 600（元） | 240（元） |
| 平均 | 200 | 102 |
| 最低额 | 70 | 30 |

1921年，由郃先生⑦指导的另一次调查，范围及于六省，其结果是：所有小学教员的年平均薪金为银洋160.25元，他们第一年服务的年薪平均为银洋125.10元。即使充分考虑到中国货币的很高购买力，我们仍然必须承认，现在付给小学教员的薪金是很低的。新的趋势是：根据教员教学经验的增长及专业知识的提高付给较高的薪金。然而，眼下的问题是如何给教员发薪更加经常些。

除了提高薪金的趋势外，还打算通过补助来鼓励教员更长时期的服务。退休金制的重要性尚未为人们充分认识，然而已有了一个良好的开端。浙江教育行政人员会议已建议施行一种计划，即为任职六年的小学教员安排一次休假年；为工作二十年，或工作十年后丧失工作能力的教员每年支付相当于他们工作最后一年年薪四分之一的退休金。此会议还建议实行一种特别补助金制度，即抽出教员总薪金的四分之一作为基金，一旦教员去世，可用这笔基金补助其家属。今年，江苏教育会已采用了一项临时退休金制度。根据这项制度，一位小学教员只要有下列情况之一者，即可得到相当于他工作最后一年年薪三分之一的退休金：（1）连续任职八年后因病丧失工作能力，或（2）他在履行公职时严重致残或丧失工作能力，或（3）连续任职20年后因年老退休。此外，他的一个子女可到所在省份的任何一所公立学校就读而不须缴费。

关于小学教员的任期，几乎还没有作什么调查。教员的聘约通常以半年为期。几年前在江苏省13所学校中收集的有关教员服务期的数据可以说明一些情况，但是切不可把这些贫乏的数据误作全国的代表性数据。

| 服务年限 | 高小教师百分比 | 初小教师百分比 |
|---|---|---|
| 1 | 6 | 26 |
| 2 | 10 | 12 |
| 3 | 23 | 20 |
| 4 | 17 | 18 |
| 5 | 44 | 24 |
| 总计 | 100% | 100% |

目前中国需要教员甚感迫切。若按四千万学龄儿童就读四年初小标准，我们至少需要为这四个年级配备100万名教员。但根据最近的报告，我们现在仅有初小教员223,279名。为了实施全国范围的义务教育，我们需要增加三倍于现在数量的教员。现在师范学校和师范讲习所共有学生总数为43,846名，即每年只能培养不到10,000名教员，而需要却是77,000名。问题是严重而紧迫的，但只能逐步解决。

## 五　若干最近的教育活动及发展

### （一）教育测验和测量

中国的教育测验运动是在四五年前，由南京的廖、陈[8]二教授，北京的刘、张[9]二教授开设科学的教育测量课程，并在测验建设方面做了某些开创性的工作时开始的。但直到1922年哥伦比亚大学师范学院W. A. 麦柯尔（William A. McCall）教授来华，这个运动才开始勃兴。麦柯尔教授与各个中心机构的中国心理学家协作，成功地拟定了供中小学之用的20套测验。今年增加的测验如下：

| | |
|---|---|
| 1. 综合英语测验 | 安德森（Anderson） |
| 2. 地理测验 | 扬格（Young） |

| | |
|---|---|
| 3. 算术练习测验 | 俞 |
| 4. 绘画测验 | 俞 |
| 5. 智力测验 | 刘—伯纳德肖（Bradshaw） |
| 6. 自我调查综合测验 | 推孟（Terman） |
| 7. 初小非语言智力测验 | 陈 |
| 8. 高小非语言智力测验 | 陈 |
| 9. 高小汉语语法测验 | 陈 |
| 10. 数学综合测验 | 廖 |
| 11. 科学综合测验 | 廖 |
| 12. 中国语言和文学测验 | 廖 |
| 13. 汉语语法测验 | 廖 |
| 14. 历史测验 | 廖 |
| 15. 地理测验 | 廖 |

中国的测验运动有两个特点值得一提：第一，所有的测验都根据统一的新体系（即T. B. C. F. 体系）来确定评分等级，以便有可能将历次测验得分进行比较，并便于将测验结果列表和给予解释。所有的用法说明书都模拟一种标准设计，以便教员只学习一种程序即可。第二，所有的测验都由一个地方（即中华教育改进社）出版，这便省却了学校教员寻求这些测验的很大麻烦。

1923年秋，燕京大学推孟教授、北京师范大学查教授[10]曾应中华教育改进社的要求，使用特别设计及自我控制的测验，进行合作性的自我调查。“这种调查的目的是使教育者熟悉各种测验，推动他们利用中华教育改进社即将出版的各种自助指南，在中小学生中间举行一次全国性竞赛。”这种调查尽管有其缺点，仍实现了它的原来目的。有关情况的最后报告，由推孟撰写，名为《中国初等学校效率》，该书已在今年春天出版。

### （二）学生的医疗及社会福利

在小学里，学生的健康及社会福利较之在中学更受到重视。一些较好的学校，如香山慈幼院、东南大学、北京男子师范大学、北京女子师范大学所办实习学校以及湖南楚怡学校等，为儿童提供了许多参加社会活动的机会，并极为关心儿童的身体健康。从北京女子师范大学实习学校我们可以得到有关该问题的报告，这所学校有590名学生。1920年开始设置校医一职，每学期进行一次体格检查，每年还注射一次预防针。在课外活动时间，强调自由活动及运动。中国式的运动项目和外国式的运动项目一样采用。矫正体操是通过体育进行的。在卫生课中，传授一般的保健常识。学校也注意通风、采光、座位等。学校园艺提供了另一种健康的娱乐。学校鼓励室外活动，每学期至少为每个班安排一次短途旅行。学校有学生自治会、文学社、班会、群众周会、合作商店、儿童俱乐部、儿童阅览室、储蓄会及数十个为丰富儿童的社会生活而提供充裕机会的其他组织。

在国立东南大学及中华教育改进社共同主持下，由麦克罗伊（C. H. McCloy）教授指导的大量研究，或许是今年进行过的最重要研究。下列研究项目已经完成：

1. 对人体测量学及体格检查的一系列研究。若干结果可列举如下：

（1）各种体型的重量的研究已经完成。采用了新的体重计算基准，据此拟定的新的体重卡片已准备完毕。

（2）胸围测定的研究已准备就绪。

（3）所有通常采用的测定都经彻底研究过，以确定它们在诊断上是否真正有用。研究的范围压缩到了少数真正重要的测定，并研究了它们如何能对学生的福利有所助益。

（4）胸围指数作为测定退化的遗传特征的基准已在编制并接近完成。

（5）研究了各项最重要的测定和学校成绩，以了解它们之间可能存在的关系。

（6）年龄、身高、体重及运动成绩的一种新的测定方法已设计出来。

(7) 对体格检查作了精细的统计研究，一种新的既用图形也用数字表示结果的形式已经设计出来。

2. 研究了若干运动比赛项目，以确定哪些十分近似的比赛项目应该加以利用。这项工作已经完成。例如，在拾土豆竞走的三种形式中，最佳的一种根据统计已予确定。

3. 细致研究了体育运动的标准测验。在300名小学男生中对11个比赛项目进行了研究，在330名中学男生中对18个比赛项目进行了研究。每一标准测验的最佳比赛项目根据统计已予确定。

4. 一种普遍适用于70余项田径运动比赛项目的记分表已设计出来。这种记分表指明，凡达到同样分数的比赛项目的难度大致相等。

5. 根据标准比赛项目及上面提到的年龄、身高、体重的测定标准，制定了确定男女儿童在运动比赛项目上肌肉的运动商的方法。这是相当准确的。

6. 在足球和篮球方面的标准测验研究也已进行，并已初步完成。

上述研究成果中若干种已出版，有些还有待出版。当一切完成时，中国的体育及体格检查至少前进10年。

### （三）平民教育——一场扫除文盲的运动

大量的文盲现象是中国的一个独特的问题。除了一亿二千万学龄前及学龄儿童，再减去八千万曾经在旧式学校平均学过三年的人，中国仍然有两亿人（或者说，占全国人口一半的人）从未受过任何教育。这是有待平民教育的倡导者去解决的一个巨大的问题。几年前，中华基督教青年会开始对平民教育进行了新实验。1923年在清华学校举行的中华教育改进社第二届年会上，以熊希龄夫人为董事长的中华平民教育促进会成立了，平民教育立即得到全国范围的赞助及支持。

实际上，所谓平民教育就是利用以大约1200个最常用汉字为基础的四册通俗读本。一个一般的文盲每天花一小时，用四个月的时间即可学完四册读本。那时他可以在所学词汇的基础上阅览书报信件，也可利用这些词汇表达自己的思想。这四册读本总共只值银洋一角二分，即使赤贫者也可买得起。有三个扫盲的方法：第一是平民学校，由一位教员在固定时间给他班上的学生上课；第二是平民读书处，它以家庭，商店以及诸如此类的地方作为单位，鼓励家庭或商店等处识字的人教他的亲人或同事识字；第三是平民问字处，不识字的人可就课本中他不明白的任何问题到问字处寻求解答。这些问字处一般由志愿干此工作的店主主持。扫盲课本即通过这些途径，引入家庭、商店、工厂、学校、教堂、寺庙、衙门、轮船、监狱及军营。两年间，这些课本发行量已达200万册。在这些课本发行后，还出版了一系列介绍各种知识的小册子。在中国实行强迫普及教育并征愚民捐的日子已经为期不远了。平民教育的朋友有这样的雄心壮志，即在30年内创造消灭两亿文盲的奇迹。

**（四）理科教学的发展**

一个时期以来，特别是在中等学校里，对理科教学成效有着越来越不满的情绪。这种不满情绪不是仅仅针对简陋的设备，而主要是针对所采用的方法。1922年，纽约国际教育研究所保罗·孟禄博士访华，他的观察证实了许多人对理科教学的意见。根据他的推荐，中华教育改进社邀请了俄亥俄州立大学推士（G.R. Twiss）博士来华，协助改进理科教学方法。他在中国进行了相当广泛的旅行，虽然逗留时间不长，建议有限，但他的来访对中国理科教员仍是一个强烈的刺激。另一个值得一提的重要事实是：为理科教员创办了暑期研究会。在研究会里，理科教员可在暑期数月中，在专家指导下，继续深入地学习研究。该研究会必须由教育团体及科学团体共同举办。第一个研究会已于1924年在北京清华学校开办。第二个研究会将在南京国立东南大学举办。

### （五）图书馆运动

远在公元前数世纪的周朝，中国就有了图书馆。但是只有极少数知识贵族方能利用，一般的学生几乎是不可能问津的，更不用说平民百姓了。随着新教育的兴起，学校图书馆逐渐出现。到今年为止，中国已有12所具有极优良现代设备的学院图书馆，以及相当数量设备良好的中等学校图书馆。这意味着为教员和学生探求知识提供了更多的机会。与此同时，位于各教育中心的古籍图书馆，不管它们怎样犹豫不决，还是逐渐向比较高级的读者开了门。

为了管理现代图书馆，需要现代方法。认识到这一点之后，一些学院已不时派遣学生出国学习图书馆学。当中华教育改进社1922年在济南举行它的第一次年会时，中国已有几位受过现代训练的图书馆专家了。在中华教育改进社的赞助下，他们立即开始组建图书馆学研究委员会。他们的目标是：推动创立更多的图书馆；推广较好的图书馆管理方法；吸引更多的人利用图书馆。为了更有效地实现这些计划，1923年在清华学校举行的第二次年会上，他们通过了一项组织地方图书馆学会的决议。这样，1924年有八个地方学会成立。当1924年7月第三次年会在国立东南大学举行时，他们自然又期待着成立中华全国图书馆学会，以便协调对图书馆运动感兴趣的个人和团体的努力。这个全国性的组织预定于1925年成立。这样一来，要求提供更多更好图书及更多更好图书馆的呼声响彻全国。我们的图书馆专家正在不失时机地做出他们特殊的贡献。与此同时，对于吁请更多的人利用书籍及图书馆的号召，平民教育倡导者正在作出响应。我们图书馆运动最好朋友之一的伍德（Wood）小姐及其他朋友正四处奔走，力求得到美国庚子赔款基金的一些份额，用来在中国建立现代公共图书馆。中华教育改进社已请求美国图书馆学会派遣一名图书馆专家来华，帮助为这一事业拟订一份系统的计划。

## 六　教会教育

据中华基督教教育会副总干事华莱士（Wallace）博士声称，现在可能有总数近30万的学生在新教教会学校学习，而且这个数字还在增长之中。从1920年到1924年的四年中，大学生增加了百分之七十六。科斯坦蒂尼（Celso Costantini）大主教说，在天主教会学校学习的学生为258,953人。因此，在中国每100名学生中，即有八名是教会学校学生。

今年教会教育突出的一件大事是：组织了中华基督教高等教育会。该会任命了一个理事会作为临时机构，该理事会也是中华基督教教育会的高等教育理事会。这样，就把高等教育与中华基督教教育会的其他活动联系起来了。理事会干事洛本斯坦（E. C. Lobenstine）牧师现正从事研究各高校，特别是这些学校的财政状况以及对它们的努力进行协调的可能性。理事会的主要目的是：使经费来源有限的基督教高等学校为满足中国的需要作出最有成效的贡献。

尽管教会教育成绩斐然，但仍受到抨击，理由有三：第一，说教会学校完全操纵在外国人手里，即使是有资格的中国基督教徒，也很难有机会担任负责的职务，这是教会教育通常受到抨击的一个理由。其次，有人批评教会教育向尚未成熟、不能自己做出明智抉择的年幼儿童灌输宗教。最后一点，中国人非常怀疑传教机构正在组织一个基督教教育系统，来同政府的教育系统平起平坐，担心它有朝一日很可能成为大群体内部的一个不能相容的小群体。

由于这些事实，在今年七月和十月举行的两次全国教育会议上，教会教育就受到了连续两次抨击。然而，比较保守的中国人却认为：在这个过渡阶段，属于比较自由类型的教会教育可以作为政府举办的教育之补充形式，为学生提供较广泛的受教育机会，并为学校纪律树立一个较好的榜样，从而作出特殊的贡献。他们也深信，教会教育应更社会化、自由化，中国化。最后，他们还感到，如果传教机构将它们的力量和资源集中于几个高等学校，而不是耗费在创立质量较差的中小学，那么它们将能够作出更大的贡献。他们相信，传教机构以及其他私立机构也许可以开办实验性质的中小学，但大量发展这类学校并由此建立一种系统的任何企图，是迟早一定要同政府的系统发生冲突的。

## 七　几句结束语

中国的办学人员正在极度的困难和逆境中工作。通常的情况是，即使在这种环境中，他们并不沮丧，而把困难和逆境看作为自己提供奋斗和尽力的机会。现在中国堪称为一块教育工作的处女地，或者可以叫做一种社会真空，无论谁愿意投入多少力量，它都能够吸收。因此，为了理解今日中国的教育，我们既要看到它的困难，也要看到为了它而付出的努力。

### 注释

①“中国的文艺复兴”　指1917年以后在中国兴起的“新文化运动”。

②“文学革命”　指“五四”时期反对旧文学、提倡新文学的运动。“文学革命”发端于《新青年》杂志。1917年初，胡适发表了《文学改良刍议》，这是提倡白话文学的第一炮。接着，陈独秀发表《文学革命论》，从形式到内容给文学革命作了理论准备。这个时期所发表的鲁迅的小说和杂文，为新文学的发表树立了典范。这次运动，是在新的历史条件下的一次思想大解放，是以民主与科学为口号的新文化运动的重要组成部分。

③ 引文据英文移译，非胡适原话。

④ 劝学所　清末创设的地方学务机构。1923年改为教育局。

⑤ 学分制　高等学校中一种以学分作为计算学生学习分量单位的教学管理制度。后扩大到中学。

⑥ 蔡校长　即蔡元培。

⑦ 郃先生　指东南大学教授郃爽秋。

⑧ 廖、陈　指东南大学教授廖茂如与陈鹤琴。

⑨ 刘、张　指燕京大学教授刘廷芳与北京高师教授张耀翔。

⑩ 查教授　即查良钊。北师大教授，《新教育评论》主要撰稿人之一。

# 中国*

## 导　　言

**影响中国教育的各种力量概况**

作为一种社会公共机构和社会进程的教育，经常受到所处环境中的政治、社会、经济以及自然力量的影响。这些力量可能有利、也可能不利于教育的发展。它们既可能促进教育活动的进一步发展，也可能阻碍有秩序地制定教育规划。为了更好地认识今年的中国教育，有必要对同期内一直作用和反作用于教育思想与实践的各种较重要的力量有所了解。

在政治上，这一年一开始就出现全国人民对于1923年10月10日曹锟被选举为大总统表示不满。人们认为，这次选举必然要孕育一场内战，虽然当时没有一个人能够说这样的一场战争何时会来临。为之担忧最甚者是中国的教师，因为他们当中许多人都已感觉到，这一次选举所开的先例有巨大的影响力量，将足以使十年的教育努力付诸东流。这就促使教师们不得不考虑：如果代议

* 本篇系陶行知以中华教育改进社主任干事身份应美国哥伦比亚大学师范学院国际教育研究所邀请，为其所编《1924年世界教育年鉴》撰写的《中国》篇。该年鉴为I.L.凯恩德尔教授主编。年鉴内容分两大部分：（一）世界各国教育现状，（二）教育问题的讨论。本文是用英文撰写的。

制政府对于中国有好处的话，那么问题就在于怎样通过教育来培养未来议员的品质。公民教育，作为一种运动，已经在这方面获得了越来越大的发展。

这次选举之后，不同政治派系的领袖们开始结成反对直系[①]的统一战线。孙逸仙博士、段祺瑞将军和张作霖将军，虽然在国策方面有分歧，在努力反对曹锟和吴佩孚方面却是一致的。不到一年，直系和反直系便在战场上交锋了，双方军事费用估计不少于两千万美元。如果连平民财产和农业收成的损失也计算在内的话，那么，在当前这场战争中已经损失的当不少于七千五百万美元。

这一年开始时，军队有一百五十万人。在将近整整一年时间里，为了准备全面战争，由公费开支的军队人数大大增加了。军费总额估计约为一亿五千万美元。这是军国主义压在中国人民身上的沉重负担。

军国主义以及由军国主义产生的当前这场战争，从两方面影响教育。首先，军国主义和战争耗尽了本来可用以发展教育的庞大资源。其次，军国主义和战争还可以促使职业教育在军队中实施。教育工作者们心中经常把士兵复员看作救国的根本方法之一，但是他们也相信，对于这些士兵中的许多人，如果不首先给予他们以能独立谋生的职业培训就把他们遣散，那是不行的。使残废军人恢复正常生活的职业培训，乃是当前战争的直接结果。

### 外交事务

在国际关系上，有三个方面需要特别提一下。迄今为止，外国与中国在不平等条件下签订的条约今年所受到的抨击，比以往任何时候都更为强烈。这些条约使中国人民蒙受耻辱，并使不少外国人采取了一种傲慢态度。一位中国作家曾经说过：“当外国人待我们以友爱时，我们也待他们以友爱；当外国人鄙视我们时，我们就憎恨他们。”这些条约引起了强烈的民族主义倾向的新发展。这甚至也表现在今年举行的历次教育会议中。在中国，目前对教会教育的抨击，除了宗教原因之外，部分地应归因于目前全国范围内反对不平等条约的间接影响。经过相互同意废除不平等条约，将使有关各方受益。人们相信，经过相互同意取消不平等条约，不仅能使中国在国际大家庭中占有一个更为适当的地位，而且将使我们的外国朋友们在中国感到更为自在得多。

应予考虑的第二件事情，是与俄国恢复外交关系。通过取消沙俄与清朝签订的所有条约，俄国赢得了中国人民热情的友谊。这在1月26日向列宁致敬和要求承认俄国而举行的游行这两件事情中表现出来了。中国人对新俄国怀有的好感，与其说是由于俄国的布尔什维主义，不如说是由于俄国不是在口头上，而是在行动上维护国际正义与平等的立场。要预测这位新朋友对我国教育的影响还为时过早。然而，我们非常肯定的一件事情是：与新俄国接触，将使中国教育不那么有利于帝国主义和资本主义在中国的进一步得势。

**取消庚子赔款**

日本政府和英国政府已经采取了一项使用庚款的政策，然而两国政府的这项现行政策，中国人民是不能接受的。法国的庚款仍以金法郎问题为转移。如果款项的管理方法得到改变，则上述三笔款项将部分地用于教育和文化目的。美国的那一份庚款，总额为12,545,438.67美元，已于5月21日由美国国会予以取消并计划用于教育和文化目的。孟禄博士（Dr. Paul Monroe）8月访问中国的结果是：成立了一个基金会，名称是“中华教育文化基金会”，由十名中国人和五名美国人组成，以掌握这笔基金的使用。可用于教育的那一部分俄国庚款总数约达四千五百万美元，已委托两名中国人和一名俄国人组成的委员会来管理。这些款项将会激发新的教育和文化活动。许多活动项目已经提出来，促进科学和乡村教育似乎已经得到最多的支持。

**中国舆论**

在结束讨论各种政治力量对教育的作用之前，必须讲一讲关于中国舆论的影响。在我国，舆论乃是一种政治力量和社会力量，它比我们通常认为的更重要。它的影响是潜在的，但无时不存在着。它的作用缓慢，但是非常稳定和实在。政治运动和社会运动的兴衰起伏，是受这支看不见的力量的支持还是为它打败而定。从民国的建立、二次革命的失败、袁世凯的倒台、清朝君主政体复辟的失败、安福系[②]的垮台和这次直系的垮台，都可以看出舆论乃是这些事件中最起决定作用的因素之一。今天的中国舆论，在对内事务中主张建立一个廉洁的、有效率的政府，在对外事务中，主张保持公平的、友好的关系。达不到这些理想，就不能够使当代明智的舆论感到满意。怎样使舆论更加公众化，更加明智，是一个普及教育的问题。普及教育的计划包括：在十年内将两亿文盲变成有知识的、有责任感的公民！

**中国是农业国**

中国人口百分之八十以上居住在从事耕作的农村。因此，了解农民的状况，对于理解有关的经济和教育问题很有必要。中国农民是知足的、保守的。他们对中国文明的稳定和延续作出了贡献。尽管困难重重，他们在种植粮食和保持土壤肥力方面还是很成功的。收成仅足养家活口的小农遍及全国。由于没有任何农村信贷组织，在需要资金援助时，农民只能典当个人的财产，所付年利竟高达百分之三十六。不利于我国农民的其他因素很多，但其中比较重要的是：糟糕的运输设施，没有合作买卖，不懂起码的文字，而文字乃是获得改良耕作所需要的许多新知识的钥匙，还缺乏环境卫生的管理，这就损害着农民及其子女的健康。这些事实促使人们从经济和教育方面着手解决农村问题，使农民的社会生活及经济生活得到更新的有效的农村教育，这被认为是当前最重要的一个问题。农民的现状与农村的教育一道，已经促进了农业教育，到了一定的时候，这将有助于农民进行科学种田。

**工业发展和劳工问题**

尽管这种农业的影响占支配地位，各种新型工业还是逐渐地、不断地兴起，而且其范围和影响正在迅速扩大。现在已有一百多家面粉厂和七十多家榨油厂开工。水泥已在上海和南京生产，山东、河南和满洲很快也将生产水泥。我们现在已能精制食糖、食盐，用国产肥皂洗涤，用国产火柴点火。现在两百多个城市用电照明。有十多个为中国人所拥有和经营的、业务蒸蒸日上的公司，资本总额达六千万元，其矿井生产能力为八百万吨，而中国所有现代矿井的生产能力则为一千四百万吨。这大致相当于在十三年增长了百分之四百〔一〕在1918至1919年期间，中国棉纺织工业突然升至显著地位，1921年之后开始下降。1923年纱锭总数为2,221,486，1924年则为2,160,406〔二〕。中国的纱锭从1923年（全国总数）的百分之六十四降至1924年的百分之五十六，而日本在中国的纱锭则在一年中从百分之二十五增加到百分之三十四。不过，织机的数量却在增加。1923年，开工的织机为7,817台，而在1924年开工的织机数已上升到9,481台。这些数字表示的乃是战前的状况；当前的战争必定已经严重地阻碍工业的自然增长。

与工业的发展同时，发生了劳工和阶级斗争问题。“许许多多各种各样的工会迅速成立了，以广州为最活跃的中心。罢工紧随劳工组织的成长而展开。虽然工人们受到那些想当劳工领袖者的拙劣领导，有时甚至受到利用，但他们还是体验到了自身的力量。……工人们正逐步意识到自己的苦难，自己的权利，以及自己的力量。”〔三〕尤其是，中国妇女和儿童的劳动受到的保护最少，而受到的剥削最重。大多数劳动者是文盲。

人们现时在中国所看到的工业状况既然如此，教育工作者便面临着诸如将人这个因素纳入工业主义，树立正确对待劳资双方的态度，在尽量不损害生活提高的条件下使工业能够满足民族和世界的需要等等问题。教育与立法必须共同从工业主义获取最充分的利益，把伴随西方采用工业主义而来的灾难减少到最低限度。

### 商业的发展

“在过去的20年中，尽管有政治上的诸多动乱，外贸还是每年都稳定地发展了，下一年的利润总是超过上一年的利润。”[四]“1923年的外贸是1,676,320,303海关两③，比上一年外贸总额增长76,378,720海关两。进口价值下跌约二千二百万两，而出口则增长了将近一万万两”，[五]这里应该充分考虑到物价波动这个因素。我国与美国的茶叶和丝绸贸易已经下降，部分原因是我们忽略了改进质量以适应美国标准，部分是由于日本的激烈竞争。这些失败激发起养蚕和茶叶加工的科学研究。近年来私人给教育事业捐款的增加，部分地可以由商业的日趋繁荣来加以说明。今年的商业因战争而大受干扰，使教育丧失了许多本来可能从商界得到的支持。正如阿诺德（Arnold）先生所说的，“当中国对外贸易总额按人口平均计算达到澳大利亚的水平时，其总额就会达到大约600亿美元而不是现在的10亿美元。”要使中国的贸易六十倍于目前的规模，须有赖于制定一个适当的与农业和工业的改善齐头并进的商业教育体制。

### 水灾和饥荒

不时降临中国的其他力量是水灾和饥荒。今年7月和8月发生的水灾，特别是在直隶、湖南、江西以及更远的南方发生的水灾，乃是一场极大的灾难。要获得全部损失的数字是不可能的。仅就张家口、湖南和福建来说，估计损失达45,000,000美元。根据华洋义赈会④的报告，至少需要花一千万美元才能救济遭受此次灾害的一千万人。这次水灾的直接后果是：第一，要求动用一切可能的财源来进行救济工作，实际上已经没有从事新的教育活动的余地；第二，需要与水利工程一道进行重新造林的有条不紊的计划，已为众所公认；第三，人们坚决主张通过一种实用的教育体制运用救济基金从事预防工作。普及教育的倡导者们还努力利用这个机会在空闲时间里教育难民中的文盲。

**交通状况**

教育通常是随着交通的进步而进步的。新教育的范围与火车和轮船交通的范围非常密切地相一致。虽然中国的面积比美国、墨西哥和中美洲的面积总和还要大，中国人口比美国人口多四倍，但与美国的265,000英里的铁路相比，中国的铁路却不到7,000英里。结果，中国人口的七分之六集中在大约三分之一的中国领土上。铁路将开拓于2,000,000平方英里现时无人定居、尚未开发的地区，将有助于人口的更好分布，有助于国家的统一，有助于根除匪患与饥荒。铁路和良好的公路是普及教育所不可缺少的，因为四通八达的教育依赖于四通八达的交通。

**中国的“文艺复兴”**

现时影响中国教育的所有各种力量之中，中国的“文艺复兴”[六]所施加的影响最为深刻。这个运动作为“文学革命”开始于1917年，当时运动的领袖胡适博士和陈独秀先生宣称：文言已经过时，白话乃是合法的继承者。由于白话是中国最广泛使用的口头语，是两千多年来语言进化的最高点，是全国最受欢迎的文学作品所使用的语言，所以“文学革命”获得了惊人的成功。尽管“文学革命”受到保守学者们的强烈反对，年轻一代却以无法抑制的喜悦心情迎接这场革命。为中国人重新发现一种活的语言，已经使中国能够产生适应新时代的新文学作品，彻底革新小学读物及教学法，并使普及教育运动得以继续进行其扫除文盲的计划。

中国"文艺复兴"的第二阶段与高等教育有关。在这场运动的最后几年里，学者们力图应用近代科学研究的方法来进行整理中国旧学的工作。用胡博士的话来说，这次"整理国故是使最近三百年汉学家们的著作富有生气的那种批判和研究精神的复活或再生"[5]。

但是中国"文艺复兴"的影响比上述更为广泛。中国"文艺复兴"是一场运动，通过这场运动，"一切传统的价值观念都要用新观点、新标准加以鉴定，传统常被抛弃，权威被废除，旧的各种信仰正逐步遭到破坏"。这说明中国的"文艺复兴"运动为什么如此透彻和深远，其影响为什么遍及民族生活的整个结构。

### 各国学者的来访

自1918年以来，杜威（John Dewey）、罗素（Bertrand Russell）、孟禄（Paul Monroe）、杜里舒[6]（Von Driesch）、泰戈尔（Rabindranath Tagore）等一批著名学者曾经访问我国。通过演讲以及与我国知识界领袖们和学生们的接触，他们对中国人的思想和生活都有很大的影响。应该特别提一下杜威博士和孟禄博士的来访，因为他们的访问对中国教育的改造具有特殊的意义。除了对高等教育的影响之外，杜威博士的实用主义教育哲学已经成为我国初等教育改革的指导方针之一。自从他访问我国以来，在初等教育中已经进行了若干实验。他的哲学促使教育系的几个学生为实现他的哲学而设计了若干技能和方法。孟禄博士强调，教育是一种应用，而不是观念的获得。他的劝告是以1921年的仔细调查为根据的，所以引起了对各种教育问题的认真思考，尤其促进了中等教育和科学教学的改革。

### 中国教育工作者的批判态度

迄今为止，我们只讲到比较重要的一些力量及其对中国教育产生的影响，但已足够说明，在中国，问题很多而且错综复杂。

人们既从中国以往的文明中，也从当代的范例中，寻求解决方法。因此，中国试图向一个又一个国家求教，到今天为止，已颇有一批可资挑选的世界性的导师。日本、德国、美国、英国、菲律宾、印度以及俄国是比较重要的国家，因为它们的教育理论和实践已经对中国的教育产生影响。中国以往曾经相当盲目地追随它的老师，但是还没有一位老师成功地为中国的问题提出满意的解决方法。

每一位老师都在某些方面对中国有所帮助，但是全盘照搬任何一种体制都把中国引上了歧途。最初，中国抛弃了一切旧的东西，采用了新的东西，然后逐渐认识到，旧的东西未必坏，新的东西未必好。因此，我国教育工作者变得比以前更加审慎得多了。现在他们对于新的理论和实践的反应，不再是照抄照搬，而是加以质疑、审查、实验和选择。这种态度的逻辑结果有助于通过吸收国内外新旧事物中最好的东西设计出最适合新中国需要的一种教育。过去的经验和外部世界的经验必须吸取，然后这些经验才能有利于增强民族的活力与福利。批判的和实验的态度是创造性的。只要人们抱着这样一种态度，适应中国人生活的真正的中国教育就有可能产生出来。这样一种创造已经开始。

## 教育行政

**中央教育行政机构**

教育体制的最高领导层是教育部，受总统节制，主管教育、艺术、科学和天文观测。下设三个司：（1）普通教育司；（2）高等教育司；（3）社会教育司。教育部中比较重要的官员有总长、次长、三位参事、三位司长、四位秘书以及十六位全国视学[七]。教育部的重大事务均经部务会议审议，出席会议者有参事、司长、秘书以及其他由总长邀请参加的人士。这种会议由总长主持。教育总长是内阁成员，负责对部务总的指导，其下属（包括次长在内）由他挑选，呈报内阁批准。

三年前，总长每年约更换两次。最近两三年来，这个职位更欠稳定；今年总长竟更换了五次之多。可是，次长的在职期通常是较长的，但也不过是总长在职期的一倍。参事、司长和他们的下属职员的在职期长得多,部的职能得以持续运行,应归功于他们。

由于国内政治纠纷和教育缺乏财政资助，教育部的活动一直受到很多限制和阻碍，以致往往被称为“北京学校管理部”，而更糟糕的是被称为“自管部”，因为教育部甚至对北京的学校也已经约束不了，有时还倒过来受这些学校的支配。然而，尽管它对各省进行建设性的活动付诸缺如，教育部仍享有不小的旧日威信。如果国家得以统一并且能任命一位适当的人选来当总长，教育部也许在未来的年月里仍能成为促进教育事业的动力，虽然地方的主动性可能因而受到更大的鼓励，过去教育部的官僚政治的影响将可能被削弱。

**省教育行政机构**

目前各省教育行政有三种现存的形式，即教育司、教育科和教育厅。广东省试行了第四项计划——教育委员会的设置，但这个形式现在已经废除了。在那些宣告独立的省份里，则采取教育司或教育科的形式。故而在云南、贵州和湖南，教育行政上就存在着教育司的形式，司长分别由云南和贵州的省长任命，在湖南则由省议会选举产生。在云南和贵州两省，在教育司之外还增设教育行政委员会，重要教育方针和计划须由该委员会审议通过。广西和四川设有教育科，被赋予的权力不多，不如教育司。其他省份采取教育厅的形式，主其事者为教育厅长，由教育总长推荐，经共和国总统任命。教育厅直接由教育部节制，但在指导本省的教育活动和监督其下属职员和县长在管理当地教育方面，教育厅长必须在省长的领导下进行工作。因此，教育厅长尽管在理论上是向教育部负责的，可是实际上是在两个主管人——总长和省长——下面工作，结果造成各省教育厅长的权限都不相同，全凭省长的意志行事。由于教育厅长接近省长胜于接近总长，教育厅长极易倾听省长的指示。

教育厅下设两个或三个科以进行主要的教育活动，每省还设有四至六位省视学。

**县教育行政**

省下面是县。县的教育行政有两种体制：一为劝学所，其职能是协助县长实施教育行政和监督各自治地区的教育工作。劝学所设置一位所长以及几名劝学员。除所长外，在县长下另设教育秘书和一名不受劝学所长指挥的县教育视学。这种类型的县教育行政体制，经证明会引起很多麻烦，现在正逐渐为第二种体制所取代，即县教育局。

县教育局在1922年创始，旨在统一县的学校管理。在这种体制下，县视学受局长的节制；局长由县长推荐，经省教育厅长委任。这项新的系统的另一尝试是，赋予一些特别城市以更大的权力来独立地管理它们的学校，并把乡村教育划归县政府节制。可是，这个原则迄今尚未积极实施，虽然已经播下了种子。今年有更多的地方，特别是吉林省，采取了教育局的体制来实施县学校行政管理。

**地方教育行政单位**

地方教育行政的最低层单位是学区。一个县划分成几个学区，每学区设置一位负责学校事务的教育委员，有时候配备一个助理员。中国的学区并未被授与足够的权限来妥善履行其职责。学区组织极为松散，效率极低。重新组织这些基层单位，使它们对本管区的教育发展负起责任来，是当今最迫切的需要之一。唯独山西省的地方单位组织得最好。县里每一个乡村以及城市里每一条街道，均有负责人员掌管教育福利事业，而且被授与较大的权限来履行其职责。

## 教育财政

粗略地说，有三级教育，由三宗经费来维持：高等教育主要依靠国家所拨的经费，中等教育主要依靠省拨经费，初等教育则主要依靠县或地方所拨的经费。也有例外，但总的来说，这个做法是一致的。

由于国家岁收来自关税、盐税，印花税，烟酒专卖证，以及电报、铁路和邮政收益、土地税、厘金等项目，所以用于国民教育的国家经费是从这个综合来源中提取的，除了清华学校，交通大学和武昌师范大学等少数几所学府的经费各有其特殊来源外，其他学府均从这项总的国家拨款中获得配额。地处北京以外的国立学校是从省财政厅长保管的国家经费中分配到拨款的。按1919年预算（这是我们能参照的唯一预算）国民教育拨款为银洋5,028,836元，占该年总拨款的百分之一弱。

虽然有省政府举办的专科学校，然而省主要关心的依旧是中等教育。各省均有举办一所正式大学的倾向，但是迄今为止，极少省份能够实现。省教育经费的主要来源出自附加税，特别是土地附加税。江苏和浙江正在征收一项烟草特别税用作省教育经费。四川在1922年试图把生猪税用于教育，但无多大结果。河南采用对契约转让和所有权转让征税，每年收入银洋100万元，用作省教育经费。在财政困境面前，已经提出了若干解决办法。为了使人们约略了解各省对教育资助到什么程度，我们可以举出下列数例：江苏每年花银洋280万元，浙江每年花银洋150万元，江西每年化银洋60万元。

县用于初等教育的经费来源通常是：土地附加税、杂捐、租金和从清朝传下来的教育机构财产上所获得的收益[八]。山西资助初等教育的方法到目前为止，是历来在中国形成的最好的方法。他们在城市里，把商店和房屋按它们的地位划分等级并确定征税金额，税款用来资助城市初等教育。在乡村，则按土地的质量征税，用以资助乡村教育。[九]

由于政局动荡，军费开支无常，各学校都面临着教育经费无肯定着落的难处。严重缺乏经费的省份计有广东、福建，江西、四川、安徽、江苏、北京地区以及湖南。教员的薪金拖欠两个月或三个月，甚至长达十个月之久。现在的中国教员是忍受着极大的个人牺牲来为国家服务的。情况好一些的省份有奉天、云南和陕西。在战争爆发前，山东和湖南给教员发薪还是照常的。

现在人们主要关注的问题是：（1）如何通过法律保障和经济措施来保证教育经费的正常支付，以便凡从事教育工作的人员都能够解除经济上的忧虑而全心全意献身于教育事业；（2）如何改订税收制度，以求对教育的负担和受教育的机会得以平等；（3）如何通过建立一个适当的分配和补贴制度来激励教育活动而又不削弱地方的积极性；（4）如何对现有经费实行节约使用，以便以最低的代价取得最大的教育效果。

## 视察和监督

中国有三级视察——国家一级、省一级和县一级。根据1913年的条例，整个国家划分为八个视察区。每个区有两位国家视学。对学校进行视察从每年8月下半月开始，下一年6月上半月结束。视察内容必须包括普通教育和社会教育的各个方面。如有教育总长的特别指令，则进行特别视察。视学不进行巡视时，必须住在部里。过去几年中，这规定已经成为一纸空文，全国视察几乎完全销声匿迹。

省教育视学由教育厅长任命。较小的省份设四名视学，较大的省份则设五至六名视学。在省以下有县视学。按旧体制，他们作为县长的代表来进行学校视察的，但是由于采取了教育局的体制，县视学由县教育局长节制。他们每年对他们所负责的学校进行一至三次视察。

视学的职责详载于教育法中，国家视学和省视学须履行七项职责，县视学则须执行十三项。但是在实际施行时，视学仅仅成为访问者、报告员，而最糟的是，成为吹毛求疵者。他们中大多数并不体会他们的使命是给在职的校长和教员们以启发、鼓励和帮助。近几年来，已经出现了一种倾向，即抗议这种消极的视察或为视察而视察，而主张以一种建设性的监督制度来取代。江苏省已经在这方面树立了可贵的榜样。从去年开始，教育厅长已经邀请东南大学和其他地方的专家，就一些专题担任监督。因此对职业教育、科学教学、体育训练以及师范教育的监督制度就建立起来了；今年还开始了对社会科学和国语的监督。这个做法在中国开辟了学校监督的新纪元。

## 新学制

“在过去20年里，中国至少有四种学制。”[十] 最新的一种在1922年采用，是在1919年各省教育会会议提倡之下经过三年讨论的结果。

这种制度所涉及的一些问题将在论述教育的分级和类型时提到。自1922年以来，各委员会一直忙于设计学习科目和全部课程，以便使总的体系更为充实完备。今年所有学习科目，除了职业教育中的一小部分之外，均已完成，并经省教育会的十月会议表决，将学习课目呈教育部，以资颁布。业经教育部第23号条令予以采用的新学制的图解说明如下。

**新学制图解说明**

## 学龄前教育和幼稚园教育

幼稚园教育在新制度下有了一席地位，并“收纳六岁以下的儿童”。师范学校的实习学校，特别是城市中的女子师范学校的实习学校，都设有幼稚园。教会也举办幼稚园。但是幼稚园合起来的总数依然很小。由于幼稚园的培育给与儿童以积极的自我表现的机会，以及儿童和教师之间的相互交往的机会，这一类型的教育是非常需要的。为了设立更多的幼稚园，首先必须有一批训练幼稚园工作人员的适当机构。1924年1月江苏教育行政人员会议通过一项增加受过训练的幼稚园工作者数量的决议，就表明人们对这种需要是有同感的。湖南教育会今年也主张在城镇设立幼稚园。江苏义务教育期成会甚至已建议在小学的最低年级采用幼稚园教育的方法[十一]。另一件鼓舞人心和更为重要的事情是陈鹤琴教授进行的幼稚园教育实验。陈教授同他手下的工作人员深深感觉到，幼稚园里所使用的内容和方法是照搬外国的，其中有一些并不适合中国儿童，因此从1923年10月开始，他们使用自制玩具、中国的“鹅妈妈”故事以及其他教材来进行实验。陈教授还试图利用幼稚园不仅作为教育年幼儿童的中心，而且作为培训母亲的中心。中华教育改进社和陈教授双方已同意合作，在他的计划里包括一项实验，即实施幼稚园教育时如何尽可能少花钱这一方面的实验，以便尽可能多的各界群众均可照样举办。



## 初等教育

根据新学制的规定，“小学的修业期限定为六年；暂时也可延长一年，以适合各地方的不同情况。小学可分成初小各年级和高小各年级，前者是四年，并且可以单独设立”。

教学科目和时间分配百分比，由小学十八人委员会制订（详见表1）[十二]。

有如下的进一步建议：第一年和第二年，学校每周上课时间至少应为1,080分钟；第三年和第四年，每周应为1,260分钟；高等小学的两个年级每周应为1,440分钟。分钟的数目应适当分配到6天的课时中去。在乡村学校里，科目可以合并和简化，但是分配给国语和算术的时间决不允许减少。

表 1

<table>
<tr><th rowspan="2">科目</th><th colspan="2">每一科目所占时间百分比</th></tr>
<tr><th>小学低年级</th><th>小学高年级</th></tr>
<tr><td>国语</td><td></td><td></td></tr>
<tr><td>会话</td><td rowspan="4">30</td><td>6</td></tr>
<tr><td>阅读</td><td>12</td></tr>
<tr><td>作文</td><td>8</td></tr>
<tr><td>写字</td><td>4</td></tr>
<tr><td>算术</td><td>10</td><td></td></tr>
<tr><td>社会科学</td><td></td><td></td></tr>
<tr><td>卫生</td><td rowspan="4">20</td><td>4</td></tr>
<tr><td>公民</td><td>4</td></tr>
<tr><td>历史</td><td>6</td></tr>
<tr><td>地理</td><td>6</td></tr>
<tr><td>自然</td><td rowspan="2">12</td><td>8</td></tr>
<tr><td>园艺</td><td>4</td></tr>
<tr><td>工艺</td><td colspan="2">7</td></tr>
<tr><td>美术</td><td colspan="2">5</td></tr>
<tr><td>音乐</td><td colspan="2">6</td></tr>
<tr><td>体育</td><td colspan="2">10</td></tr>
</table>

根据新学制，“义务教育暂定为四年”。如条件充分，可以延长以便满足地方的不同要求。接受义务教育的学龄则由各省和特别地区根据当地情况自行决定。

自清朝以来，中央当局一直有推行义务教育的打算。但直至1920年教育部才拟定了明确的步骤，在不同地区和具体时期实施义务教育。详细规定如下：

1921年——省会和通商口岸

1922年——县城和城市

1923年——500户以上的镇

1924年——300户以上的镇

1925年<br>1926年 ——200户以上的镇

1927年——100户以上的村庄

1928年——不满100户的村庄

由于政治动乱，上述明文规定很少付诸实施。然而在阎锡山省长管辖下的山西，已经实施了一项非常有效的义务教育方案。山西的方案规定七个步骤，在1918至1921年期间，用七个半年的时间来予以完成。虽然全部成功尚未达到，可是最近的统计表说明，在山西学龄儿童中，就学人数已达百分之七十二。现在，25岁以下未受过教育的成人必须进补习学校学习汉语、算术和公民课。

次于山西的情况，应该提到江苏义务教育期成会的努力。该会在袁希涛先生领导下，努力实现教育机会均等。在这方面，他们把重点放在师资训练上，作为实施义务教育的第一步。今年江苏省60个县中有50个已经举办县立师资培训所。云南省今年在义务教育方面也已取得了可喜的成绩。云南省会昆明市，在省教育厅长童玉川先生领导下[十三]，对故意反对送子女入学的父母或监护人，至少处以银洋一元的罚款。贵州省也已采取有力措施来实行义务教育[十四]。雇主阻挡儿童入学受到禁止。对十岁以下儿童的监护人，处以银洋一元到五元的罚款；十岁以上的，年龄每增一岁再加罚二元。凡反对缴纳义务教育税额者也须处以不超过银洋八十元的罚款。在今年年底，广西宣告也采取了在省内实施义务教育的十分全面的计划（详见表2）。

**表2　小学生占应受四年初等教育的学龄儿童人数的百分比**

| 省　　份 | 百　分　比 |
|---|---|
| 山　　西 | 72.0 |
| 山　　东 | 25.5 |
| 直　　隶 | 24.2 |
| 陕　　西 | 23.1 |
| 北京地区 | 22.1 |
| 东 三 省 | 22.1 |
| 云　　南 | 20.6 |

续表

| 省　　份 | 百　分　比 |
|---|---|
| 甘　　肃 | 18.8 |
| 浙　　江 | 18.4 |
| 广　　西 | 17.0 |
| 江　　苏 | 11.9 |
| 广　　东 | 11.4 |
| 湖　　南 | 10.9 |
| 福　　建 | 10.3 |
| 四　　川 | 9.1 |
| 河　　南 | 8.9 |
| 江　　西 | 8.7 |
| 湖　　北 | 7.6 |
| 贵　　州 | 5.8 |
| 安　　徽 | 4.9 |
| 新　　疆 | 2.1 |

应该讲一讲关于初等教育的另一侧面——乡村教育运动。由于中国人口的百分之八十以上居住在乡村，乡村教育应该受到最密切的关注，这是一件头等重要的事情。最近，特别是今年，回到农村去的运动已增强了声势。中华教育改进社已经设立乡村教育专门委员会。各省教育会第九次会议已于今年10月在开封召开，并且对这个重要问题也进行了仔细考虑。江苏省义务教育期成会8月在无锡举行会议，花了三天时间起草了七条改进乡村学校的实际建议[十五]。江苏义务教育期成会和中华教育改进社已经在典型社区对乡村学校作了特别调查。调查报告尽管是片断的，已经激起了人们对乡村教育的很大兴趣和热忱。因为一般乡村无力支持需要花很多钱的教育，中华教育改进社已经选定了几个乡村学校（其校长已经在新乡村的领导方面显示了才干）来进行实验，力求以尽可能少的费用来办尽可能好的乡村教育。人们希望在未来几年里，乡村教育的类型或标准均能形成，以便为全国普

遍采用。

语言问题实际上已经解决。胡适博士的“文学革命”在初等学校里已经起了最深刻的影响。白话，或称“活的语言”，受到大多数的小学的欢迎。今年奉天当局禁止初等学校使用白话，是反动的；广东对于欢迎这项变革的事仍然多少表现犹豫。然而，作为易于表达的手段，活语言是注定要在初等学校里普及的。

另一引人注意的趋势是，在小学里对教材内容和教学方法进行研究的兴趣愈来愈大。在初等教育中力求科学性的趋势正在进展，而且由于采用测量和测验（这些方法将在后面进行论述）而增强了。

## 中等教育

新学制关于中等教育作了如下的陈述：

> 中学修业期限定为六年，分成两段，每段三年，即初中三年，高中三年。……初中提供普通教育，但是可以根据当地需要，设置各种职业课程。高中课程分成普通、农业、技术、商业和师范五类。按照当地情况，可以只设置一类课程或同时设置几类课程。

在中学里，学分制已经采用。学分的定义是，一个小时的课堂教学加上预习时间。无需预习的学科的学分将按比例折算。初中要求满意地完成180个学分以后，才能毕业，其中164个学分是必修课。初中的学科和学分，由十二人委员会制定[十六]。(详见表3)

由九人委员会制定[十七]的高中全部课程，由三种类型的学习组成，即（1）所有学生必修的一般课程，占总学分的百分之四十三；（2）根据攻读专门课程制定的必修课；以及（3）纯选

表 3

| 学　　科 | 学　　分 |
|---|---|
| 社会科学 | |
| 　公民 | 6 |
| 　历史 | 8 |
| 　地理 | 8 |
| 语言和文学 | |
| 　国语 | 32 |
| 　外语 | 36 |
| 数学 | 30 |
| 自然 | 16 |
| 艺术 | |
| 　图画<br>　手工<br>　音乐 | 12 |
| 体育 | |
| 　生理学和卫生学 | 4 |
| 　体操 | 12 |
| 总计 | 164 |

**表 4　文科与社会科学组**

| 学　　科 | 学　　分 |
|---|---|
| 一般必修 | |
| 　国语 | 16 |
| 　外语 | 16 |
| 　人生哲学 | 4 |
| 　社会问题 | 6 |
| 　文明史 | 6 |
| 　科学原理概论 | 6 |
| 　体育 | 10 |
| 本学组必修 | |
| 　规定的 | |
| 　　专选中国文学 | 8 |
| 　　心理学入门 | 3 |
| 　　逻辑学入门 | 3 |

续表

| 学　　科 | 学　　分 |
| --- | --- |
| 　　　　社会科学（一门） | 4（至少） |
| 　　　　自然科学或数学（一门） | 6（至少） |
| 　　选修的 | 32（或以上） |
| 纯理论选修 | 30（或以上） |
| 总　　计 | 150 |

**表5　数学与自然科学组**

| 学　　科 | 学　　分 |
| --- | --- |
| 一般必修 | |
| 　　国语 | 16 |
| 　　外语 | 16 |
| 　　人生哲学 | 4 |
| 　　社会问题 | 6 |
| 　　文明史 | 6 |
| 　　科学原理概论 | 6 |
| 　　体育 | 10 |
| 本学组必修 | |
| 　　规定的 | |
| 　　　　三角 | 3 |
| 　　　　高等几何 | 6 |
| 　　　　高等代数 | 6 |
| 　　　　解析几何 | 3 |
| 　　　　机械画图 | 4 |
| 　　　　物理、化学、生物（三种学科任何两种，每种六个学分） | 12（至少） |
| 　　选修的 | 22 |
| 纯理论选修 | 30 |
| 总　　计 | 151 |

修课，不超过总学分的百分之二十。高中的职业课程尚未公布。普通课程分两组，即文科与社会科学组以及数学与自然科学组。这两组课程详见表4和表5。

**趋势**

正如保罗·孟禄博士在1921年对中国的教育作了一次普通调查后所说的，中等教育是中国教育制度中最大的弱点。自此以后，两个组织——中华教育改进社和中国中等教育联合会——在研究中等教育的各个不同方面时便对这一点加以仔细的考虑。不仅中学教职员的注意力，而且行政当局的注意力，也已集中在改进这一方面的教育。关于当今中国中等教育的一些更为重要的问题和趋势可以在这里简略地讨论一下。

**课程**

首先，对中等教育的科学性研究已在教育学学者以及中学教职员的脑海里，占了非常重要的地位。这是一个很有希望的进步迹象。中学学科的内容和教学方法、学校的组织以及行政管理，现在都在审查、批评、实验和重新构想之中。

中等教育所有的弱点中，最弱的莫过于科学的讲授。在这一方面，科学一直是通过讲课和按照教科书来讲授的，很少给学生本人以积极从事实验工作的机会。科学的学习所产生的结果应当是形成一种实验的态度和习得对自然加以有效的控制，但这一点历来是被忽视的。有鉴及此，中华教育改进社邀请了推士（G. R. Twiss）教授来华，对中国的科学讲授情况进行一次专门研究并作出改进的建议。推士教授在仔细调查10个省的187所学校以后，写了一个非常全面的报告，报告中有若干建设性的建议，这些建议不久将要公布。中国科学社正在着手把改进科学的讲授列为它的经常工作的一个方面。该社的成员包括了几乎所有中国的著名科学家，定能对推进科学教育起很大的影响。作为起点，江苏省已被挑选为他们的考察和实验场所。

近年来，引起人们很大注意的第二个问题是在中学里教授国语的问题。这个重要的、充满生气的学科，过去在旧文人手里竟然教得非常枯燥无味。中国是富有民族文学杰作的，但实际上选文却十分贫乏。未曾受过教育学和心理学训练的教员不得不依靠灌输式和逐词逐句解释的方法。当胡适博士于1922在中华教育改进社济南会议上宣读他关于讲授中文和中国文学的论文时，第一次唤起了全国人民的注意，觉得需要改革这门学科的教授方法。在胡适博士演讲之后，接着就有人写了30多篇文章，都是关于改进中文的讲授问题的，其中大多数在今年和去年的期刊上发表了。梁启超先生、胡适博士、孟宪承先生和朱经农先生是这个运动的主要倡导者。关于这个问题的讨论，现在正从主观和经验为依据转到客观和实验为根据。白话在中学里的地位不同于它在小学里的地位。现在的倾向是，随着学生学习的逐步提高，白话教材也越来越少，减少的部分均由文言文取代。

**纪律**

观察到的第二种倾向是，在中学里越来越强调学校纪律。自从1919年“五四”运动以来，学校纪律一直大为松弛。许多校长和教员简直对学生失去控制。在过去一两年中，有一种反作用开始发生。一方面，存在着消极控制的倾向，禁止学生参加若干活动，而在这些活动中他们一直是享有自由的。安徽为这种消极性的反作用提供了一个能说明问题的例子，他们试图牺牲教育性的课外活动来换取纪律。湖南的方法采取了比较温和的形式，他们给学生以足够的机会来进行活动，同时又严格维持纪律。最后，还有一种维持纪律的方法在一些学校里试行。这个方法是通过校长和教员以身作则，并且与学生共同过学校生活。南京的安徽中学使用了这个方法，到目前为止所获得的结果是大为乐观和有希望的。

### 民族主义

第三个是民族主义倾向，其表现是十分强烈，反对把外语作为初中必修课。尽管已经指定外语课占36个学分，可是面临如此强有力的抨击，外语课在将来究竟能否维持目前的地位还是一个疑问。

### 职业训练

第四个倾向是在中等教育里越来越着重职业训练。正如国立北京大学和国立东南大学的入学考试统计数字所显示的，不到百分之十的入学申请者可蒙录取，这个比率在过去几年里一直没有多大变动。职业教育家认为，大大削弱中等学校作为升学预备的性质，乃是绝对必要的。各学校已经响应这个号召，开设了职业训练课程，虽然现在还不清楚这些课程如何能真正使学生适合工作要求，并使他们能就终身从事的职业。

### 男女同学

第五个倾向是在中等学校里的性别隔离。有些城市的中学（为数有限）近几年来已经试行男女同学。尽管在高等学府和初等学校里人们对男女同学抱赞同态度，可是在中等学校里却明确地存在着对男女同学的强烈反对。湖南在今年3月，山东在今年8月；都禁止中学实行男女同学。江苏采取比较温和的态度；它授权给男子师范学校录取女生并允许城市的中学实行男女同学，条件是必须为这些学校作好充分的准备。

### 节约和效率

第六个倾向是讲求节约和效率。由中学支配的财源有限，因此它们花每一分钱都得顶一分钱用；不然的话，它们只能甘心为学生提供一种不能适应生活的教育，以尽可能少的费用提供尽可能良好的教育，这个倾向在中国的中等教育里也越来越明显。除师范学校外，均收学费。现在中学生数目为182,804人，不到小学生人数的百分之三。中国的中等教育，尽管对所有合格的入学者敞开大门，可是选择学生还是很严格的。

## 职业教育

新的学制已经给与职业教育一个十分重要的地位：

> 初等学校的课程可以包括职业前训练。……初中……可以开设各种职业课程。……高中分成普通、农业、技术、商业和师范课程（家政课后增）。……职业学校的修业年限与地位可以根据当地需要和情况来确定。

根据旧学制建立的中等和初等实业学校，须按新学制予以改组。

职业教育课程委员会根据这些条例已经用了三年时间来拟订16种不同的学科，这项工作实际上已经完成。在初等学校里的职业前训练课程以及大学里的专门职业训练课程之外，还拟定了职业教育的三个阶段：（1）四年初小毕业生的职业训练课程；（2）六年制小学毕业生的职业训练课程；（3）初中毕业生的职业训练课程。

关于实习工作和非职业训练学习二者之间的时间分配，职业学校联合会提出的下列建议已经及时被接受。第一，分配给实习工作的时间不应少于课堂教学，应为每周18至24学时。第二，职业学校的学科应有三种：（1）职业训练学科；（2）职业训练前必修的学科；（3）非职业训练的学科。非职业训练的学科至少应占全部分配时间的百分之二十。

今年一年中，职业教育方面的其他重要发展中有下列几项：

四川、贵州、广西、浙江和福建已经公布了根据新制度拟订的改组职业教育计划[十八]。陕西已经组织了一个省职业教育委员会，并为20个教育分区每区委任一位监督来负责职业教育、义务教育和平民教育[十九]。云南已专门拨出烟草税作为发展职业教育的经费。湖北已下令所有各县从教育基金中拨款百分之二十来推进职业教育。上海、南京、济南和武昌的职业指导周活动激起了对这个运动的很大兴趣。职业指导还被引进清华学校、东南大学附中和浦东中学。教育部已命令所有女子中学给家政学提供实习工作的机会。中华职业教育社已经筹集一项特别经费，专作推进女子职业教育之用。女子职业学校也已在8个省内建立起来。

## 师　　资

### 师资培训

关于师资培训，新的学制有如下的明文规定：

> 师范学校学生修业期限定为六年。师范学校可以只办最后两年或三年，以便吸收初中毕业生。……为了满足小学低年级的师资需要，经过适当考虑后，可以设立师范学校或师范讲习所，其学生修业期限有长有短，可不尽相同。

新制度还规定，任何适宜的学校均可创办职业教育师资培训所。至于中等学校师资的培训，由师范学院承担，学生修业期限定为四年：

> 到一定的时候，根据旧制度建立的高等师范学校应当提高水准，以吸收高中毕业生，学生修业期限定为四年，这些学校届时可以称为师范学院。……为了满足初中师资的需要，可以开设两年制的师范课程。在大学的教育学院里，以

及在师范学院、师范学校或高中里，可以组织实施两年制师范课程，录取这些院校的毕业生。

### 课程

师范学校的课程实际上均已制订完毕，共拟定了三套。第一套是供三年制师范学校实施的，相当于高中的课程。它的普通必修课与高中的课程相同，只增加四个学分的音乐课，学分总数为68。专业必修课包括心理学入门（二个学分）、教育心理学（三个学分）、一般方法（二个学分）、专门学科的教学方法（六个学分）、小学教材（六个学分）、教育统计和测量（三个学分）、小学行政管理（三个学分）、教育原理（三个学分）以及教学实习（20个学分），总共为48个学分。选修学习有两种：学组选修和纯选修。学组选修的目的在于满足三类日后将任教的学生的需要：（1）对语言、文学和社会科学具有特别爱好者，（2）对数学和自然科学具有特别爱好者；（3）对艺术和体育具有特别爱好者。每一类学生必须从学组课程中选修至少20个学分。此外，所有学生均须从九门教育课程中选修至少八个学分。纯选修课程由学校自行确定。

第二套课程是为相当于六年制中学的六年制师范学校拟定的。一般地说，在这个类型的师范学校的第一阶段中，初中的特点仍须保持，然而所有课程的目的在于形成一个连续过程，而不在中途折断。这一类比较简单，建议规模较小的学校采用。因此，这里不存在学组区别，选修课程也很少。毕业所必需的330个学分中，319个是必修课程的学分，选修课程只有11个学分。

第三套课程是为培养四个低年级的师资的，具有三种形式：（1）三年制课程，招收六年制小学的毕业生；（2）两年制课程，招收旧式高等小学的毕业生；（3）一年制课程，招收初中毕业生。所有这三种形式均已非常仔细地拟定。因为篇幅有限，不允许充分陈述，现归纳成一个简明表格，见表6。

**表 6　师范学校课程**

| 学　　科 | 形式（1）<br>三年制（学分） | 形式（2）<br>两年制（学分） | 形式（3）<br>一年制（学分） |
|---|---|---|---|
| 教育 | 36 | 24 | 14 |
| 国语 | 36 | 24 | 8 |
| 社会科学 | 26 | 18 | 8 |
| 数学 | 25 | 16 | 8 |
| 自然、园艺和农业 | 33 | 22 | 8 |
| 艺术 | 15 | 10 | 8 |
| 体育 | 9 | 6 | 6 |
| 总　计 | 180 | 120 | 60 |

**注：** 小学教材和小学学科教学方法的学习，包括在讲授的每门学科之内。教学实习在“形式（1）”和“形式（2）”中是八个学分，在“形式（3）”中则结合在每门学科之内。

在师范学校新的课程中，可以看到四个重要变化。首先，存在着更大的伸缩性和多样性，使师范学校的校长能够把他们的学校适应特殊情况的需要，而不是像旧时那样，只有一种标准课程。有适应不同情况的若干课程。其次，更着重教育学科和教育方面的新发展，可以造就更优良的师资。第三，给与教学实习更多的时间，以便学生可以通过实际工作获得教学技能。第四，大大地强调教材和小学学科的教学方法。过去，小学的需要没有被充分觉察到，没有得到满足；大多数师范学校被当作中学来办。因此，着重小学的学科表明师范教育开始了一个新纪元。

在实践中，今年高等师范学校已经在进行把学校改变成师范学院的工作。旧式师范学校也在采取步骤，按照各自的情况采用六年制或三年制课程。有些高中也开设了师范课程。已经发现的另一个重要行动是，越来越着重培训乡村师资。从去年以来，江苏已经开办了五所乡村师范学校。中华教育改进社、东南大学的教育学院和农业学院、中华职业教育社、江苏义务教育期成会以及江苏省教育厅，正在合作举办一个培训乡村师资的实验师范学校。东南大学乡村教育教授和中华教育改进社乡村教育主任赵叔愚先生已被委任为这个学校的组织者。

大多数师范学校的学生免缴学费和膳宿费，只有很少学生被录取后缴纳半费或全费。享受免费的正规学生必须为学校服务七年。几年以前，在江苏进行的一次调查表明，师范毕业生中百分之八十以上确实在毕业后当了教员。要求必须服务的规定尚未严格执行，目前有从严执行的倾向，这从开封会议的决议中可以看出。今年，江苏禁止县师范毕业生在完成强制性服务之前再进修。奉天省甚至设想在强制性服务期限尚未届满的时候，不颁发毕业文凭。

**教员资格证明**

除师范学校毕业生外，所有其他小学教员均须申请资格证明。这项资格证明有两类：（1）通过考试；（2）不通过考试。凡在中等学校攻读两年或两年以上者，或者在初等学校任教一年或一年以上者，或者经过为期六个月或六个月以上学习的师范讲习所毕业生，或者对教育原理具有充分知识并已经学习过行将任教的学科者（此点由申请者所写的文章和论文来加以证明），通过正规师范学校学科的考试后，均有资格任教，但同时应适当考虑，教什么年级和教男生或女生的问题。对助理教员的考试比较容易。无需通过教学内容考试而被证明合格者，包括：（1）已经当过一年或一年以上小学教员的中学毕业生；（2）在学习上成绩优良的中等实业学校毕业生；（3）专科学校毕业生，其专业学习确能证明其有资格讲授这些学科者；（4）具有三年教学经验并有服务良好记录的小学教员经县劝学所所长证明者。可是，所有申请资格证明者，如持有文凭则必须缴验，还须缴验由一位保证人出示县的行为端正证明书，并须接受体格检查。

在中国，小学教员的资格证明由省资格证明委员会掌管。每年必须由省长将结果呈报教育总长。中央集中和统一的资格证明制度有优点，也有缺点，这在中国也没有例外。

**薪金**

几年以前，关于江苏省教员薪金情况的一次简单调查，表明了如下结果：

**表7　江苏省小学教员的年薪**

| | 高小（银元） | 初小（银元） |
|---|---|---|
| 最　高 | 600 | 240 |
| 一　般 | 200 | 102 |
| 最　低 | 70 | 30 |

1921年郃先生进行过另一项调查，范围遍及六个省。他对他所研究过的所有小学教员的年薪进行计算的结果是：中等年薪为银洋160.25元，他们第一年服务期间的年薪则为银洋125.10元。即使充分考虑到中国货币很高的购买力，也必须承认中国小学教员目前的薪金是非常低的。教育部在1917年公布了一张薪金表并要求各学校付给教员的薪金不得低于表上的最低额（详见表8）。

**表8　小学教师薪金表**

| 类别 | 特别银洋（元） | 1 | 2 | 3 | 4 | 5 | 6 | 7 | 8 | 9 | 10 | 11 | 12 | 13 | 14 |
|---|---|---|---|---|---|---|---|---|---|---|---|---|---|---|---|
| 校长和首席教员 | 960 | 720 | 660 | 600 | 540 | 480 | 420 | 360 | 312 | 264 | 216 | 180 | 144 | 120 | 90 |
| 特别教员 | 720 | 480 | 420 | 360 | 312 | 264 | 216 | 180 | 144 | 120 | 98 | 72 | | | |
| 助理教员 | 360 | 264 | 216 | 180 | 144 | 120 | 98 | 72 | 48 | | | | | | |

目前有一种倾向，即根据教学经验和专业知识来付给较高的薪金。然而，迫切的问题是如何使发薪更加有定时。

还有人正在设法通过增加酬劳来鼓励长期服务。虽然养老金制度的重要性尚未充分被理解，但已经有了一些开端，而且有一个运动正在朝这个方向发展。浙江教育行政人员会议已经建议，服务已满六年的教员可享受进修休假，服务已满20年以后（如果残废，则在服务满10年以后），每年发给薪金的四分之一作养老金。还建议制订一项特别补助金制度，规定按已故教员薪金的四分之一或全薪付给其家属。今年，江苏教育厅已经采取了养老金暂行制度；根据这个制度，一个小学教员每年将获得他最后一年服务的薪金的三分之一。如果（1）在连续服务八年后，由于疾病而成残废；或者（2）在执行公务时成为残废或遭受重伤；或者（3）在连续服务20年后，由于年老而退休。此外，他的子女一人可以免付学费进入本省的公立学校肄业。

**在职期**

关于小学教员的在职期，一直很少进行调查。聘约一般是以半年为一期的。根据本文作者几年前收集到的江苏13所学校教员服务期的资料来看，可以对这个情况有一定的了解，但是认为这些贫乏的资料能代表全国整个的情况，那将是错误的。（详见表9）

**表9　教员在职期**

| 服务年数 | 百分比 | |
|---|---|---|
| | 高小教员 | 初小教员 |
| 1 | 6 | 26 |
| 2 | 10 | 12 |
| 3 | 23 | 20 |
| 4 | 17 | 18 |
| 5 | 44 | 24 |

中国迫切需要教员。按四千万学龄儿童估算，他们要受四年的初等教育，则估计从小学一年级到四年级就至少需要一百万名教员。根据最近的统计结果，现在只有223,279名教员在初小任

教。要实施普及全国的义务教育制度，现在的教员人数必须增加三倍多。目前的师范学校和讲习所有43,846名学生，不可能每年培养出1万名以上的教员，而其需要却是77万多名教员。这个问题是严重的。

## 教育测验和测量

四五年前，中国才开始测验运动，那时南京的廖博士和陈教授以及北京的刘博士和张教授开设了教育方面的科学测量课程并且在编制测验方面有了一些起步。直至1922年哥伦比亚大学师范学院的W·A. 麦柯尔（William A. McCall）教授来华以后，这个运动才形成很大的发展势头。麦柯尔教授同各个中心机构的中国心理学家合作，成功地编制了20个测验，供小学和中学使用。今年增加的测验如下：

| | |
|---|---|
| 综合英语测验 | 安德森（Andersen） |
| 地理测验 | 杨　氏（Young） |
| 算术练习测验 | 俞　氏 |
| 画图测验 | 俞　氏 |
| 智力测验 | 刘氏—布拉德肖 |
| 自我调查综合测验 | 推　孟 |
| 初小非语言智力测验 | 陈　氏 |
| 高小非语言智力测验 | 陈　氏 |
| 高小汉语语法测验 | 陈　氏 |
| 综合数学测验 | 廖　氏 |
| 综合科学测验 | 廖　氏 |
| 中国语言和文学测验 | 廖　氏 |
| 汉语语法测验 | 廖　氏 |
| 历史测验 | 廖　氏 |
| 地理测验 | 廖　氏 |

关于中国的测验运动有两个特点可以提出。第一，所有测验都根据统一体系——T-B-C—F体系——制定尺度，以便有可能将各个测验的得分进行比较，从而便于对测验结果制表和解释；还有所有用法说明小册子都仿效一个标准设计，以便教员只学一项程序即可。第二，所有的测验都在中华教育改进社这一个团体主持下予以发表，这一种做法能够使教员节省时间，不必为获得这些测验而费时间去寻找。

1923年秋，燕京大学推孟（Terman）教授和北京师范学院的查教授应改进社的邀请，使用特别设计的自我实施的测验，进行一次合作性的自我调查。“这个调查的目的在于使教育工作者熟悉各种测验，促使教员去利用改进社即将出版的那些自助指南，并且在中小学生中间举行一次全国性的竞赛”。以推孟教授所著《中国初等学校的效率》一书闻名的这次调查结果的最后报告今年春季出版了。

测验运动受到很大的欢迎。一批学校已经使用这些测验来替代传统的考试，有几所学校已经把这些测验包括在考试里，成为其中的一个部分。

## 医疗福利和社会福利

小学生比中学生的健康和社会福利受到更多的关注。比较好的学校，如香山慈幼院、东南大学以及北京男子师范学院、北京女子师范学院、江苏第一和第三男子师范学校、江苏第一和第二女子师范学校，以及湖南楚怡学校等院校的实习学校，已为儿童提供很多机会来积极参加社会活动，并且对学生的身体健康予以很大的关注。关于这个题目，已经看到的最佳报告是由北京女子师范学院所属有590名学生的实习学校作出的[二十]。1922年开始的体检每学期都进行一次。打预防针是规定要进行的，每年一次。今年，590名学生中226名已经打了预防针。在课外活动中则强调自由游戏和体育运动。中国的游戏以及外国的游戏都采用。矫正体操成为体格训练的一部分，一般健康知识包括在卫生学课程中。也注意到通风、灯光、坐位等等。学校园艺提供另一机会进行有益于健康的消遣。户外活动受到鼓励，为每一个班级安排短途旅行，至少每学期一次。也提供条件给学生进行自治，成立文学社，举行班级会和每周一次的全体大会，开办合作商店、儿童俱乐部和儿童阅览室，成立勤俭节约社以及许多其他团体，这些活动为发展一个社会性自我提供了充分的机会。这是办得比较好的一所学校（有代表性的一所学校）的情景。

学校生活中存在着对卫生监督惊人的无知和淡漠，这种情况在为数很多的学校里都可以看到，尤其是在内地的乡镇学校里，而在这些地方却非常需要健康之道，那里的学生最接近大自然，却又离开大自然最远。从社会意义上讲，儿童是处在专制教员统治之下的，这类教员不给儿童进行社会活动的一切自由，理由是社会活动会降低学校的尊严和教员的威信。

今年在体育方面已经进行了大量调查，是由麦克罗伊（McCloy）教授，在国立东南大学和中华教育改进社联合主持下进行的。下面各项调查已经完成：

（1）对人体测量学和体格测定的一系列研究，得出的部分结果如下：（甲）对于各种体型的体重研究已经完成。已制定出新的包括不同年龄的体重表，不久即将发行。计算体重的新的基准已经制定。（乙）对胸围测定的研究业已进行，其实用性也已逐步显示出来。这就为研究工作开辟了一个新的领域，但是这一项工作将很难进行到底。（丙）所有通常进行的测定已加以深入细致的研究，以确定它们是否真正有助于诊断。这就要把研究限制在八项真正重要的测定上面，而这些测定已经在研究之中，以便发现如何能够真正有助于学生的福利。（丁）胸围的指数作为退化的遗传特征的基准，也已在研究之中而且近乎完成。这个指数是具有重要意义的，已经获得足够的资料来弄清这个道理。（戊）已经进行了关于身体各部位测定和学校成绩的研究来看这两者之间可能存在什么关系。（己）已经拟定一个新的关于年龄—身高—体重和体育成绩的衡量标准。（庚）对体格检查的历史记录已经作出详细研究，据此来修正现在正在使用的记录卡。（辛）对体格检查已经进行了细致的统计研究，一种新的报告单业已拟定，上面载明体检结果，既使用图表形式，也使用数字形式。

（2）对几个体育比赛项目已经进行研究来确定哪些十分相同类型的比赛项目应当予以利用。例如，对拾土豆竞走的三种形式进行了研究，通过统计数字来确定哪一种为最佳形式。

（3）对体育运动方面的标准测验已经作出细致的研究。在300名小学生中间，研究了11个比赛项目，在330名中学生中间，研究了18个比赛项目，最适合这种标准测验的比赛项目已经通过统计数字加以确定。

（4）对70多个田径运动比赛项目已经拟定了一张通用的记分表。有了这张表，便获得所有具有同样分数的比赛项目大致相等的难度。

（5）逐渐形成了确定一个男孩或女孩的肌肉运动商的方法，其根据是标准体育比赛项目和在年龄—身高—体重衡量中已经提到的标准。

（6）对足球和篮球的标准测验的研究已经着手，初步研究已经结束。只是这些研究尚处在初级阶段，但是这些研究十分富于启发性，并且能够确定未来研究的路线。很可能大约再需要一年，这些研究才能完成。

上述各项研究情况，有些已经公布，其他在几个月内也将准备好。当这一切都准备好时，将意味着在中国的体育和体格检查方面前进了大约十年。

# 高等教育

根据新学制，“高等学校可以由几个学院或仅仅一个学院组成。在学院或大学修业期限定为四至六年”。再上面是研究生院，这是为学院和大学毕业生以及具有同等学力者进行研究的场所。

表10和表11将概括中国高等教育的一些情况。

**表10 学院的专业分布表**

| 院校类型 | 学校数目 | 学生人数 |
|---|---|---|
| 大学 | 35 | 13,098 |
| 师范学院 | 8 | 3,093 |
| 农学院 | 7 | 1,271 |
| 工业学院 | 13 | 2,026 |
| 商学院 | 8 | 1,890 |
| 医学院 | 7 | 832 |
| 法学院 | 33 | 10,864 |
| 其他 | 14 | 1,806 |
| 总计 | 125 | 34,880 |

今年已增加了几所大学，其中比较重要的是（1）广东大学，（2）西北大学。

高等教育目前的趋势已经由蔡元培校长予以概括如下：

大学不仅旨在为学生提供现成的课程，由他们在固定时间内去听讲，而且首要的是成为在科学研究方面进行共同工作的机构。所谓研究，我指的不仅是引入欧洲文化，而且是以西方已经做到的事情作为基础来创造性地作出贡献；也不仅是保存我们的民族文化遗产，而且要通过科学研究方法来设法显示我们的民族文化的遗产实际是些什么[二十一]。

由于创造性的研究在外界干预占支配地位时，就决不能正当地发展，所以第二个趋势是要求学术自由。政府干预已经屡遭人们的憎恨和抵制。今年，教育总长宣布“大学规程”，他就遭到国立北京大学教授们的最强烈的反对，最后他被迫收回这个规程。

**表11　按经费来源划分的学院分布表**

| 经费来源 | 学校数目 | 学生人数 |
| --- | --- | --- |
| 国　　立 | 30 | 10,535 |
| 省　　立 | 48 | 9,801 |
| 私　　立 | 29 | 10,524 |
| 教会和外国人设立 | 18 | 4,020 |
| 总　　计 | 125 | 34,880 |

也存在着各大学和学院要求更密切合作的趋势。今年7月，中华教育改进社在南京举行会议时，组织了一个中国大学联合会来处理共同关心的有关大学教育的问题。人们相信，如果管理得当，这个组织将会提高大学教育的总的水准。

第四种趋势是给予妇女以受高等教育的机会。中国大多数大学业已将大门向妇女敞开，实行男女同学。今秋，北京女子高等师范学校已升格为师范学院。

最后，私立学院异乎寻常地增多了。单在北京一处，今年已成立了约10所私立学院。上海和其他大城市的情况也相似。据说，在中国要当大人物，必须持有三样东西：一家报纸、一家银行和一所大学。然而，政府已经拒绝承认其中任何一个学院，因为这些学院的存在一律具有不可告人的动机。

# 教会教育

根据中华基督教教育会副总干事华莱士（Wallace）先生的陈述，目前新教教会所办学校的学生总人数大致为30万，而且还在继续增加。1920至1924这四年间，其大学生的人数已增加了百分之七十六。塞尔索·科斯坦蒂尼（Celso Costantini）大主教提供的数字，在天主教教会培养下的学生数目为258,953人。在中国，每100名学生中间就有八名是在教会学校里肄业的。

今年，关于教会教育最突出的事件是中华基督教高等教育会的成立，该会委任一个理事会作为临时机构，这个理事会也是中华基督教教育会的高等教育理事会，从而把高等教育与中华基督教教育会的其他活动联系在一起。理事会的干事洛本斯坦(E. C. Lobenstine）牧师正从事研究各个院校，尤其关于它们的财政状况和对各院校工作加以协调的可能性。这个理事会的主要目的是使财源有限的基督教高等教育院校能够对中国的需要作出最有效的贡献。

另一件具有重要意义的事件是农业和乡村教育会议的召开。这个会议的结果是，三所学院、20所中学和高等小学以及83个农业工人已经携起手来开展乡村教育规划的实施。

今年所作的其他重要事情中，可以提一下学校卫生会议通过的非常实际的学校卫生方案，以及把新的重点放在基督教院校的国语课和公民课的讲授上。

教会的院校，尽管有良好的成绩，却一直受到攻击，其理由有三。这些院校迄今为止都处在外国的控制之下。甚至能胜任的中国基督徒也很少得到机会担任要职。另一个批评是，它们向尚未成熟、不能自己作出明智抉择的少年灌输宗教。最后一点，中国人方面有严重的怀疑，认为这些传教机构是在组织一种基督教教育体系来同政府的教育体系并驾齐驱，他们这个体系日后也许会成为群体内部的一个不相容的群体。这些因素所产生的结果是，今年7月和10月两次全国教育会议上对教会教育进行了连续两次的抨击。可是，比较保守的一些中国人认为，在这种过渡状态下，属于比较自由类型的教会教育确实作出了一种独特的贡献，它对政府的教育活动起了补充作用，为学生提供更宽广的受教育的机会以及在学校纪律方面树立了更为良好的榜样。他们也相信，教会教育应当社会化、自由化和更中国化。最后，他们感到，如果传教机构能够把力量和财源集中在几所高等教育机构上，使它们成为第一流的学府，而不是将人力物力分散开来，去设立水平较低的中等学校和初等学校，那么他们是可能作出更大贡献的。他们相信，传教机构以及其他私立机构也许可以开设实验性质的中学和小学，而任何试图通过增设学校来建立一个体系，那必然迟早要同政府的体系发生冲突。

## 成年平民教育

**一个扫除文盲的运动**

大量文盲，在中国是一个独特的问题。从全国人口中减去1.2亿不到学龄或者属于义务教育范围内的儿童以及那些曾在旧式中国学堂里平均读了三年书的0.8亿人以后，文盲约有2亿，这是平民教育要解决的一个难题。在晏阳初先生领导下，中华基督教青年会已经开始对这个类型的教育进行实验。1923年在清华召开的中华教育改进社第二届年会上，成立了中华平民教育促进会，由熊夫人任会长，这个运动立即受到全国的支持。

实际上，运动提供了四册课本，是由朱经农教授和本文作者根据大约1,200个最普通的汉字为词汇编写出来的。一个普通的文盲每天花一个小时，能在四个月内读完这四册课本。四个月后，他便能阅读使用上述词汇所编写的报纸，小册子、书籍和信件，并且还能使用这些词汇来表达自己的意思了。这四册课本售价为银洋一角二分，所以即使最穷的人也买得起。课本以若干方式，在若干类型的学校里加以使用：第一，在平民学校，校里有一位先生在一定的时间经常给他班上的学生上课；第二，在平民读书处，这种读书处以家庭、商店等为一个单位并鼓励一家一店内的有文化者去教其他成员；第三，在平民问字处，文盲可以就课本中任何不懂之处到问字处询问。课本就这样被引进了家庭、商店、工厂、学校、教堂、寺院、衙门、轮船、监狱和军队。不到一年的时间，尽管发生水灾、饥荒和战争，这些课本和其他丛书的发行量已经达到100万册的数字。

课本出版后，接着就出版了介绍各门知识的小丛书。不要多久，义务教育将在中国实施，并征愚民捐。赞助平民教育的人们怀有雄心壮志，要在十年里创造消除文盲的奇迹。

中国的教育工作者正在极大的困难条件下工作。他们中间有些人屈服了，其他人把这些困难看作是理所当然的事，并不感到沮丧，而且把困难看作努力的机会。中国是教育工作的处女地，是一个社会真空，任何人愿意投入多少力量，她就能吸收多少。为着了解今日的中国教育，必须从其所涉及的困难和已经作出的努力方面来加以思考。

## 参考书目


**商务印书馆出版书籍**

安德森：《综合英语测验》（中译本），中华教育改进社丛书。

安德森：《综合英语测验教员手册》（中译本），中华教育改进社丛书。

赵等合编：《设计教学法实习》

陈：《儿童图书馆研究》

陈：《小学课程》，中华教育改进社丛书。

钱等合编：《学习的基本原理》

华：《汉语口语的默读测验》

华：《教育测量概要》

廖：《中等教育》

C. A. 麦克默里、F. M. 麦克默里合编：《英美教育出版物指南》（中译本）。《中国教育统计概览》，中华教育改进社丛书。

E. L. 推孟：《高中自我调查综合测验》

《中国小学的效率》（中译本），中华教育改进社丛书.

推士：《改进科学教育的全国性运动》，中华教育改进社丛书。

推士：《中国的科学与教育》，中华教育改进社丛书。

推士：《关于组织科学学科教员俱乐部的建议》，中华教育改进社丛书。

俞：《小学算术综合测验手册》，中华教育改进社丛书。

俞：《统计计算与测验设计》

岳：《小学行政管理》

岳：《设计教学》

**1924年各出版社出版书籍**

秦：《如何组织童子军》

周、欧合编：《中国文字测验实例》

徐：《论道尔顿制》

徐：《道尔顿制研究》

列：《教育心理学》

史：《教育调查的方法》

《新学制的标准课程》，江苏省教育会。

董：《小学公民课的教学法》

王：《青年职业指导》

岳："加里（Gary）学校的制度"

**教育刊物**

《义务教育》，江苏义务教育期成会。

《民主与教育》，北京师范大学。

《教育杂录》，商务印书馆。

《初等教育》，商务印书馆。

《体育季刊》，商务印书馆。

《中等教育》，商务印书馆。

《中华教育界》，中华书局。

《教育季刊》，商务印书馆。

《教育杂志》，商务印书馆。

《新教育》，中华教育改进社。

除上列全国性的杂志外，通常各省都有自己的刊物。

## 原注

［一］《字林西报》60周年专号第2版。

［二］《密勒氏评论周报》1924年9月27日第110页。

［三］《字林西报》，60周年专号第33版。

［四］《密勒氏评论周报》1924年3月22日第115页。

［五］《密勒氏评论周报》1924年7月12日第180页。

［六］《中国的文艺复兴》1923年中华教育改进社（英文简称C.N.A.A.E.）社刊第2卷第6期。

［七］《教育法规》第4页。

［八］《中华教育界》，“支持初等教育问题”第1页。

［九］同上。另见《新闻报》1924年7月13日第3版。

［十］《中国的新学制》1923年中华教育改进社社刊第2卷第8期第17页。

［十一］《江苏教育公报》1924年第1期。

［十二］《新学制的标准课程》第7页。

［十三］《义务教育》第26期第15页。

［十四］《贵州教育公报》1924年3月。

［十五］“教育与生活”《申报》第600页。

［十六］《新学制的标准课程》第1至7页。

［十七］《新学制的标准课程》中的“高中部分”第1至7页。

［十八］《职业与教育》第52期第81页;第17期第425页；第19期第549页。

［十九］《职业与教育》第57期第425页。

［二十］《中华教育界》1924年9月。

［二十一］《字林西报》60周年专号第49版。

## 注释

① 直系　即直系军阀，北洋军阀派系之一。先以直隶籍军阀冯国璋、曹锟，后又以吴佩孚为首领，横行一时。1926年被北伐军打垮，直系势力逐步消灭。

② 安福系　北洋皖系军阀的政客集团。1916年袁世凯死后，皖系军阀首领段祺瑞任国务总理，控制了北洋政府。1918年，皖系政客徐树铮、王揖唐等在北京安福胡同成立俱乐部，伪造选举，成立“国会”，推徐世昌为总统。时称该集团为“安福系”。

③ 海关两　亦称“关平两”。旧中国海关征税时使用的记账银两。

④ 华洋义赈会　国际救灾组织。实即“国际救灾委员会”。

⑤ 引语从英文移译，非胡适原话。

⑥ 杜里舒（1867—1941）　德国唯心主义哲学家、生物学家、新活力论者。认为有生命物体和无生命物体之间有不可逾越的鸿沟，1922年曾来我国宣传他的学说。

# 新的大众教育运动

一场反对同中国本身一样古老的教育制度的文化革命今天正在中国兴起。这种教育制度使得汉字十分艰深难学，以致百分之八十的人民成为文盲。因为需要花上许多年来学习，所以只有少数有特权的人才能掌握几万个汉字来达到能读会写的程度。近年来，把自己叫做“文化工作者”的那些学生和知识分子担负起将复杂的汉语拼音字母罗马化的任务并把这套罗马化字母教给群众。这种罗马化的字母共有28个，以“拉丁化”闻名。

为了把新教育带给人民，一种工农学校制度创立起来了。这种学校没有领薪的教师。学生和知识分子们每天花一至二小时来训练群众，过了一段时间，群众便培养出自己的教师。差不多每个班级总有四至五人有任教的天生才能，经过几个月的训练就主动地领导一个班级或一个小组。于是，在农村地区便可看到农民教农民的情况，在城市里可以看到工人自己当教师的工人学校。

大众教育运动的原则是：每个人，即使只学习过几个月，只要学到一点，就应把他所学到的教给别人。这是“小先生”制度的基础。甚至很小的孩子也可以当“小先生”——能力较强的可以各领导一个班级，其余的可以各教一个三四人的小组。五六岁的男孩子、女孩子教他们的父母、祖父母、佣工等读书写字是常见的事。

一种新的心理状态支撑着这种新的大众教育运动。生活的变化就是教育的变化。在普通学校里不需要、有时也不可能进行这种教育而获得成功。因此，我们的教育不限于学校的形式。既然真正的教育来源于人们生活间的接触，任何有人居住或聚集的地方实际上就是一所大众学校。于是，我们的学校是在庭院、走廊、街道、商店、庙宇、兵营中举办的。整个社会是我们的学校，全部生活是我们的课程。

文化工作者正在全中国组织这种大众的教育制度。音乐和戏剧工作者的相类似的团体也在进行同样的活动，茶馆里讲的故事也在宣传这种新的教育。因此，这一思想便广泛地传播开去。

新的课本用拉丁化文字编写，期刊用拉丁化文字出版了。北平话和上海话的拉丁化拼写体系已经编制完成，我们目前正在编制福建话和广东话的拉丁化拼写体系，因为这些省份都各有自己的方言。据估计，一个文盲无论男女，都能够在一个月内学会用拉丁化字母读和写，因此，经过很短期间的训练，群众就能够继续自己教育自己。

新的大众教育运动起源于上海，但这种教育运动不应和晏阳初[1]先生在定县所提倡的那种类型的教育方式相混淆。用汉语来说，定县类型的教育称为“平民教育”，是指普通人的教育，而新的群众教育汉语叫做“大众教育”，意思是广大群众的教育。名称上的差异包含着主要点上的根本区别。定县主张平民教育，但在实践中却成了少数人的教育，而新的大众教育则目的在于真正实现民有、民治、民享的教育。

这一运动完全靠自力维持。民族解放教育社[2]只靠每人一角钱的社员费维持。虽然对运动的同情者捐助的款子总是欢迎的，民族解放教育社的主要活动并不依赖这些捐款，而依靠人民自己。

这场文化革命理所当然地是和民族解放运动不可分离地联系在一起的。大众教育培养大众的觉悟。运动的目的不限于教人民能读会写，还教他们知道当前存在的各种问题，并引导他们懂得如何对待这些问题。测定一种教育制度的有效性在于它是否经得起现实的考验。群众需要的教育是能够帮助他们面对生活的教育。回避现实的教育制度，说明它具有一种使它不能发挥作用的内在弱点。

虽然大众教育运动进行民族解放的教育，但决不可理解为它提倡狭隘的民族主义。尽管我们面临着民族危机，我们仍然没有忘记培植国际主义精神。不言而喻，国际主义精神乃是世界和平的基础。中国大众的教师们不敢忘掉这个重要的原则。

可能除了印度之外，世界上没有任何别的国家像中国这样，教育一向成为有钱人的特权。这一新的运动发展和持续几年之后，将可能消灭中国惊人的文盲，给人民带来文化，使他们能够捍卫自己的文化，抵御外国的各种文化侵略。

原载1936年3月15日《中国呼声》（Voice of China）
英文半月刊第1卷第1期

## 注释

① 晏阳初　中国提倡平民教育的教育家之一。曾长期担任中华平民教育促进会的总干事。该会成立于二十年代中期，开始主要是在城市中进行识字教育。1929年该会总会迁到定县，1930年确定定县为实验区。1933年河北省政府根据国民政府法令，将定县作为河北省县政建设实验区，并设县政建设研究院于定县，由晏阳初任院长。1936年日本侵略者企图侵吞华北的时候，平教会南迁四川和广东、广西。新中国成立后，晏阳初仍在海外从事教育活动。

② 民族解放教育社　即国难教育社。1936年2月23日成立。领导人是陶行知。作者在这一英文论著中，把“国难教育社”译成“民族解放教育社”，是为了使英文读者更易了解该社的性质和使命。

# 中国新文字

在过去的七十年中，人们曾经作过许多努力为中国人民创造一种新的文字。本文不打算论述这些努力的历史，而仅就目前正在采取的最近、最有深远意义的步骤加以说明。一种文字已经达到完善的程度了，它必将对整个中国文化起革命性的作用。

中国新文字研究会成立于1935年12月，已经为北方方言和上海方言制定并采用了用字母拼写的文字体系。北方新文字有28个字母，上海方言的新文字有31个字母。中国新文字研究会现在正集中力量为福建方言和广东方言制定用字母拼写的文字体系，并将于最近两个月内完成。

以前叫做拉丁化的这种新文字有三个特点与其前身相区别。

1. 与中国方块字（汉字）相比，它是表音的，而不是表意的。

2. 与注音字母相比，它是独立的语言，而不是汉字的附属物。

3. 与国语罗马化相比，它能适应各地方言，因此各地区可以有适合各自方言的新文字变体。

让各地人民群众既学北京方言又学北京方言罗马化字母显然是不可能的，因此以北京方言作为唯一国语的这种权威必须取消。此外，新文字还有另一个优于国语注音字母和国语罗马化的长处，那就是：它把记录声调变化的符号取消了。这样的简化使得群众有可能不觉得有什么困难就学会新文字。

北方方言的新文字是四年前采用的。在这四年中，把新文字教给群众，进展很缓慢。然而，随着民族解放运动的日益发展，在关于大众语言和大众文学的讨论中，新文字便如旭日东升般地出现了。课本、杂志、小册子大量出版，最终结果就是中国新文字研究会的成立，它担负起领导整个运动的责任。

值得注意的是，新文字以及它的迅速为群众所接受，竟遭到强烈的反对。继《大众生活》杂志受到查禁之后，上海和其他地方的当局没收了所有用新文字出版的期刊和书籍。据公布，采取此项措施的原因有两个。第一，他们说，新文字起源于苏联，所以，任何人提倡新文字就带有“赤化”的色彩。第二，他们说，新文字会破坏中华民国的统一。

这些理由显然是胡说八道。第一，不错，北方方言新文字的最初方案起源于海参崴，但那是该市华侨的成果。现在上海、福建、广东方言的新文字方案都是在中国土地上由中国学者们制定的。至于所谓破坏国家的统一，我们认为，迅速采用新文字将有助于给中国带来日益增强的、前所未闻的国家统一。

汉字（表意的文字体系）仅仅对很少数学者保持形式上的文字统一，广大群众既没有时间也没有钱学汉字，因此必然还是没有文字。所以很明显，创造统一的手段仍付阙如，因为统一所依靠的不得不是口语或人民的相互交往。由于每个地方都有自己的方言，所以甚至口语也有很大的限制。但是，随着新文字的采用，每个地区的群众就能够比较容易学会读、写自己的方言，而且，因为知识分子不难掌握各种语言，各地区的人民便不仅能够有读报的机会，而且也有阅读本国文学和外国文学的机会。他们现时的孤立状态将被打破，他们将在实际上成为中国公民，而不是现在这样的由于口语的障碍而被相互分隔的、孤立的各省人民。

经过一个短时期，就不必依靠所谓“学者”了，因为学者将能从人民本身内部选拔出来。这必将帮助中国逐渐达到新的统一，这种统一是通过现时的表意文字永远不能达到的。

苏联各族人民有182种不同的语言拉丁化，使苏联能够成为一个真正统一的国家，这一事实指明了中国新文字运动的前景。

尽管遭到强烈的迫害，上海新文字运动仍在不断发展和普及。包括成千上万的农民、职员、工人、儿童在内的新的队伍在不到一个月的时间里学会了读和写。由一千多拥护者签名发表的宣言，表示支持新文字为战胜古老的、封建的表意文字而进行的斗争。

在中国，任何教育运动的先决条件是它经受节约时间和节约开支的考验所具有的能力。一个普通的农民能够在不到一个月的时间里学到读和写的基本要点。基础课本每册只需一分钱，再买一支铅笔和一本练习簿，一个贫苦的农民花三分钱就能学完最初的课程。甚至一个人力车夫为自己的教育也付得起所需费用。他将不再为了学习而依靠施舍。有了新文字这个新工具，属于群众所有、由群众自办、为群众服务的教育就是可能的。

因此，新文字代表着一个伟大的进步，不仅是中国文化的伟大进步，而且不久将改造中国人民的全部生活。

**附：北方方言拉丁化字母**

元音

| | |
|---|---|
| a［ah］如pap*a*中的*a* | o［o］如h*o*me中的*o* |
| e［eh］如aft*e*r中的*e* | u［oo］如f*oo*d中的*oo* |
| i［i］如*i*s中的*i* | y［ü］如德语中的*ü* |

辅音

| | |
|---|---|
| b［beh］如*B*erlin中的*b* | p［peh］如*p*art中的*p* |
| c［ts］如*Ts*i*ts*ihar中的*ts* | r［r］如*r*un中的*r* |
| ch［ch］如*ch*ild中的*ch* | rh 如ea*r*中的*r*,舌尖卷曲向后。 |
| d［deh］如won*d*er中的*d* | s［s］如*s*ee中的*s* |

f [feh] 如*f*or中的*f*

g [geh] 如*g*irl中的*g*

j [i] 如*y*es中的*y*

k [keh] 如*k*ind中的*k*

l [leh] 如*l*et中的*l*

m [meh] 如*m*an中的*m*

n [neh] 如*n*ame中的*n*

ng [ngeh] 如ki*ng*中的*ng*

sh [sh] 如*sh*e中的*sh*

t [teh] 如*t*ea中的*t*

w [oo] 如*w*ood中的*w*

x [heh] 似英语中的*h*

z [ds] 发*tz*音

zh–ch舌尖卷曲向后,压上颚发音。

原载1936年5月1日上海《中国呼声》(Voice of China)
英文半月刊第1卷第4期

# 中国大众教育运动*

中国主要是农业国，而且是一个穷国，因此没有钱按照西方的方式教育全国人民。中国要在几年内使全国人民能读会写，就必须研制出它自己的方法来。目前中国通过大众教育运动正在做这件事。中国大众教育运动开始于十二年前，但在最近两年中已经进入一个新的阶段。这个运动已下定决心要解决现时中国面临的三个最迫切的问题。首先是建立新学校的经费问题。运动的组织者们不把钱投入建筑校舍，而把整个社会看作一个学校。庙宇、戏院、休息室、私人住房的顶楼以至住房旁边的附属小屋，都已经被利用作大众的学校，从而把别的计划极为需要的钱节省下来了。

第二个问题也已经用一种新的方法解决了。中国的农民和工人没有钱买知识，没有钱付教师的薪金，因此运动的组织者们规定，凡是拥有知识的人都有责任与他人分享知识。参加夜校学习班的或者收割庄稼前后较为空闲时前来学习的三四十个农民，不仅是学生，而且也是先生。他们即使只学了第一课，也被鼓励回家去把他们刚才学到的内容教给他们的妻子和女儿。儿童们也成功地当了先生。六岁的孙儿教五十七岁的祖母读书写字。小学、中学的教师们因而受到鼓舞和帮助去训练他们的孩子们当“小先生”。

---

* 本篇是陶行知作为中国大众教育运动的组织者和领导人在1936年8月于英国切尔特纳姆市（Cheltenham）举行的“新教育联谊会”第七次世界会议上的发言。

“小先生”这个词儿听起来似乎很奇特，但是在中国，这些小先生却获得了很高的声誉。他们已经能够比成年人更有效地处理了中国的一个特殊的问题。中国妇女多数是文盲，女教师非常少。可是男教师教十六七岁的女孩子不方便。所以儿童们白天在学校，晚上当先生，教邻近的妇女和女孩。小先生制非常成功，凡是采用了小先生制的地方，男人和妇女的文化几乎相等。

当然还必须防止若干危险。小先生制须坚持自愿。但儿童们是热情的，他们一听到小先生制，多数就想当先生为国效劳。另一个危险是他们可能在教学上操劳过度，有损他们的健康。必须注意防止这样的事情发生。可能有人猜想，他们传递的知识是非常错误的。然而，实际上，人们发现，他们是非常认真的，把自己学到的东西教给别人，也使自己对学习的内容更清楚。

大众教育运动还解决了另一个问题，即简单的中文拼写字母问题。中文的方块字，一字一个图像，很难学习。中国话的一套拉丁化字母制定出来了。这套拉丁化字母已经在广州、上海和北方各省试行。它能为全国人民的四分之三所读懂，一个农民凭借这套拉丁化字母一个月之内就能学会读书写字。

随着这三个问题的解决，使大众不必等到中国工业化就能够用来自己教育自己的一种工具铸造出来了。如果中国要等待这么久，那就太晚了；没有大众教育，中国就要遭殃，丧失它的完整和自由。因为，坦率地说，现在中国的教育只有一个目的：民族解放。如果教育不能帮助中国成为一个自由、独立的国家，那么教育就没有意义了。

可是，强调民族解放，并不意味着狭隘的民族主义。一个自由、独立的中国将有助于世界和平，因为中国丝毫没有采取帝国主义政策的意思。中国力图达到的是在中国青年身上培植中国的民族解放精神和整个世界的国际谅解的精神。

出自Wyatt Rawson编“The Freedom We Seek”

（《我们追求的自由》）一书

# 在加拿大国会的讲演提纲



一九三七年十一月十九日，下午八时，加拿大国会，维多利亚剧院

一、致意。

二、中国的和平与民主。

三、我们要和平，所以我们要民主。

1. 要和平，你就享有和平。强加给我们的战争。

2. 我们要什么样的和平。我们要自由的和平，我们要正义的和平，我们要平等基础上的和平，是生与死的搏斗，还是自由与奴役的搏斗。

3. 怎样赢得和平？

A. 和平必须求索。和平不会像雨一样从天而降，也不会像雪茄烟雾喷出来。我们为追求和平就一定要付出代价。

B. 应当通过合作去追求和平。

C. 谁来合作以追求和平？

民主力量联合起来！

a. 被侵略者的联合抵抗。

b. 侵略国的民主力量采取不合作态度。

c. 世界民主力量的沟通与联合。

d. 东方和西方以两种方式汇合。

e. 世界同一。

a）战争滋生战争。

b）侵略推动侵略。

c）各国人民的自由。

d）注意不给民主与和平的敌人以帮助。

# 中国人民教育大纲

1. 民有、民治、民享。

2. 一项家庭试验：小陶教祖母。

3. 意识到模仿西方教育的灾难性失败。

4. 回归故国：从中国本土考虑发展教育（1925年）。

5. 不耻下问的善意学者看来越来越少。向农民请教。

6. 晓庄：

① 小茅屋；

② 没有围墙；

③ 跟农民在一起过简朴生活；

④ 村庄幼儿园、护卫队、“和平门”井——作为学校的一所村庄；

⑤ 生活即教育；

⑥ 带有思想活动的实际操作和教学。

7. 日本之行，日本入侵：需要唤醒国民。

8. 山海工学团：

① 工以养生；

② 学以明生；

③ 团以保生；

④ 来者不拒；

⑤ 一个医药箱、一架留声机、几个皮球；

⑥ 分解一只表；
⑦ 棉花工学团；
⑧ 小先生运动；
⑨ 像送牛奶一样送教育上门；
⑩ 习字和抄写课文；
⑪ 每个学生都养几只鸡，以助于维持学校；
⑫ 免费看电影和读书券；
⑬ 山海试验和家庭并发纠纷；
⑭ 小先生：女性教育的一个解决办法；
⑮ 小先生：起着联结学校和村庄的活导线的作用；
⑯ 小先生唤醒了学校老师的热诚，拓宽了他们的视野；
⑰ 小先生学到了更丰富的东西；
⑱ 小先生和传递先生；
⑲ 警惕：小先生对学校老师的模仿；
⑳ 防止盲目宣传——自由批评、探索真理；
㉑ 小先生遍游中国；
㉒ 小先生为着民族解放；
㉓ 小先生的三点准则：
a. 资格 b. 职责 c. 愉悦
㉔ 内容：劳动、科学、联盟、歌曲、故事、问题、活动；
㉕ 宏伟壮观的礼堂；
㉖ 新的题词；
㉗ 政府的态度：不干涉——密切注视——容许；
㉘ 将石头变成面包；
㉙ 期刊；
㉚ 正规老师；
㉛ 培训中心；
㉜ 研究中心；
㉝ 旅行指导；

㉞ 充分利用广播和电影；

㉟ 小先生修改我的诗歌的才能；

㊱ 七个小矮人；

㊲ 木匠先生；

㊳ 大学生下农村；

㊴ 小护士；

㊵ 小先生与和平；

㊶ 在敌占区的小先生：不合作与不靠书面文字传达；

㊷ 教育如同阳光、空气和水；

㊸ 将知识冷藏起来；

㊹ 与灾害竞争的教育；

㊺ 穷人让房；

㊻ 三重防御：a. 正规机动军队 b. 正规机动工业 c. 正规机动教育；

㊼ 靠自力搬迁的学校；

㊽ 夫妻学校；

㊾ 简单的医护措施：a. 接种疫苗 b. 接生 c. 卫生规则；

㊿ 翁家山的小孩教祖母；

51 书呆子；

52 手脑结合；

53 教育：作为装饰、玩具，还是作为解放的工具；

54 争取自由平等的意志；

55 朱冰如小姐的教学；

56 马老师的教学；

57 西桥；

58 盥洗间学校；

59 业余作家协会；

60 改革婚姻；

61 改革殡葬；

⑥② 小工人；
⑥③ 小科学家；
⑥④ 合作社。

# 中国的抗战是不自由就受奴役的斗争*



中国为之奋斗的理想和加拿大的理想是共同的，这种理想就是和平、自由、正义和民主。

平等的和平、足够的食品、自由和正义，这正是中国人民所需要的。

民主是中国的老传统。一位中国伟人曾经说过："天视自我民视，天听自我民听。[①]"这是中华民国的一条基本原理。

日本的眼睛比他的胃口还大。你们现在听我演讲时，在中国每分钟有五个人死伤。然而，按这个速度，日本要消灭中国人得花四百年。

中国人民已下定决心，要制止日本的进军。由于抵抗压迫者的决心，我国已经团结起来了。

日本为了辩护其侵略行径，列举了五条理由。这五条理由没有一条是站得住脚的。

1. 因为人口过多，日本必须扩张——中国以前允许日本人入境，甚至不要求护照。日本一方面宣称人口过多，同时却鼓励高出生率，而不是控制出生率。

---

* 本篇系陶行知访问加拿大时，加拿大医疗援华委员会在温哥华举行演讲会请其讲演的纪录。原文为英文，由任钟印译为中文。陶行知除讲了本篇内容外，还感谢加拿大人民和医疗援华会征集医疗物资支援中国抗战的义举。

2. 日本是为了争取与中国的友谊和合作而斗争——这是争取友谊和合作的一种古怪方式。

3. 日本想要增加同中国的贸易——他们摧毁了大宗贸易。

4. 日本想使中国开化——日本的全部文明和全世界的很大一部分文明都是渊源于中国。

5. 日本要阻遏共产主义的传播——按照这条理由，甚至去进攻英国还更合理些，因为中国是一个高度个体的国家；另一方面，当马克思撰写《资本论》时，英国庇护了马克思，而《红旗》的作者是梯帕累利②人。

日本进攻的真正原因是企图独占中国的原料并得到更廉价的劳动力。

中国的武器供应的主要来源之一是日本。我们的机动部队从背后打击日本军队，缴获了大量供应物资。

说中国是在进行游击战，这是不对的。因为我们作战的不是老百姓，而是得到正式承认的正规部队。这些机动部队只是在没有基地的情况下以高度机动的方式在作战。

中国的抗战不仅是生死存亡的斗争，它是不自由就受奴役的斗争。对我们来说，自由比生命更可贵。

1938年4月14日讲

原载1938年4月20日加拿大《太阳》报

## 注释

①“天视自我民视，天听自我民听”　这两句话出自《尚书·泰誓中》，相传为周武王伐纣，大会诸侯时的誓言。

② 梯帕累利　英国爱尔兰岛的一个郡。

# 中国的大众教育运动*

大约十二年前①，一群教授和学生深入农民生活，想研究出一种真正为农民服务的教育方法，大众教育运动就是这样开始的。大众教育运动的目的，在于尽力弥补正规学校制度所办不到的事，努力发展本国自己的教育，而不是发展从历史背景和自然条件不同的外国引进的教育；努力发展为广大劳苦大众服务的教育，而不是发展只为少数享有特权者的教育；努力发展完整的生活教育，而不是发展畸形的智力教育。为了达到这些目的，保证运动成功，我们制订了四个条件：

1. 试验者必须同群众生活在一起，向群众学习；

2. 方法必须以深思熟虑的实干为基础，而不是以书生气的思考为基础；

3. 教育费用必须最少，时间必须最短；

4. 要决心摆脱对教书这一职业的偏见和成见。

上述乃是说明“晓庄实验”部分情况中的几件事。该实验的主要成果是形成了生活即教育、社会即学校、教学做合一的理论。“山海工学团”与“小先生”对1931年及1932年外来侵略的

* 本篇原文为英文，在印度《民族旗帜》杂志上发表时，印度民族运动领袖甘地曾加按语云：“陶行知博士不久前来访问我时，我邀请他撰文介绍正在中国开展的引人注目的大众教育运动。现在，他寄来下面这篇有指导意义的文章。这篇文章对我们印度是很有用的。”

挑战作出了回答。当侵略深入到华北，北京学生奋起要求保卫华北时，我们的运动以“国难教育社”[②]的形式与“全国各界救国联合会”[③]携手合作。1935年12月以来，这一运动旨在：

1. 团结起来保卫中国的民主；
2. 通过国际合作，达到世界和平；
3. 使人民自己提高道德和文化水平；
4. 实行全民免费教育。

只有最后一个目的及实现该目的之方法才是本文详细讨论的内容。本文讨论的甚至也不只是教大众学文化，还要讨论教他们学政治、学经济。我们一直在尽最大的努力寻求最简单的方法实现民有、民治、民享的教育，使我国人民愈来愈具备条件，参加使自由的中国进入自由民族之林而进行的伟大斗争。

**死了的书呆子**

具有数百年传统的错误教育观念是我们的障碍。用旧观念来看，教育就是读书。学者被称为“读书人”，意思是读书的人。若问一位教授的职业是什么，他通常会这样回答：“我在北京大学[④]教书。”同样的，如果你问一个学生在哪儿求学，他会回答：“我在北京大学读书。”意思是他在北京大学念书。虽然我们重视书籍，把它们作为帮助我们了解过去及当代文明的重要手段，但是，我们怀疑，是否光读书就能使我们获得自由；是否只有读书，才是赏识书。在较进步的人中间，这样的读书人绰号是“书虫”。我的朋友P. C. 张博士，称他们为“书呆子”。下面是一首形容这种读书人的小诗：

我是书呆子，
家住太平洋，
读破万卷书，
想中状元郎，

农家供酒肉，
主人快饿死，
失业教蒙童，
尽变小呆子。

**手脑并用**

中国的传统教育似乎创造了两种怪人。在学校，学生的头脑被知识塞得发胀，却很少有机会使用双手。许多应该由他们自己做的事，都由仆人代做了。做泥饼与打开表检查都同样要受到惩罚。我们从人类发展史知道，手有助于形成人脑。直立使手获得自由，我们才开始工作；工作时发出的声音，逐步被我们选用为口头语言。文字及工具都是我们的双手创造的。旧学校不鼓励使用双手，的确达不到发展脑的目的。由于受到这种不正常的训练，学生只得到一大堆未经消化的、互不联系的、脱离实际的各种知识。他们看起来有个大脑袋，但不能按客观世界的情况准确地思考。因此，有机会上学的人，毕业后有个大脑袋及一双小手，用个比喻来说，他们看起来有点像只袋鼠，只有提笔写几行字的力气。另一方面，人民群众为国家做了大量的工作，却不能上学。尽管他们不断地为办学缴纳税款，他们及他们的孩子却一直被剥夺了劳动之余享受文化教育的时间。他们被迫以小脑袋及一双大手的样子而生存。生活教育运动的目的，在于使这两种怪人恢复正常生活。我们要唤醒读书人，伸出手来干活；唤醒广大人民群众学点知识好思考。让读书人与农民接触，便取得了许多近乎奇迹的成就。读书人和农民都重新发现了他们已经忘掉的东西。读书人看到农民那出色的劳动成果，禁不住喊出声来："我们不也有手吗？为什么我们不劳动？"同样地，农民重新发现了他们的脑："我们有脑袋。真的，我们有脑袋。让我们来思索吧！"确实，真正的教育必须有助于造就能思索、能建设的人。我们需要的教育，要能造就会用脑指挥手，手开动脑的人。这种教育的新概念可用一首诗来形容，诗题为《手脑相长歌》：

人生两个宝，
双手与大脑。
用脑不用手，
快要被打倒。
用手不用脑，
饭也吃不饱。
手脑都会用，
才算是开天辟地的大好佬。

**工学团**

手脑相长的原则，逐步发展形成了“工学团”的概念。“工学团”似乎是个奇怪的术语，但它阐明了新教育的内容、方法及组织形式：工以养生，学以明生，团以保生，把教育的全部内容讲得清清楚楚。而且，工、学、团的方法决定了教育的方法，教育不再是纯学术性的了。最后，该术语还表明了组织的性质。它比“学校”包含更丰富的内容，因为按传统观念来说，学校传授科学知识呱呱叫，但学生几乎没有机会劳动及合作。该术语甚至比“合作社”更合适。“合作社”除了眼前的经济需要以外，不够注意人类生活的其他方面。

“工学团”实际上采用了三种形式。第一种，是那些严格贯彻新原则，取名“工学团”的组织，如宝山的“棉农工学团”，上海的“报童工学团”。就“棉农工学团”而言，种棉花是（做）工；摸索种棉花的好方法，更加懂得整个生活是学（科学）；组织棉农，使之能保卫他们的劳动果实不受剥削，并能参加反对侵略、保卫祖国及人类的更伟大的斗争便是团（体）的真正意义。通过精选种子来改进棉花质量，使一个小小的团体能增收二千元，平均每英亩增收六元。这笔额外收入的十分之一使他们能在同一村子里成立一个“儿童工学团”，让他们的孩子受到较好的教育。

上海静安寺路的“报童工学团”成立的方式很有趣。一天，我们注意到这些报童不会念他们卖的报纸，表示要派一位年轻人去教他们识字。孩子们非常高兴地同意了。但他们找间教室很困难，孩子们担负起自己找地方学习这一任务，最后，报童吕公义的妈妈，很慷慨地把她唯一的一间房让孩子们自由使用。每天，孩子们同义务教师一起在那儿学习一小时。报纸是他们的课本，标题是他们的启蒙课文。他们受教育是免费的，但作为回报，他们有责任把所学到的知识教给邻居。报童们是自立的。卖报开始被当作光荣的劳动。一旦组成团体，孩子们的力量就强了，同报纸老板打交道，就变得容易些。有些孩子甚至还赢得了开明警察的尊敬。

“工学团”的第二种形式是学校，就是在教学计划中增添了生产活动及社会活动的内容，但还是保持着学校的名字。

第三种形式是使合作社办得朝气蓬勃，在加强合作社生产的同时，使其具备学文化及保卫生活的特点。这样的合作社，挂的是合作社之名，行的是工学团之实。这一运动及时为数以百万计的难民服务。

**小先生**

小先生是与他人分享教育的儿童。在小先生运动发展的较早阶段，最常见的小先生是自愿帮助家人及邻居学习基础知识的学童。随着时间的推移，甚至街上的孩子也即知即传，把学到的知识教给自己的朋友。大约14年前，我那57岁的母亲对学习产生了兴致。这件事启发了我，使我第一次想到小先生的可能性。母亲要读我的家信，还想了解时事，她唯一能找到的先生是我的第二个儿子，他当时6岁，刚好学完第一册读本。祖孙一边玩，一边学习。一个月以后，我母亲便学完了第一册读本。当时，这令人愉快的事并没有引起我家以外的人们的多少热情。然而，一个6

岁的男孩，没有师范学校的毕业文凭，没有督学颁发的证书，却顺利地教他57岁的祖母学完了第一册读本。这一事实使我得到深刻的印象，是发现“小先生”的决定性因素之一。

1931年和1932年，满洲受侵略，上海遭进攻。这时，我们才开始深信，不唤醒全国民众实现全民团结，就不能救国。这需要以最少的经费，在最短的时间内，实行免费全民教育。进步青年男女潮水一般涌到农村，帮助农民了解国家的危机。有些青年到我这儿来求教。我的意见很简单：来者不拒。但当农民越来越明白教育对他们及其子女的重要性时，他们及其子女便都涌到小小的学校来听课了。当时，不少教师怀疑，根据这一原则，他们能维持多久。坦白地说，有些教师还在考虑如何以收费或入学考试的办法来减少听众哩！如果允许这样做，就不能实现大众教育的全部目的了，因为它意味着又回到了只为少数人的教育。我们尽力催促他们面对现实，想出新的办法来应付这一形势。在需要的压力下，他们自然而然地委派一些能干的学生负责教那些多余的听众。1932年11月的一天，我参观了“上海工学团”，很惊奇地观看了一个12岁的男孩侣朋教一个拥有40多个儿童的班。每个幼小的心灵都掌握在他手心里！一刹那间，我的潜意识里浮现出孙儿教祖母的情景。随即召开了一个教职员会，会上我告诉他们，他们自己已经找到了救校救国的新方法，那便是“小先生”。随着小先生的兴起，我们不仅能一直遵循“来者不拒”的指导原则，还提出“不能来者免费送教上门”的新口号。从那时起，我们的小朋友就把教育送到不能参加正规班学习的家庭主妇及放牛娃的家中，这样，就不会打破他们的饭碗了。送教育上门这一特点，是小先生制所独有的，是它与兰开夏郡的“导生制”⑤的不同之处。另一个不同点是，即使放牛娃和家庭主妇，迟早也要与他人分享教育。

小先生制正以一种独特的方式为中国服务，即帮助成年女孩及妇女受点教育。在旧风俗习惯仍然盛行的农村，男教师感到很难教成年的女孩子。一个敢这样做的青年男子，会招来风言风语，女孩子们会被吓跑，他就只能教椅子和板凳了！女教师很少，多年来，让女子也受教育的问题一直困扰着我们。小先生一出现，这问题便迎刃而解，就像积雪遇到阳光便消融了一样。他们可以到新娘的卧室里给她上课。孩子比正规教师随便得多。当小先生到农民家去上课时，如果主妇还没有洗完碗，她可以让小先生等一等，小朋友何乐而不为？正好可以在院子里玩一会。小先生就是这样为推动女子教育出了力。在广东省百侯村，1934年有200名学童自愿教2,000名村民，其中1,500名是女孩及妇女。

小先生很善于说服老一代继续进步。有个故事可能大家都感兴趣。西湖附近有个烟霞洞，洞上边有个小茶场叫翁家山。山上小庙里有个小学。这所学校大约有100名“小先生”。有一次，一个年仅12岁的小先生对我讲了个非常有趣的故事，说的是他如何说服祖母跟他学习。他拿着一本漂亮的书走到祖母身边：“奶奶，如果您想学这本书，我很高兴帮助您。”老太太回答道：“好孩子，奶奶太老了，学不进去。我都是快死的人了，学习对我有什么用呢？”对一个小男孩来说，这可是个棘手的问题。一阵困惑之后，小男孩又回到祖母身旁：“您死后到哪儿去呢？”“我是个规规矩矩的好人，死后可以进天堂。”孩子说：“恭喜恭喜！如果天堂的守门天神要您签名后才能进去，您怎么办呢？”祖母似乎完全相信了孙儿的话，马上要他教她写名字：“给我一支铅笔，给我一张纸。”她开始练习写自己的名字了。半夜里，发生了一件更有趣的事。在我国，祖母通常负责照顾家里一部分孩子。这孩子同祖母一起睡。半夜里，他突然醒了，以为有小虫子顺着他的腿往上爬！伸手一摸，他大吃一惊，那不是虫子，而是祖母的手指，正在划十字、圆圈，练习笔划哩！当孙儿问她为什么这样做时，她答道：“哦！我在练习写自己的名字。”

从我们的经验来看，小先生非常热情。下面这首歌生动地描述了他们的热情：

我是小先生，
热心好比火山喷，
生来不怕霜和雪，
踏破铁鞋化愚蒙。

小先生有时被称为“蚊子先生”。我想，我们大多数人都不喜欢蚊子。但有一点我可以为蚊子辩护。若你周围有歹徒，蚊子可以使你彻夜不眠。的确，现在的小先生，已经远远不止教读和写了，他们经常教唱歌、讲故事、谈新闻、传授知识、提出问题来讨论。新安的小先生甚至自己组成旅行团，随身带着收音机、新闻缩微胶卷、唱片及演戏的道具。他们几乎走遍了北方各省，访问了公路两旁许多村庄及战场后面的兵营。他们走到哪儿，就在哪儿表演、放电影、演讲、成立识字小组或讨论小组，为的是使人民牢记民族斗争。

从小先生那里得出的原则非常简单：任何懂得一点简单真理的人，就够资格传授这个真理，并有责任与他人共享这个真理。

从我们的经验来讲，小先生运动有下述优点：

1. 通过教别人，孩子们学得更多。把知识冷藏在脑子里的人学得最少。

2. 知识不再是买卖的商品。教育成为人人可以免费得到的礼物。它像空气，人人可以呼吸；它像水，人人可以饮用；它像阳光，人人可以享受。

3. 老少共同进步。成人与儿童经常接触，共同增长知识，可以使老人年轻起来。

4. 它帮助解决了女子教育那不可克服的困难，使我们能够把初级教育扩展到全国的一半人口，而这是其他任何方法都办不到的。

5. 随着小先生的出现，学校本身也有了新的变化。从前，乡村学校在农村中是孤立的。现在，小先生就像通电的电线，把乡村学校和每家每户联结起来，全村都成了学校。教育之光照遍每个角落，而学校转过来又被众多需要解决的问题激发得生气勃勃。破庙中孤零零的教师，突然与几十个小同志相处，必然会看到他职业的新前景，为他应该完成的历史使命而振作起来。“舜帝庙”的教师曹代江先生准备辞职，因为山西乡村学校教师那微薄的薪金养不活他一家人。正准备辞职时，他在《生活教育》杂志上偶然发现了小先生教学法。他便进行试验，并发出了一封信。这封信鼓舞了许多乡村教师坚守自己的岗位。他说：“有小先生和小工人做我的同志，我相信，几年之内我们就能重建乡村生活。我感到，似乎整个国家的命运都掌握在教师手里。”在信的结尾他写道，即使给他高十倍的薪金，他也不辞职了。

小先生运动不是没有危险的。我可以举出两个：

第一，在过分热情的领导的掌握下，小先生容易操劳过度，这就可能损害孩子的健康，妨碍事业的发展。通常我们只让小先生每天教半小时。

第二，有些政客及武断的官吏为了自己的利益，利用这些孩子做小宣传员。这是违背我们的原则的。先生是传授真理的人，只传授真理而不是其他。为了传授真理，他必须追求真理。自由批评是绝对必要的。为了阻止滥用孩子作宣传工具，我们必须注射自由批评这一抗毒剂。

**传递先生**

另一类自愿教师，遵循着与小先生同样的原则，称为传递先生。它与小先生的区别在于年龄。小先生的年龄在16岁以下，而传递先生的年龄在16岁以上。“传递先生”这一术语来自接力赛跑，把旗帜传给下一个赛跑者。要说明传递教学的过程，最好的办法是邀请一些听众，让他们把自己想象为在乡村学校上夜校的中国农民，把演讲者想象为乡村学校的教师。夜校教师的任务不是把农民当学生教，而是帮助他们成为传递先生，成为不必等四至五年毕业后才出去教书的教师，成为放学后就能教别人的教师。放学后，每个学生都是教师，每个家庭都是学习中心。我们惊讶地发现，我国十分之一的农民有能力领导独立的班级。其余的至少能教两个朋友，一个坐在左边，一个坐在右边。倘若这两个朋友穷得买不起书，传递教师自己的书可以三人共用。传递教师刚刚在夜校里学了功课，也得复习一下。他一边复习功课，一边教他的两个朋友。在教朋友的过程中，他学得更多、更清楚、更深刻。一个人想与他人分享知识时,他自己的知识会有个大的飞跃。“把真理传给邻居”已成为传递教师的座右铭。看到我们这么多的农民和工人逐渐成为自己同胞的传递教师，真令人十分欣慰。

**女工的传递教学**

上海杨树浦一个烟草公司的女工朱冰如小姐，在女工中开展传递教学，成绩特别卓著。她在上海工作，住在离上海约莫5英里的浦东。她家附近有所由上海基督教女青年会主办的培养传递先生的夜校。除了星期天，朱小姐每晚在该校学习一小时。拂晓前她就过黄浦江，步行两英里左右以便按时进厂。中午，工厂午休一小时，让所有的工人到街上去吃午饭。工厂就关门直到下午一点差几分才开。在街上吃顿便饭只需10分钟。朱小姐心中有个计划，要用剩下的时间帮助她的姐妹们受教育。起初，她约伙伴们到一个空场地集中。但男工们也蜂拥而至，要看她们干什么。他们觉得这些女工很奇怪，因为他们从未见过这样的奇事——女工们聚集在露天里，手拿着书，墙上贴着地图。男工们惊讶地看见这些女工在念书、讨论问题、唱歌。男人在场令姐妹们十分讨厌。朱小姐不得不另找安身之处。这一愿望终于实现了。一位小学校长经劝服最后答应借给她一间教室上口头问答课，因为学生一点钟以后才上学。从那以后，女工听课人数猛增。几天以后，朱小姐不得不从她班上挑了一名能干的学生作第二小组的传递教师。一个月后，她不得不占用了这位好心肠校长所有的教室来适应不断增长的需要。所有的房间都挤满之后，又在姐妹们家中成立了新的小组。每组选出能干的传递教师晚上教。这样，朱小姐和她的伙伴们创办的班就成了那个地区女工传递教师的培养中心。教育之光从那儿发出，照到每个与她们有联系的家庭。随着时间的推移，其他地区的工人，闻到了这边的风声，有些人受到鼓舞，也推行类似的计划。甚至当初给朱小姐的班添麻烦的男工人也开始认识到这种教育的重要性，决定成立男工人班，贯彻类似的原则。

**一套新字母**

大众教育运动还对提倡汉语口语新字母感兴趣。70多年前，人们就开始尝试为汉语口语发明一套拼音字母，但最近的尝试才证明是最好、最有成效的。为北方、上海、广州、厦门及其他几种方言使用的字母已编造出来。新字母把汉语口语当多音节语言处理，消除了代表不同声调的那些麻烦的小符号。正是这一大优点，使这种新字母一下子超过了所有以前的发明。有了这些新字母，不同地区的农民，每天花一小时，一两个月之内就能学会用本地语言读书写字。节省了多少时间啊！

目前，把全国民众团结在抵抗日本侵略这一中心思想和行动的周围，是中国的燃眉之急。我们也须毫不犹豫地动员所有传达信息的工具实现这一团结。新字母是些听任我们支配的最好的工具。尽管有许多困难，我们也要尽可能地利用它们。

由于篇幅所限，我只介绍北方方言的新字母。6个元音是：a，就像papa中的a；e，就像after中的e；i，就像is中的i；o，就像home中的o；u，就像food中的oo；y，就像德语的ü。22个辅音是：b，就像Berlin中的b；c，就像Tsitsihar中的ts；ch，就像child中的ch；d，就像wonder中的d；p，就像part中的p；r就像run中的r；rh，就像发r音一样，舌头后缩成凹形，顶住上颚；f，就像for中的f；g，就像girl中的g；j，就像yes中的y；k，就像kind中的k；l，就像let中的l；m，就像man中的m；n，就像Brennen中的n；

ng，就像king中的ng，s，就像see中的s；sh，就像she中的sh，t，就像Terman中的t；w，就像wood中的w；x，就像Heriman中的h；z，就像zinc中的z；zh，就像发ch音一样，舌头后缩，成凹形顶住上颚。15个双元音是：ai，就像high中的i；ao，就像out中的ou；ei就像fatc中的a；ie就像legitimate中的第一个i；ou，就像pasteur中的eu，发音时下颚伸出；ia，就像yard中的ya；iao，等于发i后再发ao；iou，等于发i后再发ou；iu，就像Europe中的eu；uo，等于发u后再发o；ua，等于发u后再发a；uai，等于发u后再发ai；ui，等于发u后再发i；ye，等于发ü后再发e；yo，等于发ü后再发o。15个鼻元音是：an，ang，en，eng，ian，iang，in，ing，uan，uang，un，ung，yan，yn，yng。还有3个可以变化的辅音g，k，x，在i和y前出现时，它们发轻音。这些，就是全部北方方言新字母。我国四分之三的人口懂北方方言。倘若北方方言新字母能普遍被采用，则两三年内，就可扫除四分之三的文盲。去年，学习新字母的人越来越多。仅在一个城市，就有300,000人学会了新字母，能看懂用新字母写的文章了。我们希望政府能看清采用新字母的重要性，至少把它当做一种可以选择的方案，利用它的威信及影响，在无钱无时间，要花好多年才学会几千汉字的不太幸运的中国人中间普及。

### 社会即学校

另一个概念是把社会当成学校，利用一切现有的物力提高人民的道德和文化水平。实现这一主张的方法之一就是在庙宇、茶馆及所有空闲的地方开展识字小组及讨论小组等活动。我们的方针是尽可能少花钱建房屋。找不到房间，树荫下也可以。较大的会议总是在露天举行的。大自然造成的礼堂的确十分雄伟，青天作屋顶，大地作地板，群星作墙，当空的月亮作灯，我们的农民在那儿开群众大会和座谈会。正是在这样的礼堂里，中国的农民唱他们的歌，讲他们的故事，学习他们那简单的真理，讨论国内和国际的问题。

**新农民的诞生**

在乡村，所有这些力量都在发挥作用，在这种情况下，一旦掌握了这些力量，调动了这些力量，一代新农民就会在东方崛起。《大地》[6]中的那个竭力为自己的小家庭捞到越来越多的土地，以便成为比别的农民兄弟更富裕的农民，不再成为别人仿效的榜样。当代进步的中国农民想使每个农民都有土地，都过像样的生活。正因为如此，他们在参加抵抗日本侵略的斗争中才起这样伟大、这样英勇的作用。也正因为同一个原因，他们才要团结全国人民行动起来，以保证最后的胜利。下面这首诗便是这代新农民的写照：

**锄头舞歌**

手把个锄头锄野草呀！
锄去野草好长苗呀！

五千年古国要出头呀！
锄头底下有自由呀！

革命的成功靠锄头呀！
锄头锄头要奋斗呀！

单把的锄头不中用呀！
联合机器来革命呀！

1938年9月19日写，26日写成
原载1938年10月29日、11月5日和11月19日
印度杂志，“HARIJAN”（《民族旗帜》）

## 注释

① 大约十二年前　指1927年3月15日晓庄学校的创办。

② 国难教育社　成立于1936年2月23日。

③ 全国各界救国联合会　简称救国会。成立于1936年6月1日。

④ 北京大学　文理科综合大学。前身为京师大学堂，1893年创立于北京。1912年起改今名。

⑤ 兰开夏郡的“导生制”　亦称倍尔—兰克斯特制。为英国教师倍尔和兰克斯特所创办的教学制度。

⑥《大地》　美国女作家赛珍珠所著的小说。有中译本。

# 中国*



## 农村生活状况

**中国的村庄**——据统计，中国有一百万个村庄，平均每个村庄的人口为四百人。这些村庄遍布在黑龙江流域，长江流域，黄河流域，珠江流域，以及西北高原和华北平原。可以看到，中国村庄的结构和生活方式是大不一样的。有些村庄由同一个祖先繁衍下来的家庭所构成，它们有一个祠堂，而且或多或少受到族长的统治。还有一些村庄则为一种混合的构成。一个绅士或者一个退休还乡的官吏可以在地方行政官员和村民之间起联络作用，并且常常对地方事务有决定权。比较进步的村庄则有较为民主的统治，它们由选举出来的村长管理。在许多村庄，茶馆成为舆论的中心。不定期营业的杂货店向村民供应盐、植物油、糖、纸、煤油和其他日常必需品。除了几个地主之外，多数村民以务农为生。一般地说，每一农户有五六口人。在产稻地区，他们依靠3.5英亩地过活。在产麦地区，则依靠6英亩地过活。每户耕地一般分散在四五个地方。在多数情况下，这一小块耕地并不完全属于甚至完全不属于农民所有。一个农户如果有一条牛或一头小毛驴帮助干活，那就算幸运的了。通常一户农家都有一头猪或一只

* 本篇原文为英文，系陶行知1938年应美国哥伦比亚大学师范学院国际研究所《教育年鉴》编者之约而写。

羊，两三只母鸡，几棵树和一个屋边小菜园。根据金陵大学关于土地利用情况的研究报告，农业纯收入的百分之十五来自辅助工业和服务业。这些行业包括织布、谷物加工、榨油、土法缫丝、制茶、制糖、造纸、编竹木、稻草器皿。在工业城市周围的村民于农闲季节打零工。他们也从事贩卖水果、谷物或蔬菜。

**人口**——据专家估计，在全国总人口中，百分之十二居住在有一万或一万以上人口的城镇里。可以有把握地说，四万万五千万人口的百分之八十居住在农村。在每年新增加的四百万人口中，估计农村至少增加三百万。多余的人口从前是向东北迁移，到满洲寻找出路，或者向南迁移，到外国寻找出路；随着工业的发展，他们又到城市里寻找出路。自1929年世界经济不景气以来，海外约二十万至二十五万的中国劳工被迫回归祖国。每年有十五万至十八万农民向长城以北和东北迁移，但由于日本侵占满洲，这一人口的迁移已大大受阻。中国民族工业，既受到外国竞争的阻碍，又没有任何关税保护，其缓慢发展已经不是中国剩余农业人口的适当出路了。

**土地问题和土地政策**——中国土地问题非常严重。土地分配的不平等，农场的小规模经营，耕地收获的分成地租[①]，无地农

土地财产的不平等分配

| 地方 | 占有土地者 | | 无土地者 | |
|---|---|---|---|---|
| | 农户百分比 | 占有土地百分比 | 农户百分比 | 占有土地百分比 |
| 定县（河北） | 2.3 | 19.1 | 71.6 | 29.4 |
| 无锡（江苏） | 5.7 | 47.3 | 68.9 | 14.2 |
| 临安（浙江） | 4.7 | 52.1 | 88.9 | 21.8 |
| 南阳（河南） | 4.2 | 30.5 | 38.9 | 7.2 |
| 广东 | 6 | 66 | 74 | 19 |

民的增加，这些因素结合起来，便加速了近年来的土地革命。情况之严重，从下表可以看出：

对二十五个省占地1,148,874,000亩的58,569,000个农场的调查，表明了如下的结果（1亩=0.164英亩）：

二十五个省的土地状况

| 地区 | 灌溉状况百分比 | 每农户平均亩数 |
|---|---|---|
| 东北 | 2 | 52 |
| 东南 | 62 | 12 |
| 西北 | 8.8 | 29 |
| 华北平原 | 5.7 | 20 |
| 长江下游 | 46.1 | 15 |
| 西南 | 43.6 | 17 |
| 25个省平均数 | 24 | 19 |

国民政府认识到情况的严重性，乃于1930年颁布了《土地法》。《土地法》规定，若地主离开其土地所在地，则在该土地上经营已满十年之佃农即可根据若干合法条件开始占有该土地，地租不得超过该土地主要产物的百分之三十七点五。农民可以个别地或集体地自由使用公有耕地，但不得占有公有耕地。改良耕地的税率应为地价的百分之一，非改良耕地的税率应为地价的百分之一点五至百分之十。佃农可以随意对土地进行改良，并将由

二十二个省的地租状况

| | 22个省收取地租的习惯做法 | 700个县用地价百分比表示的地租 |
|---|---|---|
| 现金地租 | 21.2% | 11% |
| 实物地租（收获物） | 50.7% | 12.7% |
| 分成地租 | 28.1% | 15.2% |

**无土地农民的增加**

| 省份 | 占有土地农民 | | 部分占有土地农民 | | 佃农 | |
|---|---|---|---|---|---|---|
| | 1912 | 1930 | 1912 | 1930 | 1912 | 1930 |
| 云南 | 45 | 28 | 26 | 31 | 19 | 41 |
| 贵州 | 43 | 32 | 24 | 25 | 33 | 43 |
| 四川 | 30 | 20 | 19 | 27 | 51 | 58 |

地主给予补偿。除非佃农拖欠地租达两年之久或无故不经营所租土地达一年之久，否则地主不得将佃农所租土地收回。

可以举出现已合并为一个特区的中国苏区[②]的土地政策作为对照。国民党农民委员会于1926年所作的一次调查表明，农村百分之十的人口占有全国百分之七十的耕地；中农占有百分之十五；占农村人口百分之六十五的自耕农、佃农和雇农则仅占有全国耕地的百分之十至十五，据斯诺[③]报道，西北苏维埃政府于1935年颁布了一项土地法，该法规定，凡土地所有人不自行耕作之土地一律没收，并将没收之土地、荒地、以及主人已他往之土地分配给贫农。地主一词，包括主要收入来源于土地出租与他人的农人。该法之目的，在于通过提供充分之土地和消灭地租剥削来保证每一农户小康生活的基础。

**高利贷及合作社**——金陵大学于1933年对22个省共850个县的农民负债状况所作的调查表明，百分之五十的农民负债，百分之四十八的农民借粮为食。债务百分之九十以上年利高达百分之二十以上。差不多百分之二十四的债务年利竟高于百分之四十。债务中百分之九十五告贷于封建性的处所（当铺、钱庄、农村商店、地主、富农和商人），只有百分之五是向银行及合作社借的。

为了遏制高利贷和有助于解除农民的痛苦，与1918年学生运动相联系的合作社运动开始了。从1918年至1927年，合作社运动在着眼点上主要是社会的和慈善性的。自1927年以来，在提倡合作社运动方面已经注入了政治的动机。自1934年以来，中国的银行已经将越来越多的资金投入合作社。从1918年第一个合作社开始，至1936年合作社的数目已达37,318个，社员1,643,670人，股金5,139,795元（目前汇率为中国1元等于美元25分）。

由于缺乏群众的控制，由于需要财产作抵押，又由于百分之十二至十八的年利率（比一般的农业收入还高），所以，总的看来，合作社是不利于贫苦农民的。陈翰笙[④]博士研究了合作社运动之后得出了如下的结论："简言之，在中国最初发起合作社运动的是真诚希望改善国内千百万人民命运的知识分子和领袖人物。可是，在发展和扩大的过程中，合作社运动却成了中国经济所固有的一切社会弊病的牺牲品……个体的高利贷已为集体的高利贷所取代。"

中国苏区也非常重视合作社，在现时政府的领导下，这些合作社仍然继续经营，以便"提高群众的经济、政治水平"，并"鼓励社会的最低阶层参加"——这是埃德加·斯诺详细记述的许多事情中所讲到的。

**疾病和医疗中心**——农村人口比城市人口遭受大得多的疾病痛苦。农村最流行的疾病是疟疾、肺病以及眼病、牙病和皮肤病。由于缺乏医疗和卫生知识，农村产妇及婴儿死亡率也很高。诸如天花之类的传染病常常使农村人民死亡人数很多。

近年来，通过实验和示范，在力图改善农村人口的健康状况方面曾经做了许多工作。1935年，成立了一个独立的全国卫生管理机构。在江西、湖南、甘肃、宁夏、青海、陕西、浙江七个省，系统地开展了巩固卫生服务工作。每一个省的中心点都有一个行政办事处，一个卫生实验室，一所医院。各县有卫生中心和卫生站，各镇各村有卫生分站或诊疗所，更加推进了卫生工作。总共有74个县卫生中心、144个卫生站和诊疗所已经建立起来。江宁、定县、兰溪、邹平诸县则建立了示范中心，这些示范中心因战争关系已迁往华中。这些农村的卫生中心已试图在医疗人员的指导下使用农村的卫生员，这些人是从农村招收来的外行，只在简单的工作做法上经过短期的培训，例如种痘，对传染病以及出生和死亡情况作报告，几种简单药物的应用，急救，常见皮肤病和简单外伤的治疗。全国现有27所医科学校，217所护士学校，38所助产士学校，但还远远不能满足极其巨大的需要。然而，已经作出了良好的开端，而且这一项工作正在朝着正确的方向前进。

**饥荒和对自然的控制**——中国常常发生饥荒，而受害最深者则为农民。造成饥荒的原因甚多，其中可以举出如下诸方面：森林遭受毁坏，水利缺乏，河流控制不当，耕作方法原始，由于大规模土地占有的增加而致农业生产下降，耕作规模缩小。这些因素结合起来，产生水旱灾害，从而常使人民陷入饥馑。而且，由于缺乏交通工具，很难将粮食从一地区运往另一地区。

近年来，大规模的重新造林运动已在进行，政府鼓励学生、文职官员和农民于清明节种树。救灾委员会已致力于建造拦河坝，以便为西北地区提供更好的水利。在1936至1937年度，为水利工程拨款5,000,000元（国币）；用于淮河、湖北防水坝以及海河与永定河上的水土保持工程的费用约9,000,000元（国币）。在科学耕作方面，对于选种，特别是棉种，已经做了许多工作；中央棉垦局已分配改良棉种于江苏、河南、陕西、河北，从1934年的570,000亩增加到1936年的3,000,000亩。对于西北地区的畜牧业和祁门茶的改良也已予以重视。最后，公路已从1921年的1,185公里增加到1931年的66,111公里和1935年的96,345公里。

**外来侵略和团结抗战**——一百年来的外来侵略已把中国降为一个半殖民地的国家。最近日本的侵略正威胁着民族的生存。在这一事件中，受害最深者又是农民。第一，外国货已经摧毁了农村的手工业。第二，由于中国直到1929年才获得关税自主，所以中国民族工业的发展受到阻碍，农民不能在城市里得到充分的就业。第三，日本侵占满洲，关闭了农民外移的一条非常重要的出路，使他们在华北的生活更加艰难得多。第四，自1935年8月以来，日货走私进入中国市场，不缴纳关税，给予中国工业以极为严重的打击，成为失业的主要原因之一，同时也是国民政府税收损失的主要原因之一，其损失每年竟达1亿元（国币）。第五，在沦陷区，农民被迫按照几乎与没收无异的低微价格出售他们最好的土地。

由于“分而治之”乃是日本侵略的政策，所以中国人获得自由的唯一道路便是“团结抗战”。中国农民为民族解放的战斗而献身，正是他们形成了中国“看不见的军队”的群众基础，正是这支“军队”现在使得侵略者难于——确切地说是不可能——永久占领中国。的确，中国人已经日益团结起来了。所有军队现时正在蒋介石委员长的统一指挥下进行战斗，而中国农民将在这一历史性的为获得自由而进行的斗争中发挥决定性的作用。

## 教育状况

**文盲和教育**——所谓文盲，通常指不能读书写字而言。在这个意义上，中国大约有1.2亿人可以列为有文化者，其余大约3.3亿人可以叫做文盲。这种文盲的百分比，农村较城市高得多。但是，随着教育范围的扩大，所谓有文化便具有更广阔的定义。如果把生活本身看作教育，那就不仅有学校的文化，而且有社会的、经济的和政治的文化。在这个意义上，中国某些地区的农民就可能比西方某些学者或农场主具有更高程度的文化。然而，学术性的文化既然是这样一种重要的促进个人自身教育的手段，那么，中国农民中大量的文盲问题就必须解决，以便帮助他们取得更大的进步。同时，在讨论问题的这个方面时，必须不要忘记，真正的农民教育必须包括对有关农村生活所有重大问题的理解，包括对正在影响农民的一切力量的鉴别，还包括积极努力帮助他们或引导他们自行解决这些问题并达到小康生活的水准。

**初等教育**——有各种类型的初等学校。第一，是六年制的小学校，包括四年制的初级小学课程和两年制的高级小学课程。这一类型的学校通常设在县城里，在农村则很少见到。第二，是四年制的初级小学校，这一类型的学校多数在小城镇，在农村的百分比很小。第三，是主要以农村儿童为对象的一年制课程。第四，是在农村仍然流行的一种类型——私塾。

国民政府特别致力于推广一年制课程，并对私塾加以改造，引导它们或多或少符合一年制课程的标准。一年制小学校的教学科目有：国语、作文、写字、算术、公民和体育，课时为每周36节，共1,080分钟。

近二十年来，这些学校的招生人数有显著增加，在1935—1936年度，招生总数达到16,588,000名。通常未经注册的私塾学生700万名，也应该加到这个数字上去。

初等学校一般规模很小，甚至在城市里平均每所学校只有3个班左右。很少学校有10个班或20个班。在农村里和小镇上，通常只有一个班。注意到城市学校和农村学校每个学生的费用之间的差异，那是非常有意思的。在城市里，每个学生的费用高达28.71元（国币），而在农村人口占主要地位的甘肃省，每个学生的费用却只有4.77元（国币）。曾经有人说，中国农民很慷慨，给地主的孩子优良的教育，给自己的孩子低劣教育，而不给自己任何教育。

初等学校的数目，从1912年的86,318所增加到1935—1936年度的293,000所；同一时期招生数从2,795,475名增加到16,588,000名，经费从19,334,480元（国币）增加到106,594,685元（国币）。

**成人教育**——自从中国的“文艺复兴”[5]以来，成人教育已经受到重视，大众教育运动又给予成人教育以新的推动。1925—1927年的革命对成人教育提出了新的要求。自那时以来，政府已经承担起推进这一运动的责任。成人教育运动的发展情况是：从1928年的6,708所学校，206,201名学生，增加到1934—1935年度的38,000所学校，130万名学生；同一时期的经费，从466,562元（国币）增加到1900万元（国币）。所有各种类型的成人教育的经费总额，1928年是3,632,466元（国币），1934—1935年度是1690万元（国币）。

**义务教育**——1930年，教育部召开的第二次教育会议通过了一项在中国普及教育的二十年规划。1935年，颁布了《实施义务教育暂行办法大纲》。该大纲规定，1935年8月至1940年7月期间，凡属文盲成人及学龄儿童，必须上一年制小学；在1940年8月至1944年7月期间，必须学两年制课程；1944年8月以后，必须学四年制课程。每一小学区必须有一所一年制小学校。每五个至十个小学区必须有一所四年制小学校。儿童学龄定为8至12岁。对16岁至30岁成人应给予选择学校之权利。父母或监护人如不将儿童送往指定之学校，应罚款1至5元（国币）。

1936年法律最值得注意的一个特点是：成人教育应于6年内普及。教育部仅在1937年一年内，就分发了成人教科书550万册。大批无线电收音机亦经分发，以丰富教育计划。除1936—1937年度正常的教育经费外，教育部及各省政府还拨出15,847,000元（国币）专款以推广成人教育。通过这些努力，1935—1936年度共计增加一年制及四年制小学校33,000所，学生增加340万名，对1936—1937年度的预测是：一年制小学校增加46,000所，四年制小学校增加3,000所，共增招新生600万名。教育部长充满乐观情绪预言，两年内（至1937年底），中国就将有2300万名学生。

**培训农村教师**——给予农村教师以特别培训的运动开始于1927年的“晓庄实验”[6]。这一运动的倡导者们主张，农村教师应在农村环境中加以培训。未来的农村教师应在农民中生活若干时间，向农民学习，与农民同甘共苦。自1932年以来，私人实验已经停止，所有师范学校都已成为官办学堂。

现在有几种培训乡村教师的途径：第一，师范学校招收初中毕业生，给予三年制的学习课程；第二，特别师范课程，招收高中毕业生，学习一年；第三，短期师范学校，招收高小毕业生，给予四年制的学习课程；第四，附属于师范学校或中学校的师范班，招收初中毕业生，给予一年制的学习课程。

1932年，477所农村师范学校有50,150名学生，短期农村师范学校有18,712名学生；附属于中学校和职业学校的141个农村师范班的学生数字没有报道。

农村师范学校的教学科目包括公民、体育、军训（为男生设置），军事护理和家政学（为女学设置），卫生，语文，数学，地理，历史，生物学，化学，物理学，逻辑学，手工,美术，音乐，农业理论与实践，农村经济与合作社，水利，教育入门，教育心理学，小学科目、方法和管理，试验和统计，农村教育，教学实习，课外体育运动，自修。教学计划要求每周60小时，课堂教学和教学实习36小时，体育运动和自修24小时。

**农村教育实验**——在最近15年里，中国已经在农村教育这个领域内进行了若干实验，下面是其中比较出色的：

一、平民教育促进会：由晏阳初先生于1923年创建，目标有四：卫生、生计、公民、文艺。教育农村人民的全部工作是通过三个中介进行的，即学校、家庭和社会团体。促进会推行一套给农民掌握的经过精简的词汇，这套词汇通常以千字课闻名。促进会还设立了一所“乡村建设育才院”，由教育、农村经济、农业和公共卫生四个部门组成。

二、山东乡村建设研究院：由梁漱溟先生创建。该校在民政部门选定的两个县进行实验，每县分为若干区，区又再分为若干村。这一实验所根据的基本原则是“政教合一”。相应地，区的行政权力被赋予区校，村的行政权力被赋予村校。一个村校的组成人员由四个部分构成：（一）理事，即负责公共事务的乡绅；（二）校长，即被认为应该以身作则、用清规戒律教训村民的长者；（三）教师和视导员；（四）学生，即包括男、女、儿童在内的全体村民。全村经济建设的重点，放在各种形式的合作社上面。在保卫村庄方面，强调自卫和纪律。还建立了一个研究部和一个训练部。

三、江苏教育学院：由赵崇鼎博士于1928年创建。该院培训在农村教育方面从事研究和实验的农村教师和行政人员。已经进行了一次社会调查，对心理学、成人阅读材料和教育文献作了研究。该院保持着四个实验单位，其中两个单位专门以农村生活和农村问题为对象，它们具有改善大众生活条件、提高大众作公民的能力、普及大众教育这三重目的。其他实验则致力于：（一）利用农村房屋和农村教学人员从事教育活动；（二）节约学校课程的时间；（三）把儿童班与成人班结合起来；（四）组织村民进行农村改造。

由于目前的战争，所有这些实验都已移到湖南。据报道，这些实验相互间的合作，比以往更为密切了。关于这些实验较为详细的情况，在俞庆棠夫人所作《成人教育与中国农村》一文中可以看到。

**中国苏区的农民教育**——没有中华苏维埃区教育活动的报告，中国农民教育的状况就不完整。根据埃德加·斯诺的报道，红军在经过有两万万人口的各省时，召开了大规模的群众集会，演戏，课富人以重税，释放许多奴隶，宣传自由、平等和民主。他们向人民解释了土地革命和抗日政策的宗旨。他们还为传播文化、训练军队和传播政治理论而兴办了教育。许多群众组织了自学小组，在共产党人或有文化的人的领导下，用宣传材料当作课本来学习文化。

**大众教育运动**——这个运动有时叫做新的大众教育运动，指的是属于大众、由大众自办、为大众服务的一种教育组织。运动开始于大约十一年前，当时一批教授和学生从事研究和制定一种真正为农民服务的教育方法。运动的目的是在1935年定下的，就是要促进：（1）团结起来保卫中国的民主，（2）通过国际合作达到世界和平；（3）通过大众自己的努力提高他们自身的道德和文化水平；（4）免费的全民教育。

传递先生。在上述各种运动中，这最后的一种运动对我们目前的讨论很重要。运动的方法简单，使中国农民越来越能够自我教育，越来越有资格参加为获得自由而进行的伟大斗争。传递先生制已经制定出来；每次下课后，学生变成了先生，每个家庭变成了学习的中心。已经发现，有十分之一的中国农民是天生的先生，能够掌握大班级，加之，他们说的是农民的语言，又理解农民的问题，这些乃是他们独具的有利条件。

小先生。除了传递先生之外，“小先生”制也已经建立起来了。“小先生”是学校的儿童，他们上完一天学之后，回家去教自己的亲属和邻居。祖父母与孙辈玩、教、学在一块。在中国，几十万“小先生”正在帮助传播教育。他们所具有的特殊有利条件是：在女教师数量少、习惯上不赞成男教师教女孩及妇女的社会环境中，他们能够帮助妇女得到一些教育。

几年来，进步的农村学校已经遵循“来者不拒”的原则。由于农民和他们的孩子上学人数越来越多，小先生们便帮助解救困难局面，增加“不能来者免费送上门去”的口号，对于那些不能上学校学习的，小先生们便把教育送到他们的家里去。这样一来，学校的孤立状态就被打破，整个村庄成了学校，教育之光照射到每个角落。破庙里孤零零的教师顿时与几十个小同志结合起来，准能看到自身职业的新前景，并为自己应当去完成的历史使命而感到精神振奋。

新的拼写字母。大众教育运动对提倡为中国口语制定一套新的拼写字母也很感兴趣。北方方言、上海方言、广东方言和其他几种方言的拼写字母方案已经制订出来了。这些方案把中国口语作为多音节语言来处理，同时将代表不同声调的小符号取消了。有了新的拼写字母，不同地方的农民每天花上一小时，一个月之内就能用他们的方言阅读和写信。

利用公共场所进行教育。由于没有钱建造专用的房舍，人们便自愿把他们仅有的房间用来办学。不但庙宇、茶室和空房被这样利用了，而且树荫或大自然建造的露天大礼堂也足够用来开群众大会、唱歌、讲故事，学习朴素的真理，讨论国内和国际的问题。

**结束语**——有了传递先生、小先生、新的拼写字母、社会即学校，农民就能够有由他们自办、为他们服务的教育了。教育本身起了变化，它不再是少数人的奢侈品。它像阳光，人人可以享受；像空气，人人可以呼吸；像水，人人可以饮用。有了在农村共同合作的一切力量的帮助，一代新的农民正在中国崛起。赛珍珠女士所著《大地》中那个竭力为自己的小家庭捞到越来越多的土地，以便成为比别的农民兄弟更富裕的农民，不再成为别人仿效的榜样。在今天的中国，进步农民的愿望是：有足够的土地使每个农民都能过上小康的生活。新一代中国农民的情况，在下面一首诗里反映出来了：

**锄头舞歌**

手把个锄头锄野草，锄去野草好长苗。
五千年古国要出头，锄头底下有自由。

革命的成功靠锄头，锄头锄头要奋斗。
单个的锄头不中用，联合机器来革命。

## 参考文献

教育部：《中国教育年鉴》，1934年（中文版）；上海。

教育部：《月报》，第7卷第33~34期，1935年；上海。

《中国年鉴》（英文版），1936~1937，1937~1938；上海。

陈翰笙：《作为医治中国弊病万灵药的合作社》，载《远东评论》第6卷第7期。纽约，1937年3月31日。

陈翰笙：《中国现时的土地问题》。上海，1933年。

埃德加·斯诺：《西行漫记》。纽约，1938年。原载美国哥伦比亚大学师范学院国际研究所1938年《教育年鉴》

## 注释

① 分成地租　旧中国的地主向佃农榨取地租的计算方法之一。佃农每年都要把租耕土地的收获物，按一定比例上交给地主，如四六分需上交六成。

② 中国苏区　中国第二次国内革命战争时期建立的中华苏维埃共和国临时中央政府所管辖地区。

③ 斯诺　全名是埃德加·斯诺（1905—1972）。美国著名的作家，记者，曾四次来华访问，写了大量的报道和《西行漫记》、《大河彼岸》、《中国巨变》等书，较系统地介绍了我国新民主主义革命、社会主义革命和建设的史实。临终还留下遗嘱，将其骨灰一部分安葬于北京。

④ 陈翰笙　我国现代马克思主义经济学家。

⑤ 中国的“文艺复兴”　“文艺复兴”原指十四至十六世纪西欧新兴资产阶级反封建的新文化运动。陶行知说的“中国的‘文艺复兴’”，则是指起源于1917年《中国青年》的创办到1919年“五四运动”进入高峰的中国新文化运动。

⑥“晓庄实验”　即陶行知创办的晓庄学校所作的实验。

# 培养难童中人才幼苗的育才学校



## (1) 育才学校的创办

为了更好地了解育才学校，有必要说明育才是如何创办、又是如何着手发现并特别培养有科学天才之幼苗的。推动我创办育才这类学校的动力，主要来自三个人：迈克尔·法拉第[①]、托马斯.阿尔瓦·爱迪生[②]及昂多尔的桑德森[③]。

法拉第的童年是在利波先生的书籍装订店当学徒度过的。他工作速度很慢，为此，其他学徒向利波先生抱怨。但利波先生同情地说，法拉第一边装订书，一边也在看书；他还对他们说，任何人，只要像法拉第那样勤学，都能得到他的宽容。有一次，法拉第在装订一本百科全书时，发现只有两页纸论述电学这样一个有趣的题目，这当然不能满足他求知的渴望。如饥似渴地读完这两页以后，他决定："总有一天，我要写一本论述电学的书。"后来，一位顾客送票给他听汉弗莱·戴维的讲座，又帮他进了汉弗莱·戴维的实验室工作。法拉第终于实现了自己的诺言。

由于中国还未普及学校教育，可以估计到，许多天才处于繁杂的学徒工作重压之下。现代教育家可以在他们中间发现许多天才。利波的同情、理解及宽容，不仅值得店主、厂主学习，也值得学校教师学习。

托马斯·阿尔瓦·爱迪生的童年，他母亲S.纳西·爱迪生太太对儿子的同情和关心，是推动我创办育才学校的极大动力。众所周知，童年时爱迪生喜欢摆弄化学药品，由于他不能让旧式的教师满意，入学仅三个月就被学校开除了。他母亲很了解自己的儿子，允许他在地下室里继续做实验，并亲自教他历史和地理。正是在慈母的关怀之下，在他自己天才的推动之下，爱迪生才为科学、为人类的幸福作出了这样多的贡献。这两件事给我的印象颇深。有天赋科学才能的孩子，要早点学科学；天才儿童的教师，应从爱迪生母亲的态度上学到更多的东西。

到1931年底，第一次上海战争[④]爆发之前，我已为商务印书馆译完了“昂多尔的桑德森”，但不幸的是，日本人的战火，把手稿烧光了。这本书便一直未出版。从那以后，桑德森先生的思想便成了我最好的朋友和导师。他强调学识要广博的主张，在育才得到实现。这就是育才常给参观访问者留下“儿童大学”这一印象的部分原因。我还觉得他把科学人格化及社会化的思想最为重要。领导一个科学的世界，用科学原则来管理世界，这是桑德森对人类最大的贡献，是他留给子孙万代最好的忠告。我们一直在与长年的偏见、反科学的习惯和传统作斗争，努力用这些重要的思想指导我们的实践。

## (2) 育才学校的三点准则

1. 兴趣：

以少年儿童持续地对某些具体活动极感兴趣作为基本考虑，通过专门提供环境和养分，我们致力于对有才华的少年儿童进行哺育和指导，使之充分发展，进而深入到未知事物的领域中去。

2. 理解：

以少年儿童的全面智力作为基本考虑，通过施行文化教育，我们致力于对有才华的少年儿童进行哺育和指导，使之对其自身的地位和作用有更深入的理解，对生活的各个方面跟世界和人类社会的历史发展之间的相互关系有更广泛的理解。

3. 爱心：

以少年儿童乐于助人为基本考虑，通过集体生活，我们致力于对有才华的少年儿童进行哺育和指导，使之形成对人类更为崇高的爱心。

## (3) 育才学校的指导方针

1. 一副超凡出众的头脑。

2. 两只强健的手。

3. 三个圆环。——育才学校的校徽由三个圆环组成。圆环象征着开诚布公、一往无前和勤奋努力。第一个环代表学校的团结，第二个环代表中华民族的团结，第三个环代表民主和进步世界的团结。

4. 打开文化宝藏的四把钥匙：（1）中文，（2）一门外语，（3）数学，（4）科学方法。

5. 通向真理的五条道路：（1）实际行动，（2）书本知识，（3）向老师请教，（4）向朋友请教，（5）思考。

6. 六个学习组：育才学校有六个专门的学习组：（1）音乐，（2）绘画，（3）戏剧，（4）文学，（5）自然科学，和（6）社会科学。

7. 每周七天：富有创造性的集体生活。

8. 八点考虑：（1）什么？（2）为什么？（3）谁？（4）何

时？（5）何地？（6）怎么样？（7）什么数字？（8）什么方向？前面六点考虑毋须解释，（7）、（8）两点是为了确立准确的观念和富有生气的前景而新加上的。

9. 九倍于九难：有一则传奇故事告诉我们说，唐代的玄奘法师历经了八十一难才从西天取到佛经。我们应当将其当成事实，去面对生活中的艰难险阻。

10. 力量的十次乘方加上纯洁无瑕的心灵，以在生活的斗争中赢得胜利。

## （4）育才学校情况介绍

**目的**　教育天才难童。

**程度**　小学和中学。准备成立一个专科学校。

**课程**　全年上课。四分之三的时间按部颁标准学习普通课程，四分之一的时间则按儿童的兴趣和才能学习特殊课程。

**特殊学习**　包括音乐、戏剧、绘画、舞蹈、文学、自然科学和社会科学等选修课。一旦准备就绪，还要开设另外两门选修课：农业和工艺。

**教职员**　在国外获得学位的教师9名；大学毕业程度教师33名；高中毕业程度的教师及职员19名；教职员总数61名；教职员家属17名。

**学生**　正规学生320名；田间学生19名；农村识字小组学生，包括农民、煤矿工人、妇女、穷苦孩子共1500名；在音乐俱乐部学音乐的学生140名；接受育才教育总人数为1960名。320名正规学生中，男学生191名，女学生129名；难童及赤贫学生共198名，自费学生122名。他们来自全国17个省及2个其他国家。

**工人**：校工及农工40名。

**设备**：书22,000册，钢琴4架，小提琴6把，大提琴1把，科学仪器1000多件，校属土地55亩，租地300亩。

**财经情况** 美国援华联合会[5]及其他朋友为新难童提供了几笔经费。从某种程度上讲，这些钱顶住了通货膨胀带来的物价上涨。但要维持以前接收的难童及贫苦学生的费用，经费还远远不够。元月份的开支预算为590,000元，由于物价猛涨，八月份的开支预算就增加到四倍多，达2,400,000元，为支付这笔款项，美国援华联合会将提供1,400,000元，英国援华组织将提供170,000（2,000,000÷12）元，中学救济会提供160,000元，全国救济会提供15,000元，育才的朋友及其他来源还可提供468,000元，共计2,213,000元。这样一来，八月份的赤字就只有187,000元了。

**需要项目**

| | |
|---|---|
| （1）添置科学仪器 | 5,000,000元 |
| （2）教师工资将从8,500元增加到15,000元<br>共60名教师，每月需要390,000元， | 共计4,680,000元 |
| （3）增加营养费，每人每月1000元，<br>316人共需316,000元， | 共计3,792,000元 |
| （4）全年平均预算（187,000元×12） | 2,244,000元 |
| （5）扩大生活教育研究所基本建设费用 | 5,000,000元 |
| （6）成立农业系基本建设费用 | 3,000,000元 |
| （7）成立工艺系基本建设费用 | 7,000,000元 |
| （8）为50多名有才能的穷苦儿童<br>设立奖学金，每个儿童每月<br>8,000元，一年共需100,000元 | 5,000,000元 |
| 总计 | 35,716,000元 |

## （5）手脑相长歌（育才校歌）

人生两个宝，
双手与大脑，
用脑不用手，
快要被打倒。
用手不用脑，
饭也吃不饱，
手脑都会用，
才算是开天辟地的大好佬，

### 注释

① 迈克尔·法拉第（1791—1867）　英国物理学家和化学家。通过实验研究，重大发现很多。

② 托马斯·阿尔瓦·爱迪生（1847—1931）　美国发明家，在电报、留声机、电话、照明等方面有许多发明。

③ 桑德森（1857—1922）　英国的中学教育家。在昂多尔中学任教时，提出的教学法，对英国有较大影响。

④ 上海第一次战争　即1932年的“一·二八”抗战。

⑤ 美国援华联合会　美国人民在我国抗日战争时期援华的一个联合组织。

# 全民教育

**一　计划名称**　为四万万五千万中国人民推广民主教育的初步计划。

**二　主持单位**　生活教育社及育才学校。

**三　指导原则**

（一）民主第一。过民主生活以学民主。需要根据民主思想从根本上重建学校及学制，使属于大众、由大众自办，为大众服务的教育在中国蓬勃发展。民主不仅是治疗中国疾病的盘尼西林[①]，而且也是输血，使中国人民有新的活力去创造一个较好的国家。

（二）全民教育。不论宗教、种族、财富及所属阶级有何不同，男孩与女孩机会均等，男子与女子机会均等，成人与儿童机会均等。

（三）全面教育。心、脑、手并用。学政治、学经济，学文化相结合。健康、科学、劳动、艺术及民主将构成和谐的生活。

（四）终生教育。培养求知欲。学习为生活；生活为学习。只要活着就要学习。一旦养成学习习惯，个人就能终生进步不断。

（五）早在婴孩期就必须奠定民主教育的基础。或许，目前处理这个问题最好、最经济的办法是通过教父母兄弟姐妹，尤其是通过教母亲、姐妹及女佣来教婴儿。

（六）认识到中国还是个农业国，必定很穷，所以我们必须以最低廉的价格，给民众提供有益的文化粮食。让1200万名普通小学生利用写字课抄大众读本，一个月以后，就有1200万本书供民众使用了。上课最好安排在白天，以节省灯油。筷子蘸水就可以在桌上练习写字。课本没有准备好，街道上的招牌也可以当作一课。教育费用高昂就意味着没有教育或是只为极少数人的教育。

（七）社会即学校。动员社会上现有的一切可能动员的力量、学校和其他机构以及个人尽力为民众服务。庙宇、茶馆、监狱、兵营、商店、工厂、残废士兵医院、普通学校不上课的时间和空出的教室，都应给识字小组及训练中心使用。八千万受过一段时间再教育的识字成人可以作为教师，帮助家人及邻居进步。

（八）培养责任感、荣誉感及发自内心的与他人分享知识的迫切愿望。懂得了一项真理的人有传递这项真理的责任和特权。学会一个字的人就有资格教那个字，也有责任教那个字。有了与他人分享知识的欲望，才会认为这样做是一种乐趣。

（九）根据与同胞分享真理的原则，我们把小先生培养成为免费教育的先锋。大约二十三年前，我们认识了第一位小先生。从那以来，这样做的一些优点终于表现出来了，对于在像中国这样的国家普及教育，这些优点是必不可少的。

1. 已经发现，小先生制是解决女子教育难最有效的手段。

2. 拜儿童为师的成人，必然获得新生，变得像儿童一样，并受到青年精神的感染。

3. 小先生手中的知识，不再是出卖的商品，而是免费赠送给全民的礼物。

4. 通过教学，小先生对课程内容会了解得更清楚、更透彻，还从他们的教育对象身上学到很多重要东西。

5. 招生的性质改变了。来者不拒；不能来者能通过免费送教育上门的办法受到教育。

6. 学校本身也起了变化，扩大了许多倍。社会变成学校；所谓的“学校”变成一间教室，更现实地说，变成发电室，通过小先生输送光、热和力；小先生就像通电的电线一样，把学校与社会的千家万户联结起来。这样，所有的社会成员便都能享受发电室发出的光、热和力了。然后，转过来小先生又从各家各户的小发电机上带来一切，增加中心发电室的功率，使之能将更多的光、热和力送给民众。

7. 乡村学校中孤独的教师也变了。他不再孤零零地教书、生活、做饭，孤零零地奋斗了。他一下子就成了50个或100个小同志的队长。这些小同志也不再是些小书呆子，而是活跃的小先生、小工人、小战士，而首要的是，他们是中国民主的小建设者。

（十）分享真理的原则不仅产生了小先生，而且产生了传递教师。我所见到的最能干的民众教师，来自广大人民群众，来自农民、工人、工匠及商店学徒。他们一学了那么几课书，就开始不拘形式地帮助别人。换句话说，他们就成了传递教师。在这一阶段，他们非常热情，其中能干的人可以培养成为最好的传递教师。

（十一）农村及收复地区民众的教育应当最受重视。

（十二）鼓励民众边学习、边工作。决不要为一张学校毕业文凭而扔掉饭碗。

（十三）无论何时何地，只要有必要，有可能，就使用罗马化（即拉丁化）文字。

（十四）最充分地利用广播、电影、飞机、铁路、轮船，把“民主教育”的思想、人员及物资输送到我国最边远的角落，以使我国最落后的地方也能尽早实现民主。

（十五）鼓励人民的首创精神，资助地方试验。

（十六）从群众中发现和挑选人才，把他们推荐到育才学校或其他合适的学校及其他机构受特殊的、高级的训练。

（十七）本计划仅限于研究、试验、训练、出版、示范、推广和激发等活动，并向政府及其他机构提出建议，供他们参考并在全国范围内采用。

（十八）与其他国家交流教育民主化进展的情况和经验。

**四　实现的可能性**

十二年前在贯彻上述原则时，山海工学团在半年之内，不花政府一分钱，在25个村庄普及了免费教育。生活教育社领导的这场运动，在九个月内，就在23个省铺开，并继续在发展，直到思想控制介入为止。从那时起，随着民主的倒退，该运动的声势也减弱了。当然，17个解放区除外。在这些解放区，小先生制蓬勃发展，方兴未艾。小先生队伍正在扩大，为在那儿居住的1亿民众服务。最近，随着民主潮流的回归，一所学校，即育才一所学校，就为附近4,500名成人和儿童提供了受教育的机会。如果113所大学、2,278所中学、218,758所小学及79,550个属教育部管辖的社会教育组织，贯彻同样的原则，以同样的速度，做同样的事情，把它们合起来，就可以使3.5亿人继续学习和进步。当然，学校分布不平衡会打个大折扣。但在民主的鼓舞下，有政府力量的支持，有现成的读本和材料，有自愿提倡教育、竞相办教育等活动在全国的蓬勃开展，几乎不容置疑，300,699个用小先生和传递教师武装起来的学校，一年以后可以使人数达到1亿；再加上受过再教育的8000万有文化的成人的帮助，四年就可以完成全部任务了；即使把所有意外的障碍都估计在内，至多也只要十年他们就可以完全成功。一旦养成学习的习惯及与他人分享知识的习惯，他们就会依靠自身的力量向前进，因而不断朝着民主方向的进步就会得到极为可靠的保证。

**五　发动运动第一年的预算**（1945年10月1日至1946年9月30

日)：

(一) 研究所　　140,000元

根据民主的精神，研究下述问题、存在的困难及解决的方法：

1. 农民教育
2. 工人教育
3. 店主及学徒的教育
4. 残废士兵的教育
5. 女子教育
6. 适应蒙古生活的教育
7. 适应西藏生活的教育
8. 适应苗族生活的教育
9. 适应东土耳其斯坦[②]生活的教育
10. 异常儿童教育
11. 囚犯教育
12. 健康教育
13. 科学教育
14. 手工、农艺、工艺等教育
15. 戏剧作为民众教育的手段
16. 音乐作为民众教育的手段
17. 绘画作为民众教育的手段
18. 进一步研究小先生制
19. 现存教育制度的重建及军队教育
20. 有知识的人及领导人的再教育

| | | |
|---|---|---|
| 研究教授40人 | 每人1,000元 | 共40,000元 |
| 研究助手80人 | 每人500元 | 共40,000元 |
| 交通费 | | 10,000元 |
| 图书馆 | | 20,000元 |
| 房屋 | | 10,000元 |

| | | | |
|---|---|---|---|
| 设备 | | | 10,000元 |
| 函电 | | | 2,000元 |
| 杂费 | | | 2,000元 |
| 总计 | | | 140,000元 |

（二）行政费用

| | | | |
|---|---|---|---|
| 所长秘书处 | | | 60,000元 |
| 秘书 20人 | 每人500元 | 共 | 10,000元 |
| 现场指导主任30人 | 每人1,000元 | 共 | 30,000元 |
| 交通费 | | | 5,000元 |
| 房屋 | | | 1,000元 |
| 设备 | | | 12,000元 |
| 函电 | | | 1,000元 |
| 杂费 | | | 1,000元 |
| 总计 | | | 60,000元 |

（三）收复地区及普通地区之十个战略

| | | | |
|---|---|---|---|
| 中心的推广示范人员训练所 | | | 600,000元 |
| 教授100人 | 每人1,000元 | 共 | 100,000元 |
| 推广示范人员25,000人接受1—3个月训练 | | | |
| 1. 部分交通费资助 | | | 150,000元 |
| 2. 部分伙食资助 | | | 150,000元 |
| 3. 10幢房屋 | | | 10,000元 |
| 4. 学校设备10套；广播、电影、戏剧、音乐及医疗全套器材100套 | | | 150,000元 |
| 5. 25,000人的印刷材料 | | | 30,000元 |
| 6. 杂费 | | | 10,000元 |
| 总计 | | | 600,000元 |

（四）100个示范中心：收复地区及普通地区

| | | | |
|---|---|---|---|
| 共100个 | | | 100,000元 |

| | | |
|---|---|---|
| 主管人100名 | 每人500元 | 共 50,000元 |
| 助手100人 | 每人400元 | 共 40,000元 |

印刷所为1,000,000人免费提供阅读材料

训练中心免费补充的示范全部用品

| | |
|---|---|
| 杂费 | 10,000元 |
| 总计 | 100,000元 |

(五) 资助5,000个地方组织

意欲对人民实施民主教育的地方学校或组织，可以申请书籍、出版物、技术训练及示范，只要地方机构同意根据申请单位的经济情况承担部分费用（从1/10到1/2）。

书籍和出版物在5,000,000套至9,000,000套之间，在不超出预算的条件下，将由印刷所供应。

技术训练和示范将由训练中心提供部分粮食补助和交通补助，以及所需之附加费用。

(六) 要有一个编辑委员会及一个印刷所，它们能够不断供应10,000,000人的文化粮食，并且自身能够进一步发展。第一年，我们希望出4册大众读本，印数10,000,000册。人民图书馆的第一层书架上有100本一套的书，每10人的识字小组要一套，我们就需要1,000,000套，总共100,000,000本书，其次，才是供10个训练所、100个示范中心的25,000人使用的专著、期刊及各种材料，供1,000,000个小先生用的指导书籍；最后才是供1,000,000个识字小组使用的周刊。每组一份。

1,100,000元

| | | |
|---|---|---|
| 行政费用 | | 20,000元 |
| 编辑20人 | 每人700元 | 共 14,000元 |
| 印刷工人12人 | 每人700元 | 共 14,000元 |
| 印刷机及全套设备 | | 46,000元 |
| 油墨 | | 6,000元 |
| 纸 | | 1,000,000元 |

| | |
|---|---|
| 总计 | 1,100,000元 |
| 以上各项总计 | 2,000,000元 |

**六　财政运动**　我们计划从国内的朋友中募集相当于1,000,000元的资金，从对中国的进步感兴趣的盟友中募集相当于1,000,000元的资金。“中国运动”9月18日就开始了。我们希望引起100,000位中国朋友的兴趣，这些朋友的捐款能与盟友的赠款相称。

**七　预期的结果**　如果条件有利，募集到2,000,000元，我们便能在第一年，对600万到1000万人进行民主文化的基本教育，把他们都变成“钓鱼人”。这些人将把人民大众引上民主之钩。这样做，将大大推动和刺激第二年及其后每一年的运动。十年内，既有个人学习的欲望，又爱好集体分享知识的四万万五千万中国人，将成为中国和世界民主不可摧毁的栋梁，不可战胜的保卫者。这并非奢望，而是可望实现的。

出自1945年9月18日生活教育社版

Education For All 一书

## 注释

① 盘尼西林　英文Penicillin的译音，即青霉素。

② 东土耳其斯坦　指解放前新疆维吾尔族居住地区。

# 就南京“下关事件”对外国记者发表谈话*

我们相信，在南京对和平代表进行非常有组织的袭击，是中央政府内的一个小集团所为。他们需要战争，因为只有通过战争，他们才能够继续当权，因为无论民主运动还是和平运动都是同他们的野心直接对立的。

上海人民团体联合会是在5月5日成立的，有54个单位①。组织联合会的主要目的是争取民主进步，因为没有民主，中国人民就得不到进步。全国和平运动于5月间发动，并于6月23日举行的一次群众大会上正式开始，运动参加者十万人，五万人参加了这次群众大会。

上海人民团体联合会选派十一名代表至南京为和平请愿。他们刚到镇江，冒充难民的人就企图袭击他们。但未得逞。当代表到达南京时，所谓的难民就包围了他们。

若干宪兵和警察试图将代表四人带入一个房间，而将其余代表带入另一个房间。警察在场时，暴徒们没有进行袭击；而当警察一撤走，袭击就开始了。

---

* 本篇系摘自1946年6月26日上海英文《字林西报》关于《陶行知博士为下关事件等问题向外国记者发表谈话》的报道，报道中指出：“这次和平运动的主持者是上海人民团体联合会、民主促进协会和上海争取和平协会。”“下关事件”，是1946年6月23日发生在南京下关车站国民党特务殴打由上海赴南京请愿的和平代表马叙伦、胡厥文、蒉廷芳，包达三，张䌹柏、盛丕华、阎宝航、吴耀宗、雷洁琼、陈立复、陈震中等11人事件。今题为编者所拟。

袭击不是难民干的，有三个理由：第一、难民不可能得到关于代表团的情报并如此迅速地组织一次袭击；第二；南京没有收容难民的大本营；第三、我们的目的是停止战争，这对难民是有用的，因为和平协议一经签署，他们就可以回乡了。所以，我们的目的是相同的。

我们的联合会需要真正的和平与民主。我们需要民主的和平、公正的和平。那是我们的主要目的。尽管遭到袭击，我们还是要继续斗争下去，直到和平降临中国、民主占支配地位为止。我们正在为民主而战斗，因为没有民主，就不可能有和平。

这次袭击乃是一系列袭击之一，与在昆明、重庆、成都等地发生的对学生、对人民的袭击相似。这些反动势力蓄意把“三民主义”变成法西斯主义的遮羞布，C·C·集团[②]对此次事件是负有不可推卸的责任的。

**回答记者的提问**

问：你们是不是要起诉？

答：中央政府里有一个喜欢促进战争的政治集团，那是一个法西斯集团。C·C·集团对此次事件是负有不可推卸的责任的。

由于我们的伟大目的是促进和平与民主，所以决定对袭击者不予起诉，而将此事留待舆论者加以评判。

问：贴在上海许多墙壁上诸如“美国兵离开中国”等等英文标语是否和你们有关？

答：我们的人民团体联合会是负有责任。只要美军留驻中国，更多的麻烦就会发生。

我们感激美国支援中国抵抗日本侵略，但是，日本人投降之后，关于美国陆战队之类的美军却竟然仍留驻中国。我们希望采取某种措施，以便美国对政府的援助得以推迟到团结民主的政府在中国建立之时。我们不愿意让好战集团得到鼓励去进行内战，因为我们相信，如果他们得不到这样的鼓励，内战早就可以得到制止。这是我们深信不疑的。

问：美军撤退，是不是会把共产党人引进来？

答：如果共产党人有和平民主的政治纲领，我们就欢迎他们；而如果国民政府有一个类似的政治纲领，那就更好。

问：联合会里有没有共产党员？

答：联合会里没有共产党员。

问：美军撤退，是否会构成对共产党人的间接援助？

答：如果美军撤退，和平的机会就会更大。联合会不鼓励共产党人打仗，也不鼓励政府打仗，双方势均力敌时，就会妥协。然而，如果一方感觉到有一个世界强国在支持它，它就无意讨论和平。

如果共产党人利用（美军）撤退，人民就会反对他们。

问：和平代表团何时返回上海？

答：他们是去为和平请愿的。群众大会命令他们只许成功，不许失败。他们必须赢得和平之后才能回来。如果他们失败了，有些代表可能回来，但是别的代表会被派去代替他们，直到我们获得永久和平为止。

问：蒋介石是否希望和平？

答：蒋介石将军有一种心理上的过敏反应，这种心理上的过敏反应使他相信，凡是要求和平或民主的人都是共产党人。但是，正如我已经说过的，我们的团体里没有一个成员是共产党人。

问：中文报纸对你们的态度怎么样？

答：现在上海就有六家中文报同情我们的联合会进行的和平运动。

**预告将向美国人民发出呼吁书的内容**

我将在最近几天之内发布一项我们的联合会向美国人民发出的呼吁书。呼吁书要求美国人民不要做任何有助于在中国爆发内战的事情。

呼吁书还指责中国的反动势力破坏马歇尔[3]将军的工作，并把“三民主义”变成法西斯主义的遮羞布。

呼吁书还将指出，中国需要用来进行建设的援助，而不需要用来进行破坏的援助。呼吁书断言，美国继续支持政府，只会鼓励法西斯主义者促进内战。呼吁书要求美国人民在中国人民为摧毁中国的法西斯主义而进行的无情战斗方面给予帮助。

## 注释

① 上海人民团体联合会……有54个单位　这是举行这次记者招待会时已加进联合会的团体数。会后不久，请求加进联合会的上海各界人民团体就达91个单位。

② C·C·集团　亦称CC集团或中统，是国民党的特务机关——国民党中央调查统计局的简称。由于它的负责人是陈果夫、陈立夫兄弟，“陈”字的罗马字拼音为Chen，故称CC。

③ 马歇尔（1880—1959）　美国的五星上将。1945—1947年任美国驻华特使，以“调处”为名，参与国共谈判。

## 附：告美国人民书

美国人民鉴：

你们能够决定，中国是否会经历一场毁灭性的内战。战火已经点燃。战火会不会蔓延，可以说完全取决于你们。如果战火蔓延，你们也将成为这一场战争的参与者。

这场内战将在作为你们忠实而友好的盟国的中国国土上进行。遭受屠戮的，将是中国人民，中国的城镇和乡村将被摧毁，中国的理想和希望将被窒息。

国际贸易将遇到困难，而经济发展也将受到阻碍。在这种情况下，就不会有为美国商品提供的市场了。世界工会运动将丧失掉统一而强大的中国劳工运动。科学、文化和教育将被扼杀。换言之，中国将再也不是一个可以使美国感到满意的盟国了。

我们知道，美国打算给中国人民提供支援和帮助，以使他们能够振兴和建设自己的国家。我们已经获悉，美国正准备采取如下的步骤：

一、批准增加对华贷款。

二、延长租借条约。

三、销售剩余作战物资。

四、保留驻华美国海军和海军陆战队。

五、支持美国在华军事机构。

对美国人民的无私援助，我们当然深抱谢意。但是，在这样的时候提供这样的援助，却只能引起我们深深的忧患。我们不知道，美国人民是否也和我们一样，怀有这样的忧患。

对在中国发动内战，你们不会承担什么责任。中国人民充分认识到自己的责任。他们对自己的历史的发展进程并非一无所知，他们意识到，如果不付出坚定的、一致的努力，他们就不可能赢得政治上和经济上的民主。反动派的既得利益不可能轻而易举地被清除掉，而个人的自由和经济上的发展机会，如不经过斗争，也不可能轻而易举地奠定基础。在为争取自由和民主而进行的战斗中，中国人民已经向美国、法国、英国和其他国家的人民学到了不少东西。

但是，在另一方面，对于美国在中国内战中所起的作用，中国人民却不能够承担责任。中国人民已经、并且还将继续向美国人民寻求指导和理解。他们怀着尊敬和友好的情谊接待了马歇尔将军，他们接受了他所提出的、充满希望与期待的建议。马歇尔将军在去年一月所付出的努力使中国更接近于和平与民主，超过了人们在当时所能抱有的期望，这样的事实使中国人民感到欣慰。

然而，在过去的六个月中，马歇尔将军的杰出贡献却遭受到反动力量蓄意的、全面的破坏。只要这些人还能够威迫和剥削中国人民，对于会不会将中国人民推入到内战中去，他们是毫不在乎的。他们是一群恶魔，宁可毁灭自己的国家，也不肯遵从人民的意愿。这些反动力量不仅反对中国的民主，还反对美国的民主和苏联的民主。

现在，这些反动力量在国民政府中占据着显赫的领导地位。他们为了要进行法西斯主义的勾当，已经抛弃了孙中山先生倡导的“三民主义”。此刻，他们查封报纸、逮捕学生、正在使私人企业破产崩溃。

显然，美国是打算通过充斥着反动力量的国民政府向中国人民提供支援和帮助。在这种情况下，对这样的支援和帮助，我们很难表示欢迎，因为我们知道，这种援助将会被用来维持内战、扩大内战。中国需要援助，那是为了建设，但是，目前给国民政府提供的任何援助都将是为着破坏。你们所作的奉献，本意是在增进和平与民主，但我们感到，那只会用来为法西斯主义张目，为中国内战火上浇油。

换言之，你们的租借条约、贷款、剩余作战物资、海军陆战队和军事机构，将把中国引入一场持久的内战之中，因为，中国人民为了在自己的国土上消灭法西斯主义，必将进行不屈不挠的斗争。未来的形势将对中国人民不利，但他们不会忘记，在美国人民为争取独立和民主的斗争中也有过类似的不利形势。从美国历史上的这些事件中，中国人民将获得为实现理想而战的必要启示，而美国的枪炮和金钱将帮助反动力量去遏制理想的实现。

没有外来的援助，反动力量就不可能将战争进行下去。缺少这样的援助，他们就将被打败。所以，他们乞求美国为他们的战争金库解囊掏钱。他们编造神话，去欺骗美国人民给中国提供援助。

我们坚信人民的主权，这就是为什么我们要直接向美国人民呼吁的原因。你们不答应的事情，美国政府就干不了。我们请求你们，不准你们的政府将我们争取和平和民主的机会毁于一旦；我们请求你们，努力维护我们之间外交、经济和文化方面的、亲密而互惠的关系。

1946年6月29日

# 祝贺美国独立纪念日[①]

## ——中国人民团体致美国人民

美国人民：

值此贵国独立纪念日，我们——下面署名的中国人民团体——特别高兴地向你们表示祝贺。

我们从非常强调基本人权的贵国《独立宣言》以及从阿布拉罕·林肯总统对《宣言》的极其深刻的意义所作的杰出解释受到了鼓舞。对此，为在中国建立一个民主共和国而不断地奋斗了六十年[②]的人们愿意向你们表示感谢。

自从“珍珠港事件”以来，我们两国人民已经在反对帝国主义反民主势力的共同斗争中结合起来了。我们的联合努力获得了胜利，胜利给予了我们新的机会去争取和平、进步和国际合作。我们盼望我们两国人民继续友好和互助，以使战争灾祸得以从亚洲消除，民有、民治、民享的政府一定要在我们两国很好地，真正地建立起来。

上海人民团体联合委员会执行委员会

全国和平运动促进委员会

1946年7月4日于上海

## 注释

① 本篇是陶行知为中国人民两团体起草的英文书信。据1946年7月4日上海《字林西报》载，这封祝贺信还同时发与美国总领事M. 戴维斯先生、G. 马歇尔将军、A. C. 吉勒姆将军、美国新闻处费正清先生、美国商会主席W. 潘特先生。

② 此系指孙中山1886年开始致力国民革命到1946年这一段时间中国人民为建立一个民主共和国的长期斗争过程。1925年3月12日孙中山积劳病逝，其遗嘱指出“余致力国民革命，凡四十年”。从1925年至1946年又过去20余年，故信中称“六十年”。

# LETTERS

# My Résumé And My Plan Of Life Career

*—To Dean J. E. Russell*

February 16, 1916

Dear Dean Russell,

It gives me great pleasure to acknowledge the receipt of your letter of Feb. the 11th, which asks me to give a brief account of my preparation and my plan of life career for the interest of the donors of the Livingston Scholarships. I want to tell you that it is my great pleasure to comply with this order.

I am now 22 years old. I was born in Hweichow — a place where communication is almost entirely cut off from the outside world. I received my early Chinese education from my father and other teachers until I was fourteen years of age when I went to a China Inland Mission School and studied under Mr. Gibbs, who was then the only man teaching Western subjects. After two years that school was closed up and Mr. Gibbs returned to England, I was then compelled to make an adventurous move to Hangchow with an idea of studying medicine. On account of the sharp discrimination there in that institution against non-Christians even in the matter of the course of study, I finally withdrew my registration after three days' stay. With this disappointment I went back to Hweichow and devoted myself to the study of English for another year. Then I proceeded to

Nanking University, where I am glad to say both Christians and non-Christians were welcome. Three years after my entering Nanking University the first Revolution broke out. When I came back to Hweichow I was made Secretary of the Assembly of Hweichow. There I served half a year. After that I resumed my study in Nanking. With the assistance of other students and the trust of University authorities I started and edited the Chinese Edition of the University Magazine. Under the guidance of Dr. Bowen and Dr. Henke, and being deeply impressed by Prof. Jenk's "Social Significance of the Teachings of Christ" I became a Christian in 1913. I received my first degree in June, 1914, which was the end of my fifth year in Nanking. With the assistance of my parents and friends I started for Illinois University in August. There I spent one year. Besides the amount of valuable education I got there, I also secured a by-product of my labor, i.e. an A. M. degree. During my second half year in Illinois I was the Secretary of the Students' club.

Columbia University was selected three years ago as my final goal in this country, but my coming here was delayed by the lack of means. My sole purpose in this life is to create a democracy by education and not by military revolution. After seeing the serious defects of the sudden birth of our Republic I was convinced that no genuine republic could exist without a genuine public education. My devotion to educational administration as a life career was crystalized last Summer at Lake Geneva, where I received my great inspiration from the Summer Conference of the Y. M. C. A. As I looked over all the institutions I knew of, again I found your Teachers' College to be the best institution for me to go. But to select an institution is one thing; to have sufficient means to enter such an institution is another thing. Since the death of my father in January, 1915, the whole burden of my family has fallen upon me and my financial condition is almost deadly handicapped. But fortunately soon after my decision to come to your Teachers' College, our government granted me a Partial Scholarship, which, together with some other miscellaneous assistance, gave me at least courage enough to make a start. However, New York is more expensive to live in than I anticipated. After half a year's stay I found my provision not sufficient for my successful study, so with Dr. Monroe's introduction I proceeded to apply for a Livingston Scholarship, which you have so generously granted to me. Besides my hearty thanks for this kind gift, I wish to assure you and the donors of the Livingston Scholarships that after two more years' preparation under Prof. Strayer and other faculties I shall go back to cooperate with other educators to organize an efficient system of public education for our people, so that they, following the steps of the Americans, will be able to develop and maintain a genuine democracy which is the only realisable Utopia of justice and liberty.

It would be of great interest to me if you will be kind enough to give me some of the names of the donors who live nearby in the city so that I may find some chance to meet each of them.

With best wishes and regards,

Very respectfully yours,

Wen Tsing Tao

**Note**

(1) Dr. H. C. Tao gave on this letter his address as "1010 Hartley Hall, Columbia University" and the address of the addressee as "Teachers' College, Columbia University".

(2) Wen Tsing Tao: The original name of Tao Heng-Chih. (See A BRIEF BIOGRAPHY OF TAO HENG-CHIH.)

# Requested To Send Representatives To China

*—To President of International Peace Conference*

To the President of the International Peace Conference:

In order to develop more effectively the I. P. C. in the Far East and to secure close connection between the movements in the Far East and West, we, the Chinese Delegation to the Brussel's Congress, do earnestly request the General Council of the I. P. C. to send representatives to China, as soon as possible, to act as liaison officers between the General Council and the Chinese National Committee.

We believe that such a step taken by the Council would greatly facilitate and promote the movement for peace and justice in the world and would be highly appreciated by the Chinese people.

7th Sept. 1936.

Chen Min Shu, Tao, H. C.

Shelley Wang, T. S. Chien,

Chang Tching Yuan

Hu Chou Yuan, P. A. Kiang.

Per H. C.

**Note**

H. C.: Initials of Heng-Chih (Tao).

# Asked To Forward US$100 To Nat'l Salvation Ass.

*—To Mr. Tsai Chen Hsin*

April 23, 1937

Dear brother Chen Hsin,

It has been a very long time since we departed. I am very glad to learn from other friends that you are successful in your business and are doing your best for the welfare of our fellow men. Enclosed you will please find a cheque for $100 gold for the use of the National Salvation Association. If you happen to meet friends in charge, I hope you will be kind enough to cash it for them. Meantime, I hope you will favor me with an early reply. Please tell me all about the recent development of our beloved country.

With best wishes,

Affectionately yours,

W. T.

**Note**

W. T.: Initials of "Wen Tsing", for Dr. H. C. Tao was originally named Tao Wen Tsing or Wen Tsing Tao. "W. T." was sometimes used as his penname in private letters.

# Cheque For US$200 For Nat'l Salvation ASS. & All-China Students Union

*—To Mr. Tsai Chen Hsin*



May 11th, 1937

Dear brother Chen Hsin:

Under separate cover you will please find a cheque for $ 200 gold. You are requested to hand $ 100 over to the National Salvation Association, and $100 over to the All-China Students Union. If they do not happen to come, will you try to enquire Mr. Liu Liang-mo, National Committee, Y. M. C. A., Museum Road? It may be possible to locate them through Mr. Liu. This is a little sum raised here or rather voluntarily contributed by the oversea Chinese friends. The home organizations are so much in need of money. I hope you will try your best to give it to the right and responsible persons before the 25th of this month. Hoping that you will give me a receipt by return.

With hearty thanks,

Affectionately yours,

W. T.

**Note**

Dr. H.C. Tao gave his address on this letter as "International House, 1414 E 59th St, Chicago, Ill".

# Draft For US$300 For 2 Patriotic Organizations

*—To Mr. Tsai Chen Hsin*

June 24, 1937

Dear brother C. H.,

Enclosed you will please find a draft for $300 gold, a duplicate of which has been sent to the paying bank by the same steamer. You are requested to cash it at once and divide it in equal shares of $150 each to be given to our two beloved Sisters. Please pass word to them as before so that they can come to take the money.

Many hearty thanks. Remember me to Mr. Liu and Mr. Hsi.

Fraternally yours,

W.T.

**Note**

(1) C. H.: Chen Hsin, i.e. Tsai Chen Hsin.

(2) two beloved Sisters: These "two Sisters" stood for "the National Salvation Association and the All-China Students Union" as could be seen in Dr. Tao's letter of May llth, 1937, to the same ad dressee Mr. Tsai Chen Hsin.

# To Leave Los Angeles For San Francisco

*—To Miss Woo Shu Chin*

August 1, 1937

Dear Miss Woo,

Your kind letter of June 22nd has just been received, so I know that you have gone home before my answer arrives. I suppose you must have given your home address to the Health Experimental Center, which will forward letters to you. If you have not received my answer, you better write to the Health Center. I have succeeded in securing a scholarship of $ 40 gold for you, mailed through the Bank of China, Hankow Road, Shanghai. You better write to the Bank, if you have not got it. I am now in Los Angeles, and will leave for San Francisco tomorrow morning. If you want to write me, it is better to write to the above address. They will forward it to me wherever I go. With best wishes.

Sincerely yours,

W. T.

## Note

Dr. H. C. Tao gave his address on this letter as "310 W 90th Street, New York City".

# Itinerary Abroad Arranged

*—To Miss Woo Shu Chin*

August 11, 1937

Dear Shu Chin,

I am very glad to receive your kind letter of July 8th and delighted to know that everything has reached you. I shall stay here for another ten days and then go to Mexico for a month. After that I shall give two lectures in Indiana and Miami Universities. I may leave for Europe by the end of October and may go back to China by way of Siberia. I am well. Hoping that you have a good time with your mother.

With good wishes,

Sincerely yours,

W. T.

**Note**

Dr. H. C. Tao gave his address on this letter as "Chinese Y. M. C. A., San Francisco, California".

# "Join The Fight For National Freedom!"

*—To Miss Woo Shu Chin*





August 22, 1937

Dear Shu Chin,

I suppose you are still in Hweichow. How are you? This is the time for all of us to join the fight for our national freedom. You can help a great deal in the medical work. Join the Red Cross! Write me how you are getting along. Wish you success. Long live China!

I am going to Mexico tonight at 8 and shall reach there in three days.

Your friend,

W.T.

**Note**

Dr. H. C. Tao did not give his address on this letter.

# Defeat Of Jap Imperialism Inevitable

*—To Miss Woo Shu Chin*



October 5, 1937

Dear Shu Chin,

I am now back from Mexico. I had a very pleasant time there. Mexico is a most interesting and inspiring country. I have learned many things and made many friends there. Most of the Mexican Indians looklike the Chinese. Some of them have similar facial features as the Northern Chinese; others look like the Cantonese. They were kind to me and I felt at home with them. Really we were relatives thousads of years ago.

I arrived at Chicago this morning. After I make a speech here before our people, I shall proceed to Indiana University, where I shall talk to the students tomorrow morning. I shall be at Washington D.C. on the 7th. I shall decide whether I shall stay here or return to China as soon as I know where I am most needed. I shall be able to know it as soon as I reach Washington D.C.

How are you getting along all these months? There are three things which can defeat Japanese Imperialism: 1. unified and persistent resistance by China; 2. rising of democratic forces in Japan; 3. moral and economic blockade by all nations in the world. I am now doing my best in awakening the friends in western countries. If Japan cannot get war materials from these nations, she will not be able to carry on the war.

Write me often. I wish to know your plan and your health. How are your mother and father? And your brother and the other two sisters of you three?

W. T.

**Note**

(1) Dr. H. C. Tao gave his address on this letter as "310 West 90th Street, New York City".

(2) the three sisters: Miss Woo Shu Chin and her two schoolmates Shen De Hua and Huang Tung Ling, who were often referred to as "the three sisters because they were close friends from the same province — Anhui.

# Additional Strength For Life's Struggle Needed

*—To Miss Woo Shu Chin*

December 7th, 1937

My dear Miss Shu Chin,

I want to thank you for your kind letter of October 30th. From this letter I know you are still in Hweichow with your mother. Really a mother's love is the purest. I wish my mother were still alive and could be here with me. I know how happy you have been all the time under the care of your mother. I only regret that you have forgotten me for so long a time. I think I received the last letter from you in August; nothing has come from you since then. I have been worrying over you as the war situation has become more and more serious.

I shall be here for another two months. And then I shall go back to China by way of Europe. I am very well. Only the news from home is distressing. All my boys have been scattered over four places, one in Hweichow, one in Nanking, two in Shanghai but living separately.

I hope you will write me oftener. Even a word from you will save me from worrying and mean additional strength for life's struggle.

W. T.

## Note

Dr. H. C. Tao gave his address on this letter as "310 West 90th Street, New York City".

# John Dewey's Statement

*(Drafted out by Dr. H. C. Tao on Dec. 6, 1937, for Prof. J. Dewey)*



Mr. Mahatma Gandhi
Wardha,
Central provinces,
India.

Wish you join us making following statement. Same request has been sent Messrs. Romain Rolland, Albert Einstein, Bertrand Russell. Cable suggestion to 320 East 72nd Street New York. Consent understood without hearing contrary in five days.

In view of wanton destruction of Oriental civilization and for the sake of humanity, peace and democracy, we propose peoples of all countries organize voluntary boycott against Japanese goods, refuse to sell and loan war materials to Japan and cease cooperation with Japan in ways that help her aggressive policy while giving every possible assistance to China for relief and self-defence until Japan has evacuated all her forces from China and abandoned her policy of conquest.

John Dewey

**Note**

John Dewey (1859–1952): Famous American philosopher and educationist.

**Annex**

## J. Nehru's reply to JOHN DEWEY'S STATEMENT

All India Congress Committee—Dec. 23, 1937—News-letter Congress Most Willing Cooperate for Humanity Peace Democracy Everywhere:

"I have received the following cable from John Dewey, Albert Einstein, Bertrand Russell and Romain Rolland from New York: 'IN VIEW OF WANTON DESTRUCTION OF ORIENTAL CIVILIZATION AND FOR HUMANITY PEACE DEMOCRACY, WE PROPOSE PEOPLES OF ALL COUNTRIES ORGANIZE VOLUNTARY BOYCOTT AGAINST JAPANESE GOODS, REFUSE TO SELL AND LOAN WAR MATERIALS TO JAPAN AND CEASE COOPERATION WITH JAPAN IN WAYS THAT HELP HER AGGRESSIVE POLICY WHILE GIVING CHINA EVERY POSSIBLE HELP FOR RELIEF AND SELF-DEFENCE UNTIL JAPAN HAS EVACUATED ALL HER FORCES FROM CHINA AND ABANDONED HER POLICY OF CONQUEST. WISH CONGRESS ENDORSE THIS STATEMENT GIVE PUBLICITY CALL ALL INDIA JOIN ACTION.'

The following reply has been sent by me to Dr. John Dewey:

'YOUR CABLE CONGRESS ALREADY EXPRESSED CONDEMNATION JAPANESE AGGRESSION FULL SYMPATHY CHINA CALLED FOR BOYCOTT JAPANESE GOODS AGREE GENERAL POLICY AND OBJECTIVE YOUR STATEMENT GIVING PUBLICITY CONGRESS MOST WILLING COOPERATE FOR HUMANITY PEACE DEMOCRACY EVERYWHERE FEELS ONLY TRUE BASIS

FOR THESE ELIMINATION FASCISM IMPERIALISM'.

In issuing these messages to the press I should like to draw the attention of the public again to the urgent necessity of abstaining from purchasing Japanese goods. Horror piles up on horror in China and armed might and the air-bomb and poison gas kill hundreds of thousands of her children and crush her very soul. We are sickened at the brutality and inhumany of the Chinese scene. But mere sympathy is not enough. We must give such help as we can. This help can be of two kinds: refusal to purchase Japanese goods and financial assistance for medical relief. I trust that Congress Committee and other organizations will carry on propaganda for this boycott. Donations for sending medical relief will be received in the A. I. C. C. office and will be forwarded to the proper quarters. An urgent demand for medical supplies has been received by us and I earnestly trust that the people of India will give what they can for the relief of suffering and tortured humanity in China.

—Jawaharlal Nehru

## Note

(1) Jawaharlal Nehru (1889—1964): Elected President of the Indian National Congress in 1936, 1937 and 1946. After Indian independence was won in August 1947 J. Nehru was Prime Minister of India till his death.

(2) All India Congress Committee: The central leading body of the Congress Party— the Indian National Congress.

# Arrangement For Trip To India Acknowledged

*—To Meheralli*

July 27, 1938

Dear Mr. Meheralli,

I was glad to have the splendid opportunity to meet you in London, and wish to thank you for your kindness in making arrangement for my trip to your great country. I have arrived here in time to catch S. S. ARAMIS, which will sail this afternoon and will arrive at Colombo on Aug. 5 according to schedule. I have to return to Colombo from India before August 19 so that I can sail on S. S. Marshal Joffre for China on August 19. Anything you have arranged for me will be agreed upon. Wherever there are Chinese friends, I wish to have 2 or 3 hours with them. Please ask your friends to locate them and arrange with them. If my finance can be reinforced when I reach Colombo, I wish to include Dehli and Buhda's Birth Place in the programme, possibly by taking advantage of air facilities. Hope you write your friends again. My salute to your Nation: PURNA SWARAJ!

Your friend,

H. C. Tao

## Note

(1) Dr. H. C. Tao gave his address on this letter as "Hotel Misr, Suez, Egypt".

(2) PURNA SWARAJ!: A Hindi expression, meaning "Complete Home Rule! ", used in the 40s of the 20th century by the Indian people, who, more often than not, put it at the close of their letters to show their strong will to win the final victory in their struggle for total independence against the then British colonial rule. The Indian people struggled for TOTAL independence because, though they were allowed to elect their own ministers at provincial level, the supreme power of a province was vested in the governor.

# Thanks For "Introducing Me To Your People" Expressed

*—To Mr. Meherallí*





Dear Mr. Meheralli,

I want to apologize for my failure to send you my article on *Chinese People's Education*. Unfortunately my manuscript has been packed by my friends for China and I could not take it out. However, I will tell your friends in India in person.

Your letter informing me about the arrangements in India must have already come on the steamer, and I may have the opportunity to read it this afternoon.

Thank you again for all the trouble you have taken in introducing me to your people. Following your advice, I am writing to Gandhiji, Mr. Tagore, Mr. Bose, Mr. Bannerji and Mr. Sinha this morning.

Your friend,

H. C. Tao

**Note**

(1) Dr. H. C. Tao did not give his address and the date of writing on this letter, but it is reasonable to judge, from what he stated in the letter, that he wrote it

also on July 27, 1938, at Hotel MisR, Suez, Egypt, and intended to send it along with the dated and addressed letter to Mr. Meheralli in London.

(2) Gandhiji: Mr. Gandhi or Mahatma Gandhi was very frequently referred to as "Gandhiji" in India, because, according to Mr. Jawaharlal Nehru in his *Autobiography*, it was Mr. Gandhi himself that preferred this to being otherwise addressed. The Hindisuffix"ji", according to Mr. Nehru, "conveys an idea of respect, something equivalent to Mr., Mrs., or Miss" (p. 29).

# Informed Of Arranged Visit To India

*—To Mr Gandhi*





July 27, 1938

Dear Mr. Gandhi,

Your teachings and sacrifice are always an inspiration to the Chinese people. I have long dreamed of a visit to your great country, and am very glad at last to have an opportunity to visit her now. Mr. Meheralli in London must have already written you about my proposed trip and the approximate date when I am to pay you my respect. I am leaving here tonight and scheduled to arrive at Colombo on Aug. 5. I can stay in India for 2 weeks. Mr. Meheralli's friends in Colombo or Calcutta are taking care of my itinerary. The time is too short for my purpose, but under your guidance I may learn the first lesson from New India. I anticipate the joy to see you soon.

Wish you Purna Swaraj!

Respectfully yours,

H. C. Tao

陶行知

**Note**

Dr. H. C. Tao gave on this letter his address as "Hotel MisR, Suez" and the name and address of the address as "Mahatma Gandhi, Shegan, Wardha District, India".

# Informed Of Visit To India

*—To Pres. Chandra Bose*

July 27, 1938

Dear Pres. Bose,

I am very glad that at last I have an opportunity to visit India on my way back to China. Mr. Meheralli in London must have already written you about my proposed trip and the time I am expected to reach Calcutta. I sail tonight on S. S. ARAMIS and reach Colombo on Aug. 5. From there I shall come to pay you my respect. I have read your great speech before the 51st Indian National Congress. I agree with you on every point except as regards Mr. de Valera's politics and the Labor Service Camp in Germany, on which I wish to be further enlightened when I see you.

Wishing you great success in leading your nation to freedom,

Respectfully yours,

H. C. Tao

**Note**

(1) Dr. H. C. Tao gave on this letter his ad dress as "Hotel MisR, Suez, Egypt" and the name and address of the addressee as "President S. S. Chandra Bose, Elgin Road, Calcutta, India".

(2) The Indian National Congress: The largest political party in India, founded in 1885. Before the British colonial rule in India came to an end in August 1947, the Congress party had played an important role in the struggle of the Indian people for independence against the then British colonialists.

# "Anticipating The Joy Of Seeing You Again"

*—To Dr. Tagore*

July 27, 1938

Dear Dr. Tagore,

It is about two decades since I had the splendid opportunity to meet you in Peking. Your message always remains a treasure of our people. I am glad to report that at last I shall have an opportunity to pay a short visit to your great country on my way back to China. I shall arrive at Colombo on Aug. 5 on board S. S. ARAMIS. I can spend about 2 weeks in India and sail on S. S. Joffre on Aug. 19. As soon as I reach Calcutta I will write you again about the date when I shall pay you my respect.

Anticipating the joy of seeing you again very soon,

Respectfull yours,

H. C. Tao

**Note**

Dr. H. C. Tao gave on this letter his address as "Hotel MisR, Suez" and the name and address of the addressee as "Dr. Robindranath Tagore, Sandimkedan, Bengal".

# Wish To Understand Most Important Work In India

*—To Dr. Bannerji*



July 27, 1938

Dear Dr. Bannerji,

Mr. Meheralli in London must have already written you about my proposed trip to your great country. I have long desired to learn firsthand about New India and I am glad that I can pay a brief visit to her on my way back to China. I shall arrive at Colombo on August 5 and leave Colombo on the 19th. So I have about 2 weeks' stay in India. The time is too short, but with your help I hope I may understand some phases of the most important work that is going on in India. Anticipating the joy to see you soon, and with thanks for your help in making my visit instructive,

Yours very sincerely,

H. C. Tao

**Note**

Dr. H. C. Tao gave on this letter his address as "Hotel MisR, Suez" and the name and address of the addressee as "Dr. Suresh Bannerji, 18 Herrison Road, Calcutta, Inrdia".

# Object Of Visiting India "Is To Learn"

*—To Mr. Sinha and Mr. Brakash*



July 27, 1938

Dear Sirs,

In London I was introduced to Mr. Meheralli, your friend, who has written you about my proposed trip to India on my way back to China. My object of coming to your great country is to learn. I wish to learn something from your peasants, your workers, your teachers and your great leaders. The limited amount of time, 2 weeks, can only permit me to get a glimpse of your great civilization. At the same time if opportunity offers, I may report to your people what is going on in China. I shall arrive at Colombo on August 5 and leave there for China on the 19th. I have not seen Mr. Meheralli's letter yet in regard to the arrangements in India, but I shall follow whatever arrangements he has made with you during my 2 weeks' stay in India. Anticipating the joy to see you,

Yours very sincerely,

H. C. Tao

**Note**

Dr. H. C. Tao gave on this letter his address as "Hotel MisR, Suez" and the address of the addressee as "c/o Geneda Office, Badna, India".

# Answers To Questions About Yu Tsai School

*—To Mrs. Louise K. Rugg*

(June or July) 1942

My dear Mrs. Rugg,

Two copies of your kind letter of March 16th have just been forwarded to me by YWCA from Chengtu. It reminds me of the pleasant hours we spent together when you and Professor Rugg visited China years ago. I heartily congratulate you upon serving on the China Aid Council and participating in the splendid work of the United China Relief, which is interested in giving material as well as cultural help to Chinese War Orphans to some of whom have had the honor to render my service during the last three years. It is most delightful to learn that at last my brief conversation with Miss Gerlach has been made known to friends so far away in space. You are right, "We are now at War together." Indeed, we are fighting together for a common victory—the victory of liberty over fascism and Hitlerism. The war may not be a short one. Children grow fast. Whosoever give the best care to their children will win the real victory. It is a most noble act to extend love of one's own children to children of other lands.

In compliance with your request, let me answer your questions in the order you asked them:

1. We have 165 children in our school. Nine tenths of them are refugee children who have lost their homes because of Japanese invasion. Of the refugee children, more than half are without parents and are real orphans. But even those who have parents can not receive any support from them either because family fortunes have been lost or because high cost of living has reduced their parents to marginal existence. Therefore, the entire burden of subsistence and education of 150 children falls upon the school.

2. The school started in the fall of 1939 with a budget of 3,000 Chinese dollars a month. It has been steadily increasing until now it amounts almost to 40,000 Chinese dollars a month. Still, our budget is lagging far behind in view of the fact that the index of the cost of living has had a much greater increase during the same period.

Average Monthly Appropriation for the first 5 months, 1942

| | |
|---|---|
| A. Administrative Expenses | $1,500 |
| B. Salaries and Food of Staff | 8,000 |
| C. Housing Cost | 2,000 |
| D. Food of Refugee Children | 18,000 |
| E. Clothing | 3,000 |
| F. Medical Care | 1,000 |
| G. Equipment | 2,000 |
| H. Light and Fuel | 1,000 |
| I. Printing and Text Books | 1,500 |
| J. Miscellaneous Expenses | 1,500 |
| Total | $39,500 |

3. The total cost per child in our school is about $240 a month, including medical care, clothing and education. For food alone, the monthly cost per child is about $120 Chinese dollars. It is still on the increase.

4. Children in our school are given opportunities for play, work and study. For play, we have basketball, volleyball, gymnastics, table tennis, chess, ets. As to work, our children do the cleaning of the dormitories and classrooms, and carry on other domestic activities. Besides, every student is given a piece of land, 1/10 of a *mow*, for growing vegetables for community consumption, but each is entitled to a portion of the produce for his own benefit. As to study, the students are allowed 2/3 of the time to pursue general studies and 1/3 of it to pursue special studies fit for their respective interest and aptitude. As the school is running all the year round, not only can our children be promoted at the same rate as those in other schools, but also they can acquire a more solid foundation in special studies.

5. The general studies follow the elementary and junior middle school curriculum prescribed by the Ministry of Education. The special studies consist of elective courses in Music, Dramatics, Painting, Literature, Natural Sciences and Social Sciences. To these, Agricultural and Mechanical Arts will be added soon when new students are selected. Each student is allowed to select one special course to pursue, provided he has shown evidence of a special aptitude for it.

6. We have now a staff of 26 teachers. On the average each special course has two specialists as directors, the rest being teachers of general subjects. Two-thirds of the teachers are college graduates or returned students and are trained. We have no training school as such in connection with the institution. But our Research Institute, bringing all teachers together by study of problems, reading of books, periodical conferences and inspection tours, is actually a training centre for teachers in service.

7. We have about $20,000 a month available, of which $ 8,500

come from the Central Relief Commission. About $ 20,000 Chinese dollars have to be raised.

8. We have a plan to increase our student population to 400 and wish to take in more talented refugee children. For the purpose of improving nutrition of students and staff, we hope you will find it possible to propose to the United China Relief to give us a monthly grant of $2,000 gold or an yearly grant of $ 24,000 gold so as to enable us to carry out our new plan. Of the sum, $15,000 gold will be used for food, $5,000 gold for reinforcing our technical staff, and $4,000 gold for the increase of our equipment and the improvement of our medical service.

You will have a better understanding of Yu Tsai School if I tell you some stories of how it has come into existence. "The childhood of Thomas Alva Edison and the sympathetic care of his mother, Madame S. Naney Edison, has given a profound impetus to my founding of Yu Tsai. As you know, Edison, when a boy, was fond of playing with chemicals. Being dissatisfied with by his old-fashioned teacher, he was dismissed after only three months' schooling. His mother had a better understanding of her boy, allowed him to continue his experiments in the cellar and taught him history and geography herself. It was under the care of a kind mother and the push of his own genius that he made so many contributions to science and to the welfare of mankind. Two things impressed me: for one who is gifted with scientific aptitude, the study of science should begin early and teachers of gifted children should learn more from the attitude of Edison's mother." This is one of the five influences that have led me to found this institution. In order that this letter should not be too long, I have to satisfy myself in telling you just this one story and leave the rest for the future. Your kind letter gives me a sense of relief because the major part of my time has been spent in a new form of athletics — racing with rice, and need to find some way to raise enough fund so that I and my colleagues may devote our energy to the real education of our refugee children.

I thank you for your kind endeavour and look forward to hearing good tidings from you. Kindly give my best regards to Prof. Rugg and Miss Gerlach.

Your friend,

Heng Chih Tao





## Note

(1) Dr. H. C. Tao gave on this letter his address as "Yu Tsai School, Beipei, Chungking, China" and the address of the addressee as "The Walt Whitman School, 25 East 78th Street, New York, U.S.A.".

(2) Miss Gerlach: Talitha Gerlach (1896— ), born in U.S.A.; served as an expert from the U. S. in China Welfare Fund (renamed China Welfare Institute in 1952)for many years; adviser to China Welfare Institute and to Soong Ching Ling Foundation since 1984.

(3) *mow* (or *mou*): Measure of land in China, 0.1518 acre.

# Urged To Appropriate US$2,000 As Monthly Subsidy For Yu Tsai

*—To Miss Mildred Price*



Sept. 9, 1943

Dear Miss Price,

It is almost a miracle that I could meet Dr. Ed ward C. Carter on the eve of his leaving China and could grip this opportunity of sending you more materials which will enable friends to have a better understanding of our experiment. Since we have been in a great hurry to prepare materials for you, the time left is too short to write a lengthy letter.

First of all, in behalf of our refugee children and the whole school, allow me to convey our hearty thanks to United China Relief, China Aid Council and the American Committee For Chinese War Orphans for the generous and timely contributions sent to us. Especially we want to thank you, Miss Krueger and Mrs. Carter for the kind interest in our project and the enthusiastic support given towards its realization.

On January 31 I sent through the kindness of Mr. Edwards, a Project Report and some photos of the school life of Yu Tsai, which I hope will be of some use for your reference.

Enclosed you will please find a duplicate of the Semi-Annual Statement of the Receipts and Expenditures of Yu Tsai relating to the

Fund from China Aid Council, January 1 — June 30, 1943, audited by a chartered Accountant; a list of the amount of money we have received from you by installments to date; 24 photos of Yu Tsai School Life; 13 Duplicates of Wood-Engravings made by pupils of our Drawing Course, and 7 songs written by myself, the Threefold Criteria and Ten Guiding Principles of Yu Tsai School.

To date we have received $10,500 U. S. Gold from you which are equivalent to $250, 225.81 Chinese National Currency. Besides, we have received a fire relief of $50,000 CNC direct from the Chungking Office of U.C.R. and the bank interests for the temporary deposit of your subsidy totalling $2,206.36 CNC. Balance in banks and in hand is $62, 313. 57 CNC.

The expenditures for August, 1943, is $100,000 CNC as compared with $12,516 for January, 1942, and $50,379.80 December, 1942. Of this $100,000 CNC, about 1/10 comes from the Central Relief Commission, less than 1/10 from the National Self Welfare Committee, 3/10 from China Aid Council and U.C.R. and more than 5/10 from Friends of Yu Tsai in China which have to be raised from month to month. The continual increase of cost of living has prevented us from enrolling more new students. September begins with a budget of $110,000 CNC. It is rather conservative to estimate that a big jump may happen after the Moon Festival, and most likely our budget for December may reach $150,000 CNC. It is our earnest desire that before the year ends, preferably by October, you will be able to send us $ 2,000 U.S. Gold per month. About thirty students of older age and less promise will be transferred to other schools, thus leaving some vacancies for younger children to come in. We are planning to take in 10 young children into the Music Course and another 20 into the Natural Sciences Course, all to be below ten years of age.

In the near future I shall send you some songs with the melodies composed by children, stories of Yu Tsai School Life, in addition to the pictures which may come to my hand.

Kindly give my best regards to Mrs. Carter, Miss Krueger, and other friends

With best wishes for the success of your great work.

Very sincerely yours,

Heng Chih Tao

**Note**

Dr. H. C. Tao gave on this letter his address as "Yu Tsai School, Beipei, Chungking" and the name and address of the addressee as "Secretary Mildred Price, China Aid Council and American Committee For Chinese War Orphans, 200 Fifth Avenue, New York City".

**Encl. (1)**

## Report On The Activities Of Yu Tsai School During The Period Of Jan.—Mar., 1943

### (I) General Activities

1. In January, according to the Regulations prescribed by the Ministry of Education, semester examinations of various courses were given, and then the winter vacation began. As ours is a refugee school and most of the students are homeless, New Year's Activities had been inaugurated for those who remained in school. One activity was mobilizing those in the school to attend the performance of the play "Mozart", originally written by Baratz, with the hope of their learning

something from the life of this great musician.

2. The Chinese Spring Festival Celebration had been held 2 times, and a general exhibition of the school had been opened for 2 days, in order to entertain the neighboring villagers.

3. Outstanding members, selected from the mass education service, were dispatched, in cooperation with the local Center School, to lead the students of the village Elementary School to serve as little teachers, sharing truth with others, and establishing "Study Posts" for illiterates, in order to propagate education to a wider population.

4. The writers who have been engaged in editing the "Yu Tsai Series" had had several meetings at which they exchanged experiences with one another, and discussed probemls which they had met in their work.

5. A Producers and Consumers' Cooperative Society had been established.

6. A United Athletic Meeting was organized and participated in by students from other schools and farmers from other villages.

7. A movement of Land Utilization was promoted so that every inch of our soil would be utilized for growing vegetation.

8. All the girl students remaining in school celebrated Women's Day on March 8.

9. Studies of news and Current History had been emphasized by giving a test every week.

### (II) Departmental Activities

*Music Course*

1. In January the members of the Music Course went to Chungking to attend field studies, in order to learn the necessary theories and techniques from the musicians in the city.

2. A concert was given in the middle of February under the

auspices of Youth Training Dept, Central Training Corps.

3. In March, students of the Music Course gave a concert under the auspices of Executive Training Dept., Central Training Corps.

4.20 songs were composed by the students.

*Dramatic Course*

1. The operetta "Dancing of the Oranges' was introduced to our home stage.

2. On the Spring Festival, the play "Children Corps and the operetta"Dancing of the Oranges" were performed.

3. Going to Chungking at the beginning of March to pursue field studies and make arrangements for the performance of the play "Little Masters" written by Mister Lincoln Tung.

*Literature Course*

1. The famous play, "The Hypocrites" was performed during the Spring Festival.

2. Invitations were sent to leading authors and writers in Chungking to participate in a discussing meeting on Children's Literature, and a Special Number under the title "Children's Literature" was edited for the Wartime Education Monthly.

3.30 essays and 2 poems were written during the three months.

*Drawing Course*

1. A New Year's exhibition of children's drawings was given.

2. An Exhibition of Chinese Drawings by Friends of Yu Tsai was given at the YMCA Mar. 19–21.

An Exhibition of the wood engravings, Chinese drawings, water-color paintings, by the students of the Drawing Course was given at Li Chih Sheh from March 20–23.

An Exhibition of wood engravings by Friends of Yu Tsai and Photos of world-famous Fine Arts was held at our Children's Arts

Gallery March 20—23.

*Social Sciences Course*

2 plays, "The Lotus Boat" and "Our Headquarters", were performed during the Spring Festival.

*Natural Sciences Course*

In the middle of February the members were dispatched to various factories, including chemical works, electrical works and machine works, in the vicinity of the Wartime Capital to acquire some field training.



**Encl. (2)**

## Report On The Activities Of Yu Tsai School During The Period Of Apr.—Jun., 1943

### (I) General Activities

1. A great Celebration of Children's Day was held on April 4. Village children and their parents and relations were invited to attend the celebration meeting.

2. Competitive examinations on Oration, Composition and World and National Affairs were held.

3. Studies relating to May Events were emphasized.

a) Speeches on the problems of May Days were delivered.

b) A general discussion assembly dealing with the Significance of the Student Movement was held on May 4.

4. A congratulation message was telegraphed to Gens. Chen and Sun and all the soldiers taking charge of Western Hupei Front for their latest victory against the Japs on June 7, and $10,000 CNC were sent to them as our humble present on the Dragon [Boat] Festival, which is now called the Muse Festival in honor of the Great Poet

Chu Yuan.

### (II) Departmental Activities

*Music Course*

2 concerts were given consecutively on Apr. 3 and Apr. 4 at The Banker's Club in celebration of the Children's Day and in response to the National Call of inaugrating May as the Month of Music.

April 5. A concert was given at the Central Broadcasting House entertaining the intellegentsia of the wartime capital; and at the same time a broadcast was given and a phonographic recording of the songs was made.

April 18. The songs were broadcast to the South Seas, India, USA, and USSR, and further phonographic recording was made.

April 19. A concert was given in the National Farmer's Bank of China.

On May 1, a concert was given at the request of the Political Department of the Military Council in honor of American and British military officers at the North Spring.

The programmes in all the concerts as mentioned above contained Music and Songs composed by Great Masters of the World and also those composed by our own children.

During the 3 months from April to June 22 songs were composed by the students themselves.

*Dramatic Course*

The 4-acts play "Little Masters" was performed on Chungking Stage for 7 nights consecutively from Apr. 8 on.

On Children's Day "The Children's Corps" and "Dancing of the Harvest" were performed by our children under the auspices of the Sino-Soviet Cultural Association for the Social Meeting of Sino-Soviet Children.

April 19. Another performance of "Children's Corps" was given in the Farmer's Bank of China.

Toward the end of April, "Little Masters" was given 5 performances consecutively at Beipei.

All the above-mentioned performances were attended by an audience of 15,000 persons.

In May "Little Masters" was performed 4 times consecutively at Hochuan, a shire-town near Chungking, attended by an audience of 5,000 persons.

*Literature Course*

A Poem-recital Evening Party was given on each of the following Days: Chinese Poets' Day, the 2221st Anniversary of a Patriotic Chinese Poet Chu Yuan's Birth, and the Seventh Anniversary of Gorky's Death.

A Short-story Evening Party was given.

30 essays were written.

*Drawing Course*

In May Professor Hsu Shi-chi, taking charge of the Course, secured 13 plaster busts and brought them back to the Children's Arts Gallery for study and practice.

On June 5, this department and the Children Arts Gallery were partly destroyed by fire owing to the carelessness of neighbors. All the plaster busts and part of the collections were burned, making a total loss of about $250,000 CNC. The work of reconstruction has already been going on with full strength.

*Social Sciences Course*

1. Volunteers had been dispatched to Salt-Well Town in helping a primary school there to teach the students singing and drawing, twice a week.

2. Volunteers had been dispatched to the Local Town with the same aim.

3. A Story Evening Party was given in celebrating the Second Anniversary of the Russian War of Resistance Against the Nazi Invasion.

*Natural Sciences Course*

Lu Chang-chuen, a student of the course, in co-operation with a student of the Music Course, made 2 sets of simple magic lanterns with wasted material, adding a good tool for propagating mass education in villages.

# Requested Not Base Increase In Subsidy On Enrolling New Students

*—To Miss Mildred Price*



Feb. 9, 1944

Dear Miss Price,

Your very kind letter of December 7 and the January Payment of $1,000 gold which came to hand a week ago, I received with hearty thanks. The question, "Would you prefer that we send the money some other way? ", has given me food for thought. The next day I cabled you to use February payment to buy and send us by air Haliverol oil and Haliverol Capsules. This will greatly help to recover the physical health of many children and improve the financial condition of the School. I also asked you to hold future payments until further request so that time will enable me to form judgement as to the best way or ways to receive your subsidies in order to do the greatest good to the children under our care.

On February 7, through a friend, I received $90,000 Chinese National Currency (including $39,024.38, which is the equivalent of the official exchange rate and 100% government subsidy for $1,000 U. S. Gold,the rest being donations to the School) from Mr. Brownell, who wishes to have $ 1,000 U.S. Gold to be sent to Mrs. Brownell by our School. Since it is beneficial to both parties I have agreed to the proposal.You are requested to give $1,000 U. S. Gold against your March payment for Yu Tsai to Mrs. Mary Hester Brownell upon presentation of this letter and my receipt for the same. I hope you will ask Mrs. Brownell or her representative to give me a receipt to the same effect so that I can show it to my friend.

According to agreement the payment should be made before the end of March. In case you do not approve the method or for some other reason you can not possibly comply with my request, you will feel free to act. Anyway I hope you will kindly send me a cable (DLT) with a short message "Approved" or "Not approved", so that I could judge as to whether I should refund the money to my friend.

In case you do not approve my suggestions, you are requested to send the monthly payments in the usual way or any other way you see fit. Then you are requested to destroy my February and March receipts.

As to the other nine thousand dollars gold per quarter, we have never received it. Mr. Edwards said, it was probably due to the fact that we did not enroll new students (such enrollment was laid down as a condition for increase in appropriation by the Committee on Child Welfare in China). Will it be proper for you to request the Programme Committee to take away this clause of condition, because the mere increase in prices would justify your making this additional grant. We are doing our best to enroll new students but by all means, do not make this a rigid condition for the increase in subsidy. Since last week we have added ten new students with high I.Q.; two of them have been admitted to the Music Course.

Anticipating to receive your cable very soon, and with best wishes,

Very cordially yours,

Heng Chih Tao

Director, Yu Tsai School

## Note

Dr. H. C. Tao gave on this letter his address as "Yu Tsai School" and the name and address of the addressee as "Miss Mildred Price, Executive Secretary, China Aid Council, 200 Fifth Avenue, New York City, N.Y., U.S.A. "

**ANNEX**—Receipt For US $1,000 From C.A.C.

Received from the China Aid Council U.S. Dollars One thousand for the Month of March, 1944.

Tao Heng Chih
Director, Yu Tsai School
For Talented Refugee Children

February, 1944

# British Postcards Interest Young Artists Of CAFA

*—To Mr. S. Smith*

March 10, 1944

Dear Sir,

The news of the arrival of Postcards of British Paintings has aroused admiration in the young artists of the Children's Academy of Fine Arts, under the auspices of the Yu Tsai School for Talented Refugee Children. I wonder whether it is possible for you to donate a set of these postcards to our Academy. I can assure you that our young artists will make the best use of these in their deep appreciation of your generous contribution.

With thanks in advance,

Very sincerely yours,

H. C. Tao

Director, Yu Tsai School

## Note

Dr. H. C. Tao gave on this letter his address as "Chungking Office, 28 Kuan Chia Hang, Chungking" and the name and address of the addressee as "Mr. Stanley Smith, Press Attache's Office, British Embassy".

# Seeking Financial Aid From Foreign Friends For Yu Tsai School

*—To Lady Cripps*

April 10, 1944

Dear Lady Cripps,

First of all, please allow me to express our hearty appreciation of what you and your noble organization have done for the Chinese nation in her long struggle for liberation. I am sure you will be glad to hear from a school in China's Wartime Capital, which has been fighting for the education and nurture of children whose parents and homes have been sacrificed and ruined as this great struggle is going on. Its full name, Yu Tsai School for Talented Refugee Children, will show you at a glance the object which we are trying to achieve. These children have been selected through intelligence and special tests from Wartime Children's Homes, Orphanages and children's own organizations which once flourished during the first stage of the war. We devote 3/4 to 2/3 of their time to general studies and 1/4 to 1/3 of it to special studies fit for each one's own special interest and aptitude. Thus we have organized them into seven groups or departments to meet their own different needs, namely, Music, Painting, Dramatics, Literature, Ballet, Natural Sciences and Social Sciences.

The school started with 150 refugee children thus selected and organized for general and special studies. All the expenses including food, clothing, lodging, education and medical care were taken care of by the school. On account of rising prices, we have been compelled to take in some partially selfpaid students. Beginning with this spring our enrollment has reached 320. And through the little teacher system we are offering our service in extending educational opportunities to 1,158 less fortunate children and adults outside our school.

Because of the abnormal rise in prices, our faculty and children have been suffering from undernourishment and from the lack of sufficient scientific equipment. Therefore on behalf of the Yu Tsai School For Talented Refugee Children I am presenting to you this application for financial aid in order to improve the nourishment of our refugee and poor children, to ameliorate the living condition of our teaching staff and to reinforce the equipment for effective education.The subsidies we are applying for will be used in the following ways:

(1) Reinforcement of scientific apparatus

CN $5,000,000

(2) Raising 60 teachers monthly salaries from
$ 3,000 to $10,000 each for 12 months

CN $ 5,040,000

(3) Improving nourishment for 316 members
including the food for refugee children,
faculty and families, workers at $1,000 each
per month for 12 months CN $ 3,792,000

(4) Balancing the monthly deficit of
$170,000 for 12 months CN $ 2,040,000

Total CN $16,072,000

Enclosed you will please find a copy each of "Facts About Yu

Tsai", "The Threefold Criteria of Yu Tsai", "The Ten Guiding Principles", "The Founding of Yu Tsai School", and "Report on Yu Tsai School," by Lennig Sweet, Program Direcor, UCR. I hopet hese materials and this letter will give you a true picture of Yu Tsai and an understanding of its aspirations, efforts and difficulties. Anything you can do by way of creative relief to enable Yu Tsai to help the refugee children and teachers to obtain more wholesome food and lead a more healthy life as well as give a more effective education in order to make the experiment more fruitful and successful will be greatly appreciated.

Anticipating to hear from you as soon as there is good tidings,

Very respectfully yours,
Heng Chi Tao
Director, Yu Tsai School

**Note**

(1) CN$: Chinese National dollars.

(2) The mailing list attached to this letter is as follows:

1) Lady Cripps, British Aid to China, London.

2) S. Exc. Sir Horace James Seymour, British Aid to China, British Embassy.

3) Secretary K. K. Kuok, British Aid To China, Central Bank of China.

4) Mr. John Blofeld.

5) Dr. Dorothy Needham.

6) Mr. Blunt.

7) Mr. Wright.

8) Lady Seymour.

# Estimate Of Request For 1944—1945 Explained

*—To Mr. Dwight Edwards*

May 30, 1944

Dear Director Edwards,

Your letter of May 24 has been forwarded to Beipei for me to answer. The estimate of our request for the period Oct. 1, 1944—Sept. 30, 1945, is based on the average monthly increase in expenditure for the last 9 months. Our budget for August, 1943, was CN $100,000 while that for May, 1944 is CN $300,000 with a monthly increase of CN $ 22,000. By Oct., 1944, it will probably jump to CN $410,000 and by Sept., 1945, it may reach the figure CN $674,000. Therefore for the whole year Oct., 1944—Sept., 1945 our total budget should be CN $6,504,000 or CN $542,000per month. We wish that 2/3 of this amount be raised locally in China and 1/3 of the amount or CN $2,168,000 be subsidised by your organization. This serves as an explanation of our request in behalf of Yu Tsai School.

Very sincerely yours,

Heng-Chih Tao

Director, Yu Tsai School

**Note**

(1) Dr. H. C. Tao gave on this letter his address as "Yu Tsai School" and the name and address of the addressee as "Director Dwight Edwards, United China Relief, No. 218 Shan Nan Chu Road, Chungking ".

(2) CN $: Chinese National dollar (s), known also as CNC $=Chinese National Currency dollar(s).

# Seeking Support From Home & Abroad For Yu Tsai School

*—To Friends of Yu Tsai*

June 30, 1944

Dear Sirs,

On behalf of the Yu Tsai School for Talented Refugee Children I am presenting to you this application for financial aid in order to improve the nourishment of our children, to reinforce the equipment for effective education, to make preparations for enrolling some new students and to ameliorate the living condition of our teaching staff. With a view to maintaining the present status of the school, we need CN $2,562,000 for the second half of 1944. However, we have a reliable income of only CN $1,440,000 for the same period with a financial deficit of CN $1,222,000 which we wish to raise from our friends at home and abroad. In improving the nourishment of the children we need another monthly increase of CN $28,000 and in raising the scale of salaries we need another CN $35,000 per month. For adding new refugee children, seeing that the present per capita cost is more than CN $2,000 a month, a ten per cent increase from month to month should be provided in order to prevent financial collapse in the mid-way. The School can be much more effectively operated if we have financial backing sound enough for enrolling one hundred more children. We welcome your aid in any one or more of these phases of improvement as well as the maintenance of the present status of the School.

……………………………………………………………………………………

Enclosed please find a copy each of "Facts About Yu Tsai", "The Threefold Criteria of Yu Tsai", "Ten Guiding Principles of Yu Tsai", and "Financial Condition of Yu Tsai". I hope these and the letter will give you a true picture of Yu Tsai and an understanding of its aspirations and efforts. Anything you can do to enable Yu Tsai to give a more effective education to its students and to conduct a more successful experiment in Scientific Education will be greatly appreciated.

Anticipating to hear from you as soon as there is good tidings to us.

Very respectfully yours,
H. C. Tao
Director, Yu Tsai School

**Note**

(1) Dr. H. C. Tao gave on this letter his address as "Yu Tsai School, 28 Kuan Chia Hang, Ho-ping Rd., Chungking" and the addressee as "Friends of Yu Tsai School."

(2) ……: The dotted line represents the omission of 4 paragraphs which are actually the content of "The Founding of Yu Tsai School" included in YU TSAI SCHOOL FOR TALENTED REFUGEE CHILDREN.

# Asked To Help Simplify Procedure For Carrying Books Abroad

*—To Dr. Dorothy Needham*

July 27, 1944

Dr. Dorothy Needham,

My son, Shao-kwang Tao, will go to Calcutta within a week to offer his service in China National Aviation Corporation. He has with him some Chinese and English books including printed bulletins of Yu Tsai School and reference books for his own study. It has been reported that passengers bringing books abroad, especially those in foreign languages other than English, would often be detained for de tailed inspection. Is there any way to have the printed matter examined beforehand by British authorities in Chungking so that Shao-kwang Tao can cross the frontier of India without unnecessary delay. Any advice and help you can give him in this matter will be greatly appreciated. With many thanks,

Very sincerely yours,

H. C. Tao

Director, Yu Tsai School

## Note

Dr. Dorothy Needham: An English scientist, wife of famous English scientist Dr. Joseph Needham. She was working for the Sino-British scientific cooperation in the wartime capital Chungking when Dr. Tao wrote this letter to her.

# Budget For Project Of Enrolling 100 New Refugee Children

*—To Dr. Lennig Sweet*

Oct. 20, 1944

Dear Dr. Sweet,

I am delighted to receive your kind letter of October 17. During our last interview your fear of our possible becoming a Chinese Dartmouth has kindled my inherent fire for the refugee children which has been imbedded under the pressure of rising prices. A new decision has taken form when three days' cold has given me enough leisure to lie down for creative meditation: Yu Tsai will be dedicatad for ever to the poor, the unfortunate, the neglected, the parentless, especially now the refugee children.

Enclosed you will please find a budget for this long-delayed and seemingly new project of enrolling 100 more gifted refugee children especially from the different active war zones. The budget indicates a per capita cost of $15,000 for permanent expenses which, once appropriated, will last for several years, and a per capita cost of $2,500 for current expenses. The total for the first year amounts to CNC$ 4,500,000. Of this sum, nearly all the permanent expenses, with the exception of that for mosquito nets, amounting to CNC $1,300, 000 have to be ready before the arrival of newcomers; while the current expenses of $250,000 can be appropriated month by month. Besides, provision of a 10% monthly increase in current expenses should be made in order to safeguard us against a financial collapse in the mid-way.

From Kweilin and Hunan fronts are pouring in hundreds of thousands of refugee children. Let no time be lost in hesitation. To fight to save children is to save the future of China. To give a right education to the children thus saved is to give a dose of spiritual and intellectual Penicillin to our future generation which will help to fit China to make healthy contributions in a better world of Democracies.

Plans have been made. With enough money we can take in a thousand; we can take less, say a hundred or a dozen, if we could get only so much to support them. Day before yesterday, the 18th, Mr. Chow Tsungchin promised to support two children. This morning Mayor Ho has given special permission for us to present Prof. Tai Ai Lian's Ballet and our own Music at Kan Kian Tang on Nov. 3rd—7th at 8 p.m. to raise a fund, that, if house full, will be enough to support eighteen children. Our surplus room and staff can take care of these twenty with less cost than the budget I am presenting you. It is my earnest hope that your noble organization will give us financial backing to take in at least another 100 children.

With best wishes for an early realization of our common dream.

Sincerely yours,

H. C. Tao

Director, Yu Tsai School

**Note**

(1) Dr. H. C. Tao gave on this letter his address as "Yu Tsai School, Beipei,

Chungking" and the name and address of the addressee as" Dr. Lennig Sweet, Acting Field Director and Programme Director, United China Relief, Chungking".

(2) Dartmouth: Dartmouth College, at Hanover, a town west of New Hampshire. It is one of the oldest educational institutions in the United States, having its origin in a school for poor Indian youths founded in 1754. It was moved to Hanover in 1769 and was granted a state charter on the authority of King George III. Thanks to William Legge (1731—1801), second Earl of Dartmouth (from which the name of the school derives), who donated and collected funds that enabled the school to move to Hanover, the school developed into a full-fledged university, no longer a school for poor Indian youths.

(3) Mayor Ho: Mr. Ho Yao-zu, mayor of Chungking, the wartime capital of China.

**Encl. (1)**

## Budget For The Project Of Enrolling 100 New Gifted Refugee Children

——*Submitted by Yu Tsai School*——

Permanent Expenses:

| | No. Unit Cost in CNC$ | Total in CNC $ |
|---|---|---|
| Double Beds | 50×5,400 | 270,000 |
| Double Desks | 50×1,600 | 80,000 |
| Double Benches | 50×400 | 20,000 |
| Wash Basins | 100×180 | 18,000 |
| Mosquito Nets | 100×1,300 | 130,000 |
| Bedding Mattresses | 100×4,000 | 400,000 |
| Reference Books | | 50,000 |
| Tools | | 30,000 |
| Laboratory Equipment | | 100,000 |

| | |
|---|---|
| Medical Equipment | 50,000 |
| Musical Equipment | 200,000 |
| Repair of a temple for school use including bathrooms, lavatory and cooking equipment | 100,000 |
| TOTAL | 1,448,000 |
| Per capita cost in round number | 15,000 |

Current Expenses:

| | Average Monthly per capita cost CNC$ | Monthly cost for 100 children CNC$ | Annual cost CNC $ |
|---|---|---|---|
| 1. Food | 1,226.00 | 122, 600 | 1,471,200 |
| 2. Clothing | 400.00 | 40,000 | 480,000 |
| 3. Towels (4 per year×90) | 30.00 | 3,000 | 36,000 |
| 4. Hats (2 per year×60) | 10.00 | 1,000 | 12,000 |
| 5. Shoes (3 per year×22) | 66.00 | 6, 600 | 79, 200 |
| 6. Soap (12 per year×40) | 40.00 | 4, 000 | 48, 000 |
| 7. Tooth brushes (3 per year×40) | 10.00 | 1,000 | 12,000 |
| 8. Textbooks (2 sets per year×90) | 15.00 | 1,500 | 18,000 |
| 9. Medical care | 100.00 | 10,000 | 120,000 |
| 10. Materials | 50.00 | 5,000 | 60,000 |

| | | | |
|---|---|---|---|
| 11. Lighting | 50.00 | 5,000 | 60,000 |
| 12. Pocket money | 40.00 | 4,000 | 48,000 |
| 13. Teachers' salaries (10 persons×2,000) | 200.00 | 20,000 | 240,000 |
| 14. Teachers' food (10 persons×1,226) | 122.60 | 12,260 | 147,120 |
| 15. Workers' wages (2 persons×1,000) | 20.00 | 2,000 | 24,000 |
| 16. Workers' food (2 persons×1,226) | 24.52 | 2,452 | 29, 424 |
| 17. Administrative and miscellaneous expenses | 90.00 | 9,000 | 108,000 |
| TOTAL | 2,493.52 | 249,412 | 2,992,944 |
| Total in round nos. | 2,500.00 | 250,000 | 3,000,000 |

**Encl.（2）Monthly Pay On & Before Arrival Of New Students**

| | Monthly Pay On Arrival | Before Arrival |
|---|---|---|
| 1. Food | $1,471,200 | |
| 2. Clothing | 180,000 | 300,000 |
| 3. Towels | | 36,000 |
| 4. Hats | | 12,000 |
| 5. Shoes | | 79,200 |
| 6. Soap | | 48,000 |
| 7. Tooth brushes | | 12,000 |
| 8. Textbooks | 9,000 | 9,000 |
| 9. Medical care | 120,000 | |
| 10. Materials | 60,000 | |
| 11. Lighting | 60,000 | |

| | | |
|---|---|---|
| 12. Pocket money | 48,000 | |
| 13. Teachers' salaries | 160,000 | 80,000 |
| 14. Teachers' food | 97,120 | 50,000 |
| 15. Workers' wages | 24,000 | |
| 16. Workers' food | 29,424 | |
| 17. Administrative expense | 36,000 | |

# Thanks For Support To Yu Tsai Enrolling 100 New Refugee Children

*—To Dr. Lennig Sweet*

November 15, 1944

Dear Dr. Sweet,

Mr. Tang Kunheng has been asked to represent me in receiving from you the balance of subsidy for August, September and, if any, for October as well as the allowance of $140,000 for November.

Mrs. Wang told me that the Child Welfare Committee had passed your recommendation of supporting 100 more refugee children in Yu Tsai. I am sure this will bring an earlier realization of our common project. As some articles are steadily rising in prices (for instance, wash basins, $180 each in my budget, have risen to 280 each in so short a time) , I hope you will find some way or other to advance us the Permanent Expenditure $1,448,000 as soon as possible so that I can secure the necessary equipment for the newcomers ahead of time in order to prevent financial strain later.

Thanking you heartily for your warm interest in our new project and your strong support to our application,

Ever sincerely yours,

H. C. Tao

## Note

(1) Dr. H. C. Tao gave on this letter his address as "Yu Tsai School, Beipei, Chungking" and the address of the addressee as "UCR, Chungking".

(2) Child Welfare Committee: A committee of UCR which concerned itself with the welfare of Chinese refugee children and war orphans. The full name of the committee was the Committee on Child Welfare in China.

# 3-Point Note On Chen Yi-shin's Autobiography

*—To Dr. Ruth Weiss*

Nov. 15, 1944

Dear Dr. Weiss,

Herewith I am sending you Chen Yi-shin's autobiography. Three points should be added:

(1) Before Yi-shin was admitted into Yu Tsai, he had been rejected once by our Travelling Examination Committee because the Musician on the Committee did not want him on account of his head disease. It was through my recall of his ability in directing chorus singing and through my persistent search of the little bald-headed musician that he finally secured admission to Yu Tsai.

(2) His head disease got cured through the sympathy of Marshal Feng, who secured Dr. Liu, a Christian Physician in Luchow, through the kindness of Mr. Hwang Tse-han, General Secretary of Y. M. C. A. Dr. Liu gave him a grain of Thallium Acetate, which caused all hairs with germs to fall off and after a while gave birth to new hairs. He is now no longer bald-headed.

(3) Yi-shin has shown a superability not only in producing songs but also in teaching music to our still younger generation.

Ever sincerely yours,

H. C. Tao

Director, Yu Tsai School

## Note

(1) Dr. Weiss: Dr. Ruth F. Weiss (1908— ), born in Vienna, capital of Austria; came to Shanghai in 1933 and actively took part in progressive cultural work, especially during the War of Resistance against Japan; became a friend of Dr. H. C. Tao and Yu Tsai School; worked in foreign languages publishing departments in Beijing since 1952; acquired Chinese nationality in 1955; member of the Chinese People's Political Consultative Conference since 1983.

(2) Chen Yi-shin: Mr. Chen Yi-shin has been for many years a well-known conductor and professor at the Central Music Conservatoire of China.

(3) Marshal Feng, Feng Yu-xiang (1882—1948) a distinguished Kuomintang general, usually called "Marshal Feng" by his subordinates and the ordinary people. He used to be very friendly to Dr. H. C. Tao and had done a great deal to help him in his educational activities. Gen. Feng died as a result of a fire in a motor vessel on the Black Sea when he was on his way back to China from abroad in 1948.

(4) Luchow: A city of Sichuan Province in Southwest China.

# Thanks Expressed For Securing Scores In India

*—To China Relation Office in Calcutta*

Nov. 15, 1944

Dear Sir,

It gives me great pleasure to refund you rupees 144 by draft against Bank of China, for the 17 musical scores you have so kindly secured and sent to Yu Tsai School through Mr. John Blofeld. The faculty and students of our Music Department and myself wish to express our hearty thanks for your very kind service.

My son, Tao Shao-kwang, has also secured some music strings for our Music Dept. and water colors for our Painting Dept.—all for refugee children. (He will call on you soon. ) I shall be greatly obliged if you will try your best to send them to Chungking. As we need them very urgently, anything you can do to facilitate an early transport will be greatly appreciated.

Sincerely yours,

H. C. Tao

Director, Yu Tsai School

# Urged To Forward Tonics To Chungking By Air

*—To Mr. W. P. W. Barnes*





Nov. 15, 1944

Dear Mr. Barnes,

Upon receiving your kind letter of August 3rd in regard to the Navitol Oil and Orifices, sent to us from Miss Mildred Price, China Aid Council, I wrote to ask you to send them direct to Chungking by C.N.A.C. So far we have not yet received them. Herewith I am sending you a draft for Rupees 200 against Bank of China; you are requested to draw it out in order to defray any expenses involved. In case there is any surplus, you are requested to keep it for us and buy things in India for our refugee children, the list of which I will send you later.

With hearty thanks,

Sincerely yours,

H. C. Tao

Director, Yu Tsai School

**Note**

(1) Dr. H. C. Tao gave on this letter his address as "Yu Tsai School, Beipei,

Chungking" and the address of the addressee as "Friends' Ambulance Unit, China Convoy, India Office, 1 Upper Wood Street Calcutta".

(2) C. N. A. C.: China National Aviation Corporation.

# Requested To Subsidize Yu Tsai

*—To Mr. Arthur B. Coole*



December 5, 1944

Dear Mr. Coole,

Your kind letter of November 27 reached me this evening and I am very thankful to you for your considerate advice.

Beginning with this fall, we have added quite a large number to our student body as well as to our staff. We have now a total enrollment of 280 students including 182 regular students, 10 students in field observation and investigation, and 88 continuation students. The teaching staff in our middle school, not counting office secretaries and elementary school teachers, has reached the round number of fifty, including 9 returned students, 33 with college graduation standing, 3 with junior college graduation standing and 5 senior middle school graduates: Of these 30 are full-time and 20 are part-time teachers. Most teachers in our Music and Painting departments and the Continuation Middle School classes are part-time teachers. The other departments have full-time teachers. But we are sure that the part-time teachers in the arts department have been arranged in the best possible way under the present circumstances, and they have a good sacrificing spirit, forming an integral and essential part of our scheme. As our salaries are really too low and nearly all teachers, or most of them, still lead a single life. Part-time teachers receive the same salaries as full-time teachers, considering their travelling expenses. This accounts for the difference between our part-time teachers and those of other schools.

Our part-time teachers are as devoted as our full-time teachers and they are among the best friends of Yu Tsai. The teaching staff in our school is comparatively larger than in the ordinary middle schools, because it is our purpose to allow the teachers to spend 1/3, even 1/2 of their time to improve their learning in service. As our experiment is new, our teachers have to learn more than others; otherwise the students may get ahead of them. Another reason for our larger staff is to make preparations for taking in more talented refugee children in the near future and for possibly establishing new schools of this kind in other localities. We hope to take in ten more teachers of high calibre before the coming of new students.

Besides, I wish to take this opportunity to report the receipts and expenditures of the second semester of 1943 and the first semester of 1944 and the budget for 1944—1945 as asked by Secretary Mather.

| January—June 1944 | | July—December 1943 | |
|---|---|---|---|
| Receipts | $3,572,119.24 | Receipts | $1,169,989.18 |
| Expenditures | $2,482,997.70 | Expenditures | $1,106,896.50 |
| Designated | | | |
| Sinking Fund | $1,056,000,00 | | |
| Balance | $32,621.54 | Balance | $63,092.68 |

Budget for July—December 1944

| Month | Estimated Expenditure | Reliable Receipt | Estimated Deficit to be raised |
|---|---|---|---|
| July. | CN $372,000 | CN $240, 000 | CN $132,000 |
| Aug. | 394,000 | 240,000 | 154,000 |

| | | | |
|---|---|---|---|
| Sept. | 416,000 | 240,000 | 176,000 |
| Oct. | 438, 000 | 345,000 | 93, 000 |
| Nov. | 460, 000 | 345, 000 | 115,000 |
| Dec. | 482,000 | 345,000 | 137,000 |
| Total | CN $2,562,000 | CN $1, 755, 000 | CN $807,000 |

The budget for the first semester of 1944 is to be computed by adding successively $22,000 the average monthly increase since August 1943 to $482,000 for January, and progressively for the months to come.

Beginning with October 1944, the reliable receipts have increased to $345,000 per month, resulting in lowering the monthly deficit amounting to $105,000.

To date we have received the following appropriations from your Committee:

| | |
|---|---|
| January 5 | |
| Special Contribution | $20,000 |
| Subsidy for November and December 1943 | $15,000 |
| March 14 | |
| Subsidy for January and February | $15,000 |
| April 8 | |
| Subsidy for March and April | $15,000 |
| June 29 | |
| Subsidy for May and June | $15, 000 |
| October 18 | |
| Subsidy for July and August | $15,000 |
| Total | $95,000 |

The $20,000 special contribution has been used for medical supplies end special nutrition. The bimonthly subsidy of $15,000 or a monthly appropriation of $7,500 has been used for increasing the salaries of teachers amounting to $300 per teacher per month, 25 teachers being benefited by your subsidy.

The amount of our salaries is $1,500 per month. It is imperatively necessary to bring it to the level of at least $3,000 a month. On the basis of 50 teachers in our middle school we apply to your Committee for an additional subsidy of $75,000 per month in order to retain our teachers by relieving them somewhat from the hard life under which they are serving our younger generation with the utmost devotion.

As to detailed information about our teaching staff, we shall send it to you later when I return to school. It may take $10,000 to audit the book of Yu Tsai by a registered accountant. This has prevented us from doing so. But we are willing to comply with your wish if you think it necessary for us to do so.

Ever sincerely yours,

H. C. Tao

Director, Yu Tsai School

**Note**

Dr. H. C. Tao gave on this letter his address as "Yu Tsai School, Beipei, Chungking" and the address of the addressee as "Middle School Relief Committee, Chungking".

# Report On Preparations For Enrolling 100 New Students

*—To Dr. Lennig Sweet*

December 13, 1944

Dear Dr. Sweet,

These are the preparations I am making for enrolling the 100 new students.

(1) On December 7 two representatives were appointed to go to Nanchung to find the Emergency Site. In case there is no difficulty to remain here, we have provided a temple for the purpose.

(2) Since we received your approval of our application, we have proceeded to secure the additional teachers needed. I hope to complete the selection of personnel before the 20th of this month.

(3) The Board of Examiners will be formed on the 18th.

(4) Intellegence tests are ready and persons who conduct the tests are being trained.

(5) Application blanks begin to be sent to the two refugee camps on South Bank. We decide to give the first examination on the 22nd, so that the successful examinees will have a good time this Christmas.

(6) We are negotiating with the National Relief Commission, Pao Yu Hwei, and the China Children Welfare Association as to the best way of selecting their children.

It is my wish to receive the monthly current appropriation from December as there is no other fund available to advance for the salary of additional teachers, travelling and other expenses for the Board of Examiners and the new refugee children who may come before Christmas and whose number is not known yet.

Anticipating an earlier answer from you, and with thanks in advance,

Ever sincerely yours

H. C. Tao

Director, Yu Tsai School

**Note**

(1) Dr. H. C. Tao gave on this letter his address as "Yu Tsai School, Beipei, Chungking" and the address of the addressee as "UCR, Chungking".

(2) Pao Yu Hwei: Wartime Child Welfare Committee, with Mme Chiang, wife of Generalissimo Chiang Kai-shek, as its president, and Mme Ho, wife of Mr. Ho Yao-zu, the then mayor of the wartime capital Chungking, and Mme Chow, wife of Mr. Chow En-lai, the then vice-chairman of the Communist Party of China, as its Vice-Presidents.

# Seeking Funds For Starting New Departments of Yu Tsai

*—To Dr. Lennig Sweet*





December 23, 1944

Dear Dr. Sweet,

In response to your notice of December 18 I wish to make two applications on behalf of Yu Tsai School:

Application I. Revision of estimates for the present year. The estimates for the maintenance of the present school have been too low in regard to the following items. First, the basic salary schedule of our staff is not satisfactory and up to date in spite of occasional increases, each member is getting only CN $1,500 per month. It is imperative to increase the minimum salary to CN $3,000 per month. In order to accomplish this for 50 paid teachers we need an additional appropriation of CN $75,000 per month or CN $645,000 for January—September. Second, since last September, the price of controlled rice for schools and private orphanages have jumped from CN $1,100 to CN$3,000 per *tan*. We are consuming 34 *tans* of this rice per month, so the cost exceeds our monthly estimate by $64,600. We need an additional appropriation of CN $581,400 to balance the budget for the nine months. Third, beginning with October, the controlled prices of material for clothing has increased 150%, with the effect that our estimate for winter clothes has run into a deficit of CN $500,000. So, together with deficit for summer clothes, we need another appropriation of CN $700,000 for making up the deficits. Fourth, we need CN $50,000 a month or CN $450,000 for nine months to raise the minimum standard of nutrition for the refugee children. In order to make it clearer, I tabulate the funds applied for as follows:

| | |
|---|---|
| CN$645,000 | Increase of basic salary |
| 581,400 | Balancing sudden increase in rice price |
| 700,000 | Balancing sudden increase in price of clothing |
| 450,000 | Raising basic standard of nutrition |
| CN $2,376,400 | Total amount to be applied for in revising estimates of maintenance |

The above amount can not be covered by the 15% set aside against price rising because the sudden rise in prices of the controlled rice and clothing materials do not affect to any appreciable extent the general index of price rising and the basic standards for the salary of staff and nutrition were set rather too low.

Application II. A new project of Creative Relief. Yu Tsai needs a Department of Agriculture and a Department of Industrial Arts to complete its full programme. Plans can be worked out so that these departments can take form by selecting refugee scientists as professors, talented refugee foremen and talented disabled soldiers as leading workmen and farmers and talented refugee children of preadolescent age as student-apprentices. We aim at a creative relief by enabling creative talents to carry on creative studies and creative work. In this way relief is transformed into a creative force. These new departments will be operated according to the principle of the unity of labour, science and union. It will be an industrial or agricultural cooperative plus science permeated by democracy. The Agricultural Department will engage in experimental and productive activities in vegetables, fruits, animal husbandry, forestry and manufacture of farm products. The Department of Industrial Arts will carry on experimental and productive activities in electrical, mechanical, chemical, and civil lines. Different shops and laboratories will be set up for productive and research activities. On the productive side, we aim to produce agricultural implements, simple machines, scientific apparatus and chemical products for daily use. After a subsidy for initial expenses has been secured, these departments will do their best to approach self-supporting by October 1945.

On the basis of these principles and considerations we apply for an endowment of CN $3,000,000 for opening the Department of Agriculture and CN $7,000,000 for opening the Department of Industrial Arts. These will be the foundation for the Agricultural and Engineering Colleges when Yu Tsai becomes a full-fledged university dedicated to Truth, Love and Service. I shall submit a detailed plan if the general principle is approved.

Sincerely yours,

H. C. Tao

**Note**

(1) Dr. H. C. Tao gave on this letter his address as "Yu Tsai School, Beipei, Chungking" & the address of the addressee as "UCR, 218 Shang Nan Chu Malu, Chungking".

(2) CN$: Chinese National dollars, also known as CNC$: Chinese National Currency dollars.

(3) tan: a picul=100 catties or 133.33 pounds.

# On "Creative Relief"

*—To Dr Lennig Sweet*

Dec. 25, 1944

Dear Dr. Sweet,

This is four o'clock on the morning of Xmas Day. A moment ago, I was in bed. A thought, bathing in the grand magnetic field of Creative Relief, the Frontiers of Wisdom, and the Great Love of Christ, has driven me to get up and write this letter to you. I take delight in racing with daybreak and am glad to have risen before the rising sun.

Creative Relief can not be less than the emancipation of creative geniuses, giving them enough food and sunshine, so that they can pioneer into the frontiers of Wisdom, and continue to advance the creative work of the Creator. When such Wisdom is transformed into forces that are making a better world and a better mankind we have the highest manifestation of Christian Love. If the opportunity for the Creative Genius to emancipate itself is not confined to a few but is open to the greatest number of a nation or the whole world, then that nation or the whole world has achieved the highest form of Creative Democracy.

During this long war of resistance, thousands of talented scholars including many promising unknown scientists of high calibre have been reduced to utter poverty and driven to the margin of existence or compelled to change professions which do not fit. Then, since before the war and especially since the war, tens of thousands of talented young men and women have been prevented from college education by sheer poverty and debarred from research institutes by the consequent lack of college diploma. These are compelled to lead a harder life even than the schollars and waste their creative energy in vocations which do not fit into their aptitudes or in refugee life which does not offer opportunity or encouragement of the expression of their talents. Finally, under the deep bedrock of authority, prejudice, poverty, ignorance of bosses and overlords, tight work schedule, false theory of education, and agelong tradition are buried the talents of the great masses of apprentices, workers, artisans, farmers, chamber maidens and poor children, which are waiting to be awakened, and can be awakened with a whisper of democracy.

Six years ago on December 15, the Morning Village Research Institute was founded to start an attack on this problem. With our meagre resources, we are carrying on two projects. You are acquainted with Yu Tsai School. I ought to tell you that the mother who gave birth to Yu Tsai was the Morning Village Research Institute. Yu Tsai is simply an experimental school, under the auspices of the Education Division of the Institute. The mother is an unknown soldier, more exactly an unknown nurse. She has another unknown son — The Laboratory of Inner Combustion Engine, under the Science Division. Mr. Lee Hwa, the research professor in charge of the experiment, has sacrificed everything for conducting the experiment and I am glad to say that most probably he has nearly completed his model for a new engine.

The Morning Village Research Institute, in order to be true to the ideal that originated it, plans to take in ten more such professors of various lines, and select as many as possible research fellows from promising refugee poor youths and also recruit young research fellows from Yu Tsai. We have books worth $2,000,000 serving as a foundation. But we need more money to maintain a larger staff, to buy more reference books and to set up more laboratories. It is my wish to apply for $2,000,000 endowment for the Institute to expand its work and enhance its service. This will give us a good lift. In case you don't have enough fund to distribute, then any amount available in a lump sum or in installments will be welcome. Or if you think it is more proper to make this subsidy through Yu Tsai, we have no objection, and the Institute could be organized into Yu Tsai as its highest peak. But at this stage, we prefer to run the Institute as an independent organization and receive the subsidy direct from you.

I am rather convinced that if half of your resources or the whole of the surplus fund could be used for creative relief in China, you may see, in less than a generation, miracles in this suffering nation and her millionfold contributions to be rendered to the world and mankind. Isn't this magnificent?

Ever sincerely yours
H. C. Tao
Director, Morning Village
Research Institute

**Note**

(1) Dr. H. C. Tao, Director of the Morning Village Research Institute and Yu Tsai School, gave his address on this letter as "28 Kuan Chia Hang, Chungking" (the Chungking Office of Yu Tsai School).

(2) The Morning Village Research Institute: A research institute which aimed at training senior research workers in certain fields of natural and social sciences through advanced studies based on experimentation. The name of the institute "Morning Village" had its origin in "Xiao Zhuang", or "Morning Village" in meaning, a village near Nanjing where the well-known "Xiao Zhuang (Morning Village) School" was founded by Dr. H. C. Tao in March 1927, a school which had conducted a series of experiments in order to find a new system of education fit for China's conditions and had achieved considerable success in experimentation.

# Requested Not To Base Appropriation On Arrival Of New Refugee Children

—*To Dr. Lennig Sweet*





Jan. 19 '45

Dear Dr. Sweet,

Enclosed you will please find a receipt of the check for $1,050 from the Victory Restaurant.

Your letter of January 18th has given me a difficult problem to solve. I hope you will find it possible not to stick to the per capita basis on the arrival of the new refugee children, because even beginning with November we have gone ahead to spend money in making preparations for the new comers not covered by the permanent expenses. Before the arrival of the new refugee children, we have to complete the following preparations with the current allowance:

1) 10,000 copies of General Intelligence Tests for 10,000 pupils;

2) A staff of six persons to be selected forming the Committee of Tests;

3) Travelling expenses and salaries for the Committee for two months;

4) Ten teachers to be secured and trained beforehand, and their salaries and food to be paid; some began their pay in December, all to be paid from this month on;

5) Materials for winter clothing should be provided at once, and the Bureau of Cotton Goods Control has just ratified our purchase;

6) Finally, if towels, hats, shoes, toothbrushes, etc. can be purchased now, we can save lots of money.

In looking over the list of items of current expenses which I submitted to you on Oct. 20th, I found the only things that warrant a per capita pay basis on arrival of new refugee children are food, lighting, text-books, pocket money.

Therefore I request you to continue to pay $250,000 per month for making adequate preparations for the admission of new refugee children, and not to deduct the previous payment from the amount due for the first appropriation. The withholding of this payment until their arrival can only delay their coming, because, if that is the case, I have to spend too much time filling the financial gap which could be more advantageously used for the new children.

In regard to the period covered by the requests which I made in my letter of Dec. 23, 1944, for increase in teachers' salaries and cost of grain, I wish to state that it covers the period between January and September inclusive, 1945.

You told me that our application for $50,000 a month to raise the minimum standard of nutrition was voted down because the new refugee children have not come yet. I have reviewed my letter of Dec. 23, and I have not found the word "new" before "refugee children". I meant the refugee children already in school as against self-paid children. When the Child Welfare Committee is convened again, I hope you will kindly ask them to reconsider my application in this respect.

Ever sincerely yours,

H. C. Tao

**Note**

(1) Dr. H. C. Tao gave on this letter his address as "Yu Tsai School, Beipei, Chungking" and the address of the addressee as "UCR, Chungking".

**Encl.**

**Current Expenses Before**
**The Complete Arrival Of New**
**Refugee Children**

| | | |
|---|---|---|
| Cost of Tests | $360,000 | (can be reduced) |
| Winter Clothing | 300,000 | |
| Teachers' Salaries (3M) | 75,000 | |
| Teachers' Food (3M) | 36,780 | |
| Car Fares of Testing Committee(2M) | 120,000 | |
| Hotel Expenses of Testing Committee (2M) | 72,000 | These two can be reduced. |
| Food of Testing Committee (2M) | 150,000 | |
| TOTAL | $1,113,780 | |
| Receipt for 4 months (Nov.—Feb.) | $1,000,000 | |

# Estimates For 2 New Depts Of Yu Tsai & An Inst.

*—To Dr. Lennig Sweet*

January 31, 1945

Dear Dr. Sweet,

I am glad to receive your letter of January 25th, which has been forwarded to me. In compliance with your wishes I am enclosing the estimates for the Agriculture Department, the Industrial Arts Department and the Morning Village Research Institute. The conservative estimate of monthly yield of the Endowments/Funds is 8%, which can cover the current expenses. A greater part of the appropriation has to be used for initial expenses of the Industrial Arts Department, and a lesser part for initial expenses of the Agriculture Department.

In the Agriculture Department 40 students will be aided; in the Industrial Arts Department 40 students and 5 skilled workers will be aided; and in the Morning Village Research Institute 5 full-time professors, 5 outside professors, 10 research fellows and 20 young research fellows will be aided.

Your letter has made a mistake regarding the amounts we applied for. My letter of December 23rd applied for

$3,000,000 for the Agriculture Department,

$7,000,000 for the Industrial Arts Department, and my letter of

December 25 applied for

$ 2,000,000 for the Research Institute.

I hope you will kindly make a correction on the duplicate copy of your letter of January 25th to me.

I am returning to City on the 5th of February, and wish very much to receive No. 1 and No. 2 appropriations for January and, if possible, the appropriations for Increased Price of Winter Clothing Materials, Increased Price of Rice, and Increase in Teachers Salaries.

With best wishes,

Ever sincerely yours,

H. C. Tao

Director, Yu Tsai School

**Note**

(1) Dr. H. C. Tao gave on this letter his address as "Yu Tsai School, Beipei, Chungking" and the address of the addressee as "UCR, Chungking".

(2) Morning Village Institute: For the origin of the name "Morning Village" and the purpose of founding the institute see Dr. Tao's letter to Dr. Lennig Sweet dated December 25, 1944.

**Encl. (1)**

## Estimates For Founding The Agriculture Department Of Yu Tsai School

1) Initial Expenses

| | | |
|---|---|---|
| Students | 40×15,000= | $600,000 |
| Teachers | 5×15,000 = | $75,000 |
| Workers | 2×15,000 = | $30,000 |

| | | |
|---|---|---|
| Building | = | $300,000 |
| Equipment | = | $300,000 |
| Total | | $1,305,000 |

2) Current Expenses 40×3,000 per month $120,000

including students food, clothing,

miscellaneous expenses,

Teachers' Salaries, Food,

Workers' Wages, Food,

Medical care, Administrative expenses.

3) Receipts

| | |
|---|---|
| UCR Appropriation for Initial Expenses | $1,305,000 |
| UCR Appropriation for Capital Outlay | $1,695,000 |
| (with a monthly 8% yield of | $135,600 |
| which will cover the Current Expenses) | |
| Total | $3,000,000 |

4) Farm Produce will off-set the rise in price due to inflation and will take care of future maintenance and development.

**Encl. (2)**

**Estimates For Founding The Industrial Arts Department Of Yu Tsai School**

1) Initial Expenses

| | | |
|---|---|---|
| Students | 40×15,000 | =$600,000 |
| Teachers | 5×15,000 | =$75,000 |
| Workers | 5×15,000 | =$75,000 |
| Building | | $500,000 |
| Equipment | | $3,750,000 |
| Total | | $5,000,000 |

2) Current Expenses

| | | |
|---|---|---|
| including all expenses of students, teachers, workers, materials, medical care and administrative expenses | 40×40,000 per month | =$160,000 |

3) Receipts

| | |
|---|---|
| UCR Appropriation for Initial Expenses | $5,000,000 |
| UCR Appropriation for Capital Outlay (will yield 8% per month to cover the $160,000 for current expenses | $2, 000,000 |
| Total | $7,000,000 |

4) Shop service will off-set the rise in price due to inflation and will take care of future maintenance and development.

**Enel. (3)**

**Estimates For Developing**

**The Morning Village Research Institute**

(1) Initial Expenses

| | |
|---|---|
| Books and Equipment (Already Provided) | $2,400,000 |
| Building (Already Provided) | $300,000 |
| Total | $2,700,000 |

| (2) Current Expenses | Staff No. | $per month | Total |
|---|---|---|---|
| Research Professors | 5 | $10,000 | $50,000 |
| Research Fellows | 10 | $5,000 | $50,000 |
| Young Research Fellows | 20 | $500 | $10,000 |
| Subsidies for Outside Research Projects | 5 | $3,000 | $15,000 |

| | |
|---|---|
| Monthly addition of Equipment and Books | $35,000 |
| Administrative Expenses | $10,000 |
| Total | $170,000 |

(3) Receipts

| | |
|---|---|
| Initial Expenses provided by Institute | $2,700,000 |
| Original Income per month | $10,000 |
| UCR appropriation for capital outlay $2,000,000 will give a monthly yield | $160,000 |
| Total Income for Current Expenses | $170,000 |

(4) Publication sales, royalties, patent rights will meet inflation and take care of future maintenance and development.

# World Famous Violinist Ma Sze-Tsung To Give Concert To Raise Money For Yu Tsai

*—To. Dr. Ruth Weiss*

January 31, 1945

Dear Dr. Weiss,

Mr. Ma Sze-Tsung, the most accomplished, Chinese artist of world renown, will give a violin concert, under the auspices of Yu Tsai, for adding new refugee children, on February 13th, 14th, 16th and 17th at 7:00 p.m. with a different programme for each evening. We have reserved 100 best seats every evening for friends of Yu Tsai, who are admitted by Invitation Cards instead of tickets. I am asking Mr. Chen Yuan-chi to take to you as many Invitation Cards as you need for friends who are interested in Violin Concert as well as in the cause for the education of talented refugee children. Any contribution above $5 gold or its equivalent in round numbers from each friend invited to each performance will be appreciated. I expect that you will do your best to win fifty Allied friends for Yu Tsai, but certainly not less than twenty. I hope to hear good news from you as soon as I return from Beipei on the 5th Inst. With the combined effort of four hundred friends to be invited, I expect to achieve the result of raising enough money to take care of 40 more new refugee children for one year.

Ever sincerely yours,

H. C. Tao

Director, Yu Tsai School

**Note**

(1) Dr. Ruth Weiss: (See Dr. Tao's letter to Dr. Weiss dated November 15, 1944.)

(2) Allied friends: Friends from Allied countries which were at war with the Axis Bloc (Germany, Italy and Japan) during World War II.

# Appreciation Of YMCA's Generosity Expressed

*—To Mr. Hwang Tse-Han*

Feb. 23, 1945

Dear Mr. Hwang,

On behalf of the refugee children of Yu Tsai School, I wish to express my hearty thanks for your generosity of not requiring us to pay for the balance short of full house 6—8 p.m. on the 17th Inst. on account of our short notice to cancel the contract of using your auditorium. You are also requested to convey my hearty thanks to Mr. Way, whose kindness is equally appreciated.

Ever sincerely yours,

H. C. Tao

Director, Yu Tsai School

**Note**

(1) Dr. H. C. Tao gave on this letter his address as "28 Kuan Chia Hang, Hoping Rd., Chungking" and the address of the addressee as "Y. M. C. A., Chungking".

(2) Mr. Hwang Tse-Han: The then General Secretary of Y. M. C. A., Chungking.

# Appreciation Of Foreign Friend's Presents For Yu Tsai's Children Expressed

*—To Mr. Frederic Douglas*

Feb. 25th, 1945

Dear Mr. Douglas:

On behalf of the refugee children of Yu Tsai School I wish to express my hearty thanks for your kind presents consisting of 2 boxes of chess, 6 table-tennis balls, 3 feathered tennis balls, and 2 packages of colored crayon, which were forwarded to me just before New Year's Eve, old calendar. These new treasures have been welcome to the play room and field with great enthusiasm and excitement.

It has taken me some time to trace the donator of these gifts, so I ask your pardon of not sending this letter of appreciation earlier.

Anticipating to see you personally before long,

Ever sincerely yours,

H. C. Tao

**Note**

(1) Dr. H. C. Tao gave on this letter his address as "28 Kuan Chia Hang, Hoping Rd., Chungking" and the address of the addressee as "AIS, Liang Fu Chi Lu, Chungking".

(2) AIS (or A. I. S.): American Information Service.

# Report On Selection Of Refugee Children

*—To Dr. Lennig Sweet*

Feb. 26, '45

Dear Dr. Sweet,

It gives me pleasure to report that between December 23rd and February 25th we had given six successive tests to 290 children of whom 22 refugee children successfully passed the standard set up by our Board of Examiners. It seems to be very slow.

It was not until last Friday that we received introduction letters from Pao Yu Hwei permitting us to select children from the children's homes of different localities. This will enable us to make a schedule of field tests and begin to give them in a few days.

We hope with all the introduction letters in hand we can speed up the work and make quicker progress in the future.

I am leaving for Beipei tomorrow, hoping that the February grant for our school will be ready when I return on March 5th.

Many thanks for showing me the films you took in our school and at the North Spring. I will return them to you as soon as copies are made.

Ever sincerely yours,

Heng-Chih Tao

Director, Yu Tsai School

## Note

(1) Dr. H. C. Tao gave on this letter his address as "28 Kuan Chia Hang, Hoping Rd.,Chungking" and the address of the addressee as"U. C. R., Chungking".

(2) Pao Yu Hwei: For the meaning of Pao Yu Hwei, see Dr. Tao's letter to Dr. Lennig Sweet dated December 13, 1944 (Note 2).

# Educational Plan Mapped Out For Int'l Home

*—To Dr. Lennig Sweet*





March 20, 1945

Dear Dr. Sweet,

Your kind letter of March 16 has just come to hand. It has travelled too slowly indeed, especially in the countryside.

(1) The International Home will give an elementary education from the 1st grade to the 6th grade.

(2) Beginning with the 5th grade, vocational studies and preparation should be started. The nature and details will be decided by the Board of Trustees upon the recommendation of the Director.

(3) Cultural Equipment will consist of:

a) Reference Books for teachers and pupils,

b) Musical instruments,

c) Medical apparatus,

d) Farm implements,

e) Carpenter's tools,

f) Simple scientific apparatus,

g) Other tools and equipment of production.

I have had no time to ascertain the cost of each before I give you the application. Another reason is that I have intended to give the director more freedom to make his decision.

Hoping this will comply with your wish,

Ever sincerely yours,

H. C. Tao

**Encl.**

**Int'l Home For**
**Refugee Children**

I Initial Expenses

| | No. | | Unit Cost in CN$ | Total in CN$ |
|---|---|---|---|---|
| 1. Double bed | 50 | × | 8,000 | 400,000 |
| 2. Double desk | 50 | × | 2,400 | 120,000 |
| 3. Double bench | 50 | × | 600 | 30,000 |
| 4. Washbasin | 100 | × | 300 | 30,000 |
| 5. Mosquito net | 100 | × | 2,000 | 200,000 |
| 6. Bedding | 100 | × | 6,000 | 600,000 |
| 7. Cultural equipment | | | | 620,000 |
| 8. Building and repairs | | | | 1,000,000 |
| Total for 100 children | | | | 3,000,000 |
| Per Capita Cost | | | | 30,000 |

II Current Expenses

| Items | Monthly per capita cost CN $ | Monthly cost for 100 children CN $ | Annual cost CN$ |
|---|---|---|---|
| 1. Food | 1,500 | 150,000 | 1,800,000 |
| 2. Clothing | 500 | 50,000 | 600,000 |
| 3. Towels | 40 | 4,000 | 48,000 |
| 4. Hat | 20 | 2,000 | 24,000 |
| 5. Shoes | 80 | 8,000 | 96,000 |

| | | | |
|---|---|---|---|
| 6. Soap | 50 | 5,000 | 60,000 |
| 7. Tooth brush | 20 | 2,000 | 24,000 |
| 8. Textbooks | 20 | 2,000 | 24,000 |
| 9. Medical care | 100 | 10,000 | 120,000 |
| 10. Materials | 60 | 6,000 | 72,000 |
| 11. Lighting | 60 | 6,000 | 72,000 |
| 12. Pocket money | 50 | 5,000 | 60,000 |
| 13. Teachers' salary | 300 | 30,000 | 360,000 |
| 14. Teachers' food | 150 | 15,000 | 180,000 |
| 15. Workers' wages | 30 | 3,000 | 36,000 |
| 16. Workers' food | 30 | 3,000 | 36,000 |
| TOTAL | 3,010 | 301,000 | 3,612,000 |

(10% increase per month against inflation)

# Requested To Help Set Up Int'l Home

*—To Dr. Lennig Sweet*

March 24, 1945

Dear Dr. Sweet,

Mr. King has reported to me Mme Ho's interview with you. I wish only to express my opinion in regard to maternal love and institutional care in connection with the refugee children on South Bank.

1) The refugee families on South Bank have been reduced to the margin of existence. Both adults and children are suffering. If the children are well taken care of, it will be a relief to both mothers and children.

2) Maternal love can not be the panacea for all the antisocial attitudes. When both the mother and the child are suffering from lack of means of subsistence, both may assume an antagonistic attitude toward society, which may be reduced in proportion to the extent of substantial assistance and sympathy applied.

3) The question whether this assistance should be given to the home direct or through some institution can only be answered by a careful comparison and investigation. It should not be dealt with by one general principle. If it is an educated home and the mother is well educated, I should suggest supporting the child through giving

relief to the home, or, alternatively, putting the child in a well managed institution.

4) To put the child in an environment so that both his body and his soul could grow is certainly better than to keep him in the home wherein only the body is taken care of.

5) An institution under the direction of Mme Ho can not fail to be up to the standard, and it is safe to infer that such an institution would be better than the best home that the South Bank refugees could establish.

6) The steamer does not allow me to write longer. I hope you will find it possible to help in laying the foundation of the International Home.

Ever sincerely yours,

H. C. Tao

**Note**

(1) Int'l Home: International Home for refugee children.

(2) Mme Ho: Wife of Mr. Ho Yao-zu, the then mayor of the wartime capital Chungking.

(3) South Bank: An area south of the Yangtse River which runs past Chungking proper.

(4) the steamer: The regular passenger steamer which was sailing along the Jialing River from Chungking to a neighboring town Beipei when Dr. Tao wrote this letter.

# Financial Report Of Yu Tsai For 1944

*—To Dr. Lennig Sweet*

March 28, 1945

Dear Dr. Sweet,

Enclosed you will please find 2 copies of the financial report of Yu Tsai School for the period of 1944, audited by a registered auditor, Mr. Pai Chingshin.

I notice that you need another copy of the audited report for the year 1943 for the file of your Chungking Office, which will be furnished by the auditor in a few days.

Very sincerely yours,

H. C. Tao

## Note

Dr. H. C. Tao gave on this letter his address as "28 Kuan Chia Hang, Ho-ping Rd., Chungking" and the addressee as "UCR, Chungking". No copy of the financial report of Yu Tsai School for 1944 has been found attached to this letter. Instead of the financial report, a copy of "Monthly Food Cost of Yu Tsai School for New Refugee Children Already Arrived" has been discovered in the relative file and is made to serve as an enclosure here.

Encl.

**Monthly Food Cost Of Yu Tsai School**
**For New Refugee Children Already Arrived**

| | | October Budget | Corrected Budget according to changes in conditions | Expenses Extra |
|---|---|---|---|---|
| January 10 | New Refugee Children | $12,260 | $25,460(1) | $13,200 |
| February 22 | 〃 | 26,972 | 70,532(2) | 43,560 |
| March 32 | 〃 | 39,232 | 50,832(3) | 17,600 |
| April 62 | 〃 | 75,012 | 185,720(4) | 110,708 |

Foot Notes

(1) Original estimate of food in October application consists of $660 per capita for rice on the basis of official rate rice $3,000 per *tan*, and $666 per capita for supplementary food including everything besides rice. In January market common grade rice averaged at $9,000 per *tan*. The 10 children's official price rice was not yet approved and had to take market rice, resulting in a per capita cost of $1,980 totaling $13,200 extra.

(2) In February 22 children still had to take market rice which rose to $12,000 per *tan*, resulting in a per capita cost of $2,640 totaling $43,560 extra.

(3) 22 children were allowed official price rice, totaling $26,972 for their rice and supplementary food. The 10 new comers took market rice at $11,000 per *tan*, resulting in a per capita cost of $2,420, totaling $17,600 extra.

(4) 22 children have official price rice, $660 per capita, amounting to $14,520; supplementary food has increased to $1,200 per capita, 62 children totaling $74,400; 40 children take market rice $2,420 per capita, totaling $96,800. The grand total runs up to $185,720 for 62 new children for food alone.

# Revision Of Yu Tsai's Budget Requested

*—To Dr. Lennig Sweet*

April 27, 1945

Dear Dr. Sweet,

Yu Tsai is facing a most serious financial crisis. I am presenting you some essential data which may help you to consider and judge as to the best way of solving the present difficulties and preventing more serious development. At the same time I wish to make some recommendations for your reference and to report a few specific things which need to be reconsidered and acted upon as soon as possible.

This year we began with a budget of $590,000 for January and, through periodic high jumps of prices we have been compelled to adopt a minimum budget of $1,678,000 for April. This means an increase of 283% for the first quarter. The month of April alone will have a deficit of $841,000. Our total deficit since January 10 has run up as high as $1,500,000.

The first jump of prices occurred about January 10, the second jump, about February 20, and a little drop since March so far as rice is concerned. We have reasons to believe that in May rise will go up again.

There is an urgent need for revision of the budget of all agencies including ours, and I think the revision should begin with January if it is possible and not later than February. Don't you think it would be a better plan to grant the agencies a budget in gold and pay them from month to month according to the rate of exchange? Gold will rise with the prices and in general a little more slowly than other prices. It will save the trouble of redistribution and also relieve different agencies from constant worrying over financial difficulties.

The budget for enrolling new refugee children was drafted on October 24, 1944. On November 28 we received the appropriation for initial expenses. The lease of Hwei Lung Temple was finally approved by the local government as late as January. The following main items of Initial Expenses have exceeded the original budget:

| | Original appropriation | Actual cost | Amount Exceeded as deficit |
|---|---|---|---|
| Repair of a temple | $100,000.– | $300,000.– | $200,000.– |
| Double beds | 270,000. – | 400,000.– | 130,000.– |
| Double desks | 80,000.– | 130,000.– | 50,000.– |
| Mosquito nets | 130,000.– | 200,000.– | 70,000.– |
| Total | CN $580,000.– | $1,030,000.– | $450,000.– |

We hope you will find it possible to pay us the $450,000. The October budget for rice was based on the official price rice which is $3,000 per *tan*. Only 22 new refugee children have been allowed to take official price rice; 40 refugee children have not yet been given permission to take such rice and are still taking market rice which costs $10,000 per *tan*; the remaining 38 refugee children, if enrolled now, have to take market rice right through until the Autumn session begins. Then the supplementary food, including fuel, oil, salt, vegetable, meat, water, etc. beginning with March has increased from $556 per capita in October estimate to $1,200 per capita and should be increased to $2,000 per month per capita besides rice, applicable to teachers and workers as well as students.

The monthly food cost for new refugee children has been worked out and enclosed for your reference. From January to April the total appropriation for food is $490,400. On account of the necessity of buying market rice for newcomers before the governmental approval of official price rice and the increase in price of supplementary food, the actual food expense for the newcomers will be $338,544 for the 4 months. Thus there is only a surplus of $151,856 from previous food approprtation which is far from being enough for all the expenses if UCR should withhold our April appropriation.

As to the remaining 38 new refugee children, it would be impossible for them to get official price rice before September and with the proposed rise of supplementary food to $2,000 per capita in May, the per capita food cost will be about $ 4,640 as against $1,226 according to October Budget, resulting in an additional appropriation of $129,732, which needs your approval before I dare to admit them.

In regard to my application to British Aid To China, I hope you will do your best to support the following requests:

(1) Reinforcement of scientific apparatus $5,000,000

(2) Raising teachers' salary from 3,000.– to $10,000.– 60 teachers $5,040,000 totaling $420,000 a month

(3) Improving nutrition $1,000×316 totaling $316,000 per month $3,792,000

You seem to disapprove my effort for science apparatus. This is however the essence of my plan. I need this money to make simple apparatus ourselves. If this project should fail the whole plan of Yu Tsai would fail. I hope you will do your best to help my experiment to achieve its perfect success and contribute our best to mankind.

Very sincerely yours,

H. C. Tao





**Note**

(1) Dr. H. C. Tao gave on this letter his address as "28 Kuan Chia Hang, Ho-ping Rd., Chungking" and the address of the addressee as "U.C.R., Chungking".

(2) Hwei Lung Temple: A temple in which the Social Sciences Department of Yu Tsai School was housed.

# Requested Grant-aid For Yu Tsai Budget('45–'46)

*—To Mr. Dwight W. Edwards*

June 1, 1945

Dear Director Edwards,

On December 23, 1944, I had the pleasure of submitting two applications to Director Sweet, "Application Ⅰ" had received immediate consideration, for which I wish to express my hearty thanks, but "Application Ⅱ" concerning the establishment of the Agricultural and the Industrial Arts Departments had not been brought up for discussion when the Child Welfare Committee convened. It is my earnest wish that you will kindly bring this application up to the next meeting of the Child Welfare Committee and make a strong recommendation in favor of its adoption. The essence of "Application Ⅱ" is quoted with slight modifications as follows:

"Application Ⅱ. A new project of Creative Relief. Yu Tsai needs a Department of Agriculture and a Department of Industrial Arts to complete its full programme. Plans can be worked out so that these departments can take form by selecting refugee scientists as professors, talented refugee artisans, foremen and talented disabled soldiers as leading workmen and farmers and talented refugee children of preadolescent age, say 10—13, as student-apprentices. We aim at a creative relief by enabling creative talents to carry on creative studies and creative work. In this way relief is transformed into a creative force. These new departments will be operated according to the principle of the unity of labor, science and union. It will be an industrial or agricultural cooperative plus science permeated by democracy. The Agriculture Department will engage in experimental and productive activities in vegetables, fruits, animal husbandry, forestry and manufacture of farm products. The Department of Industrial Arts will carry on experimental and productive activities in electrical, mechanical, chemical, civil and native crafts lines. Different shops or laboratories will be set up for productive and research activities. On the productive side, we aim to produce agricultural implements, simple machines, simple scientific apparatus or chemical products for daily use. After a subsidy for initial expenses these departments will do their best to approach self-supporting by October 1945. On the basis of these principles and considerations we apply for an initial expense and capital outlay of CN $3,000,000 for opening the Department of Agriculture and CN $7,000,000 for opening the Department of Industrial Arts."

In the original application, the word "endowment" was a misnomer. I mean by it, "capital outlay". As you have noticed this change has been made in the above quotation and in the budget that is attached to this letter.

The age limit of children whom I wish to select is the preadolescent period. In order to make it clearer I have inserted "10—13" following "preadolescent age".

The budget was estimated on the basis of prices half a year ago. If funds were available I wish the budget could be doubled. However I consider the budget still workable on a smaller scale, if more funds are difficult to procure. As a wise Chinese proverb says, one begets two,

two beget three, three beget all things (一生二,二生三,三生万物), I consider a small beginning better than none. Yu Tsai, without a nursery for refugee young talents of agriculture and industry, remains a deformed being and cannot hope to make wholesome and healthy contributions that New China needs. It is for this that I request that you recommend this application to the Child Welfare Committee and help to pull it through all the stages of deliberation so that we may win another victory not only for the refugee children who are in and may come to Yu Tsai but also for a greater progress of New China.

Very sincerely yours,

H. C. Tao

Director, Yu Tsai School

**Encl. Budget Request Form (1945–1946)**

**UNITED CHINA RELIEF**

**218 Shang Nanchu Malu, Chungking**

**BUDGET REQUEST FORM**

**1945–1946**

**CHILD WELFARE**

To: Director Dwight W. Edwards, United China Relief and China Aid Council.

From: H. C. Tao, Director, Yu Tsai School.

We hereby request you to make a grant-in-aid for the orphanage or welfare center named below:

1. Name of institution: Yu Tsai School.

2. Location of institution: Beipei, Chungking, China.

3. Name of organisation or person responsible for carrying out the program: Life Education Association through the personal direction of H. C. Tao.

4. Amount granted by UCR in 1944—1945: $10,862,300 ($3,000,000, $4,464,300, $1,448,000, $1,950, 000)

5. Amount requested: $81,665,200 (Based on May appropriation with 15% monthly increase compound)

| | | |
|---|---|---|
| Oct. 1, 1945 | Dec. 30, 1945 | $9,778,100 |
| Jan. 1, 1946 | Mar. 30, 1946 | $14,871,300 |
| Apr. 1, 1946 | June 30, 1946 | $22,617,500 |
| July 1, 1946 | Sept. 30, 1946 | $34,398, 300 |
| Total | | $81,665,200 |

6. It is expected that the institution will be financed as follows:

| | |
|---|---|
| a) From the Chinese Government National Relief Commission | $180,000 |
| b) From private Chinese sources, Friends of Yu Tsai | 3, 600,000 |
| c) From abroad, other than by this request British Aid to China or others possible | 4,260,000 |
| d) From fees, rent, sale of products | 800,000 |
| e) From present request | 920,000 |
| Total amount needed for the year | $91,425,200 |

7. Write below why this money is needed from UCR, and cannot be obtained elsewhere.

In the past, before 1944 the friends of Yu Tsai in China were the major supporters of the school, but as business condition has become more and more serious their financial ability can not cope with the rising inflation, and the British Aid to China has only promised to increase our monthly from $4,425 to $10,000 per teacher and there is no hope for an increase from government subsidy, we earnestly hope that UCR will grant the $81,665,200 which is estimated on the basis of UCR's May Appropriation of $1,400,000 in round number, computed at the rate of 15% increase compounded from month to month, giving the figure $2,815,900 for October, 1945; $13,100,600 for September, 1946; $81,665,200 as the total of the whole year.

8. Below is the expense budget of the Child Welfare Center, listing the major expense items together with number of staff:

| | | |
|---|---|---|
| Oct. 1, 1945 | Dec. 30, 1945 | $9,778,100 |
| Jan. 1946 | Mar. 1946 | $14,871,300 |
| Apr. 1946 | June 1946 | $22. 617,500 |
| July 1946 | Sept. 1946 | $34,398,300 |
| Total | | $81,665,200 |

| | |
|---|---|
| 1) Total Buildings | |
| 2) Repairs and Upkeep | $1,000,000 |
| 3) Living Subsidy for 250 Children | |
| a) Food | 22,500,000 |
| b) Clothing | 9,250,000 |
| c) Bedding | 800,000 |
| d) Necessities | 6,400,000 |
| 4) Productive Work | |
| a) Equipment | 1,000,000 |
| b) Materials | 1,000,000 |
| c) Transportation | 240,000 |
| 5) Educational Program | |
| a) Books | 1,800,000 |
| b) Equipment | 750,000 |
| c) Misc. | 500,000 |
| 6) Salaries | |
| a) Staff 61 teachers with 17 family members | 21,560,000 |

| | |
|---|---|
| b) Wages of servants 40 school and farm workers | 6,000,000 |
| 7) General | |
| a) Office Expenses | 1,200,000 |
| b) Travel | 240,000 |
| c) Light, water and fuel | 3,625,200 |
| 8) Welfare Program | |
| a) Medical | 3,000,000 |
| b) Recreation | 600, 000 |
| c) Magazines etc. | 200,000 |

9. Other

10. Write below what you expect to accomplish with the money given as a result of this request.

This grant-aid from UCRwill enable our 61 teachers to continue to help 250 refugee and very poor children to grow and to learn according to their aptitudes, and at the same time to help 1,500 peasants and their children to improve their health and to acquire the rudiments of knowledge and the urge for learning and progress.

# New Project Under Way Dem. Ed. For 450m People

*—To Miss Mildred Price*

CABLE—To Miss M. Price, China Aid Council, 1790 Broadway, New York (Sept. 21, 1945).

---

Victory greetings! There is no change in the Yu Tsai budget for the coming half year. There is a new project under way to bring democratic education to 450 million people. It is under the joint auspices of the Life Education Association and the director of Yu Tsai School—myself. It has been worked out on a four-year plan. The first-year plan aims at reaching six million people. The four-year experimental plan includes the study of health, labor, science, and preparation for democracy. There will be one research institute to study problems and methods, ten training institutes for training personnel including staff and tcachers, 100 demonstration centers, the printing of materials, including books and periodicals, and we plan to subsidize 5,000 local experimental centers. The total amount of money needed is two million dollars gold. We can raise one million dollars gold and request you to grant us one million dollars gold. H.C. Tao.

## Note

"Victory greetings! ": "Victory" means "Victory over Japan." During World War Ⅱ, Japan was a member country of the Axis Bloc headed by Germany, Italy being another member country. After Germany and Italy were defeated in Europe, Japan, having lost one battle after another in China and elsewhere in the Far East, was compelled to announce "unconditional surrender" on August 14,1945, and, on September 2 in the same year, the statement of "unconditional surrender" was formally signed and made public all over the world. Hence "Victory greetings! " in Dr. H. C. Tao's cable to Miss M. Price.

**Annex—**

## Miss M. Price's Reply To Dr. Tao's Cable

September 27, 1945

Dear Dr. Tao,

Thank you for your cable which arrived September 21. As I understand it the cable said as follows: "Victory greetings! There is no change in the Yu Tsai budget for the coming half year. There is a new project under way to bring democratic education to 450 million people. It is under the joint auspices of the Life Education Association and the director of Yu Tsai School—myself. It has been worked out on a four-year plan. The first-year plan aims at reaching six million people. The four-year experimental plan includes the study of health, labor, science, and preparation for democracy. There will be one research institute to study problems and methods, ten training institutes for training personnel including staff and teachers, 100 demonstration centers, the printing of materials, including books and periodicals, and we plan to subsidize 5,000 local experimental centers. The total amount of money needed is two million dollars gold. We can raise one million dollars gold and request you to grant us one million dollars gold. "

Please let me know as soon as you can if that is what you intended to say as we want to go to work to help you. Mrs. Carter spoke to the Girls Scouts about giving their $10,000 appropriation to your work.

Would you mind giving us a little more information on the Life Education Association? Please be a little more specific about how you intend to reach six million people. Who will run your research institute? Where will you get the personnel for the 10 training institutes? Who will man the 100 demonstration centers, and what will be their program? You said you plan to subsidize 5,000 local experimental centers. How will you get personnel for them? How will you supervise them? What will be their program? Where will they be located? The more details you give us the better it will be in trying to raise the money for your work. Do you expect to get any from Britain or Canada?

Mr. Douglas brought us pictures of your school and I must say they are beautiful. We are so glad to have those of you handing out the books from the treasure chest. These pictures will do a great deal towards the filling of more treasure chests to send to China. If you will let us know the type of books you want we can get treasure chests to you filled with those. We can also send you other materials in treasure chests such as pencils, paper, drawing books, paints. In fact anything that will go in a box of the same size which you received before.

Mr. Douglas was very much impressed with you and your work.

I think it might be a good idea if you can see the Interim International Information Service (old O. W. I.) and get them to give you some publicity.

Mr. Arthur Calvin of the American Red Cross was in the office yesterday. I told him about your needing haliver oil and the fact that the haliver oil we sent you never reached you. He said that you should go to one of the relief agencies such as the International Relief Committee and ask for haliver oil from the stocks given to the IRC by the American Red Cross. He first said you should go to the Committee from the Ministry of Education but I told him that I didn't think that Committee would be interested in seeing that your children get haliver oil. However, I may be wrong on that score. In case you get no satisfaction from the IRC or the Ministry of Education Committee try to see Mr. Calvin and tell him what you need.

Do you plan to move your headquarters from Chungking? We look forward to the publicity material you are sending us. Mr. Douglas brought us some but it is all material we have had before. We must have some new things if you can possibly send them.

With greetings to you from us all and with hopes of hearing from you soon, I am

Sincerely yours,
Mildred Price
Executive Director
China Aid Council

# Asked To Help Find A Meeting Place

*—To Mr. Peter Townsend*

July 23, 1946

Dear Mr. Townsend,

The bearer Mr. Wang will take my letter to Miss Gerlach. Will you please let him have the car you plan to lend me.

Is it possible to hold the Committee Meeting in your place, and what time of the day will be convenient for you? Please reply by the bearer. If your place is not convenient, please contact the Y. W. C. A. for us.

Very sincerely yours,

H. C. Tao

**Annex— Mr. Peter Townsend's Reply**

Dear Dr. Tao,

Any time Wed. evening or Thursday evening Wed. evening after 7 p.m. Thurs. evening any time.

Peter T.

**Note**

Miss Gerlach: See Dr. Tao's letter to Mrs. Louise K. Rugg dated 1942, Note 3.

# 书信

（译文）

# 我的学历及终身志愿

——致 J. E. 罗素

亲爱的罗素院长[①]：

2月11日手示敬悉，欣喜何似。所嘱就自身曾受训练及终身事业之计划向利文斯通奖学金捐助人作一简略报告，自当乐于从命。

余现年二十有二，生于徽州，此乃一鲜与外界交往之地。余之早期汉学教育受业于家父及其他师长，至十四岁始入一中华耶稣内地会学堂，受教于唐进贤师（Mr. Gibbs），彼当时为仅有之西学教员也。两年后，该学堂停办，贤师返回英国，余乃不得不冒险前往杭州意欲习医。旋以医学堂严重歧视非基督教徒，甚至事关学科问题亦然，余乃撤回注册，而入学仅三日耳。余于失望之余，仍返徽州专习英文复经一年，然后前往南京入金陵大学，校中基督教徒与非基督教徒均受欢迎，此乃余今日仍乐于称道之事也。三年后，第一次革命爆发[②]，余返徽州，任徽州议会干事[③]甫及半载，回南京复学。蒙学友之助及大学当局之信任，余倡办《金陵光》学报中文版并任主笔。1913年，余成为一基督信徒[④]，因得包文博士（Dr. Bowen）、汉克博士（Dr. Henke）之指导，复因詹克教授（Prof. Jenk）讲授"基督教义之社会意义"予余印象至深，有以致之也。1914年6月，亦即余就学于南京之第五年末，余获学士学位。8月，蒙父母及友人相助，余启程赴伊利诺大学攻读一年，除获可贵之诸多教益外，复得余辛劳之副产物，即硕士学位是也。于伊利诺一年中之下半年期间，余曾任学生俱乐部干事。

三年前，余选就哥伦比亚大学为余在美之最终目标，然因资力不济而未能及时来校就读。余今生之唯一目的在于经由教育而非经由军事革命创造一民主国家。鉴于我中华民国突然诞生所带来之种种严重缺陷，余乃深信，如无真正之公众教育，真正之民国即不能存在。余矢志以教育管理为终身事业，始于去夏，是时正值基督教男青年会于日内瓦湖举行夏季大会，余于此受极大启迪。余曾查阅既知之所有学府，再次发现贵院乃其中最佳去处。然而，选定一学府为一事，有无充足资力进入该学府则为另一事。自1915年1月家父逝世以还，家庭全部负担即加于我身，余之经济状况乃陷于极大困境。所幸者，在余决定来师范学院之前不多时，蒙我国政府授予"部分奖学金"，连同其他种种援助，至少已予我以作一起步之足够勇气。然而，纽约生活费用之高，竟超出余所预料。留纽约半载，已觉余之准备不足以供顺利完成学业之用，因之，蒙孟禄博士介绍，余乃着手申请利文斯通奖学金，并已蒙慷慨授予。衷心谢领此项厚礼之余，受业愿向您及利文斯通捐助人保证，在斯特雷尔教授及其他科、系教职员之教导下，再经两年之培训，余将回国与其他教育工作者合作，为我国人民组织一高效率之公众教育体系，以使他们能步美国人之后尘，发展和保持一真正之民主国家，因此乃唯一能够实现的正义与自由的理想之国。

如蒙告知居于纽约附近之若干捐助人姓名，俾便设法一一前往拜会，则对余当为一极有意义之事。

谨致最佳祝愿及问候，

陶文濬敬上

1916年2月16日于哥伦比亚大学

哈特莱学生宿舍1010室

## 注释

①J. E. 罗素　当时任美国哥伦比亚大学师范学院院长。

② 第一次革命　指1911年孙中山领导的资产阶级民主革命，即辛亥革命。

③ 据安徽省陶行知纪念馆《陶行知纪念馆五岁》97页所载，已故休宁县教师程管侯1954年亲笔写的《自传》中有“1911年，31岁、宣统三年、辛亥，参加余德民、陶行知、汪章瑞、程则裴等在屯溪湖余家庄起义……余德民失败走依黎宗岳”的记载。起义领导人余德民之子，祁门县退休干部余芳提供的书面材料亦说：解放后听父亲余德民口述参加起义的有平民教育家陶行知、金慰农、余家榴先生等。

④ 基督信徒　此系由英文Christian翻译过来，可作基督徒、基督教徒、基督信徒以及按基督教义行事的人解。据陶行知的亲属和友人提供的回忆材料(其中有儿子陶宏、陶晓光；老同学、原金陵大学校长陈裕光，同辈亲属、当时曾长时间在一起工作的曹子云等）说明：陶行知曾经信仰基督教义，但他从未参加基督教会组织的教仪活动。

# 敦促国际和平会议速派代表来华

——致国际和平会议主席



致国际和平会议主席：

为了在远东更有成效地开展国际和平会议并在远东与西方的运动之间取得密切联系，我们出席布鲁塞尔会议的中国代表团恳切要求国际和平会议全体会议尽速派遣代表来华，以便在全体会议和中国全国委员会之间起联络作用。

我们相信，全体会议采取此一步骤将大大便利和促进争取世界和平与正义的运动，并将受到中国人民的高度重视。

陈铭枢、陶行知、王锡礼、钱俊瑞、
张清源、胡秋原、P. A. 江
于1936年9月7日

## 注释

此信是1936年9月出席比利时首都布鲁塞尔召开的国际和平大会第一次会议的中国代表，致大会主席英国西薛尔爵士的信。该会接受了中国代表的建议，于是年底派代表来中国，参加在上海由宋庆龄主持召开的远东和平大会。此信是由陶行知起草并呈交的。

# 汇100美元请转交救国会[①]

——致蔡承新

亲爱的承新兄弟：

阔别已非一日。自友人处得知你在业务上很有成就并乐为友辈福利尽力，喜甚。随函附上100美元支票一张，供救国会使用。倘有机会遇见负责朋友，望费神代为兑款转交他们。同时，望能早日见复，并以可爱祖国近况见告。

谨致最良好祝愿。

你的挚友

W. T[②]

1937年4月23日于纽约市

第90大街西310号教育促进会

**注 释**

① 此件原是陶行知从美国寄给时在上海的蔡承新的英文书信。当时陶行知在国外执行“国民外交使节”任务，他将募捐来的款子，陆续通过当时在中国银行工作的蔡承新转交给全国各界救国联合会。

② W. T. 是“文濬”二字开头的英文字母。是陶行知最早见于英文书信中的笔名。

# 汇200美元请转交救国会和全国学联

——致蔡承新



亲爱的承新兄弟：

兹另函附上200美元支票一张，希将100元交与救国会，另100元交与全国学生联合会。如他们正好不来，可否请向博物馆路基督教青年会全国委员会刘良模①先生询问？通过刘先生可能找到他们。这是在此间筹集到的——确切些说是由海外的中国朋友们自动捐助的一笔小款。国内各团体急需钱用，务希于本月25日前将款交与可收此款的负责人。望即将收据寄来。

谨致衷心的感谢。

你的挚友

W. T.

［附言］由陆璀记名的旅行支票，你可以从通济隆银行(Thomas Cook）领取。

1937年5月11日于伊利诺斯州芝加哥第59大街东1414号国际大楼

## 注释

① 刘良模　当时在上海基督教青年会工作。

# 汇300美元请转交救国会和全国学联

——致蔡承新

亲爱的C.H.[①]兄弟：

随函附上300美元汇票一张，汇票副本已交同班邮轮寄交付款银行。望立即兑款并平分两份各150元，分别转交我们“两位敬爱的姐妹”。[②]请一如既往传话给她们以便他们能来取款。

顺致衷心的感谢，并代向刘、施两位先生致意。

你的兄弟

W. T.

1937年6月24日

## 注释

① C. H. 是承新英文Chen Hsin的第一个字母。

②“两位敬爱的姐妹”即“两联”，指“全国各界救国联合会”和“全国学生联合会”。

# 明天到旧金山去

——致吴树琴

亲爱的吴女士：

6月22日惠书刚才收到，得悉在你收到我的复信前你已经回家了。我想，你一定已将你家地址告知卫生实验站，由该站转信。如果还未收到我的复信，最好写信给卫生站。我已经为你取到40美元的奖学金，经由上海汉口路中国银行邮寄给你。如尚未收到该款，最好写信去问该银行。我现在洛杉矶，明天早上到旧金山。如果你要给我写信，最好寄到我在此信写明的地址。无论我到哪里，他们都会将信转给我的。

致最良好的祝愿。

你忠实的W. T.

1937年8月1日

于纽约市第90号大街西310号

**注释**

此件和1937年8月11日、8月22日、10月5日、12月7日致吴树琴信，原稿均为英文。

# 国外行程安排

——致吴树琴

亲爱的树琴：

接七月八日来信，喜甚。得知所寄各物均已收到，很为高兴。我再留此间十日，然后到墨西哥一个月。尔后将在印地安纳和迈阿密两个大学作两次演讲。我可能于十月底到欧洲去，并可能取道西伯利亚回国。我身体很好。希望你同你母亲生活愉快。

致良好祝愿。

你忠实的W. T.

1937年8月11日于加里福尼亚

旧金山中国男青年会

# 参加红十字会，为民族自由而战

——致吴树琴

亲爱的树琴：

我猜想你仍在徽州。你好吗？该是我们大家都参加为我们的民族自由而进行战斗的时候了。在医药工作方面，你能够帮助做许多事情。参加红十字会吧！来信告知你进行得怎样。祝你成功。中国万岁！

我今晚八时要到墨西哥去，三天可以到那里。

你的朋友
W. T.
1937年8月22日

# 日本帝国主义必败

——致吴树琴

亲爱的树琴：

我现在已从墨西哥回来。我在那里过得很愉快。墨西哥是个非常有趣和鼓舞人心的国家。我学到了许多东西，交了许多朋友。多数墨西哥印第安人看起来像中国人。他们当中有些人面貌像北方人，还有些人像广东人。他们待我很好，使我觉得就像在家里一样。确实，几千年前我们还是亲戚呢。

我于今晨抵达芝加哥。我将向这里的同胞们发表演说，然后于明晨前往印第安纳大学同该校学生谈话。七日，我将在首都华盛顿。只要知道哪里最需要我，我便可决定是留在这里还是回国。这一点，我一到首都华盛顿就会知道。

你这几个月生活得好吗？有三件事可以打败日本帝国主义：(1) 中国的团结、持久抗战；(2) 日本国内民主力量的兴起；(3) 世界各国对日本进行道义上的谴责和经济上的封锁。我现在正尽力唤醒西方各国的朋友们。如果日本不能从这些国家获得战争物资，它就无法进行战争。

望常来信。我想知道你的计划和健康状况。你母亲身体好吗？你父亲呢？你的兄弟以及你们"三姐妹"①中的另外两位呢？

W. T.

1937年10月5日

来信仍寄"纽约市第90号大街西310号"。

## 注释

①“三姐妹”指吴树琴和她的同学沈德华、黄彤麟。三人同时毕业于安徽隆阜第四女子中学。

# 增添生活斗争的力量

——致吴树琴

我亲爱的树琴女士：

十月三十日来信收到，谢谢你。从来信得知，你仍在徽州。和你母亲在一起。确实，母爱是纯真的。但愿我的母亲还活着、能和我在一起就好了。我知道，你在母亲的关怀下一直生活得多么愉快。只是我觉得遗憾的是，你竟然把我忘记得这么长一段时间。我想，我收到你上一次来信是在八月，此后即未得到你的任何信息。由于战局越来越严重，我一直在为你担心哩。

我将在这里再逗留两个月，然后经欧洲回国。我身体很好，只是家中来的消息令人苦恼。我的孩子们分散在四个地方：一个在徽州，一个在南京，两个在上海，但是分开住。

我希望你来信比以往更勤一些。即使只言片语也可令我免于躭心并意味着增添生活斗争的力量。

W. T.

1937年12月7日于纽约市

第90号大街西310号

# 陶行知代拟《杜威声明》[1]

## ——致甘地等

印度中央省瓦尔达
圣雄甘地[2]先生

希望您与我们共同作如下声明。同一请求已送交罗曼·罗兰[3]、阿尔伯特·爱因斯坦[4]、伯特兰·罗素[5]。如有建议，请电纽约第72号大街东320号。如五日内未闻相反意见，即视为同意。

鉴于东方文明正遭恣意摧毁，为着人类、和平与民主，我们提议各国人民组织自愿的抵制日货运动，拒绝将战争物资出售和租借给日本，在有助于其侵略政策之各方面停止与日本合作，同时尽可能给予中国各种援助以进行救济和自卫，直至日本自中国撤退其一切武装力量并放弃其侵略政策为止。

约翰·杜威

1937年12月6日

**附录：印度国民大会党复杜威函**

……

我已收到约翰·杜威、艾伯特·爱因斯坦、阿尔特兰·罗素和罗曼·罗兰自纽约发来的如下电文："鉴于东方文明正遭恣意摧毁，为着人类和平与民主，我们提议各国人民组织自愿的抵制日货运动，拒绝将战争物资出售和租借与日本，在有助于其侵略政策之各方面停止与日本合作，同时尽可能给予中国各种援助以进行救济和自卫，直至日本自中国撤退其一切武装力量并放弃其侵略政策为止。”希望国民大会赞同此一声明并加以宣传，号召全印度共同行动。

下列答复已由我发送与约翰·杜威。

“来电悉。国民大会党对日本侵略已予谴责，完全同情中国，号召抵制日货，同意声明之总方针、总目的，并正加以宣传。国民大会党极愿为人类、和平与民主普遍进行合作，认为达到此等目标之真正基础乃消灭法西斯及帝国主义。”

在向报界发布此等信息时，我应再度提请公众注意不买日货之迫切必要性。在中国，恐怖层出不穷，武力、空袭、毒气杀死了几十万中国儿童，恰恰是在摧毁它的精髓。对于在中国这个事件发生出现的暴行和不人道，我们感到憎恶。但仅仅同情是不够的，我们必须尽可能给予援助。这项援助可以有两类：一是拒绝购买日货，一是经济上支援其医药救济。我相信国民大会党委员会及其他团体将会对此抵制日货运动进行宣传。全印国民大会党委员会办公室将会收到医药救济的捐赠并转交适当处所。我们已经收到对医药用品的紧急要求。我真诚相信，印度人民将会尽其所能救济遭受苦难、备受折磨的生活在中国的人类。

J. 尼赫鲁⑥（签名）

原载1937年12月23日《时事通讯》第30期

## 注释

①《杜威声明》指杜威致甘地、罗曼·罗兰、阿尔伯特·爱因斯坦、伯特兰·罗素等人的信电，是陶行知代杜威草拟并经杜威同意发出。据陶行知《衔备忘》所载，信电稿发出时间是1937年12月6日。此件过去曾译为《杜威宣言》。

② 甘地（Mohandas Karamchand Gandhi，1869—1948） 印度民族运动领

袖，在印度被尊称为“圣雄”(Mahatma)。

③ 罗曼·罗兰（Romain Rolland，1866—1944） 法国作家、音乐学家、社会活动家。1915年获诺贝尔文学奖。受十月革命鼓舞，同高尔基建立友谊。热烈支持无产阶级革命。

④ 阿尔伯特·爱因斯坦（A1bert Einstein，1879—1955） 物理学家。生于德国，1933年因受纳粹政权迫害，迁居美国。因创立广义相对论以及理论物理学方面的卓越贡献，于1921年获诺贝尔物理学奖。

⑤ 伯特兰·罗素（Bertrand Russell，1872—1970） 英国哲学家、数学家、逻辑学家。1921年曾来华讲学。在政治态度上反对侵略战争，主张和平主义。

⑥ 尼赫鲁（Jawaharlal Nehru，1889—1964） 1929年任印度国大党全国委员会总书记。1936年当选为该党主席。1947年8月印度独立后任内阁总理直至逝世。

# 函谢为访印作安排

——致谟罕拉里

亲爱的谟罕拉里先生：

非常高兴在伦敦有幸认识您。承蒙为我访问你们伟大的国家作出安排，谨表谢意。我已抵达此间，正好赶上“阿拉密斯”号班轮，该轮今午即将启航，预定于8月5日到达科伦坡。我必须在8月19日之前从印度返回科伦坡，以便于8月19日乘“霞飞元帅”号班轮启航回国。您为我所作的一切安排，我都会同意。凡有中国朋友的地方，我都想同他们在一起呆上两三个小时。请转告贵友设法找到他们并与他们一道作出安排。到科伦坡后如经济上能得到补充，我将把德里和佛祖诞生地包括在我的旅行计划内，可能乘飞机。望再函告贵友。谨向你们的民族致敬——完全的自治！

您的朋友　陶行知

1938年7月27日于埃及

苏伊士米斯尔旅馆

# 为介绍本人给印度人民表示感谢

——致谟罕拉里





亲爱的谟罕拉里先生：

未能送上拙作《中国大众教育》一文，特此向您道歉。我的手稿已由敝友装运回国，不能取出送上，殊觉遗憾。不过，我要在印度亲自告诉贵友。

您通知我关于访印安排的信想必已到船上，今午我可能有机会看到这些安排。

蒙费神将我介绍给贵国人民，再次表示感谢。今晨，我正遵嘱执笔写信给甘地先生、泰戈尔先生、博斯先生、巴姆勒基先生和辛哈先生。

您的朋友

陶行知

## 注释

此件未注明写信日期及地点。

# 将从新印度学习到首要的一课[①]

——致甘地



亲爱的甘地[②]先生：

您的教导和牺牲精神，永远鼓舞着中国人民。我久已梦想着要访问你们伟大的国家，现在终于有机会如愿以偿，感到十分高兴。在伦敦的谟罕拉里先生想必已将有关我计划中的此行以及抵印的大致日期函告，届时我一定前来拜会您。我今晚离开这里，预计8月5日抵达科伦坡。我在印度可逗留两星期。我的旅行计划正由谟罕拉里先生在科伦坡或加尔各答的朋友作具体安排。就我的目的而言，时间实在太短，但是，在您的指导下，我可以从新印度学习到首要的一课。期待着与您愉快地会见。并祝愿完全的自治。

尊敬您的陶行知

1938年7月27日

于埃及苏伊米斯尔旅馆

**注释**

① 1938年7月27日于埃及苏伊士米斯尔旅馆，陶行知连续写给印度友人七封英文信，这是其中之一。

② 甘地（1869—1948） 印度民族运动领袖。陶行知于1938年8月14日访问甘地，并曾赠送甘地《中国大众教育运动》讲稿。后该文发表在印度《民族旗

帜》杂志上时，甘地作了以下按语："陶行知博士不久前来印度访问我时，我曾请他送一份令人注目的中国进行大众教育情况的小册子给我。如今他已送给我，我不得不认为这份具有指导意义的小册子，对我们印度是非常有用的。"

# 希望当面领教

——致博斯[①]

亲爱的博斯主席：

我终于有机会在回国途中访问印度，感到十分高兴。在伦敦的谟罕拉里先生想必已将有关我计划中的此行以及预定到达加尔各答的时间函告。我将于今晚乘“阿拉密斯”号班轮启航，8月5日到达科伦坡。我将从那里前来拜会您。您在第五十一届国民大会上的演讲，我已拜读。除了与您会晤时我希望进一步领教的有关德瓦勒拉[②]先生的政治和德国的劳动服务营之外，我同意您的每一个观点。祝您在领导你们的民族走向自由的事业中取得伟大的成功。

尊敬您的陶行知

1938年7月27日于

苏伊士米斯尔旅馆

**注释**

① 博斯（Chandra Bose） 时任印度国大党第51届主席。

② 德瓦勒拉（Eamon de Valera 1882—1975） 爱尔兰总统(1959—1973)。早年参加爱尔兰独立运动，曾任新芬党主席(1919—1962)，后另组共和党，四次出任政府总理（1932—1959），任期内宣布爱尔兰独立（1937）和脱离英联邦(1948)。

# 函告将到印度拜会

## ——致泰戈尔

亲爱的泰戈尔博士：

上次在北京有极好的机会会见您，至今已近20年了。您的教言永远是我国人民的宝贵财富。我在返回中国途中终于有机会对你们的伟大国家作短期访问，非常高兴，特此奉告。我将乘搭“阿拉密斯”号班轮于8月5日到达科伦坡。我可以在印度度过约两周时间，于19日乘“霞飞”号班轮启航。我抵加尔各答时，将立即再度函告我拜访您的日期。期待着很快再次与您愉快地会见。

尊敬您的陶行知

1938年7月27日

于苏伊士米斯尔旅馆

**注释**

泰戈尔（1861—1941） 印度作家、诗人和社会活动家。1924年4月曾来华讲学。

# 希望了解新印度

——致巴姆勒基

亲爱的巴姆勒基博士：

在伦敦的谟罕拉里先生想必已将有关我计划中访问你们伟大国家之行函告阁下。我早欲直接了解新印度，我在回国途中能够对印度作短期访问，感到很高兴。我将于8月5日到达科伦坡，19日离开科伦坡，所以我大约有两个星期在印度逗留。时间太短，但是有您的帮助，我希望我可以对正在印度进行的最重要工作的若干方面有所了解。期待着很快与您愉快地会见。感谢您为使我的访问获得许多教益所提供的帮助。

您非常忠实的陶行知

1938年7月27日于埃及

苏伊士米斯尔旅馆

# 访印目的在于学习

## ——致辛哈和布拉卡舒

亲爱的先生们：

在伦敦，有人介绍我认识你们的朋友谟罕拉里先生，他已将有关我计划在返回中国途中访问印度之行函告。我访问你们的伟大国家，目的在于学习。我希望向贵国的农民、贵国的工人、贵国的教师以及贵国的伟大领袖学习到一些重要的东西。但两周的有限时间只能允许我对贵国的伟大文明作一片段的领略而已。同时，如有机会，我可以向贵国人民报告当前中国的情况。我将于8月5日到达科伦坡，并于19日离开科伦坡回国。我尚未看到谟罕拉里先生有关在印度的安排，但是在我逗留印度两周期间，我将遵从他与你们一道作出的安排。期待着愉快地与你们会见。

您的非常忠诚的陶行知

1938年7月27日于苏伊士米斯尔旅馆

# 就育才学校情况回答罗格夫人提问

——致罗格夫人[①]

亲爱的罗格夫人：

顷接3月16日惠书副本两份，皆由基督教女青年会自成都转来。尊函令我忆及数年前您及罗格教授访华期间我们一同度过的愉快时光。衷心祝贺您在美国援华联合会任职，参加该会的光辉工作。美国援华联合会对中国战争孤儿深为关怀，不仅在文化上，而且在物质上给他们以帮助。三年来，我本人也有幸为这些孤儿竭尽绵薄。得知上次我与耿丽淑女士所作简短之谈话，竟能传至远方朋友，殊觉快慰之至。“我们如今是在共同作战。”夫人此言极是。诚然，我们正在为一个共同的胜利——为自由击败法西斯主义、希特勒主义的胜利而战斗在一起。战争不会很快结束，但孩子们成长很快。凡能给予他人的孩子以最大关怀者，即能赢得真正的胜利。以对本国孩子之爱施于他国之孩子，乃一极为崇高之举。

兹遵大函所嘱，依所提问题之先后次序答复如下：

（1）我校现有165名儿童，其中十分之九为难童，他们因日寇侵略而丧失家园。难童中，半数以上为无父无母者，他们乃真正之战争孤儿。但即使是父母双全之难童，亦无法获得彼等父母之任何资助，或因其家财已丧失殆尽，或因生活指数过高，其父母已陷于无法生存之境地。因此，150名儿童生存及教育之全部重任乃不得不由我校承担。

（2）我校创办于1939年秋，每月预算3,000元，嗣后预算不断增加，目前几高达国币40,000元。然而，由于同一时期内生活指数增长过速，故我校预算瞠乎其后远甚。

| | 1942年头5个月的月平均拨款 |
| --- | --- |
| A. 行政费用 | 1,500元 |
| B. 工作人员薪金及伙食 | 8,000元 |
| C. 住房费用 | 2,000元 |
| D. 难童伙食 | 18,000元 |
| E. 服装 | 3,000元 |
| F. 医药 | 1,000元 |
| G. 设备 | 2,000元 |
| H. 照明及燃料 | 1,000元 |
| I. 印刷和课本 | 1,500元 |
| J. 杂费 | 1,500元 |
| 总计 | 39,000元 |

（3）我校儿童每月每人费用总额约为240元，包括医药、服装及教育费用。仅伙食一项，人均每月费用约为国币120元。看来开支还将不断增加。

（4）我校给予儿童游戏、劳动和学习之机会。游戏方面，有篮球、排球、体操、台球、象棋等等；劳动方面，我校儿童打扫宿舍、教室，并有其他校内活动。此外，还给每个学生一分土地种植蔬菜供集体食用，同时可留一部分产品归己支配；学习方面，学生可用三分之二的时间攻读普修课，而用三分一的时间攻读适合个人兴趣和才能之特修课。我校全年开课。因此我校儿童不仅能以与其他学校儿童大致相同之速度升级，而且能在特修课方面打下更为坚实之基础。

（5）我校普修课系根据教育部规定之小学及初中课程设置。特修课包括音乐、戏剧、绘画、文学，自然科学和社会科学诸方面之选修科。不久，当新生入学时，还将增加农艺和机械工艺两门课。就每个学生而言，他可以选定一门选修科作专攻对象，只要他在这方面表现出确具特殊之才能。

(6) 我校现有教师26位。每一特修课平均有两位专家作指导，其余则为普修课教师。教师中三分之二为大学毕业生或留学生并经培训。我们没有培训学校这样的专门机构，但我们的研究所通过研究问题、阅读书籍以及定期开会和外出考察将所有教师凝聚在一起，它实际上就是在职教师的培训中心。

(7) 我们每个月约有国币20,000元可以动用，其中8,500元由中央救济总会[2]拨给，尚需筹募约国币20,000元。

(8) 我校计划将学生人数增至400人，希望多招具有天赋之难童。为了改善我校学生和工作人员的营养，我们希望您能够向美国援华联合会提出建议，每月给我们拨款2,000美元，每年总计24,000美元，使我们的新计划得以实现。拨款总额中，15,000元将用于伙食，两千美元将用于加强我校的技术人员，4,000元将用于添置设备和改善我校的医疗服务。

夫人，如果我把关于育才学校诞生的几个小故事告诉您，您一定会更加了解育才。托马斯·A.爱迪生的童年给了我创办育才的巨大推动力。如您所知，爱迪生小时候喜欢玩弄化学品，他的老师是个老派先生，对此大为不满，所以爱迪生在学校只三个月就被开除了。他的母亲对自己的孩子很了解，允许他在地下室继续进行实验，并亲自教他历史和地理。正是在一位慈母的关怀和自身天资的推动下，爱迪生才对科学和人类福利作出了这么多的贡献。有两件事给了我很深的印象：一是具有科学才能的人应该尽早开始学习科学；二是有天赋儿童的老师应该更多地学习爱迪生母亲的教育态度。这是促使我创办育才学校的五种力量之一。为使此信不致过长，我暂且讲这个故事给您听也就满意了，其余的留到将来再说。您的信给了我一种轻松感，因为我的大部分时间都用在进行一种新型的“运动”——与粮价赛跑，并设法筹措足够的基金以使我和我的同事们能够致力于真正的难童教育。

承蒙为育才尽力，谨表谢意，并伫候佳音。请代向罗格教授和耿丽淑女士问候。

您的朋友陶行知

1942年6—7月[③]

## 注释

① 罗格夫人（Mrs. Louise K. Rugg） 时在美国纽约第78大街东25号华尔特·惠特曼学校。

② 中央救济总会 即当时的国民政府赈济委员会。

③ 原信打字稿未注明写信日期，据信中所列“1942年头5个月平均拨款”一语推断，写信日期可能是1942年6—7月。

# 为育才学校申请每月资助2000美元

## ——致毕来思女士

亲爱的毕来思女士[①]：

我能在爱德华·卡特博士离华前夕与其晤面，并能趁此机会奉上更多可资朋友们对我们的实验作进一步了解的材料，几可视为一大奇迹。因准备材料事出极大仓促，所余时间过于短暂，致未克于函中详报有关各情。

首先，请让我代表我校难童及全校员工向美国援华联合会、美国援华会及美国救济中国战争孤儿委员会给予我们慷慨的、及时的捐助致以衷心的感谢。我们特别要感谢您、克鲁格女士和卡特夫人对我们的规划所给予的亲切关怀以及为促其实现而给予的热情支持。

1月31日，蒙艾德敷先生慨允相助，曾委托他奉上规划报告一份及育才学校生活照片数张，希望对您有一定参考价值。

随函附奉与美国援华会资助有关的、业经合格会计师审计的1943年1月1日至6月30日育才学校半年收支报告副本一份；迄今为止从您处收到分期付款清单一张；育才生活照片24张；我校绘画课学生所作木刻复制品13份；拙作歌曲7首；《育才三方针》《育才十字诀》各1份。

迄今为止，已从您处收到10,500美元，折合中国国币250,225.81元。此外，我们还直接从美国援华联合会重庆办事处收到火灾救济金中国国币50,000元以及贵会补助金临时存款的银行利息总计中国国币2,206.36元。银行结余及手头现款结余共为中国国币62,313.57元。

1943年8月的支出为中国国币100,000元，而1942年1月的支出则为中国国币12,516元，1942年12月的支出增为中国国币50,379.80元。在上述中国国币100,000元中，约十分之一来自中央救济总会，十分之一弱来自中华自救会，十分之三来自美国援华会和美国援华联合会，十分之五强来自在华的育才朋友，但此款须逐月筹集。生活费用不断增长使我们无法多招新生。9月的预算为中国国币110,000元，比较保守的估计是：中秋节后生活费用将会猛增。12月份我们的预算很可能到达中国国币150,000元之数。我们，恳切期望，年终之前，最好不迟于10月，您每月能给予我们2,000美元。大约有30名年龄较大，培养前途不大的学生将转学到别的学校， 这样空出的名额可供招收年龄较小的儿童。我们计划音乐组收10名幼童，自然科学组收20名，年龄都在10岁以下。

不需多久，我将寄上由儿童谱写旋律的歌曲、育才生活故事以及可能到手的照片。

请代向卡特夫人、克鲁格女士及其他朋友问好。祝您的伟大工作成功。

您的极忠诚朋友陶行知

1943年9月9日

**原信附件一：1943年1—3月期间育才活动报告**

一、一般活动

（一）在一月份，根据教育部规定，举行各课程的期终考试，然后放寒假。因我校是难童学校，大多数学生无家可归，故为他们安排了新年活动。一种活动是动员留校学生观看原为巴拉兹所著戏剧《莫扎特》的表演，希望从这位伟大音乐家的一生中获得教益。

（二）中国春节庆祝活动进行了两次，学校综合展览会举行了两天以招待附近村民。

（三）选派群众教育工作的杰出人员，与当地中心学校合作，引导农村初等小学学生担任小先生，与别人同享真理，为文盲建立“学习岗”，以便将教育普及到更大范围的群众中去。

（四）参加编辑“育才丛书”的作者们开了几次会，会上相互交流了经验，讨论了各自在工作中遇到的问题。

（五）建立了一个“生产消费合作社”。

（六）组织了一次联合运动会，其他学校的学生和其他村庄的农民也来参加。

（七）开展了土地利用运动，以使我校的每寸土地可种植蔬菜。

（八）所有在校女生都在3月8日庆祝了妇女节。

（九）新闻及现代史课程每周测验一次以资强调。

二、分组活动

（一）音乐组

1. 音乐组学生于一月份赴重庆参加现场观摩，以便向市内的音乐家学习必要的理论和技能。

2. 2月中旬，在中央训练团青年训练处赞助下举行了一次音乐会。

3. 3月，在中央训练团行政人员训练处赞助下，音乐组学生举行了一次音乐会。

4. 学生作曲20首。

（二）戏剧组

1. 首次在国内舞台上演出《橘子舞》。

2. 春节，演出戏剧《儿童团》和小歌剧《橘子舞》。

3. 3月初赴重庆进行现场观摩并安排演出董林肯先生所作戏剧《小主人》。

（三）文学组

1. 春节期间，演出名剧《伪君子》。

2. 邀请重庆主要权威人士参加“儿童文学”讨论会并为《战时教育》月刊编辑“儿童文学”专刊。

3. 在这3个月期间，写了30篇论文，创作了两首诗。

（四）绘画组

1. 举办了一次新年儿童绘画展览会。

2. 自3月19日至21日，在基督教青年会举办了一次育才之友中国画展览会。

自3月20日至23日，在励志社举办了一次绘画组学生创作的木刻、中国画、水彩画展览会。

自3月20日至23日，在我校儿童美术馆举办了一次育才之友木刻及世界著名美术照片展览会。

（五）社会科学组

春节期间，演出《莲舟》和《我们的总部》两剧。

（六）自然科学组

2月中旬，学生被分派到战时首都附近包括化工厂、电厂、机器厂在内的各工厂去接受现场训练。

**原信附件二：1943年4—6月期间育才活动报告**

一、一般活动

（一）4月4日，举行了盛大的儿童节庆祝活动，邀请了村上儿童及其父母、亲戚参加庆祝大会。

（二）举行了演讲、作文及关于国内外时事的比赛性考试。

（三）强调“五月诸事件”的研究。

1. 就五月份有纪念意义诸日的问题发表了演讲。

2. 5月4日举行了“学生运动之意义”的讨论大会。

（四）6月7日，向鄂西前线陈、孙两将军及全体战士发出贺电，祝贺他们于最近取得的抗日胜利，并于“龙舟节”（现在又叫“诗人节”，以此纪念伟大诗人屈原）汇去国币10,000元作为我们的一份薄礼。

二、分组活动

（一）音乐组

4月3日和4月4日连续两天假座银行俱乐部举行音乐会，以庆祝儿童节并响应以五月为“音乐月”的全国号召。

4月5日，在中央广播大楼举行了一场音乐会，招待战时首都知识界人士，同时广播并灌制歌曲唱片。

4月18日，向南洋各地、印度、美国及苏联播放歌曲，并灌制了更多的唱片。

4月19日，在中国农民银行举行了一场音乐会。

5月1日，应军事委员会政治部的要求，在北温泉举行了一场音乐会，招待英美军官。

上述所有音乐会的节目，既有世界伟大的作曲大师创作的乐曲，也有我们自己的儿童创作的乐曲。

在四月至六月3个月内，由学生自己创作的歌曲共22首。

（二）戏剧组

从4月8日开始，四幕剧《小主人》在重庆舞台上连续演出了七个夜场。

儿童节，在中苏文化协会赞助下，我们的儿童为中苏儿童交谊会演出了《儿童团》及《丰收舞》。

4月19日，在中国农民银行再一次演出了《儿童团》。

四月底，《小主人》在北碚连续演出了五场。

所有上述演出的听众和观众达15,000人次。

五月，《小主人》在重庆附近的合川县城连续演出了四场，观众达5,000人次。

（三）文学组

在下列每个纪念日都举办了诗歌朗诵晚会：诗人节，中国爱国诗人屈原诞生2221周年。高尔基逝世七周年。

举办了一次短篇故事晚会。

撰写了论文30篇。

（四）绘画组

五月，负责美术组的许士骐教授征集到13尊石膏半身塑像携回儿童美术馆以供研究和实习。

6月5日，因邻居不慎失火，本组及儿童美术馆部分受灾，全部石膏半身塑像及部分收藏品被焚毁，损失达国币250,000元。重建工作正全力进行中。

（五）社会科学组

1. 派遣志愿人员每周两次赴自贡市，帮助那里的一所小学教学生唱歌、绘画。

2. 派遣志愿人员到本地镇上教小学生唱歌、绘画。

3. 举行了故事晚会，以庆祝苏联抵抗纳粹侵略两周年。

（六）自然科学组

本组的一个学生吕长春与音乐组的一个学生合作，用废料制作了两套简单的幻灯，为在农村推广群众教育增添了一个良好的工具。

## 注释

① 毕来思（Miss Mildred Price）女士当时在美国纽约"美国援华会"任执行主任。曾积极支持陶行知的教育事业，并给予一定的援助。

# 请勿以招收新生作为增加补助的条件

——致毕来思

亲爱的毕来思女士：

12月7日手示及1月份汇款一千美元均已于一周前收到，谨表衷心的感谢。承蒙垂询“是否愿意以他种方法提供此等款项”，此问题使我沉思良久。次日我即电告，请将2月份拨款购买哈里弗鱼肝油及胶囊航寄我们，这将大有助于恢复众多儿童的身体健康和改善育才学校的财政状况。我又曾请求您，在我们进一步提出要求前暂停待发之款，使我有时间考虑接受贵会补助的某种或某些最佳方式，以使我们照料下的儿童能获得最大的裨益。

2月7日，布朗内尔先生曾通过余友转交给我中国国币90,000元，他希望将其中39,024.38元按官定外汇比率（政府补助1,000美元的百分之百折合价）折合1,000美元由我校转与布朗内尔夫人，余额作为捐款赠与学校。因此事能令双方受益，故我已同意此一建议。见此信以及我所出具之1,000美元收据，请即将此数额交与玛丽·赫斯特·布郎内尔夫人，该款请在给予育才的3月份补助款额中扣除。惟望布朗内尔夫人或其代表出具1,000美元之收据，俾能以之出示我友。

根据协议，该款应于3月底前交付。倘未蒙同意上述支付办法，或以其他原因未蒙允余所请，则请自便处置，但望惠发一加急电报，简复“允”或“不允”即可，俾便考虑应否原款璧还余友。

若上述建议均未蒙俯允，则请照常拨付或以您认为合适之其他方式拨付每月资助款额。如是则请将余出具之2月份及3月份收据予以销毁。

至于按季度拨付之9,000美元，则迄今仍未收到。艾德敷先生曾言，原因很可能是我们没有招收新生，而这是中国儿童福利委员会作为增加拨款的一个条件规定了的。您看是否可以要求计划委员会取消有关此一条件之条款，因为仅物价增长这一因素即可证明您增加对我们的补助是正确的。我们将尽力招收新生，但无论如何不要以此作为增加补助费的一个严格条件。自上周以来，我们已增加了10名新生，他们的智商都很高；其中两名被吸收进了音乐组。

盼早日电复。祝好！

您的极忠诚朋友陶行知

1944年2月9日

## 收　据

——致援华会

兹收到

援华会1944年3月份1,000美元，此据。

为培养有特殊才能的难童而设立的育才学校校长

陶行知

1944年2月

# 函请馈赠英国画明信片给儿童美术馆

——致史密斯①

亲爱的先生：

闻印有英国绘画之明信片业已到达贵处，消息传来，令育才学校主办之儿童美术馆的小美术家们深表钦慕（按：育才学校系为招收天才难童而创立之学校）。未卜阁下能否惠赠此等明信片一套与儿童美术馆。我可以向阁下保证，我们的小艺术家们必能充分发挥其作用，并对阁下之慷慨馈赠深表感谢。

特此预致谢意。

您的忠实朋友育才学校校长陶行知

1944年3月10日

## 注释

① 史丹莱·史密斯（Mr. Stanley Smith）时在英国大使馆任新闻专员。

# 吁请外国友人资助育才学校

——克里普斯夫人[①]



亲爱的克里普斯夫人：

首先，请允许我向您及贵会表示衷心的感谢，感谢你们在中华民族的解放斗争中为它所作的一切。我相信，您定会乐于听到关于中国战时首都一所学校的情况。由于当前这场伟大斗争还在进行，这所学校便继续在为教育和培养父母双亡、家园被毁的儿童而进行战斗。这所学校的全名是：为招收具有特殊才能之难童而设立的育才学校。学校的名称就会让您一望而知我们所力图达到的目的。这些儿童都是通过智力测验和专门测验从战时儿童收容所、孤儿院以及战争第一阶段曾经一度勃兴的儿童自己的组织中选拔出来的。我们安排学生用四分之三到三分之二的时间攻读普修课，而以四分之一到三分之一的时间攻读适合他们各自的兴趣和才能的特修课。因此，我们将他们分成七个组以满足他们的不同要求。这七个组就是：音乐、绘画、戏剧、文学、舞蹈、自然科学和社会科学。

学校开始时有150名难童，都是按上述办法选拔和分组攻读普修课和特修课的。包括伙食、服装、住宿、教育和医疗在内的全部费用都由学校负责。由于物价上涨，我们不得不招收若干部分自费的学生。自今年春季开始，学生注册人数已达320名。而且我们还通过小先生制向校外失学的1,158名儿童及成人提供受教育的机会。

由于物价暴涨，我校教师及儿童均深受营养不良和科学设备不足之苦。因此，我代表为招收具有特殊才能之难童而设立的育才学校向您申请财政援助，以改善我校贫苦难童之营养，改进我校教师的生活状况，添置为实施有效教育所需要的设备。我们所申请的补助款将用于以下各项：

| | |
|---|---|
| （1）添置科学仪器 | 国币5,000,000元 |
| （2）提高60位教师的薪金，<br>从3,000元至10,000元，<br>12个月 | 5,040,000 |
| （3）改善316人的营养，<br>包括难童、教师和家属以及<br>工人之伙食，每人每月1,000元，<br>12个月 | 3,793,000 |
| （4）抵销每月170,000元的赤字，12个月 | 2,040,000 |
| 总计 | 16,072,000 |

随函附奉《育才实况》《育才三方针》《育才十字诀》《育才学校之创办》，美国援华联合会计划主任甘霖林《关于育才学校之报告》各一份。我希望这些材料和我的这封信将使您看到育才学校的真实情景并对学校的抱负、努力和困难有所了解。如蒙鼎力相助，以创造性的救济使育才能够帮助难童及教师得到更卫生的食品，过更健康的生活，实施更有效的教育，以使实验更富成果、更有成效，则不胜感激之至。

谨此伫候佳音。

育才学校校长陶行知敬上

1944年4月10日

## 注释

① 收信人除当时在英国援华会任职的克里普斯夫人外，信末尚附有以下收

信人名单：英国大使馆，英国援华会H.J.塞摩尔爵士（Sir H. J. Seymour）；中国中央银行，英国援华会秘书K.K.柯克（K. K. Kuok）；英国大使馆，约翰·布洛菲尔德（John Blofeld）先生；D.尼德哈姆（Dorothy Needham）博士；布朗特（Blunt）先生；赖特（Wright）先生；塞摩尔夫人（Lady Seymour），以及英国援华会各位先生。

# 为1944—1945年度育才概算作解释

——致艾德敷

亲爱的艾德敷①主任：

5月24日手示已转来北碚我处作复。我校申请1944年10月1日至1945年9月30日经费概算，是以最近9个月经费支出月平均增长额为根据的。我校1943年8月之预算为国币100,000元，而1944年5月之预算则已增至国币300,000元，月增长额为国币22,000元。1944年10月，预算将很可能跃至国币410,000元，到1945年9月，预算则可能到达国币674,000元之数额。因此，1944年10月至1945年9月全年之总预算应为国币6,504,000元，亦即每月为国币542,000元。我们的愿望是：预算的三分之二在国内筹集，三分之一即国币2,168,000元则由贵会给予补助。

以上乃代表育才学校对1944—1945年度概算所作的解释。

您极忠诚的朋友育才学校校长陶行知

1944年5月30日于育才学校

**注释**

① 艾德敷（Dwight W. Edwards）时任美国援华联合会驻华主任。

# 为维持和改进育才学校向国内外呼吁支援

——致国内外育才之友



亲爱的先生们：

育才学校是为招收具有特殊才能的难童而创办的学校。我现在代表育才学校向你们申请财政支援，以期改善我校儿童们的营养，添置为进行有效教育所需要的设备，为招收若干新生而进行准备，以及改进我校教师的生活状况。为了维持学校的现状，1944年下半年就需要国币2,562,000元。然而，我们在同一期间的可靠收入只有国币1,440,000元。财政赤字为国币1,222,000元，这笔款子我们准备向国内外的朋友们筹集。在改善我校儿童们的营养方面，我们需要另行增加每月国币28,000元，在提高薪金方面，则每月另需增加国币35,000元。为了增招新难童，因鉴于目前每月人均费用为国币2,000元以上，必须逐月增加10%以免中途发生财政危机。如能获得增招100名儿童所需的充分可靠的财政支援，则育才学校将能办得更为有效得多。不仅为了维持学校现状，而且为了改善学校现状，我们欢迎您在任何一方面或几个方面给我们以支援……

随函附奉《育才实况》《育才三方针》《育才十字诀》《育才财政状况》各一份。我希望这些材料以及我写的这封信，能给您看到育才学校的真实情景，并对育才的抱负和努力有所了解。如蒙鼎力相助，使育才能对学生实施更为有效的教育，并对科学教育进行更为富有成效的实验，则不胜感激之至。敬希赐复，伫候佳音。

育才学校校长

陶行知敬上

1944年6月30日于重庆和平路管家巷28号育才学校

# 请代设法在渝预检印刷品

——致陶露西·尼德姆





陶露西·尼德姆博士[1]：

小儿陶晓光将于一周内赴加尔各答中国航空公司工作。他携带有中英文书籍，包括育才学校铅印刊物及他自己学习所用参考书籍。据说旅客携带之书籍，特别是英文以外的外文书籍，往往被扣留作详细检查。不知有无办法将印刷品交由驻重庆英国当局先行检查，以便陶晓光能够通过印度国境而不致遇到不必要的耽搁。如蒙给他指点和帮助，当感激不尽也。诸多谢谢。

您的极忠诚的朋友、育才学校校长陶行知
1944年7月27日于重庆管家巷28号育才学校

**注释**

①陶露西·尼德姆博士（Mrs. Dorathy Needham）（女） 英国著名学者、《中国科学技术史》作者李约瑟博士（Dr. Joseph Needham）的夫人。当时是英国科学委员会驻华代表团成员，时在中英科学合作馆任职。

# 育才学校增收100名难童的计划及预算

——致甘霖林

亲爱的甘霖林博士：

10月17日手示敬悉，十分高兴。上次晤谈时，您表示担心我们可能变成“中国的达特默思”①一事，使我内心固有的、由于物价不断上涨而暂受压抑的对难童的炽热感情之火烧得更旺了。三日来我因感冒卧病在床，得以足够的闲暇作一番创造性的思考，由此作出了一个新的决定：育才学校将永远服务于贫苦儿童、不幸儿童、无人关心的儿童、无父无母的儿童、特别是当前的难童。

随函附奉一项计划的预算，此项计划看似新的，实则久经酝酿而未能实施耳。该项计划旨在额外招收100名具有天赋的难童，特别是来自战争正在进行的各战区的难童。预算包括人均15,000元的固定经费，拨款后可维持数年；还包括人均2,500元的日常费用。第一年的经费总额为国币4,500,000元。总额中除用以购置蚊帐之费用外，数额为国币1,300,000元之固定经费在新生入校前几乎全部必须备齐；日常费用250,000元则可按月拨付。

此外，日常费用还应增加10%，以防中途发生财政危机。

湘、桂前线的战事迫使数十万难童不断涌来，拯救难童之工作刻不容缓。为拯救儿童而奋斗亦即为拯救中国之未来。对获得拯救的儿童施以正当的教育无异于给我们的后代注射一剂精神上、智力上的“盘尼西林”，他们将会有助于使中国在一个更好的、由各民主国家组成的世界中作出有益的贡献。

计划业已制定。如有足够经费，我校能够招收1,000名；如只筹措到少量经费，亦可少收，比如说一百名或十几名。前天，即18日，周宗琼先生许诺资助两名儿童。今晨贺市长[②]已给我们特别许可，让我们在“抗建堂”演出戴爱莲教授的舞蹈和我们自己的音乐以筹措经费，时间定于11月3日至7日下午8时。如满座，义演所得足以资助18名。我校校舍及工作人员尚有多余，足以照顾这20名新生，开支可少于我此次所呈交之预算。恳切希望贵会给予我们财政支援，使我们至少能够再多招收100名儿童。祝愿早日实现我们的共同理想。

您的忠实朋友、育才学校校长陶行知

1944年10月21日

**原信附件一：**

**关于招收100名具有特殊才能的难童计划预算表**

——育才学校呈交

**固定经费**

| | 数量、单位价格（国币元） | 总计（国币元） |
|---|---|---|
| 双人床 | 50×5,400 | 270,000 |
| 双人桌 | 50×1,600 | 80,000 |
| 双人凳 | 50×400 | 20,000 |
| 脸盆 | 100×180 | 18,000 |
| 蚊帐 | 100×1,300 | 130,000 |
| 被褥 | 100×4,000 | 400,000 |
| 参考书 | | 50,000 |
| 工具 | | 30,000 |
| 实验设备 | | 100,000 |
| 医疗设备 | | 50,000 |
| 乐器 | | 200,000 |

续表

| | 数量、单位价格（国币元） | 总计（国币元） |
| --- | --- | --- |
| 庙宇(作校舍用)修缮费(包括浴室、厕所与烹饪设备) | | 100,000 |
| 总　计 | | 1,448,000 |
| 人均费用(整数) | | 15,000 |

**日常使用**

| | 人均月开支（国币元） | 100名儿童月总开支（国币元） | 年总开支（国币元） |
| --- | --- | --- | --- |
| 1. 伙食 | 1,226.00 | 122,600 | 1,471,200 |
| 2. 服装 | 400.00 | 40,000 | 480,000 |
| 3. 毛巾(每年4条×90) | 30.00 | 3,000 | 36,000 |
| 4. 帽子(每年2顶×60) | 10.00 | 1,000 | 12,000 |
| 5. 鞋子(每年3双×22) | 66.00 | 6,000 | 79,000 |
| 6. 肥皂(每年12块×40) | 40.00 | 4,000 | 48,000 |
| 7. 牙刷(每年3支×40) | 10.00 | 1,000 | 12,000 |
| 8. 课本(每年2套×90) | 15.00 | 1,500 | 18,000 |
| 9. 医疗费用 | 100.00 | 10,000 | 120,000 |
| 10. 材料 | 50.00 | 5,000 | 60,000 |
| 11. 照明 | 50.00 | 5,000 | 60,000 |
| 12. 零用钱 | 40.00 | 4,000 | 48,000 |
| 13. 教师薪水(10人×2,000) | 200.00 | 20,000 | 240,000 |
| 14. 教师伙食(10人×1,226) | 122.60 | 2,260 | 147,120 |
| 15. 校工工资(2人×1,000) | 20.00 | 2,000 | 24,000 |
| 16. 校工伙食(2人×1,226) | 24.52 | 2,452 | 29,424 |
| 17. 行政费与杂费 | 90.00 | 9,000 | 108,000 |
| 总　计 | 2,493.52 | 249,412 | 2,992,944 |
| 总计整数 | 2,500.00 | 250,000 | 3,000,000 |

**原信附件二：**

**新 生 月 开 支 表**

| | 入校后 | 入校前 |
|---|---|---|
| 1. 伙 食 | 1,471,200元 | |
| 2. 衣 服 | 180,000元 | 300,000元 |
| 3. 毛 巾 | | 36,000元 |
| 4. 帽 子 | | 12,000元 |
| 5. 鞋 子 | | 79,000元 |
| 6. 肥 皂 | | 48,000元 |
| 7. 牙 刷 | | 12,000元 |
| 8. 课 本 | 9,000元 | 9,000元 |
| 9. 医 疗 | 120,000元 | |
| 10. 材 料 | 60,000元 | |
| 11. 照 明 | 60,000元 | |
| 12. 零 用 | 48,000元 | |
| 13. 教师薪水 | 160,000元 | 80,000元 |
| 14. 教师伙食 | 97,120元 | 50,000元 |
| 15. 校工工资 | 24,000元 | |
| 16. 校工伙食 | 29,424元 | |
| 17. 行政费 | | 36,000元 |

## 注 释

①“中国的达特默思” “达特默思”（Dartmouth）指美国“达特默思学院”。该院前身是由美国教育家伊·惠洛克(Eleazar Wheelock，1711—1779）在1754年创办的一所专收贫苦土著民族印第安人青年入学的学校。1769年迁至新汉普夏州的汉诺佛镇，受“达特默思第二世伯爵”威廉·列治（William Legge，1731—1801）之私人捐助，学院因之用“达特默思”命名，这时已实际上是一所门类齐全的文理科大学。甘霖林博士担心育才会“变成中国的达特默思”，意即担心育才会变成一般的正规大学，不再是为穷孩子办的学校了。

② 贺市长指当时重庆市长贺耀祖。

# 为获准资助新招100名难童表示感谢

——致甘霖林

亲爱的甘霖林[①]博士：

兹委托唐堃珩（译音）先生代表我向贵会领取8月份和9月份的补贴余额（10月份如有，也一并领取），以及11月份140,000元的补贴。

据王夫人告知，儿童福利委员会[②]已经通过您的提议，再资助100名难童进育才。我可以肯定，此举将有助于早日实现我们的共同计划。由于若干物品不断涨价（以面盆为例，在我的预算中其价格为每只180元，然而时隔甚短，现已涨至280元。）所以希望将固定经费1,448,000元尽快预支给我们，以便预为新来难童购置必要设备，防止日后经济拮据。

我校新计划备蒙关怀，申请资助，亦蒙鼎力支持，谨在此表示衷心的感谢！

永远是您忠诚的朋友、育才学校校长陶行知

1944年11月15日

## 注释

① 甘霖林（Lenning Sweet） 美国人。当时在美国援华联合会任职。他曾在致陶行知信中批评过育才学校不宣传宗教，但对育才学校为培养有特殊才能

的难童的教育仍热心支持，并积极协助提供经济援助。

② 儿童福利委员会系美国援华联合会协调委员会下面的一个组织，其职能是研究美国援华联合会的儿童福利计划，并向协调委员会提出相应的建议。它有权通过或否决有关为中国儿童福利拨款的提案或申请。抗日战争胜利后，该委员会曾邀请“上海育才学校陶行知博士”担任该委员会的委员。

# 关于陈贻鑫自传的三点说明

——致魏璐诗



亲爱的魏璐诗[①]博士：

随函附奉陈贻鑫的自传。应该附加三点说明：

（1）贻鑫在被录取入学之前，曾经被我校流动考试委员会中的音乐家拒绝录取过，原因是他患有头疾。由于我回忆起他指挥合唱队的能力并坚持不懈地寻找这位秃头的小音乐家，他才终于被育才学校录取了。

（2）他的头疾已经治愈。这要归功于冯大帅[②]的同情，是他从泸州请来一位基督教徒医生刘大夫；也要归功于基督教青年会总干事黄次咸先生的善意。刘大夫赠给贻鑫醋酸铊，使其病发全部脱落。长出新发。贻鑫现已不再秃头。

（3）贻鑫才华出众，不仅精于作曲，而且善于向更为年幼的一代人教授音乐。

永远是您忠实的朋友，育才学校校长陶行知

1944年11月15日

## 注释

① 魏璐诗（Ruth Weiss） 女。奥地利人。抗日战争时期来华。当时在重庆“联合国影闻宣传处”任职。（即摄影、图片和电影新闻宣传处）曾与史沫

特莱、马海德等编辑出版《中国之声》《中国大众教育运动》。热心支持中国人民抵抗日本帝国主义侵略的正义事业和陶行知的人民教育运动，积极为育才学校募集经费。1946年7月25日陶行知逝世，魏当时在美国，参加了美国友人发起的陶行知追悼会，并著文纪念陶行知。中华人民共和国成立后，加入了中国国籍，长期在北京外文出版社任德文编辑，为全国政协委员。

② 冯大帅　指冯玉祥。

# 为在印代购乐谱致谢

## ——致印度加尔各答中国联络处



亲爱的先生：

承蒙代为购到乐谱17本并通过约翰·布洛菲尔德[①]先生送至育才学校，我校音乐组全体师生及我本人对阁下之鼎力相助特表衷心的感谢。兹寄奉144卢比汇票一张，请向中国银行兑取，用以清还阁下代垫书款。

小儿陶晓光亦曾为我校音乐组购到琴弦若干并为我校绘画组购到水彩颜料，均系为难童所购之物。他日内当登门拜访。如蒙设法将小儿所购之物送来重庆，当不胜感激之至。因此等物品均为我校所急需，在运输方面如蒙赐予方便，使之早日到渝，当感激不尽也。

您的忠诚朋友，育才学校校长陶行知

1944年11月15日

### 注释

① 约翰·布洛菲尔德（John Blofeld）时在重庆英国大使馆任职。

# 函催营养品运渝并委托在印购物

——致巴恩斯

亲爱的巴恩斯[1]先生：

关于美国援华会M.毕来思女士送与我们纳维妥油和奥利菲斯两种营养品一事，蒙8月3日大函告知，当即函请阁下将营养油交中国航空公司径送重庆，然迄今尚未收到。兹随函附奉200卢比汇票一张，请向中国银行兑取此款，以支付任何有关之费用。倘有结余，请代保留，以便为我校难童在印购物，购物单容稍后寄上。

致衷心的感谢！

您忠诚的朋友、育才学校校长陶行知

1944年11月15日

## 注释

① 巴恩斯（W. P. W. Barnes） 印度人。时在中国护运队印度办事处工作。

# 向中学救济委员会申请补助

——致库勒

亲爱的库勒[①]先生：

11月27日惠书已于今晚奉悉。对您提出的恳切意见，谨表谢意。

自今秋开始，我校师生人数均有大幅度增加。现在学生注册人数为280名，其中正式生182名，作实地观察和调查之学生10名，业余补习学生88名。我校教师除办公室秘书和小学教师外，已达50之整数，其中归国留学生9名，大学毕业生33名，大专毕业生3名，高中毕业生5名。教师中，专职者30名，兼职者20名。音乐和绘画组以及业余补习中学各班级的教师多数为兼职，其余各组教师则都是专职的。不过工艺美术组的兼职教师乃是在目前情况下我们所能够做得到的最佳安排，他们情绪甚佳，并富于牺牲精神，成了我校规划中必要的组成部分。由于我校薪金太低，所以几乎所有教师都过独身生活。我校的兼职教师与专职教师领取同样数额的薪金以支付往来车费。这是我校兼职教师与他校兼职教师的区别所在。我们的兼职教师与专职教师具有同样的献身精神，他们也是育才最好的朋友。我校的教师数量比普通中学的教师数量相对地大些，因为我们要让教师们有三分之一甚至二分之一的时间用于在职进修。由于我们的实验是新的，我校教师必须比他校教师学得多些，否则学生就可能超过他们。我校师资队伍较大的另一个原因，是我们准备在不久的将来招收更多有天赋的难童，还可能在其他地区建立同类的新型学校。我们希望在新生入学前再增聘10名教师。

此外，我想借此机会应马瑟秘书的要求就1943年第二学期和1944年第一学期以及1944—1945年度的预算作一报告。

| 1944年1—6月 | | 1943年7—12月 | |
|---|---|---|---|
| 收　入 | 3,572,119.24元 | 收　入 | 1,169,989.18元 |
| 支　出 | 2,482,997.70元 | 支　出 | 1,106,896.50元 |
| 指定偿债基金 | 1,056,000.00元 | | |
| 结　余 | 32,621.54元 | 结　余 | 63,092.68元 |

**1944年7—12月预算**

| 月 | 估计支出（国币元） | 可靠收入（国币元） | 估计需要募集的款额（国币元） |
|---|---|---|---|
| 7 | 372,000 | 240,000 | 132,000 |
| 8 | 394,000 | 240,000 | 154,000 |
| 9 | 416,000 | 240,000 | 176,000 |
| 10 | 438,000 | 345,000 | 93,000 |
| 11 | 460,000 | 345,000 | 115,000 |
| 12 | 482,000 | 345,000 | 137,000 |
| 合计 | 2,562,000 | 1,775,000 | 807,000 |

1944年第一学期预算的计算方法是：将1943年8月以来月平均增长额22,000元连续加上，直到1944年1月达到482,000元，以后逐月递增。

自1944年10月开始，可靠收入已增至每月345,000元，这就可以减少每月亏空数额达105,000元。

迄今为止，我们已从贵委员会获得的拨款如下：

1月5日

特别赠款　　　　国币20,000元

| | |
|---|---|
| 1943年11月及12月补助 | 15,000 |
| 3月14日 | |
| 1月及2月补助 | 15,000 |
| 4月8日 | |
| 3月及4月补助 | 15,000 |
| 6月29日 | |
| 5月及6月补助 | 15,000 |
| 10月18日 | |
| 7月及8月补助 | 15,000 |
| 总计 | 国币95,000元 |

特别赠款20,000元已用于购买药品和特别营养，两个月一次的15,000元即每月7,500元的补助已用于增加教师的薪金，每人每月增加300元，受益于贵委员会补助的教师共25名。

我们的月薪是1,500元。将月薪增至3,000元的水平，实属当务之急。根据我们中学的50名教师计算，我们向贵委员会申请每月增加补助75,000元，以留住我校教师，使他们解除生活困顿之苦，而他们却正是在这样的条件下以最大的献身精神为我们的下一代服务。

有关我校教师的详细情况，俟日内我返回学校后自当送呈。聘请注册会计师审计育才收支帐目，大约需化10,000元。这一考虑使我们一直未能办成此事。如您认为必要，当遵嘱办理。

永远是您忠诚的朋友、育才学校校长陶行知

1944年12月5日

## 注释

① 库勒（Mr. Arthur B. Coole）当时在重庆中学救济委员会任职。

# 为育才招收新生100名作准备的情况

——致甘霖林



亲爱的甘霖林博士：

下面是我为招收100名新生所作的准备工作：

一、12月7日派两名代表去南充找应急校址。如果留在这里并无困难，我们已准备一座庙宇作应急之用。

二、自从我们获得您批准我们的申请以来，我们已着手增聘所需要的教师。我希望在本月20日之前结束遴选人员的工作。

三、18日将组成考试委员会。

四、智力测验已准备就绪，进行测验的人员正在受训。

五、报名申请单已送到南岸两处难民收容所。我们决定在22日举行第一次考试，以便考试及格的人能欢度圣诞节。

六、我们正在跟全国救济总会、保育会[①]、中国儿童福利协会[②]磋商关于考选他们的儿童之最佳方式。

我的愿望是从12月份起能够收到每月日常费用的拨款，因为手头已无其它款项可资垫付新聘教师的薪金、考试委员及新难童的旅费等费用。这些新难童可能在圣诞节前报到，他们的人数尚不能确知。

盼望早日回音，预为致谢。

永远是您的忠实朋友、育才学校校长陶行知

1944年12月13日

## 注释

① 保育会　全称是“战时儿童保育总会”。1938年3月30日成立。领导人是宋美龄、李德全、倪斐君、曹孟君等人。

② 中国儿童福利协会成立于1944年12月16日。在成立大会上，陶行知曾到会讲演并发表文章提出十点建议。参见《创造的儿童教育》。

# 为创办育才农业组和工艺美术组申请拨款

——致甘霖林



亲爱的甘霖林博士：

奉12月18日通知，自当遵办。兹谨代表育才学校提出两项申请：

申请一：修正本年度概算。为维持目前学校所作的概算中，下列各项实属过低。第一，我校工作人员的基本薪金不能令人满意。直至目前为止，虽然偶尔有所增加，每人每月仍仅有薪金国币1,500元。因此，将每月最低薪金增至国币3,000元，实乃当务之急。我校领薪教师50名，为其增加薪金，每月需增加拨款国币75,000元，自1月至9月需增国币654,000元。第二，自今年9月份以来，供应学校及民办孤儿院之限价米每担价格已从国币1,100元猛涨至国币3,000元。我校每月消费这种米34担，故超出月概算国币64,600元。我们需要增加国币581,400元的拨款方能令9个月的预算获得平衡。第三，自10月份开始，限价衣料之价格已上涨150%，以致我们的冬衣概算赤字达国币500,000元。因此，加上夏季服装费之赤字，我们需要另行增加国币700,000元拨款，方能弥补服装方面之亏空。第四，我们需要每月国币50,000元用以提高难童最低营养标准，9个月共国币450,000元。为求更为清晰，兹将申请之各项费用列表如下：

| | | |
|---|---|---|
| 国币 | 645,000元 | 增加基本薪金 |
| | 581,400元 | 平衡米价猛涨 |

| | |
|---|---|
| 700,000元 | 平衡服装价格猛涨 |
| 450,000元 | 提高基本营养标准 |
| 2,376,400元 | 申请用以修正维持费概算之总额 |

上升数额非原定用以防备物价上涨之15%补贴所能抵销者，因为限价米及衣料价格暴涨对物价上涨总指数并无任何显著影响，而工作人员薪金及营养之基本标准又规定过低。申请二：实施“创造性救济新方案”，育才需要办一个农业组和一个工艺美术组来完成其全部计划。可以作出规划使两个组能够通过如下途径得以形成：挑选难民中的科学家作教授，有能力的工人领班和有才干的残废军人作领头的工人和农民，有才能的、年龄在青春期前的儿童既作学生又作学徒。我们的目的在于：使有创造才能的人能够进行创造性的研究和创造性的工作，以实施创造性的救济。这样一来，救济就被转变成为一种创造的力量。这两个新的组将根据“工、学、团合一”的原则来进行工作。它们将是既有科学精神又充满民主气氛的工业/农业合作社。农业组将在蔬菜、水果、畜牧、造林及农产品加工方面开展实验和生产活动。工艺美术组则在电气、机械、化学及民用各个行业方面开展实验和生产活动。各种车间及实验室将建立起来以进行生产活动及研究活动。在生产方面，我们的目标是生产农具、简单机器、科学仪器、日用化学产品。在获得开办费补助金之后，两个组将尽力争取在1945年10月以前达到自给。

根据这些原则和考虑，我们为开办农业组申请国币3,000,000元赠款，为开办工艺美术组申请国币7,000,000元赠款。当育才成为羽毛丰满的、献身于真理、博爱和服务的大学时，这两个组将是农学院和工学院的基础。总的原则如蒙批准，我将呈奉一项详细的规划。

您的忠实朋友

育才学校校长陶行知

1944年12月23日

# 关于“创造性的救济”

——致甘霖林

亲爱的甘霖林博士：

这是圣诞日之晨四点钟。顷刻之前，我尚卧床未起。沉浸在创造性救济、智慧尖端和基督伟大之爱的宏大磁场中的一个想法驱使我起床给您写这封信。我很高兴与黎明赛跑，乐于在日出之前起身。

创造性的救济，与创造性天才的解放相比，不能稍有逊色。创造性的救济必须给他们以充分的食物和阳光，使他们能够首先进入智慧的尖端，继续推进造物主的创造性工作。当这样的智慧转变为能将世界和人类改造得更好的那种力量时，如果创造性天才解放自己的机会并非限于几个人而是敞开于一个国家或全世界，那末，这个国家和世界就获得了最高形式的民主。

在此长期抗战的过程中，成千上万有才能的学者，包括许多有发展前途而且很有能力的无名科学家，陷入了极度的贫困之中，被逼到几乎无法生存的地步，或不得不改行干不适当的工作。而且，甚至在抗战开始前，尤其是抗战开始以来，数以万计的有才能的男女青年仅仅由于贫穷而无法受高等教育，继而因为没有大学文凭而被摒于研究所门外。这些青年人被迫过着比学者们还要艰难的生活，把他们的创造能力空耗于不适合他们才能的职业，或者过着难民的生活，没有机会、也得不到鼓励来表现他们的才干。最后，在权威、偏见、贫穷、上司或把头的无知，时间紧迫的工作计划，错误的教育理论，以及古老传统的重压下，埋葬了大批艺徒、工人、手艺人、农民、女佣以及贫苦儿童的才能。这些人的才能有待唤醒，而且只要民主的一声轻唤就能唤醒。

六年前的12月15日，建立了晓庄研究所来着手解决这个问题。凭我们少得可怜的经费，我们正在进行两个项目，您是熟悉育才学校的，我应该告诉您：生下育才的母亲是晓庄研究所。育才不过是在研究所教育处赞助下举办的一个实验学校。母亲是一位无名战士——更确切些说，是一位无名的保姆。她还有另一个无名的儿子——科学处下面的内燃机实验室。负责该项实验的研究员李华，牺牲了一切来指导这项实验。我很高兴地说，他大概已快要完成一架新内燃机的模型了。

晓庄研究所为了忠于原来创办这个研究所的理想，计划增聘十位各种学科的研究员，并从有发展前途的贫苦难民青年中挑选尽可能多的研究人员，也从育才吸收年轻的研究人员。我们有价值两百万元的书籍作基础。但是我们需要更多的钱来维持更多的工作人员，购买更多的参考书，创办更多的实验室。我想为研究所申请两百万元捐款以扩大其服务范围。这将会给我们很大的鼓舞。如果您没有足够的基金可供分配，则现有的任何数额的整笔款或分期付款均受欢迎。或者，如果您认为通过育才提供这项补助更为合适，我们也无异议，研究所可以组织进育才成为它的最高峰。不过，在目前阶段，我们宁愿把研究所作为一个独立机构来办，并且直接从您那里接受补助。

我很相信，如果您的一半财源，或者说，全部剩余基金，能够用于中国的创造性救济，那么，在不出一代人的时间里，您将会在这个灾难深重的国家看到奇迹，看到她对世界和人类作出的百万倍的贡献。这岂不宏伟、壮观么?

您的永远忠实的朋友

晓庄研究所所长陶行知

1944年12月25日

## 注释

这是陶行知谈“创造性救济”的重要信件。在国民党当局对晓庄研究所不断削减经费直至完全停止资助的情况下，陶行知不得不请求美国援华联合会予以援助。这是研究陶行知办学思想的重要材料。

# 请求不要对新来难童按人头计算拨款

——致甘霖林

亲爱的甘霖林博士：

兹附奉胜利饭店1,050元支票收据一纸。

1月18日尊函提出的问题，令我难以解决。我希望您能够不坚持对新来难童按人头计算拨款。因为，甚至从11月份开始，我们就已为准备接受新难童而超支，而这些超支费用并未包括在经常费用之内。在新难童到来之前，我们已不得不使用目前的补贴费来完成下列准备工作：

一、10,000名学生的10,000份一般智力测验卷。

二、挑选6名工作人员组成测验委员会。

三、测验委员会人员两个月的旅费及薪金。

四、10名教师必须预先聘请并加以培训，他们的薪金及伙食费必须支付，有的从12月份起即已支付，而从本月份起，全部教师的薪金及伙食费均须支付。

五、冬令服装材料必须立即提供，而且棉织品管制局刚刚批准了我们购买。

六、最后，如果毛巾、帽子、鞋子、牙刷等能够现在购备，我们就可以节省许多钱。

在查阅我10月20日奉上之日常费用项目表时，我发现其中只有伙食、灯光、课本、零用钱这些东西在新难童到来时是应按人头计算费用的。因此，我请求您继续付给我们250,000元以便为招收新难童作好准备，而不要从首次拨款应有数额中扣出以前的历次已付款额。将此款推迟到新难童到来之时才拨付，结果只能推迟他们的到来。因为，如果拨付此款真的推迟了，则我不得不花太多的时间去弥补财政差额，而这些时间用在新来难童身上应当是更为有利的。

关于我在1944年12月23日信中请求增加教师薪金及米贴所包括的一段时间，我想说明一下，这是指从1945年1月至9月（包括9月份在内）这一段时间。

您告诉我，我们为提高最低营养标准而要求每月50,000元拨款的申请已被否决，理由是新难童尚未到达。我重读了我12月23日的信，发现在“难童”前面并无“新”字。我原来指的是已经在学校的难童，以别于自费儿童。儿童福利会下次开会时，希望您请求他们重新考虑我在这方面的申请。

永远是您忠实的朋友

育才学校校长

陶行知

1945年1月19日

**原信附件：育才学校新难童全部到达之前的日常费用**

| | | |
|---|---|---|
| 测验费用 | 360,000元 | （可以减少） |
| 冬令服装 | 300,000元 | |
| 教师薪金（3个月） | 75,000元 | |
| 教师伙食（3个月） | 36,780元 | |
| 测验委员会车费（2个月） | 120,000元 | |
| 测验委员会旅馆费（2个月） | 72,000元 | （这两项可减少） |
| 测验委员会伙食费（2个月） | 150,000元 | |
| 总计 | 1,113,780元 | |
| 4个月（11月—2月）的收据 | 1,000,000元 | |

# 为育才学校及晓庄研究所申请拨款

——致甘霖林

亲爱的甘霖林博士：

1月25日手示已转给我，十分高兴。兹遵嘱附上育才农业组、工艺美术组及晓庄研究所的概算。捐款及基金的月息，保守估计为8%，此数足敷应付日常开支。拨款大部分必须用作工艺美术组之开办费，小部分用作农业组之开办费。

受援者有：农业组学生40名，工艺美术组学生40名，熟练工人5名，晓庄研究所专职研究员5位，兼职研究员5位，研究人员10名，青年研究学员20名。

您信中对我们申请的数额有一处错误。我于12月23日信中申请的数额是：

| | |
|---|---|
| 农业组 | 3,000,000元 |
| 工艺美术组 | 7,000,000元 |

我于12月25日信中申请的数额是：

| | |
|---|---|
| 晓庄研究所 | 2,000,000元 |

希望1月25日尊函副本能予更正。

我将于2月5日回城，恳切希望收到1月份的1号及2号拨款，如有可能，并希望收到为冬装材料、米价涨价以及教师薪金提高所提供的拨款。

致最佳的祝愿！

永远是您的忠实朋友

育才学校校长陶行知

1945年1月31日

## 原信附件一：开办育才学校农业组概算

(1) 开办费

| | | |
|---|---|---|
| 学生 | 40×15,000 | = 600,000元 |
| 教师 | 5×15,000 | = 75,000元 |
| 工人 | 2×15,000 | = 30,000元 |
| 建筑 | | = 300,000元 |
| 设备 | | = 300,000元 |
| 合计 | | 1,305,000元 |

(2) 日常开支　每月40×3,000　120,000元

包括学生伙食、衣着、杂项开支，教师薪金及伙食，工人工资及伙食，医药费，行政开支。

(3) 收据

| | |
|---|---|
| 美国援华联合会为开办费拨款 | 1,305,000元 |
| 同上为捐助拨款 | 1,695,000元 |
| 合计 | 3,000,000元 |

(135,600元的月息8%可敷日常开支)

(4) 农场生产将应付由通货膨胀引起的物价增涨并照管未来的维持及发展。

## 原信附件二：开办育才学校工艺美术组概算

(1) 开办费

| | | |
|---|---|---|
| 学生 | 40×15,000 | = 600,000元 |
| 教师 | 5×15,000 | = 75,000元 |
| 工人 | 5×15,000 | = 75,000元 |

| | |
|---|---|
| 建筑 | = 500,000元 |
| 设备 | = 3,750,000元 |
| 合计 | = 5,000,000元 |

(2) 日常开支

包括学生、教师、工人、材料、医药所有开支以及行政开支。} 每月40×4,000=160,000元

(3) 收据

| | |
|---|---|
| 美国援华联合会为开办费拨款 | 5,000,000元 |
| 同上为捐助拨款 | 2,000,000元 |
| 合计 | 7,000,000元 |

(160,000元的月息8%可敷日常开支)

(4) 商业服务将应付由通货膨胀引起的物价增涨并照管未来的维持及发展。

**原信附件三：发展晓庄研究所的概算**

(1) 开办费

| | |
|---|---|
| 书籍及设备（已提供） | 2,400,000元 |
| 建筑（已提供） | 300,000元 |
| 合计 | 2,700,000元 |

(2) 日常开支

| | 人数 | 每月金额 | 合计 |
|---|---|---|---|
| 研究员 | 5 | 10,000元 | 50,000元 |
| 研究人员 | 10 | 5,000元 | 50,000元 |
| 青年研究人员 | 20 | 500元 | 10,000元 |
| 院外研究规划津贴 | 5 | 3,000元 | 15,000元 |
| 每月添置设备及书籍 | | | 35,000元 |
| 行政开支 | | | 10,000元 |

合计　　　　　　　　　　　　　　　　　170,000元

(3) 收据

| | |
|---|---|
| 研究院提供的开办费 | 2,700,000元 |
| 原来每月收入 | 10,000元 |
| 美国援华联合会作为捐助的拨款2,000,000元的月息 | 160,000元 |
| 作为日常开支的总收入 | 170,000元 |

(4) 出版物销售、版税、专利，将应付通货膨胀及未来的维持和发展。

## 注释

由于经费不足，育才学校开办农业组、工艺美术组以及发展晓庄研究所的计划，均未能实现。

# 请邀盟国友人参加马思聪小提琴演奏会

## ——致魏璐诗

亲爱的魏璐诗博士：

驰名世界的、中国最有才华的艺术家马思聪先生将于2月13日、14日、16日及17日下午7时在育才学校主持下为该校新招难童举行小提琴演奏会，每晚均有不同的节目。我们为育才学校的朋友们每晚保留100个最好的座位，凭请柬而不凭门票入场。我托陈元祺（译音）先生送上尽您所需数量之请柬，以便您邀请对小提琴演奏会有兴趣并关心天才难童教育的朋友们前来参加。如被邀参加的每位朋友能捐助5美元以上或其等值之整数，我们将不胜感激。我盼望您能尽力为育才邀请到盟国朋友50位，当然最好不少于20位。我希望下月5日我从北碚回来时就从您那里听到好消息。有400位受到邀请的朋友们的共同努力，我期待取得的结果是：筹集到的钱足供维持新招收的40名难童之需。

永远是您的忠诚朋友

育才学校校长陶行知

1945年1月31日

# 为免收租金差额致谢

——致黄次咸

亲爱的黄先生[①]：

由于我们临时通知取消租用贵会礼堂的合同，以致本月17日晚上6—8时演出不满场，而您慨允我们免付因之造成的差额，对此，我谨代表育才学校的难童，向您致以衷心的感谢，并请您代向韦先生（Mr. Way）致谢，我们对他的厚意同样表示感激。

永远是您的忠诚朋友

育才学校校长

陶行知1945年2月23日

## 注释

① 黄先生即黄次咸。当时任重庆基督教青年会总干事。

# 为育才受赠礼物向外国友人致谢

——致道格拉斯

亲爱的道格拉斯[①]先生：

蒙惠赠象棋2盒，台球6只，羽毛球3只，以及彩色蜡笔2盒，兹谨代表育才学校难童向您表示衷心的感谢。这些礼物均已于旧历新年除夕之前转给我。

此等珍品在我校文娱室及运动场均已受到热烈和激动的欢迎。

此感谢信未能早日奉达，因打听礼物之馈赠人颇费时日，务望见谅。切盼不久能当面致谢。

永远是您忠实的朋友

陶行知1945年2月25日

**注 释**

① 道格拉斯（Mr. Frederick Douglas） 美国人。当时在重庆“美国新闻处”任职。

# 关于选拔难童的情况

——致甘霖林

亲爱的甘霖林博士：

非常高兴地向您报告：在12月23日和2月25日之间我们对290名儿童连续进行了六次测验，儿童中有22名难童成功地通过我们考试委员会所定的标准。此事似乎进行得很慢。

直至上星期五我们才接到保育会的介绍信，允许我们从各地儿童保育院选拔儿童。这将使我们能作出现场测验的时间表，并在几天之内就开始测验。

我们希望有了手头的所有这些介绍信，我们能加快工作，将来进展得更快。

明天我将去北碚。希望当我3月5日返回时，我校2月份拨款已准备好。

承蒙将您在我校及北温泉所拍影片①见示，不胜感谢之至。该片经复制后当立即奉还。

永远是您的忠实朋友

陶行知

1945年2月26日

**注释**

① 北温泉所拍影片指甘霖林为育才学校所拍的照片和幻灯片。

# 关于国际难童学校教育实施计划

——致甘霖林

亲爱的甘霖林博士：

顷接3月16日手示。此信确实行程太慢，在农村尤甚。

一、国际难童学校将实施一年级至六年级的初等教育。

二、从五年级开始实施职业教育及职业准备。其性质及细节将由理事会根据主席推荐予以决定。

三、文教设备将包括：

a）教师及学生的参考用书

b）乐器

c）医学仪器

d）农具

e）木工工具

f）简单科学仪器

g）其他生产工具及设备

我在向您提出申请前没有时间估定每一项目的费用。另一理由是我想让理事会主席有更多的选择自由。

希望这能符合尊意。

您的忠实朋友

陶行知

1945年3月20日

## 原信附件：

### 国际难童学校

I 开办费

| | 数量　单价(国币元) | 总计(国币元) |
|---|---|---|
| 1. 双人床 | 50×8,000 | 400,000 |
| 2. 双人桌 | 50×2,400 | 120,000 |
| 3. 双人凳 | 50×600 | 30,000 |
| 4. 面　盆 | 100×300 | 30,000 |
| 5. 蚊　帐 | 100×2,000 | 200,000 |
| 6. 被　褥 | 100×6,000 | 600,000 |
| 7. 文教设备 | | 620,000 |
| 8. 房屋及修缮 | | 1,000,000 |
| 100名儿童总计 | | 3,000,000 |
| 人均费用 | | 30,000 |

II 日常费用

| 项　目 | 人均每月费用(国币元) | 100名儿童每月费用(国币元) | 一年费用(国币元) |
|---|---|---|---|
| 1. 伙　食 | 1,500 | 150,000 | 1,800,000 |
| 2. 服　装 | 500 | 50,000 | 600,000 |
| 3. 毛　巾 | 40 | 4,000 | 48,000 |
| 4. 帽　子 | 20 | 2,000 | 24,000 |
| 5. 鞋　子 | 80 | 8,000 | 96,000 |
| 6. 肥　皂 | 50 | 5,000 | 60,000 |
| 7. 牙　刷 | 20 | 2,000 | 24,000 |
| 8. 课　本 | 20 | 2,000 | 240,000 |
| 9. 医　药 | 100 | 10,000 | 120,000 |
| 10. 材　料 | 60 | 6,000 | 72,000 |
| 11. 照　明 | 60 | 6,000 | 72,000 |
| 12. 零　用 | 50 | 5,000 | 60,000 |

续表

| 项目 | 人均每月费用（国币元） | 100名儿童每月费用（国币元） | 一年费用（国币元） |
|---|---|---|---|
| 13. 教师薪金 | 300 | 30,000 | 360,000 |
| 14. 教师伙食 | 150 | 15,000 | 180,000 |
| 15. 工人工资 | 30 | 3,000 | 36,000 |
| 16. 工人伙食 | 30 | 3,000 | 36,000 |
| 总计 | 3,010 | 301,000 | 3,612,000 |

（为抵销通货膨胀每月增加10%）

## 注释

国际难童学校　1945年初，陶行知依靠国际援华机构的帮助，计划开办一所国际难童学校，后因形势变化，经费无着而未能实现。

# 吁请帮助建立国际难童学校

——致甘霖林

亲爱的甘霖林博士：

关于贺夫人[①]同您的晤谈，金先生（Mr. King）已向我报告。我只想就有关南岸难童的母爱和公共机构的收容救济发表自己的意见。

一、南岸的难民家庭已经到了几乎无法生存的境地，成人及儿童都在遭受苦难。如果儿童得到好的照顾，则母亲和儿童均将得到宽慰。

二、母爱不可能是治疗一切反社会态度的灵丹妙药。当母子均因缺乏生存手段而挨饿受冻的时候，两者都可能采取与社会对抗的态度，但这种态度可因给予的实际援助和同情的程度而得到相应的缓解。

三、这种援助究应直接给予家庭或通过某种机构提供的问题，只能依靠仔细的比较和调查来回答，而不应当用一个一般原则来处理。如果那个家庭是受过教育的家庭，母亲又是受过良好教育的，那么，我建议将救济给予家庭来援助儿童，否则我建议将儿童送往管理良好的机构收容。

四、将儿童置于某种可使其身心均能成长的环境，肯定比将他放在只有身体受到照顾的家中为好。

五、在贺夫人指导下的一个机构决不会不够标准，并且可以有把握地推断，这样一个机构将比南岸难民所能建立起来的最好的保育院更好。

六、轮船不容许我继续写下去。我希望您将发现，帮助建立国际难童学校的基础是可能的。

永远是您忠实的朋友

陶行知

1945年3月24日

## 注释

① 贺夫人　指当时重庆市贺耀祖市长的夫人倪斐君。

# 育才学校1944年度财务报告

——致甘霖林



亲爱的甘霖林博士：

育才学校1944年度财务报告两份随函附奉，报告已由注册审计员白清兴（译音）审计过。

我注意到您需要另外一份1943年审计过的财务报告为您的重庆办事处存档，该报告将于日内由审计员提供。

您的忠实朋友
育才学校校长
陶行知
1945年3月28日

## 原信附件

### 育才学校报账单

**已到校新来难童每月伙食费**

| | 10月份预算 | 根据已变化情况修改预算 | 额外开支 |
|---|---|---|---|
| 1月份新难童10名 | 12,260 | 25,460 | 13,200 |
| 2月份新难童22名 | 26,972 | 70,532 | 43,560 |

| | | | |
|---|---|---|---|
| 3月份新难童32名 | 39,232 | 50,832 | 17,600 |
| 4月份新难童62名 | 75,012 | 185,720 | 100,708 |

## 原件附注

① 10月份申请中原来伙食估算的根据是：官价米每担3,000元，人均660元；除米之外，副食品统算人均666元。1月份，市场普通米价每担平均9,000元。10名儿童尚未被批准吃官价米，不得不买市场米，结果人均费用1,980元，共多支出13,200元。

② 2月份，22名儿童仍须吃市场米，而每担米价已涨至12,000元，结果人均费用2,640元，共多支出43,560元。

③ 22名儿童被允准吃官价米，米粮及副食合计为26,972元。10名新难童吃市场米，每担11,000元，结果人均费用2,420元，共多支出17,600元。

④ 22名儿童吃官价米，人均660元，共14,520元，副食品人均已增至1,200元，62名儿童共74,400元；40名儿童吃市场米，人均2,420元，共96,800元。62名新儿童仅伙食一项总支出就达185,720元。

# 因物价上涨为育才新来难童申请增加拨款

——致甘霖林



亲爱的甘霖林博士：

育才学校正面临一场最严重的财务危机。兹奉呈若干主要数据以期有助于您考虑及判断最好的方法来解决目前的困难并防止更严重的发展。同时我想提出供您参考的几个建议以及报告若干有待尽快加以重新考虑和处理的具体情况。

今年我们从一月份590,000元预算开始，历经周期性物价飞涨，我们不得不在四月份采用1,678,000元的最低预算。这就意味着第一季度增加283%。单是四月份我们就短缺841,000元。我们从1月10日以来亏空总额已高达1,500,000元。

物价第一次飞涨约发生于1月10日；第二次飞涨约于2月20日，3月份以来米价略有回跌。我们有理由相信，5月份米价将再度上涨。

修正所有服务机构的预算，包括我们的预算，实属当务之急，我认为，如可能修正，应从1月开始而不应迟于2月。您是否认为较好的办法是准许各服务机构采用金本位预算，按月照兑换率支付？金价将与物价一同升值，大体上比其它物价升得较慢。这将减少重新分配的麻烦，同时使各服务机构为财务困难而经常焦虑的心情得到缓解。

招收新难童的预算是1944年10月24日编制的。在11月28日我们收到开办费拨款。租借迴龙寺迟至1月才经地方政府批准。下列开办费主要项目已超过原来的预算。

| | 原来拨款 | 实际费用 | 不敷数额 |
| --- | --- | --- | --- |
| 庙宇修理 | 100,000元 | 300,000元 | 200,000元 |
| 双人床 | 270,000元 | 400,000元 | 130,000元 |
| 双人桌 | 80,000元 | 130,000元 | 50,000元 |
| 蚊帐 | 130,000元 | 200,000元 | 70,000元 |
| 总计国币 | 580,000元 | 1,030,000元 | 450,000元 |

我们希望您能够付给我们国币450,000元之数。

10月份米粮的预算是根据官价计算的，每担为3,000元。只有22名新难童被批准吃官价米；40名新难童尚未被批准吃这种米，故仍继续吃市场上的米，每担为10,000元。剩下的38名难童，若现在招收进来，仍需吃市场米直到秋季开学时为止。还有副食品，包括燃料、食油、食盐、蔬菜、肉、水等，从3月份开始，已从根据10月份估计的每人566元增加到每人1,200元，而按师生员工通算，除米之外，每人副食品应增加到2,000元。

新难童每月的伙食费已经算出，附呈参阅。从1月至4月伙食总拨款额为490,400元。由于在政府批准新难童吃官价米之前仍须购买市场上的米，以及副食品价格的上涨，新难童4个月的实际伙食费用将为338,544元。因此，以前的伙食拨款只剩下151,856元。如果美国援华联合会不给我们4月份的拨款，则此项余款将远不足以应付全部开支。

至于其余38名新难童，在9月份以前他们不可能吃到官价米，5月份副食品价格估计将增至每人2,000元，所以每人伙食费将为4,640元左右，而根据10月份预算则仅为1,226元，以致拨款须增加129,732元，这需要先得到您的批准，我才敢招收这一批新难童。

至于我向英国援华会提出的申请，我希望您尽力支持下列要求：

1. 增添科学仪器　　国币5,000,000元

2. 提高教师薪金

从3,000元增至10,000元。

教师60人，每月合计420,000元。　　国币5,040,000元

3. 改善营养1,000元×316人，

每月合计316,000元。　　国币3,792,000元

您似乎并不赞同我争取科学仪器的努力。然而这是我计划的精粹。我需要这笔钱自己动手制作简单仪器。如果这个规划失败，则育才学校的整个计划也归于失败。我希望您将尽一切努力来帮助我的实验取得最后胜利并对人类作出我们最大的贡献。

永远是你的忠实朋友

育才学校校长陶行知

1945年4月27日

# 为育才1945—1946年度预算请求资助

——致艾德敷



亲爱的艾德敷主任：

1944年12月23日我曾有幸向甘霖林主任呈送两项申请。“申请Ⅰ”已蒙迅速加以考虑，对此我谨表示衷心的感谢。然而有关创办农业组和工艺美术组之“申请Ⅱ”，于儿童福利委员会召开会议时却未蒙提交会议讨论。中国儿童福利委员会下次开会时，敬希将上述“申请Ⅱ”提交会议讨论并望鼎力推荐，使其得以通过。兹将“申请Ⅱ”的主要内容稍加修改后引述如下：

“申请Ⅱ：创造性救济的新规划。育才需要一个农业组和一个工艺美术组以完成其全部计划。可以订出方案来，使两个组通过如下的途径得以形成：从难民中挑选科学家作教授，挑选有特殊才能的手工艺人、工人领班和有特殊才能的残废军人作领头的工人和农民，挑选前青春期年龄（例如10—13岁）的儿童既作学生又作学徒。我们的目的在于使具有创造才能的人能够进行创造性的学习和创造性的工作，以实现创造性的救济。这样，救济就被转变成创造力。这两个组将根据‘工、学、团合一’的原则进行活动，是与科学相结合的、充满民主气氛的工业合作社或者农业合作社。农业组将在蔬菜、水果、畜牧、造林和农产品加工方面既有实验活动，也有生产活动。工艺美术组则在电气、机械、化学、民用及地方手工艺等行业方面既有实验活动，也有生产活动。各种车间或实验室将建立起来进行生产活动和研究活动。在生产方面，我们准备生产农具、简单的机器、简单的科学仪器或日用化学品。在获得开办费的补助之后，两个组都将尽最大努力争取在1945年10月接近自给。根据这些原则和考虑，我们为开办农业组申请3,000,000元，为开办工艺美术组申请7,000,000元，用作开办费和基本建设费用。”

在原来的申请书中，“赠款”一词实为误用。我用该字本来是指“基本建设费用”。正如您已经看到的，我已经在上面的引文中和本函所附的预算中作了改动。

我准备挑选的儿童之年龄限制是青春期以前。为了讲得更清楚些，我已经在“前青春期年龄”后面加了“10—13岁”字样。

所附预算是根据半年前的物价作估算的。如有可用之款，我希望预算能加一倍。不过，倘若更多的款项难于获得，那么，我认为这项预算在缩小规模的基础上还是可行的。中国有句名言说，“一生二，二生三，三生万物。”我认为开始少些比没有要好些。育才，如果没有一个保育室来培养难童中年幼的工农业人才，就仍然像一个畸形人，不能指望作出新中国所需要的那种有益的、健康的贡献。正是由于这个原因，我请求您向中国儿童福利委员会推荐这个申请并望鼎力相助，使之能通过仔细研究的各个阶段，以便我们能够赢得另一个胜利——不仅是已经在育才和可能来育才的难童们的胜利，而且对新中国的更大进步来说，也是一个胜利。

您忠诚的朋友

育才学校校长陶行知

1945年6月1日

**注释**

① 原信附件：1945—1946年度育才学校预算表

## 附录：预算请求表

### 美国援华联合会
### 重庆上南纪马路218号

**预算请求表**

1945-1946

**儿童福利**

致：美国援华联合会及美国援华会主任艾德敷
(Dwight W. Edwards)
制表人：育才学校校长陶行知
兹申请给予下列孤儿院或福利中心以资助

一、机构名称：育才学校

二、机构地点：中国 重庆 北碚

三、负责实施所报计划之团体或个人：陶行知亲自领导的生活教育社

四、1944—1945年美国援华联合会资助款额：
10,862,300元（3,000,000元，4,464,300元，1,448,000元，1,950,000元）

五、申请资助款额：81,665,200元（以五月份拨款数额为基数，逐月递增15%）

| | |
|---|---|
| 1944年10月1日 1945年12月30日 | 9,778,100元 |
| 1946年1月1日 1946年3月30日 | 14,871,300元 |
| 1946年4月1日 1946年6月30日 | 22,617,500元 |
| 1946年7月1日 1946年9月30日 | 34,398,300元 |
| 总 计 | 81,665,200元 |

六、预期该机构将获得如下财政援助：

1. 中国政府全国救济总会 180,000元

2. 中国私人方面——育才之友　　3,600,000元

3. 国外（不包括本申请），英国援华会或其他可能来源　　4,260,000元

4. 收费，租金，产品出售　　800,000元

5. 本申请　　920,000元

该年度所需资助款总额　　91,425,200元

七、下面写明为何此款须向美国援华联合会申请而不能自他处获得：

过去，在1944年以前，在中国的育才朋友是育才学校的主要资助者，但由于营业状况日益恶化，它们的财政能力无法应付不断加重的通货膨胀，而英国援华会只同意对我校教师每人每月的资助从4,425元增加到10,000元，亦无希望从政府获得增拨资助款项；因此，我们恳切希望美国援华联合会能资助81,665,200元之数额，此项数额是以美国援华联合会五月份1,400,000元拨款整数为基数、逐月递增15%来估算的，估算结果的数额是：1945年10月2,815,900元；1946年9月13,100,600元；全年度总额81,665,200元。

八、以下为儿童福利中心的费用预算，仅列主要费用项目以及工作人员数目：

| | |
|---|---|
| 1945年10月1日　1945年12月30日 | 9,778,100元 |
| 1946年1月　1946年3月 | 14,871,300元 |
| 1946年4月　1946年6月 | 22,617,500元 |
| 1946年7月　1946年7月 | 34,398,300元 |
| 总　　计 | 81,665,200元 |

1. 房屋

2. 维修　　1,000,000元

3. 250名儿童之生活补助

| | |
|---|---|
| (1) 伙食 | 22,500,000元 |
| (2) 服装 | 9,250,000元 |
| (3) 被褥 | 800,000元 |
| (4) 日用必需品 | 6,400,000元 |
| 4. 生产工作 | |
| (1) 设备 | 1,000,000元 |
| (2) 材料 | 1,000,000元 |
| (3) 运输 | 240,000元 |
| 5. 教育计划 | |
| (1) 书籍 | 1,800,000元 |
| (2) 设备 | 750,000元 |
| (3) 杂项 | 500,000元 |
| 6. 薪金 | |
| (1) 工作人员：教师61名（家属17人） | 21,560,000元 |
| (2) 佣工工资：学校及农场工人40名 | 6,000,000元 |
| 7. 总务 | |
| (1) 办公室费用 | 1,200,000元 |
| (2) 旅费 | 240,000元 |
| (3) 灯光，水，燃料 | 3,625,200元 |
| 8. 福利计划 | |
| (1) 医疗 | 3,000,000元 |
| (2) 娱乐 | 600,000元 |
| (3) 杂志等 | 200,000元 |

九、其他

十、下面写明，打算用申请所得之款达到什么目的：

从美国援华联合会所得之补助将使我校61位教师能继续帮助250名极穷苦之难童成长起来并根据他们各自的才能进行学习；他们同时还帮助1,500名农民及其子女增进健康、获得基础知识和要求学习、进步的迫切愿望。

# 实施中的民主教育新计划*

——致毕来思

亲爱的毕来思女士：

庆贺胜利！下半年育才预算无变化。将民主教育带给四亿五千万人民的新计划在实施中。新计划是由生活教育社和育才学校校长（我自己）联合赞助下实施的。新计划作为四年规划制定出来。第一年规划对象为六百万人。四年实验规划包括对卫生、劳动、科学和为民主作准备的研究。将设立一个研究院研究问题和方法，十个训练所训练工作人员（包括职员和教师），一百个示范中心，印刷包括书籍和期刊在内的材料，我们计划补助五千个地方实验中心。所需总额为两百万美元。我们能够筹措到一百万美元，请求你们给予我们一百万美元。

永远是你忠实的朋友

育才学校校长

陶行知

1945年9月21日

* 此件是陶行知致毕来思女士的电报。

## 附：毕来思致陶行知函

亲爱的陶博士：

接9月21日来电，谢谢。根据我的理解，电报内容如下："庆贺胜利！下半年育才预算无变化。将民主教育带给四亿五千万人民的新计划在实施中。新计划是由生活教育社和育才学校校长（我自己）联合赞助下实施的。新计划作为四年规划制定出来。第一年规划对象为六百万人。四年实验规划包括对卫生、劳动、科学和为民主作准备的研究。将设立一个研究院研究问题和方法，十个训练所训练工作人员（包括职员和教师），一百个示范中心，印刷包括书籍和期刊在内的材料，我们计划补助五千个地方实验中心。所需总金额为两百万美元。我们能够筹措到一百万美元，请求你们给予我们一百万美元。"

上述是否您要说的内容，请尽快见告，因为我们需要进行工作来帮助您。关于用女童子军的10,000元拨款来支持您的工作，卡特夫人已跟她们谈过。

对于生活教育社，可否请您给我们提供多一点情况？关于如何与6,000,000人取得联系，请您讲得更具体一点。谁来办研究院？从哪里得到十个训练所的工作人员？一百个示范中心的工作人员是些什么人，他们的工作计划怎样？您说您将补助5,000个地方实验中心。您怎样为它们弄到工作人员？您怎样监督它们？它们的工作计划又是怎样的？它们将设置在什么地方？给我们提供的情况越详细，对于设法为您的工作筹措费用就越有利。您期望从英国或加拿大弄到一些钱吗？

道格拉斯先生给我带来了贵校的若干照片，我必须说，这些照片很漂亮。你们有人将"宝箱"中的书籍分发出去，我们非常高兴。贵校的这些照片很有助于装满更多的"宝箱"送往中国。如果您把你们需要什么样的书告诉我们，我们就能够把装满这类书的"宝箱"给你们送去。我们还可以给你们送去其他东西，例如铅笔、纸张、绘画书、绘画颜料。实际上，甚么东西都可以放进一个箱子，其大小与你们过去收到的“宝箱”大小一样。

道格拉斯先生对您和您的工作有很深的印象。我想如果您能够去看望一下“临时国际新闻处”（过去“美国战时新闻处”）并请他们给你们作一些宣传，大概不失为一个好意见。

美国红十字会的阿瑟·凯尔文先生昨天来过我们的办公室，我告诉他你们需要哈里弗鱼肝油，而我们送给你们的哈里弗鱼肝油你们一直没有收到。他说，你们应当去找一个救济团体，例如“国际救济委员会”，向他们要库存的哈里弗鱼肝油，那是美国红十字会给该委员会的。他起初还说，你们可以去找教育部的一个委员会。但是我告诉他，我认为那个委员会对于让贵校的孩子们得到哈里弗鱼肝油不会感兴趣。然而，在这一点上我可能是错误的。如果你们从国际救济委员会得不到满意的结果，不妨去找凯尔文先生试试看，告诉他你们需要什么。

您打算将你们的指挥部迁出重庆吗？我们盼望你们将不断送来宣传资料。道格拉斯先生给我带来了一些，但都是过去我们已经有了的。我们必须得到一些新的东西，或许你们能够给我们送来一些。

我们大家祝贺您，并希望很快得到您的信息。

您的忠实朋友

美国援华会执行主任

M. 毕来思

1945年9月27日

于美国纽约

# 请借用或代租用开会地点

——致唐森

亲爱的唐森[①]先生：

传信人王先生将代我把信送给耿丽淑[②]女士，请您把准备借给我的汽车给他用。

委员会开会是否能在您处举行，哪一天的什么时间对您方便？答复请交传信人带回。如果您处不方便，请代我们与基督教女青年会联系。

您的极忠诚的朋友

陶行知

1946年7月23日

## 注释

① 唐森（Peter Townsend） 即彼得·唐森，当时在中国工业合作协会国际协会（简称"中国工合"）任职。

② 耿丽淑（Talitha Gerlach） 女，美国友人。陶行知的老朋友，也是中国人民的老朋友。中国福利会及宋庆龄基金会上海分会顾问、北京分会理事。

## 附：唐森先生回复

亲爱的陶博士：

星期三或星期四晚任何时间均可。

星期三晚7时以后或星期四晚任何时间均可。

彼得·唐森

# STORIES, FOLK TALES, FABLES, MYTHS AND JOKES

(*Translated From Chinese*)

# Look In Vain

Men who expect to get rid of poverty would naturally ask the God of Wealth（财神）for help. This is why, during the new year's season, so many persons, men and women, boys and girls, gather in the temple of the God of Wealth, praying, fasting and burning paper gold and silver in the hope of gaining the so-called philosopher's stone in return. I would call it useless, because here is a story to illustrate it.

Once in the land of Wu-ho a husband and his wife, on the last night of the year, sat silently in a wretched cottage. With no money and no food they could only bend their heads and sigh: "Why doesn't the God of Wealth come? " No sooner did they murmur than the sky became clear; the clouds, bright; the doors of heaven opened and the God of Wealth, dignified and magnificent, came down before the poor pair. Then the wife knelt down, and the husband followed, kissing the God's feet. "I will give you three things you two first think of," said the God. They were both glad to hear that. But the wife, having suffered hunger for three days, could endure no longer. "If the God should give me a piece of bread I would be very glad," she thought within herself. The bread came down as soon as she thought. The husband, at the first glance, supposed that gold was coming, because the bread appeared yellow in colour. Laughing to himself, he took up the supposed gold. He found it to be light and soft. Instead of the precious metal, it was a piece of bread which cost no more than ten cash. He was filled with anger and cursed his wife, saying, "You great fool, let the bread fill up your mouth." The bread jumped into the wife's mouth at once, which seemed to obey his command. Of the things two had gone. The hunsband with anger on the one hand and despair on the other began to think of something he most needs. His wife's mouth was blocked, breathing was checked, speaking was not permitted. She now wished to free herself from the bread which she formerly eagerly demanded. As she thought thus, the bread flew away, and the God disappeared. The man and the woman, with their frowning faces, blamed each other till the dawn of day when they were exhausted and fell asleep. The Chinese proverb says, "Look in vain".

**Note**

LOOK IN VAIN, translated from a Chinese folk, translated into English by Tao Wen Tsing (one of Dr. H. C. Tao's old names), was first published in "THE UNIVERSITY OF NANKING MAGAZINE", No. 1, Vol. IV, February 1913.

# Three Famous Chinese Stories

## (Ⅰ)

## Tong Fang Soh (东方朔), the Humorist

Emperor Wu (武帝) of the Han Dynasty (汉朝), though a man of great genius, was very superstitious. Believing in fairies, many times he sent men to Peng Lai (蓬莱) to seek "ambrosia" (不死之药) so that he might live eternally in this world by eating it. Once a Taoist claimed to have some sort of such ambrosia, the so-called honeydew (甘露) and deceitfully presented it to the Emperor in the hope of gaining a high position. The Emperor heard of it gladly and appointed Tong Fang Soh, one of his ministers to receive it and to see that it was carefully protected. But as soon as Tong Fang Soh received the bottle, he boldly drank all the honeydew. Taking the empty bottle in his hand, he went back to the Emperor Wu. "Have you got the honeydew? " asked the Emperor. "Yes, "replied Tong Fang Soh, "but, I beg your pardon, I have drunk all of it." Hearing this with unbearable anger, the Emperor condemned him to death, "May I be permitted to speak a word before I go to the execution ground? " "You may," remarked the Emperor. "What will you say? " Then the humorist sarcastically said. "If the honeydew is a true medicine for giving eternal life, then you can never put me to death because I have drunk it. But if it is false, it will be worth nothing to you, and what use can it be to take your revenge upon my life by means of a false medicine? " Hearing this, the Emperor could only laugh and finally forgave him.

## (II)
## The Spear and the Shield

Han Fei （韩非）was a well-known debater, in the time of Lih Kwoh （列国）, whose famous work, Han Tze （《韩子》）, tells us about a spear-and-shield maker. We derive our idiom "spear and shield", which signifies any self-contradiction from this short and interesting story.

There was once a man who wished to sell his spear and shield. Holding up his shield, he said to the passers-by, "This shield I made is impregnable; nothing can penetrate it." But when he took up his spear he would say, "Sharp is my spear; nothing can resist its point." Then some one asked him, "What would you say if I should pierce your shield with your spear? " The seller was forced to be silent.

## (III)
## The Kingfisher and the Clam

This fable was uttered by Su Tai （苏代）in the attempt to persuade the country Chao （赵）and the country Yen （燕）to join forces against the country Tsin（秦）.

Just then a clam came out and opened its shell to receive a little sunshine, a kingfisher tried to pick at its meat. The clam immediately closed its shell and firmly held the bird's beak. The kingfisher said to the clam, "If it does not rain today, and does not rain tomorrow, surely I shall have your life." "If today you cannot get out and tomorrow you cannot get out, there will be a dead kingfisher, too," replied the clam. So these two would not loose each other till a fisherman came calmly by and, laughing up his sleeve at the feast, caught both of them.

**Note**

THREE FAMOUS CHINESE STORIES, translated from Chinese into English by Tao Chih-Hsin (one of Dr. H. C. Tao's old names), was first published in "THE UNIVERSITY OF NANKING MAGAZINE", No. 3, Vol. IV, April 1913.

# Special Trenches

A fellow was trying to dodge military service.

"I am afraid my short-sightedness will prevent me from doing any actual fighting," he said. The M. O. replied cheerfully: "That's Okay, old chap. We've got special trenches for the short-sighted ones. Right up close to the enemy—you just can't miss seeing 'em."

## Note

SPECIAL TRENCHES AND ANATOMY SCHOOL RECTOR MAY EXECUTE CRIMINALS: Two jokes, sources unknown, duplicate copies found in the files of the Tao Heng-Chih Museum at Xiao Zhuang Normal School in Nanjing.

# Anatomy School Rector May Execute Criminals

The rector of a school of anatomy wrote to the executioner asking if the executions could be carried out with less savagery so that the bodies would be better suited for scientific purposes.

The executioner politely replied: "I am happy to be able to render a service to science, and in order to avoid further error I will from now on send you the bandits living so that you may kill them in the manner that seems best to you."

# Mencius (1)

Mencius was talking with the King Hsuan of Ch'i.

"Can I care for the people?" asked the King.

"Yes, you can," said Mencius.

"How do you know that I can?"

"I have heard Hu Heh say," answered Mencius, "that Your Royal Highness was one day sitting in the hall, and some one led a cow past the hall, and Your Royal Highness asked, 'Where are you leading the cow?' and the man said, 'We are going to smear the bell with the cow's blood.' Your Royal Highness said, 'Let the cow go. I cannot bear to see the cow shuddering, like an innocent man going to his execution ground.' The man said, 'Then shall we dispense with the ceremony of smearing the bell with blood?' Your Royal Highness said, 'How can we abolish this ceremony? I do not know if it would do to substitute it with a sheep.' 'It would.' was the reply. Now this kindly heart will enable you to rule over the whole country. The people think that you love the cow, but I know that you just could not bear to see the cow die."

"Yes," replied King Hsuan, "there are indeed people who say such things. However small my kingdom is, why should I love a cow? It was rather because I could not bear to see it shuddering, like an innocent man going to his execution ground, so I substituted a sheep for it."

"Do not be surprised," said Mencius, "that people think you love the cow. You substituted a small animal for a big one. How could they know your intentions? If you could not bear to see an animal die innocently, what difference was there between a cow and a sheep?"

King Hsuan laughed and said, "How could I have the heart to do such a thing? I did substitute the sheep for the cow because I considered the cow was worth more money. I am not surprised that people should think that way."

"That does not matter," said Mencius. "It is the way of the kind-hearted. You saw the cow, but you did not see the sheep. In regard to animals, a gentleman can see them live, but cannot bear to see them die. When he hears their cries, he cannot bear to eat their flesh. Therefore the gentleman always keeps away from the kitchen." —Liang Huiwang.

**Note**

Mencius (1) is a passage translated by Dr. H. C. Tao from MENGZI (MENCIUS), Vol. I.

# Mencius (2)





"There was once a man in Ch'i Kingdom, who had a wife and a concubine. Whenever this man went out, he always had meats and wines, and when his wife asked him who he had dined with, (he said) it was always with wealthy and noble friends. So the wife said to the concubine: 'Whenever our good man goes out, he always dines on meats and wines, and when we asked him who he had dined with, it was always with wealthy and noble friends. But we never see any of his noble friends come to our house. I am going to watch him and see where he goes.' She got up early and followed her good man to see where he went. In the whole Kingdom, no one talked with him. Finally he went to the Eastern Outer City, and begged of the people who were offering sacrifices (at the temples) to give him the left-overs, and having not yet been satisfied, he went on to beg of other people. This was the way he ate and drank his fill. The wife returned and told the concubine: 'A good man is a person we wish to rely on for life. But our good man behaves like this.' So the two women joined in railing against their husband, and were weeping in the courtyard. The husband, knowing nothing about all this, came back in his usual suave manner, and boasted as usual before his wife and concubine. From the gentleman's point of view, people who seek for power and glory and wealth and whom their wives and concubines have not to be ashamed of and weep for are very few indeed."—Li Lou.

**Note**

Mencius (2) is a passage translated by Dr. H. C. Tao from MENGZI (MENCIUS), Vol. VIII.

# The Tiger And The Donkey





Mere talk has always been another of our banes, which reminds me of a story (perhaps, with a moral) about a tiger and a donkey in Kweichow Province. In that remote region there lived a Tiger, but never any other quadruped of any size, until someone imported a Donkey. One day the Tiger met the Donkey and; was startled by its size and formidable appearance; sat back on its haunches and soliloquized: "Is this threatening looking stranger going to conquer me?" He mused, as he meticulously surveyed the armament of the Donkey. "Golly! He has four hard rocks on the ends of his legs; he has a big head, full of great teeth. And I ask you just to look at those ears."The Tiger crept slowly around the Donkey. "By gun," said Old Stripes, "I must be careful. He may be as dangerous as he looks. I'll find out." The Donkey grazed quietly, as donkeys usually do. The Tiger crept about as silently as he could. He studied the Donkey from behind, gave a quick nip at his fetlocks. A hee-haw, a squeal, a fast-flying pair of heels—and back the Donkey went to his grazing. "So that's that," quoth the Tiger with a sigh of relief, "I'll try the front side." He pondered as the Donkey's strong array of teeth bit at the grass. Then he deftly nipped the Donkey's long ear. The Donkey brayed, squealed in panic, swiftly pivoted, lashed the atmosphere with his heels, and settled down once again to the job of feeding on the grass. "Ah ha, " laughed the Tiger, stroking his whiskers, and licking his chops, "You can only talk; you are not half as dangerous as you look; you can only squeal and kick; you are—why, bless me! You are one of those pacifists. Dang it, I'll eat you." And he did.

**Note**

THE TIGER AND THE DONKEY is apparently a free translation of the fable entitled"A Donkey In Gueizhou (Kweichow) Province" in a work by Liu Zongyuan (773–819 AD), a famous Chinese writer of the Tang Dynasty(618–907AD).

# The Appointment Of Kuan Yu For The Defence Of Chingchow





Man Chung was well received and conducted into the city and into the presence of Sun Chuan. He presented his letter at the conclusion of the ceremonies of reception and declared his mission.

"Wu and Wei have no fundamental quarrel, and their dissension has been brought about by Liu Pei. My master sends me to covenant with you for an attack on Chingchow, while he goes against Han and Chuan. This double attack being successful, the conquered country can be divided between you two and you can both swear to respect each other's territory."

Having read the letter, Sun Chuan prepared a banquet in honur of Man Chung and then sent him to the guest-house to rest while he discussed the matter with his council of advisors.

Said Ku Yung, "Although the messenger's speech was correct in form, it was a special pleading. I propose that the messenger be allowed to return and that a covenant be made with Ts'ao Ts'ao for a joint attack. In addition, let spies be sent over the river to find out Kuan Yu's movements, and then we may act."

Chuko Chin said, "I hear that since Kuan Yu has been in Chingchow, Liu Pei has found him a wife, who has borne him a son and a daughter. The daughter is too young to have been betrothed, therefore let me go to ask for her to be married to your heir. If Kuan Yu consents, we can arrange with him to attack Ts'ao; otherwise, if Kuau refuses, then we can aid Ts'ao in an attack on Chingchow."

Sun took this advice. So he sent Man Chung away and sent Chuko Chin to Chingchow to try to arrange for the betrothal. Chuko Chin was received; and when the time came to state the reason for his coming, Kuan Yu asked him bluntly what he had come for.

"I have come to try to ally the two houses. My master the Marquis of Wu, has a son who is quite clever. Hearing that you have a daughter, General, I ask for their marriage, whereby the two houses may join in an attack on Ts'ao Ts'ao. This would be an admirable result and I pray you to consider the proposal."

But the warrior flared up. "How can my tiger daughter marry a dog's whelp? Were it not for your brother, I would take your head. Say no more!"

Kuan Yu called his servants to hustle off the hapless messenger, who ran away with hands over his head, too astonished to look anyone in the face, and reaching his own place, he dared not hide the manner in which he was received, but told the whole truth.

"What ruffianism!" exclaimed the marquis.

Thereupon he ordered the council again to consider an attack on Chingchow.

**Note**

THE APPOINTMENT OF KUAN YU FOR THE DEFENCE OF CHINGCHOW is a story from THE ROMANCE OF THE THREE KINGDOMS, a world famous historical novel by Lo Guan-zhong (1330–1400 AD). The novel described the intricate relations between the Three Kingdoms (220–280 AD), namely, Wei, Shu Han and Wu. Kuan Yu was one of the "three sworn brothers", Liu Bei (Liu Pei), King of the Kingdom Shu Han, being the eldest, and Guan Yu (Kuan Yu) and Zhang Fei (Chang Fei) the younger and the youngest.

# POEMS AND SONGS

*(Translated from Chinese)*

# Wood Orchid

A soft sound steals upon the ear.
Before the window sits Wood Orchid weaving.
But the soft sound is not the humming of the
loom and the shuttle;
'Tis the sigh of the maiden.

Whither wend the maiden's memories?
Whither wend the maiden's fancies?
Lo, it was neither memory nor fancy that gave
birth to the maiden's sigh.

Yesternight came war's dread mandates;
Ko-han is mustering a great army;
Many were the mandates,
Each bore my father's name.
No elder son hath my father,
Wood Orchid hath no elder brother;
I would buy saddle and charger,
I, even I, would fain battle in the stead of my sire.

In the East Street I buy a sqeedy charger,
In the West Street I buy a steed's housings,
In the South Street I buy reins and saddle,
In the North Street I buy whip and spurs.

At dawn I go forth from my mother and my father;
At eve I breathe my steed at the bank of the Yellow River:
No longer can I hear the lamentation of my parents;
It is only the lapping of the swift current upon the river's strand.

At dawn I go on from the foaming Yellow Rivers,
At eve I seek repose at the fountain of the Black Water;
No longer can I hear the lamentation of my parents;
It is only the death moaning of the stricken foe.

For ten thousand *li* we speed on, bearing over our
engines of battle.
Through many a mountain pass sounds the hurrying tread
of our horses;
The biting north wind flings afar the clang of our night
sentinel's clapper,
Ghastly the cold moon beams glint as they seek out the
dents in our armour.

Thus passed a full decade of warfare,
A century of victories, costing many a leader's life.
Then they came back, strong hearted comrades,
Came back, to see the Emperor, enthroned in his palace halls.

The achievements of the warriors are inscribed on the bamboo,
Myriads of cash are bestowed with lavish hand.
Emperor Ko-han bids me say what reward I would wish for.
But what reck I of rewards and Shang Shu Lang titles?
I would fain have a steed that can course over a thousand *li* daily.
I would fain haste me back to the home of my parents.

When the word comes that at last their warrior
daughter returneth,
Forth from the city walls hurry father and mother to meet me;
When the word comes that at last her younger sister returneth,
Gayly the elder sister bedecks her garments to greet me;
When the word comes that at last his elder sister returneth,
Quickly the younger brother prepares with a feast to entreat me.

Then once more I pass through the door of my morn
lighted chamber,
Once more I rest on the couch that I often had sought
at the sunset,
Doff the dusty armour, heavy and worn from the fighting,
Attire myself once more in the garments soft of my girlhood;
Plait back my glossy hair, with a maidenly glance at the mirror,
Coyly adorning its sable strands with a fair Yellow Flower.
And then I step forth from my chamber,
Bashfully greeting my erstwhile comrades of warfare —
Blankly they gaze in amazement:
Can it be that their long-time companion,
Who had shared their privations and dangers?
Is really Wood Orchid a maiden?

The rabbit pairs run close to the ground,
Blindly intent on their little path;
How should they know or care whether I be male or female?

## 木　兰　诗

唧唧复唧唧，木兰当户织。
不闻机杼声，惟闻女叹息。

问女何所思，问女何所忆。
女亦无所思，女亦无所忆。

昨夜见军帖，可汗大点兵。
军书十二卷，卷卷有爷名。

阿爷无大儿，木兰无长兄。
愿为市鞍马，从此替爷征。

东市买骏马，西市买鞍鞯。
南市买辔头，北市买长鞭。

朝辞爷娘去，暮宿黄河边。
不闻爷娘唤女声，但闻黄河流水鸣溅溅。

旦辞黄河去，暮至黑水头。
不闻爷娘唤女声，但闻燕山胡骑声啾啾。
万里赴戎机，关山度若飞。

朔气传金柝，寒光照铁衣。

将军百战死，壮士十年归。
归来见天子，天子坐明堂。

策勋十二转，赏赐百千强。
可汗问所欲，木兰不用尚书郎。
愿借明驼千里足，送儿还故乡。

爷娘闻女来，出郭相扶将；
阿姊闻妹来，当户理红妆；
小弟闻姊来，磨刀霍霍向猪羊。

开我东阁门，坐我西阁床。
脱我战时袍，著我旧时裳。
当窗理云鬓，对镜贴花黄。

出门看伙伴，伙伴始惊惶：
同行十二年，不知木兰是女郎。

雄兔脚扑朔，雌兔眼迷离。
两兔傍地走，安能辨我是雄雌？

## Note

(1) Wood Orchid: A word-for-word translation of 木兰 ([mu:, lain]), *Magnolia liliflora* in the botanical term, the name of a girl described in a folk song handed down from ancient times (about 439-534AD) as a heroine who, when her aged father was to be drafted into the army to resist foreign invasion, disguised herself

as a young man and served in the armed forces under her father's name.

(2) This folk song, translated from Chinese into English by Tao Chih-Hsin (or Tao Tchi-shin, one of Dr. H. C. Tao's old names) was first published in "THE UNIVERSITY OF NANKING MAGAZINE", No. 8, Vol. Ⅳ, January 1914, in which the translator's note said as follows:

This poem is a translation from a Chinese poem written in the Tang Dynasty. The translator is indebted to Mr. Henry Clemons for the poetical form.

(3) Ko-han (or Ke-han): The highest ruler of any of the several minority nationalities (including the Mongols) populating areas north of the ancient "China proper".

# A Stanza Of The Short Songs

*by Tsao Tsao*



When the moon is bright and stars are rare,
The black crow's taking a southward flight.
Round a tree it's soaring[①] thrice[②] with care[③];
Which branch may be fit to stay[④] for the night?

## 短 歌 行

曹操

月明星稀，
乌鹊南飞，
绕树三匝，
何枝可依？

**Translator's note**

① soaring 飞
② thrice 三次
③ with care 留神
④ may be fit to stay 可依，可停

## Note

Tsao Tsao (or Cao Cao)(155–220 AD): Prime Minister of the Kingdom of Wei, one of the Three Kingdoms (220–280 AD) in Chinese history. He was also known as a poet in the history of Chinese literature.

# Home-coming

*by Ho Chi-chang*

I left home when a boy;
And return as an old fogy.
Native tongue I can still speak,
Frost is on my hair, you see.
Children do not know me;
When they meet me,
Smilingly they ask,
"Where from comes he?"

## 回乡偶书

贺知章

少小离家老大回，
乡音无改鬓毛衰。
儿童相见不相识，
笑问客从何处来。

**Note**

Ho Chi-chang (or He Zhi-zhang) (659－744 AD): A poet of the Tang Dynasty (618－907 AD).

# Night Meditation

*by Li Pai*

In the front of my bed, the moon sheds her light,
I suspect on the floor, frost has come.
With my head up, I see the moon bright;
Down, I am thinking of my old sweet home.

## 静 夜 思

李 白

床前明月光，
疑是地上霜。
举头望明月，
低头思故乡。

# Drink Alone Under Moon Light

*by Li Pai*

In the midst of flowers, is a pot[1] of wine.
Lonely I drink, with no beloved[2] of mine.
Fair Moon!  I raise my cup to greet[3] thee.
With my shadow[4] we've a party[5] of three.
The moon knows no delight[6] of drinking[7].
In vain[8] the shadow follows[9] my being[10].
For a short time can I join them both[11].
Let us enjoy[12] when it is still[13] spring[14].

The moon lingers[15] as I am singing.
My shadow confused[16] as I am dancing.
Awake[17] we are happy together.
After drunk, each of us goes his own way.
This loveless[18] friendship[19] we keep forever[20].
May we meet again in the distant[21] Milky Way.[22]

# 月下独酌

李白

花间一壶酒，独酌无相亲。
举杯邀明月，对影成三人。
月既不解饮，影徒随我身。
暂伴月将影，行乐须及春。
我歌月徘徊，我舞影零乱。
醒时同交欢，醉后各分散。
永结无情游，相期邈云汉。

## Translator's note

① pot 壶 ② beloved 亲爱者 ③ greet 邀
④ shadow 影 ⑤ party 团，党 ⑥ delight 乐
⑦ drinking 饮 ⑧ in vain 徒然 ⑨ follow 随
⑩ being 存在，身 ⑪ them both 他俩 ⑫ enjoy 行乐
⑬ still 还是 ⑭ spring 春 ⑮ linger 徘徊
⑯ confuse 乱 ⑰ awake 醒 ⑱ loveless 无情
⑲ friendship 友谊，交游 ⑳ keep forever 永结
㉑ distant 邈，远 ㉒ Milky Way 天河，云汉

# Departure[1]

*by Do Mu*

Overlove[2] appears[3] to be loveless[4]:
When cups abound[5] we can't have smiling face[6].
The candle[7] has a heart[8] of sympathy[9],
Shedding[10] tears[11] for us[12] till[13] break of day[14].

## 赠　　别

杜 牧

多情却似总无情，
惟觉樽前笑不成。
蜡烛有心还惜别，
替人垂泪到天明。

**Translater's note**

① departure 别离　② overlove 多情　③ appears 似
④ loveless 无情　⑤ cups abound 杯满　⑥ smiling face 笑容
⑦ candle 蜡烛　⑧ heart心（代替芯）　⑨ sympathy 同情
⑩ shedding 流，垂　⑪ tears 泪　⑫ for us 替我们

⑬ till 到　　⑭ break of day=day break 天明

## Note

Du Mu (803-about 852 AD): A well-known writer in the history of Chinese literature, also known as a poet of the Tang Dynasty.

# The Bride

*by Wang Chien*

The third day after wedding, the Bride enters kitchen.
She washes her hands and makes a soup of chicken.
Without knowing what her mother-in-law likes best,
She asks first her Groom's sister① to have a taste②.

## 新 嫁 娘

王 建

三日入厨下，
洗手作羹汤。
未谙姑食性，
先遣小姑尝。

**Translator's note**

① groom's sister 新郎之妹，小姑　　② have a taste 尝一尝

**Note**

Wang Chien (about 767–830 AD): A well-known poet of the Tang Dynasty.

# A Traveler

*by Ma Chih-yuan*

Withered vine, old tree, a dusky crow;
Little bridge, streaming water, a cottage;
Ancient road, West wind, a bony horse.
The sun is setting,
A broken-hearted man on sky's edge.

## 征　　人

马致远

枯藤，老树，昏鸦；
小桥，流水，人家；
古道，西风，瘦马。
夕阳西下，
断肠人在天涯。

**Note**

Ma Chih-yuan (? —after 1321 AD): A well-known composer of traditional Chinese operas of theYuan Dynasty(1279–1368 AD).

# Chrysanthemum

*by Chu Yuan-chang*

**(First Emperor of the Ming Dynasty)**

When all are in full blossom.
I do not bloom.
When I am in full bloom.
Be sealed their doom.
For fighting the West wind in October,
I have put on my golden armor.

## 菊　花　诗

朱元璋（明太祖）

百花发，
我不发。
我花发，
都骇杀，
要与西风战一场，
遍身穿就黄金甲。

# Bamboo And Snow

*by Chu Yuan-chang*

Bamboos become downcast in a snowfall.
Though down they never touch the mud at all.
Once more when the red sun rises high.
They again measure up to the blue sky.

## 雪 竹 诗

朱元璋

雪压竹枝低，
虽低不着泥。
一朝红日出，
依旧与天齐。

# Rock Bamboo

*by Cheng Ban-chiao*

The Green Mountain① is tightly② in its grip③,
In the rugged rock④ it has struck its root⑤ deep.
Thru⑥ thousands of rubs and worries⑦,
It's made invincible⑧ and strong⑨.
Wind from East or West, South or North,
Accept this challenge⑩ of its own⑪.

## 岩　竹　诗

郑板桥

咬定青山不放松,
立根原在破岩中。
千磨万击还坚劲,
任尔东西南北风。

## Translator's note

① green mountain 青山　② tightly 不放松　③ grip 握住=咬定　④ rugged rock 崎岖之岩　⑤ strike its root 立根　⑥ thru=through 经过　⑦ rubs and worries

（西成语）千磨万虑=千磨万击　⑧ invincible 坚不可破，常胜　⑨ strong 强，劲　⑩ accept this challenge "任尔"，含有挑战之意。对风说，你们来吧，随便你们来吧！　⑪ of its own 竹自己的（挑战）(凑韵）

## Note

Cheng Ban-chiao （1693–1765 AD）：A painter, calligrapher and man of letters of the Qing Dynasty（1644–1911 AD）.

# On Congee

*by Chen Shi-guan*

To cook rice or congee[1], which is better[2]?
With our boys and girls discuss[3] this matter[4].
One litre[5] of grain[6] may have the use[7] of three.
Two days' food[8] may last[9] for six days, believe me[10].
Should guests[11] come, we add[12] water and fuel[13] only.
No need for soup[14] if our purse[15] be empty[16].
Avoid[17] not plain[18] food for lack of [19] delicacy[20].
Plain taste[21] in plain food will feed[22] us a long way[23].

## 煮 粥 诗

陈世倌

煮饭何如煮粥强?
好同儿女细商量。
一升可作三升用,
两日堪为六日粮。
有客只须添水火,
无钱不必作羹汤。
莫嫌淡泊少滋味,

淡泊之中滋味长。

## Translator's note

① congee 粥 ② better 强些 ③ discuss 商量 ④ this matter 此事 ⑤ litre 升 ⑥ grain 米粒 ⑦ use 用 ⑧ food 粮 ⑨ last 贯彻 ⑩ believe me 信我 ⑪ guests 客 ⑫ add 添 ⑬ fuel 火，煤 ⑭ soup 汤 ⑮ purse 钱袋 ⑯ empty 空 ⑰ avoid 避嫌 ⑱ plain 平淡 ⑲ lack of 少 ⑳ delicacy 美味 ㉑ taste 滋味 ㉒ feed 喂 ㉓ a long way 长途

# New Year Snow

*by Hsiung Shi-yi*

Wine brings a double cheer if snow be here.
Snow takes a brighter white from song's delight.
Ah, but when cups abound, and song is sweet,
And snow is falling round, the joy's complete.

## 新 年 雪

熊式一

对雪饮酒酒更香；
高歌一曲雪增辉。
但愿杯长满，歌长好，雪长飘，
欢乐极兮人忘归。

# Cloth-selling

*by Liu Ta-bai*

Sister-in-law weaves cloth;
Elder brother sells the cloth.
Selling cloth, buying rice,
To obtain a meagre meal for hungry mouths.

Sister-in-law weaves cloth;
Elder brother sells the cloth.
Little brother's trousers are worn,
There is no cloth to mend the trousers with.

Sister-in-law weaves cloth;
Elder brother sells the cloth.
Who is it that buys the cloth?
The rich man in the town beyond.

Native cloth is coarse,
Foreign cloth is fine;
Foreign cloth is cheaper,
The rich man is glad.
Native cloth now nobody wants,

Starved must be brother and sister-in-law.

## 卖 布 谣

刘大白

嫂嫂织布，哥哥卖布。
卖布买米，有饭落肚。

嫂嫂织布，哥哥卖布。
小弟弟裤破，没布补裤。

嫂嫂织布，哥哥卖布。
是谁买布，前村财主。

土布粗，洋布细，
洋布便宜，财主欢喜。
土布没人要，
饿倒了哥哥和嫂嫂。

# Little Cabbage

Like a cabbage small,
Yellow on the ground.
Seven or eight was I when my mother died,
Good as gold I then followed after Dad.
La, le, la, le, la,
Father now I fear
Will re-wed a wife.
La, le, la, le, la,
Children that she brings, favours will receive.
Noodles they will eat, leaving me the soup.
Chopsticks bring to mind,
My mother dear.
If she thinks of me, is it any use?
La, le, la, le, la.
I shall long for her many, many days.
La, le, la, le, la.

# 小　白　菜

（山东临清民歌）

小白菜，地里黄，
七岁八岁没了娘，
跟着爹爹还好过，
就怕爹爹娶后娘。
生个弟弟比我强，
他吃面，我喝汤。
拿起筷子想亲娘。
亲娘想我有何用？
我想亲娘泪汪汪。

# All Rise

Arise, we who are not willing to be slaves!
With our blood and flesh,
We shall build our New Great Wall.
Our nation has reached
The most dangerous crisis,
Every one of us is compelled at last
To raise the Lion's roar.
Arise, arise, arise,
Let us unite!
Under the enemies' gunfire,
We march on!
Under the enemies' gunfire,
We march on, march on, march on and on!

## 义勇军进行曲

起来，不愿作奴隶的人们！
把我们的血肉，筑成我们新的长城。

中华民族到了最危险的时候，
每个人被迫着发出最后的吼声，
起来！起来！起来！我们万众一心，
冒着敌人的炮火，前进！
冒着敌人的炮火，前进！前进！前进！进！

# Growing Up

Oh, pear flowers in spring!
The pear tree top is each year growing.
Mother! Please don't have those tears.
I can carry the water in two years.
And in four years from now,
I can take care of the cow.

## 长 起 来

春天梨花开！
梨树每年长个头。
妈妈别把泪来流。
过两年儿能挑水，
四年后儿能守牛。

# Miss Autumn Fragrance The Lonely Shepherdess

**1**

Warm be the sunshine
Sunshine,
Sunshine remembers:
It's kissed Miss Gold's face.
It's kissed Miss Silver's coat.
It's kissed the Childhood of Autumm.

**2**

Gold has papa.
Silver has mama.
Autumm! Where's your papa?
And your mama?
She, a shepherdess, still on the lawn
Taking care of
Her lambs! Her lambs! Her lambs!
The lonely Autumn, the lonely Autumn.

## 3

Gold has a brother.
Silver has a lover.
Autumn! Where's your brother?
And your lover?
She, a shepherdess, still on the lawn
Taking care of
Her lambs! Her lambs! Her lambs!
The lonely Autumn, the lonely Autumn.

# 可怜的秋香

## 一

暖和的太阳,
太阳,
太阳它记得:
照过金姐的脸,
照过银姐的衣裳,
照过幼年时候的秋香。

## 二

金姐有爸爸呀,
银姐有妈妈呀。

秋香，你的爸爸呢？
你的妈妈呢？
她呀每天只在草场上
牧羊，牧羊，牧羊，
可怜的秋香！
可怜的秋香！

三

金姐有哥哥呀！
银姐有爱人呀！
秋香，你的哥哥呢？
你的爱人呢？
她呀，每天只在草场上，
牧羊，牧羊，牧羊，
可怜的秋香！
可怜的秋香！

# A Farmer's Picture Of Confucius

Oh! That man toils not his hands and feet,
Distinguishes not the corns that he likes to eat.
What is he that pretends to teach?

## 一位农人之孔子观

四体不勤，
五谷不分，
孰为夫子?!

# Self-independence

Drop our own sweat.
Earn[①] our own rice.
Do our work with all our might,[②]
They who depend on others[③]
Can never rise[④].

## 自　立　歌

滴自己的汗，
吃自己的饭，
自己的事自己干，
靠人靠天靠祖上，
不算是好汉。

### Translator's note

① earn 赚　② might 力量　③ others 别人（可包括祖上）
④ rise 上升（指精神之崇高）

# Dancing Of The Hoe (1)

I

Cut off the weeds with your hoe,
You'll have good crops if weeds go.
Jijaxei Jaxoxei!
You'll have good crops if weeds go.
Jaxoxei Jijaxei!

II

Old China will win her day.
Under the hoe is Liberty.
Jijaxei Jaxoxei!
Under the hoe is Liberty.
Jaxoxei Jijaxei!

III

Revolution, hoes will defend.

Hail hoe, hail hoe, fight to the end!
Jijaxei Jaxoxei!
Hail hoe, hail hoe, fight to the end!
Jaxoxei Jijaxei!

## IV

A new world is in sight[①]
When Machines and Hoes unite.
Jijaxei Jaxoxei!
When Machines and Hoes unite[②]
Jaxoxei Jijaxei!

# Dancing Of The Hoe (2)

## I

Take up your hoe,
Take up your hoe,
Cut off the weeds,
The crops will grow.

## II

Drive off your foe!
Song of the Ancient Country.
Under the hoe,
There is liberty.

## III

Hail Revolution!
The hoe must defend.
Long live the Hoe,
Fight to the end.

## IV

When fighting alone,
The hoe cannot stand long.
Machines and Hoes unite,
A new world is in sight.

# 锄　头　歌

## 一

手把个锄头锄野草，
锄去野草好长苗。

## 二

五千年古国要出头，
锄头底下有自由。

## 三

革命的成功靠锄头，
锄头锄头要奋斗。

四

光杆的锄头不中用，
联合机器来革命，
新世界在眼前。

## Translator's note

① A new world is in sight 新世界在眼前

② Machines and Hoes unite 机器锄头相连

## Note

This song was composed in Chinese by Dr. H.C. Tao on November 9, 1927. The 4th stanza was added to the song on March 15, 1933. The song was translated into English in two different ways by Dr. Tao himself on September 9, 1938.

# The Song Of The Dancing Of The Sickle

## I

The sun's rising, dundun, yahohei.
The sickle's shining, hoho.
Cutting off grasses, meyitseso.
Good for cooking.
'T will please popo, hoho.

## II

The sun's over head, dundun, yahohei.
Cut! Cut! hoho.
Maidens, listen! meyitseso.
'f flowers are cut off.
Nothing to deck, hoho.

## III

The sun's westing, dundun, yahohei.
Cut! Cut! hoho.

Maidens, look out! meyitseso.
'f sprouts are cut off,
Autumn'll have bald head, hoho.

## IV

The sun's setting, dundun, yahohei.
A clean sweep's made, hoho.
Spring gives life again, meyitseso,
For seeds survive,
Sickle! Sickle! hoho.

# 镰刀歌

## 一

太阳起山墩墩，雅荷海。
镰刀雪亮，荷荷。
遇着草儿割，梅绮紫梭，
捆去好烧锅，
见得婆婆，荷荷。

## 二

太阳当顶墩墩，雅荷海。
砍啊砍啊，荷荷。
大姑娘听啊，梅绮紫梭，

好花儿砍掉，
没有戴了，荷荷。

三

太阳偏西墩墩，雅荷海。
砍啊砍啊，荷荷。
大姑娘看啊，梅绮紫梭，
树苗若不留，
秋山秃头，荷荷。

四

太阳下山墩墩，雅荷海。
砍干净了，荷荷。
春风吹又生，梅绮紫梭，
留下种子多，
刀儿刀儿，荷荷。

**Note**

(1) This song was composed in Chinese by Dr. H. C. Tao on December 4, 1927.

(2) popo： mother-in-law.

# The Little Workers' Song

We are little Pankus.
We'll remake seas and lands.
No hardship can scare us.
See the axes in our hands.

We are little Newtons,
Though look as a fool.
Searching truth in Nature,
We've to keep our head cool.

We are little workers,
These hands, nothing mightier.
We'll make a rich society,
That all will be happier.
We are little workers.
Mighty hands we have pairs.
Good care we must take
Not to make millionaires.

# 儿童工歌

我是小盘古，
我不怕吃苦。
我要开辟新天地，
看我手中斧！

我是小牛顿，
让人说我笨。
我要用我的头脑，
向大自然追问。

我是小工人，
双手有万能。
我要造富社会，
不造富个人。

## Note

（1）This song was composed in Chinese by Dr. H. C. Tao in the spring of 1931.

（2）The 4th stanza of the song in the English version actually is the 3rd stanza translated in a different way.

（3）Panku（or Pangu）：The all-mighty god in Chinese myth who brought into existence the Heaven and the Earth.

# Hands and Brain Unite

## I

Two treasures with us life-long remain:
A pair of free hands and a great brain.
He who does not use his hand
Belongs to the dethroned King's band.
He who does not use his brain
Has to endure hunger and pain.
He who uses both his brain and hand
Can set up Heaven's Kingdom on Satan's Land.

## II

Treasures we have two:
Hands and brain will do,
He, using no hand,
Will soon① lose② his stand③.
He, using no brain,
Will face hunger and pain.
He who uses brain and hand,

Can set up Heaven's Kingdom④ on Satan's Land⑤.

## 手脑相长歌

人生两个宝，
双手与大脑，
用脑不用手，
快要被打倒。
用手不用脑，
饭也吃不饱，
手脑都会用，
才算是开天辟地的大好佬。

### Translator's note

① soon 快 ② lose 失 ③ stand 立脚地 ④ Heaven's Kingdom 天国 ⑤ Satan's Land 魔鬼之地

### Note

This poem was composed in Chinese and translated into English by Dr. H. C. Tao in the winter of 1931.

# Children's Day

Longdong longdong ji longdong,
Let's celebrate today with a song.
The world once owned by upsgrown,
Now all to children belong.

Longdong longdong ji longdong,
Let's celebrate today with a song.
Dead books we no longer hang on.
With brain and hands, work shall be done.

Longdong longdong ji longdong,
Let's celebrate today with a song.
Ivory tower youths[①] chewing gum[②],
Enjoy the moment, the future is gone.

Longdong longdong ji longdong,
Let's celebrate today with a song.
With the hoe and the axe we come.
A New World'll be built without the rule of thumb[③].

Longdong longdong ji longdong,
Let's celebrate today with a song.
The world shall be shaped by a child's heart.
Failing this, 't will fall apart.

Longdong longdong ji longdong.
Let's celebrate today with a song.
In Children's world there are no old men.
All old men are reborn as children.

Longdong longdong ji longdong,
Let's celebrate today with a song.
Aggressors[4] against the weak can't live long.
Toward them all are mobilized[5] to dash on.

## 儿童节歌

弄冬弄冬一弄冬，
今天过节热烘烘。
从前世界属大人，
现在世界属儿童。

弄冬弄冬一弄冬，
今天过节热烘烘。
儿童不再读死书，
手脑相挥来做工。

弄冬弄冬一弄冬，
今天过节热烘烘。
少爷小姐是废物，
贪图享福必送终。

弄冬弄冬一弄冬，
今天过节热烘烘。
拿起锄头和斧头，
造个世界大不同。

弄冬弄冬一弄冬，
今天过节热烘烘。
世事须从小儿意，
不从儿意不成功。

弄冬弄冬一弄冬，
今天过节热烘烘。
儿童国里无老翁，
老翁个个变儿童。

弄冬弄冬一弄冬，
今天过节热烘烘。
谁要欺负弱与小，
总动员向他进攻。

**Translator's note**

① Ivory tower youths 象牙塔上之少年=少爷小姐

② chewing gum 吃胶皮糖，少爷小姐只会吃糖，含有“不中用”之意。

③ rule of thumb 按部就班　without the rule of thumb 不依常规，含有“维新，不同”之意。

④ aggressors 侵略者

⑤ mobilize 动员

## Note

This song was composed in Chinese and translated into English by Dr. H. C. Tao on April 2, 1933.

# Little Teachers

## I

Longdong yi longdong,
Heaven and Earth to children belong.
We are angels spreading the truth.
To every village, we dash on.

## II

I am a little teacher, you know.
My heart is like a volcano.
I am not afraid of frost and snow.
I melt ignorance wherever I go.

# 小 先 生

## 一

弄冬一弄冬，
乾坤属儿童。
我们是真理的传布者，
瞄准乡村向前冲。

## 二

我是小先生，
热心好比火山喷。
生来不怕霜和雪，
踏破铁鞋化愚蒙。

**Note**

This song was composed in Chinese and translated into English by Dr. H. C. Tao in the spring of 1934.

# Feng Yang Song

## I

Sing Feng Yang, Dance Feng Yang.
Feng Yang was a good farm.
Since Imperialism came in,
Nine out of ten years, it's done harm.
It's done lots of harm. Jijarxei.
Dr langdang piao ji piao, dr langdang piao ji piao,
Dr langdang piao piao ji piao ju ji piao.

## II

You beat th' drum; I beat th' gong.
All come to hear a good song.
Other songs we want not to sing,
Let us sing a Feng Yang Song.
Indeed a Feng Yang Song! Jijarxei.
Dr langdang piao ji piao, dr langdang piao ji piao.
Dr langdang piao piao ji piao ju ji piao.

# 凤 阳 歌

一

唱凤阳，舞凤阳，
凤阳本是个好地方。
自从来了帝国主义，
十年倒有九年荒。

二

你打鼓，我打锣，
大家来听一个好歌。
别的歌儿我不唱，
让我们唱个凤阳歌。

**Note**

This song was composed in Chinese and translated into English by Dr. H. C. Tao in 1935.

# New Leadership

The world turns up-side-down.
The cap becomes the crown.
Torch lights change bearers.
Youths shall lead their elders.

## 青年领导

世界将起变化，
火把要换人拿。
但愿天翻地覆，
青年领着老大。

### Note

NEW LEADERSHIP was composed in Chinese and translated into English by Dr. H. C. Tao on October 5, 1936.

# Summer Of 1925

On board a Japanese steamer,
A mass meeting was called to order;
All Chinese seamen joined hands:
The chairman a 3rd class passenger.

"Down with Japanese imperialism!"
As the shouts were led by a speaker.
The Japanese captain leaning on the upper deck,
From below came storm and thunder.

Down, he stared at the sea.
Up, he stared at the sky.
Then he stared at the mass,
Giving a deep, deep sigh.

# 1925年之夏

（从汕头坐日本船到香港）

日本船上，
水手开会。
三等客人，
主席就位。

打倒日本，
呼声如雷。
日本船主，
无法作对。

抬头看天，
低头看水。
再看众人，
自叹倒霉。

## Note

This poem was composed in Chinese and translated into English by Dr. H. C. Tao in July 1936.

# Full Moon

When the Moon is full,
And the air is cool,
I think of a lady,
With whom I read the Devil's Pool.

When the Moon is full,
And the air is cool,
I think of the League,
Ruined by a Tory① fool②.

When the Moon is full,
And the air is cool,
I think of China,
She has to fight a bull.

When the Moon is full,
And the air is cool,
I think of my nation,
She will come under people's rule.

When the Moon is full,
And the air is cool,
I think of myself,
When to graduate from the World School?

May 13th, 1938

## 月　　圆

月亮圆，
清风吹入心田，
我想到一位姑娘，
当年同读魔沼缘。

月亮圆，
清风吹入心神，
我想到国际联盟，
毁灭于贪利蠢人。

月亮圆，
清风吹入心头，
我想到我的祖国，
她要斗一头牛。

月亮圆，
清风吹入心里，
我想到我的民族，
快要受民主的洗礼。

月亮圆，
清风吹入心窝，
我想到我自己，
何时毕业于世界大学？

## Translator's note

① Tory 英国保守党之绰号。
② Tory fool 贪利蠢人，指张伯伦。

## Note

This poem was composed in Chinese by Dr. H. C. Tao in July 1936, and was translated into English by Dr. Tao himself on May 13, 1938.

# Work

Doing no work,
Eating much rice.
What are you?
A bunch of lice①!

## 做　　工

不做工，
要吃饭。
什么人，
王八旦。

### Translator's note

① lice 虱子，寄生虫。

### Note

This poem was composed in Chinese and translated into English by Dr. H. C. Tao on September 18, 1935.

# Study

With the belly full.
Reading no book.
What are you?
Just a hog!

读　　书

吃饱饭，
不读书。
什么人，
老母猪。

## Note

This poem was composed in Chinese and translated into English by Dr. H. C. Tao on September 18，1935.

# Teaching

Reading a lot,
Teaching not.
What are you?
A hard nut[①]!

## 教　　人

死读书，
不教人。
什么人，
木头人。

## Translator's note

① hard nut 硬壳果

## Note

This poem was composed in Chinese and translated into English by Dr. H. C. Tao on September 18, 1935.

# Resist Japan

Teaching dead book,
Seeing China broke①.
What are you?
Just a joke②!

## 抗　　日

教死书，
不抗日。
什么人，
狗放屁。

### Translator's note

① Seeing China broke 坐视祖国被侵而不救
② joke 笑话

### Note

This poem was composed in Chinese and translated into English by Dr. H. C. Tao on September 18, 1935.

# Two Sisters

Dedicated to French and Chinese friends who participated in the celebration in Paris of the 25th Anniversary of the Founding of the Republic of China on October 10, 1911.

Two Sisters are born,
You know where and when;
One, on July Fourteen;
One, on October Ten.
One is called China;
Miss France is the other's name.
They fight with sword.
They fight with pen.
They have joined hands
For Democracy they defend.

# 两位姊妹

献给参加双十节25周年巴黎庆祝会之中法友人

两位好姊妹，
生辰有意义：
一是七一四，
一为十月十。
姊名大中华，
妹名法兰西。
拿起笔与剑，
保卫德谟克拉西。

## Note

This poem was composed in Chinese and translated into English by Dr. H. C. Tao on October 10, 1936.

# The Scholar Ghost

I am a scholar ghost.
I live on the Pacific coast.
I have bookish knowledge to boast.
I have my eyes upon the official post.
I like delicious food,
And make the half starved farmers my hosts.
When jobless, I teach children,
And make all of them little scholar ghosts.

# 书 呆 子

我是书呆子,
家住太平洋,
读破万卷书,
望中状元郎,
农家供酒肉,
主人快饿死,
失业教蒙童,

尽成书呆子。

## Note

This poem was composed in Chinese and translated into English by Dr. H. C. Tao in 1937.

# Peace Power

(*Dedicated to Canadian Friends*)

Jan.16, 1938

## I

Silently I stood before the Niagara.
What a magnificent Water Orchestra!
Through her thrilling and inspiring music,
I received a wise message from Canada.

## II

May we imagine, these little drops of water,
Tiny and insignificant as they are,
Once united from a high plain, move forward,
Posseses the power that reaches near and far.

## III

May friends who love peace and democracy,
Leaning high from the ivory tower,
Unite and move forward toward the same goal.

Only then are sentiments made a power.

## IV

This power greater than the Niagara
Can stop the War that is forced on China.
When Peace without slavery comes to earth
'T will bring prosperity also to Canada.

# 和平之威力

（献给加拿大的朋友）

1938年1月16日

## 一

默无一言我面对着尼嘎拉，
洋洋乎大哉这水之交响曲！
在动人心灵之美乐中，
我接到了加拿大之智慧的忠告。

## 二

让我们想象这小小的水点，
何等的渺小而微细！
在高岩上一经联合而向前，
便成为打破距离之威力。

三

爱护和平与民主的朋友，
高高的倚在象牙塔之上。
要对准着一个目标团结前进，
只有这时情感才能变成力量。

四

这力量大于尼嘎拉，
能阻止侵略战争之加于中华。
等到无奴隶的和平降临在大地，
自然而然的也会繁荣加拿大。

# Love What The People Love

## I

Love what the people love.
Hate what the people hate.
Teachers of the people
Take lessons at the people's gate.

## II

Love what the people love.
Hate what the people hate.
He who serves the people
Becomes the people's mate.

## III

Love what the people love.
Hate what the people hate.
Defenders of the people
With blood write the people's Iliad[①].

1945. 10. 27.

# 民之所好

## 一

民之所好好之，
民之所恶恶之。
教人民进步者，
拜人民为老师。

## 二

民之所好好之，
民之所恶恶之。
为人民服务者，
亲民庶几无疵。

## 三

民之所好好之，
民之所恶恶之。
为人民奋斗者，
血写人民史诗。

**Translator's note**

① Iliad伊利亚特，包括24篇诗。相传古希腊时代荷马(Homer) 作两首史诗，

即奥德赛（Odyssey）和伊利亚特(Iliad)。

people's Iliad人民的史诗。

## Note

This poem was composed in Chinese and translated into English by Dr. H. C. Tao on October 27, 1945.

# Petticoat
## —A Gift To A General

You proclaim yourself a hero,
But bow down to China's foe.
With orders to retreat,
You let mountains and rivers go.
    My Petticoat is fit for you.
    Let women face the foe.
    Give me your uniform,
    Towards the battlefield I go.
Petticoat says, "no."
"What makes you think so?"
The North has Lady Lee,
Down South is Maiden Ho.
Then China's Joan of Arc
Whose name is Miss Loh
With petticoats
They have fought the foe.
What a disgrace
To let me go!

**Note**

The manuscript of this poem, in English only, is in the custody of the Tao Heng-Chih Museum at Xiao Zhuang Normal School in Nanjing.

# All China Unite

The iron will of the four hundred million people
Shall steer our ship towards her Destiny.
Eight million hands shall join together,
Rowing the oars to the Land of Liberty.
All cheer in the same joys,
And share in the same sorrows.
Look! There comes a strange boat.
It is the pirates who shoot the arrows.
Countrymen! Think of nothing else.
Stop all your eloquent debates.
Dash to the threatening enemy,
And clear off the menacing pirates.
The iron will of the four hundred million people
Shall steer our ship towards her Destiny.
Eight hundred million hands shall join together,
Rowing the oars to the Land of Liberty.

## Note

The manuscript of this poem, in English only, is in the custody of the Tao Heng-Chih Museum at Xiao Zhuang Normal School in Nanjing.

# 译 诗

# 一位美国博士之自述

布希那葛原作

爸爸轻信书本：
书中自有富贵。
一生做牛做马，
拼命为儿缴费。
我也用功读书，
连得三个学位。
毕业找到差使，
洗碗洗盘洗碟。

二十六年五月十五日

# 我决定[①]

斯特森(Charlotte Parkins Stetson)作

要保持我的健康;
做我的工作;
求生存;
留心看是否长进,取来给去;
绝不白费光阴往后看,
不在懦弱中等待,不在权势中奔走;
只是常常的朝着光明迈进,
常常的常常的面向着正义。
夺去了,饿坏了,失败了,跌倒了,打散了,
向前,拿出我所有的力量,
回转到大路上来。

三十年十月二十一日译

**注释**

① 此诗参见本全集第十卷1941年10月5日所记:"王牧师出示焕公所读诗及其译稿。"

# 箭与歌

朗费罗[①](H. W. Longfellow) 作

我向空中射了一枝箭，
落下地来，我不知道它在何方，
只见它一去如飞，
眼光跟不上箭的去向。

我向空中唱了一首歌，
落下地来，我不知道它在何方；
谁有如此敏捷健强的眼光，
跟得上歌声的飞扬？

好久好久以后，在一棵橡树上，
我寻着了这枝箭，仍旧没有破；
在一个朋友的心里，
我寻着了这首歌，一个字也不错。

三十一年四月

## 注释

① 朗费罗（1807—1882）美国诗人。作品反对民族压迫和种族歧视，主观上同情印第安人和黑人的不幸遭遇。主要诗集有《夜吟》《奴隶之歌》等。《海华沙之歌》是他的代表作，是美国文学中第一部反映印第安民族的史诗。

# 言论自由

福尔泰[①]对杜德夫人说：
我反对你所说的话语，
但你说这话的权利，
我要拼命为你争取。

三十三年十月十日

载1946年2月17日《民主生活周刊》创刊号

## 注释

① 福尔泰，通译伏尔泰（1694—1778）。法国启蒙思想家、作家、哲学家，反对当时的封建专制制度，强调资产阶级的自由和平，批判天主教的黑暗与腐朽。著有《哲学通信》《形而上学论》；文学作品有《查第格》《查伊尔》，长诗《奥尔良少女》等。

# 今天

无名氏作(英诗)

每逢太阳上升，
想到开始一生。
昨天已被埋葬，
让它睡得沉沉。

只有今天可贵，
紧紧抓住在手，
教它由你支配，
变为你的朋友。

“今”为光阴骄子，
人有高贵精神。
你俩天作之合，
前进，勇敢，完成！

# 你的任务

S. M. Gnannis 原作

假使你不能在海洋中，
驾驶飞快的舰队，
摇荡最高的浪涛，
笑对着迎头来的暴风，
你也该立在
碇泊的海湾内水手群中；
拿你的一臂之力，
帮助他们将船开出去。

假使你没有力量，
攀上高险的山峰去旅行，
你也该站在众人必经的山谷；
你能唱一只快乐的歌，
当他们慢慢走过，
他们或者忘记歌者之名，
然而忘不了所唱之歌。

假使你没有金和银，
在手边任你分配，
假使你不能对于穷人，

伸出一只常愿援助的手，
你也该安慰受难的人，
对犯过的人，滴你的同情之泪；
你也该做一个忠实的门徒，
坐在基督的脚边。

假使你不能在收获的时期，
搜集那粗心的农夫遗漏掉，
丰富成熟的金黄色的麦粒，
你也该到墙边，
收拾那长在荆棘中的麦子；
因为麦子被阴影所掩护，
或者比一切还长得丰富。

假使你在战斗中，
不能证明你是一个真正的兵士，
假使你在炮火密集的地方
没有工作能担任，
当战场寂静的时候，
你也该小心地走去——
将受伤的战士抬出，
将死去的掩埋。
那末不要懒洋洋的站着，
等候那更大的工作去做；
幸运是一个懒惰的女神——
她决不会来找你。
去到生命的葡萄园中去操劳吧；
不要怕工作，不要怕冒险，
假使你要一个工作的园地，

你到处都可以找得着。

注：这是林肯总统所喜爱的一首歌，当1864年华盛顿礼拜学校大会中唱着这首歌时，林肯呼重唱至少有十八次之多。

# 和气的说吧[①]

大卫贝茨原作

和气的说吧，
以爱待人远胜于以威吓人。
和气的说吧，
不要让恶言来毁坏我们在此地可做的好事。
和气的对小孩子说话吧，
这样必能得到小孩子的爱。
教导他要平心静气，
小孩的时代不会久留。

和气的对青年人说话吧，
因为他们的担负是够重了。
他们要尽力过这一生，
这一生充满着忧患。
和气的对老年人说话吧，
不要使伤心过的人再忧愁。
他的生命漏壶中的沙粒将要流尽了，
让他在和平中离别。

和气的对犯过的人说话吧，
要知道，他们已经是劳而无功；

或者是因为受了虐待才做错事，
啊！争取他们回心转意吧！
和气的说是件小事，
却能打到人心的深处。
它所带来的福气和快乐，
将来会有事实告诉你。

## 注释

① 此诗由陶行知选题，吴树琴初译，陶行知修改定稿。

# 命运（前途）[1]

歌德[2]原作

藏在未来的怀抱中，
是欢乐与忧患；
我们得贯彻始终，
没有东西能阻挡
我们——冲锋。

庄严的在我们面前，
是挂了帘幕，漆黑的小门，
一切世人的目的——
抬头是静默的星辰，
低头是静默的坟地。

当你认真而四顾，
有恐怖的预兆来到；
同来的有幻影和错误，
用怀疑与烦恼，
叫勇士颠倒。
但是听啊，那儿来的忠告。
古今世界的圣贤说给你听：
慎选啊，选你要走的路。

选是一霎那就选好，
路是一辈子也走不尽。

“在永存的寂寂中，
有眼睛注视你；
这里有一切宝藏，
勇士啊，报酬你；
努力吧，不要丧气。”

## 注释

① 此诗系按陶行知手迹收入。

② 歌德（1749—1832） 德国大诗人、剧作家、思想家。代表作有小说《少年维特之烦恼》、诗剧《浮士德》等。

# 自家人[①]

森斯特

我若知道在早上
当你走开的时候，
对你说话不和气
怎样使我懊悔
烦恼了一整天。
亲爱的，我应当更小心，
使你不致受不必要的痛苦。
但是我们懊恼“自家人”，
声调脸色一出，
或是永远收不回来。

虽然是在这平静之夜，
你或者能给我一个和平之接吻，
然而我心里的痛苦，
或者永远不会停止。
多少人早上出去，
晚上不复回来，
为了恶声的说话，
使人心碎，
这忧愁是永不能重新改正。

但是对“自家人”说话，
是以难受的音调，
虽然最爱的是“自家人”，
那不耐烦的曲唇啊！
那谴责的眉峰啊！
只好付给残忍的命运，
如果到了夜里已是太迟，
再来取消早上所做的事。

## 注释

① 此诗由陶行知选题，吴树琴初译，陶行知修改定稿。

# 坚强起来[1]

巴比科克原作

坚强起来！
我们不是在这里玩耍——做梦流荡。
我们有困难的工作要作，有重的担子要挑。
不要逃避斗争——面对着它，这是上帝的
恩赐。

坚强起来！
不要埋怨时运不好。
是谁该受责备呢？
垂手，屈服，不要脸！
大胆的，用上帝的名义，站起来说话。
坚强起来！
不问事情错得怎样的深，
斗争如何的艰难，日子如何的长久，

不要消沉——向前作战！
胜利的歌声明天会来到。

注释

① 此诗陶行知选题，吴树琴初译，陶行知修改定稿。

# 黄昏①

莎孚②原作　西蒙英译



莎孚（公元前6世纪），抒情诗人中最伟大者之一，古希腊抒情文学时代之光荣诗人。

黄昏把一切招回来——
把黎明前所分散的招回来：
把小绵羊招回来，
把小山羊招回来，
把小孩子招回来，
都招到母亲的怀抱里来。

## 注释

① 此诗由陶行知选题，吴树琴初译，陶行知修改定稿。

② 莎孚　通译萨福（公元前7—前6世纪），古希腊女诗人，出身贵族，曾在故乡教授妇女诗歌和音乐。写有诗集9卷，现仅存两首完整的诗和一些残句。

# 苹果

公元前6世纪，希腊女诗人莎孚（Sappho）写了一首苹果小诗，我从罗塞蒂（D. G. Rossetti）之英译，译了出来。这苹果是多么像那“胜利之果”啊！那攀不上的摘者又是多么像中国的老百姓啊！但是时代不同了。莎孚的苹果无论结在怎么高的高枝上，终有会飞的人把它一摘而光，决不肯留一个给人瞻仰。

苹果甜，苹果香，
红上第一枝头上。
有果堪摘何不摘？
怕是摘者善遗忘。
遗忘，未必是，
是他攀不上。
到如今，还只是，
可以瞻仰不可尝。

三十二年九月二十八日

# 鹰[1]

狄尼生[2]男爵原作

他用弯曲的脚爪抓住巉岩，
在寂寞的上空与太阳为邻。
被蔚蓝的世界所环绕它屹然而立，
有皱皮的大海在它的下面爬行。
他从高山的峭壁上瞄准，
像一道闪电而降临。

## 注释

① 此诗由陶行知选题，吴树琴初译，陶行知修改定稿。

② 狄尼生　通译丁尼生（1809—1892）。英国诗人。1850年被封为桂冠诗人。主要作品有《公主》《毛黛》《悼念》《国王之歌》等。

# 风信子[①]

莎孚原作　罗塞蒂英译

风信子，风信花，
山坡好比他的家。
牧童上山来牧羊，
来来去去不惜花。
人也糟踏他，
可叹是爱方便，
紫艳隳入污泥下。

## 注释

① 此诗由陶行知选题，吴树琴初译，陶行知修改定稿。

# 光阴，您这吉卜西老人呀！[①]

R. 赫森原作

光阴，您这吉卜西[②]老人呀！
您不愿安顿您的旅行队，
屈留一天吗？

只要您愿做我的客人，
我把一切都送给您：
为您的小马挂上上等的银铃；
叫银匠为您打大的金戒指；
孔雀向您鞠躬；
小孩对您唱曲；
啊，还有小姐用花为您编领圈。
光阴，您这吉卜西老人，
为什么忙着要去？
上礼拜您在巴比伦[③]，
昨晚在罗马，
今早在伦敦，
在保罗礼拜堂之日晷[④]下，
您系了缰绳，
一忽儿，
又去了，

去到一个个城，
在娘胎里尚未开眼睛；
去到另一个城，
则在它进坟墓之前。

光阴，您这吉卜西老人啊！
您不愿安顿您的旅行队
屈留一天吗？

## 注 释

① 此诗由陶行知选题，吴树琴初译，陶行知修改定稿。

② 吉卜西人　通译吉卜赛人，又叫茨冈人。以过游荡生活为特点的一个印度民族，主要以歌舞、卖艺、占卜算命等为生，原住印度西北部，10世纪后开始外移，现几乎遍布世界各地。第二次世界大战中惨遭法西斯种族主义者残害后，人口有所减少。诗中把光阴比作吉卜赛老人，是因吉卜赛人从不在一处久住。

③ 巴比伦　原址在西亚伊拉克首都巴格达以南幼发拉底河和底格里斯河之间。建于公元前3000年。是当时两河流域最大的城市，是古巴比伦王国和新巴比伦王国的首都。公元2世纪时，遭异族入侵后化为废墟。

④ 日晷　利用太阳投射的影子测定时间的古代仪器。又叫日规。

# 送给西丽雅[①]

边觉生原作

让我在您的秋波里喝一杯，
我也拿我的明眸把您灌醉；
你只须在杯子里亲一亲嘴，
我再也不必去寻那酒的美味。

从灵魂里发出来的渴望，
是想喝一口神妙的仙酒；
即使有天上的甘露给我畅饮，
我也不愿把你的去换一口。

我新近送给你一束玫瑰花，
与其说是向你致敬；
不如说是抱着一个希望——
在你的手中它不致凋零。

你只须对它吹一口气；
送回来给我培养；
它滋长时，我闻到的，能发誓，
不是花香而是你的芬芳。

## 注释

① 此诗由陶行知选题，吴树琴初译，陶行知修改定稿。

# 斑鸠

英国诗人丹尼森[①]（1809—1892）作

我听一斑鸠，
会说也会唱。
说的是故事，
唱的是胜仗。
永远无止息，
只是咕咕咕。
它也想求爱，
心事向谁诉。
于是唱情歌，
宁静能中节；
缓缓以开始，
滔滔而不绝。
庄严唱信仰，
也唱心中乐；
好像为我唱，
不愧我的歌。

**注释**

① 丹尼森　即狄尼生。通译丁尼生。

# 阿布本阿第亨[①]

利亨特原作

这是杜威提督所爱的一首诗，并且由他投稿来，同时亦是许多竞选者送来的一篇。

阿布本阿第亨，（愿他的部落昌盛）
一天晚上自一个和平的甜梦醒来，
觉得他的卧室在月光下更显得华丽，
好似一朵盛开的百合花，
只见一个天使正在一本金书上写着。
充分的和平，
使阿第亨胆壮起来，
对着室中的天使说：
“你写的什么？”——天使抬起头来，
和颜悦色的回答，
“我写着爱神者的名字。”
阿布说：“我也是一个吗？”
天使回答：“不，并不是。”
“那末，请你把我写为一个爱人的人吧。”
天使写完，
就不见了。
第二夜，天使在令人清醒之大光辉中又出现了

发表因爱神而得福的人名，
看啊！阿第亨是名列第一！

## 注释

① 此诗由陶行知选题，吴树琴初译，陶行知修改定稿。

# 林肯的心[①]

布特沃尔斯

“孩子，您受伤了，原野是您的帐篷，
　在最后一分钟，我能为您做点什么？”
“是的，我受伤了，我已精疲力竭，
　您愿意将看见我的经过，为我写封信？”
这高个儿折着几张纸，
　在那阳光朦胧的空气下写着信。

“我怎样署名呢？”这样能给她一点快乐。
　朋友，无论怎样，签上您的大名，
假使您所写的正适合您孩子的心，
　又将您的名字写在这里，他看见了：
“谁如此温和的为我写这封信？”
　“林肯”激动的写在这里。
流着血的孩子，从一个不认识的人的手里，
　拿着这封信。
“什么？‘林肯！’不是他吗？
　仅有我一个人，拿着我的手，
看我经过的，您就是他吗？”
　在那隐退所，这个国民的心，
维持着微弱的脉搏，直到它停止。

太阳穿过树林，好像是个凸悬窗，
　由天穹反射下来。
鸟在唱，鸠在呻吟，
　紫红色的空气充满这空间！
两个人闭上了眼睛，两颗心在祈祷，
　走上这冷静阶梯之级。

他，这个小孩，仍握着他的手，
　他爱的心，永不复回；
让他驾着彩虹，向远地的南方飞去。
　树林在歌唱，太阳烧灼得裂开，
这个领袖在紫红色的空气下，
　闭上眼睛，交叉着手，
我们的林肯在这里上了生命之一课。

## 注释

① 此诗由陶行知选题，吴树琴初译，陶行知修改定稿。

# 当我们别离[1]

拜伦[2]原作

当我们别离，
沉默，流泪，
心儿几乎碎了，
感到后会无期，
那时你的脸惨白冰冷，
更冷的是你的接吻；
预告我，
忧愁的来临！

早上的清露，
寒冷的落在眉睫；
好像是暗示我，
现在我所感到的是什么？
您的誓约完全抛弃，
您的名誉是受着轻视，
我听见你的名字，
如同身受着耻辱。

他们在我面前提及您，
好似凶钟惊我耳；

我听得不寒而栗——
您为何如此可爱？
他们不知道我知道您，
知道您那样的深；
长久长久的为您忧愁，
真不是语言所能形容。

于秘密中初会，
在静谧中独愁，
您的心肠善忘，
您的灵魂会变。
假使我们重逢，
在多年之后，
叫我怎样招呼您？
沉默，流泪。

## 注释

① 此诗由陶行知选题，吴树琴初译，陶行知修改定稿。

② 拜伦（1788—1824）　英国浪漫主义诗人。出身贵族。早年受启蒙主义思想影响，反对专制压迫和侵略。代表作有讽刺诗《唐璜》和长诗《哈尔罗德游记》等。

# 珍钟[①]

本金原作

珍钟常常和我说，
你必定立下一条规矩，
努力读书，工作，学习，
始终不缺课。
记住伊立胡巴勒梯的故事，
他怎样流落在铁匠铺里？
也得到他所要知道的知识，
攀上了知识的最高峰，
珍钟诚实的说这故事是真的！
　　或者他是如此——
　　　我不知道？
当然，什么阻碍了我攀上山顶，
是因为我没有铁匠铺。
珍钟常常说，佛兰克林是个非常
　苦的孩子，
但是，他有大志和头脑，
他用一生研究哲学，
看，他从痛苦中得了什么！
用了一只纸鸢，一个瓶和一个钥匙，
他把空中的电取下来了，

现在我们从他那里得到的光明，
比什么人还多。
珍钟诚恳的说，这故事是真的。
　　或者他是如此——
　　　我不知道！
当然，什么阻碍了我，
因为我没有纸鸢、闪电和钥匙。
珍钟说林肯连一本书也没有，
孩时常以劈木为生；
格兰特将军曾以皮匠职业，
住在伊利诺州。
在南方发生大战之初，
他坚决站在正义的一边。
当林肯请他担任大事，
他每一次都在要失败的战场上打胜仗。
珍钟诚恳的说这故事是真的，
　　或者他是如此——
　　　我不知道！
不算我的错，也并不是眼高，
因为现在没有仗要打。
他说当哥伦布想出他的大计划，
而要求人使他实现时，
他就告诉西班牙和意大利人。
大家都说这是一个梦，
但是伊沙伯拉皇后却听了他的话，
她将所有的金珍宝贝都押掉，
并且替他买了圣玛利亚船，
对他说：
“把地球上的新地找来！”

珍钟诚恳的说这故事是真的。
　　或者他是如此——
　　　我不知道！
当然，容或是这样，但是你
必定要原谅我，
现在是没有新地可以被发现了。

**注释**

① 此诗由陶行知选题，吴树琴初译，陶行知修改定稿。

# 译 文

# 中华民国之将来*

贵大民国之将来，果何如乎？中国近日所处之境遇，实自有历史以来最危难之境遇。就目前而论，固已将四千年之政局一革而新。其进步之速，世界实罕有其匹。然其将来之前途果何如乎？欲知中国将来之前途，必揆世界已往之历史与中国、亚东现在之情形。迪历游日本、高丽、印度、俄罗斯、巴尔干等国，知东亚大势疾趋于变。愈变而愈进化，有如欧洲十六世纪焉。欧洲中古之进化，约有五端，知此则论亚洲，中国不难矣。

一、政治之进化。中古以前，欧洲人民涣漫无纪。至十六世纪，爱国心生，各扞其类，各御其侮。列国以次成立，政局一新。

二、智育之进化。自东学西渐，学者趋之若鹜。不数年，而学校林立，人才叠兴。他若印刷之技，航海之术，远镜[①]之制，亦胥于此时代相继发明焉。

三、工商之进化。中世以前，欧民渔猎以外，农事而已。迨至学术有进步，则发明日多，而工业以兴。航海有术，则交通便利，而商业以盛。工业兴，商业盛，进化愈速矣。

---

* 本篇系艾迪先生演讲词，由陶行知翻译发表。原文无标点，译文篇末附有译者按语："兹篇乃按原文译述，未稍损益，诚恐读者对于先生之引用《四书》语，有疑译者失其本来面目，故及于此。"原载 1913 年 3 月《金陵光》第 4 卷第 2 期。

四、社会之进化。前此人民箝制于群，不克自由。自民权之主义发生，而后个人之位置以高，税值以贵，此为人道昌明之始。

五、道德之进化。中古之世，人民行违其心，宗迷其教。自路德[②]革命以后，天良始免于澌灭，宗教乃趋于正轨。

此五者，皆欧洲中世进化之大端，亦为欧洲近代文明之基础。以亚概欧，则亚之地面较欧为更大，亚之人民较欧为更多。就历史观之，则亚洲实学术之师、文明之母、宗教之主。夫以偌大之土地，偌大之人民，而承古昔之余烈，其前途必远大，较欧洲更远大！（鼓掌）

舍亚洲而论中国，则亚东诸邦，土地以中国为最广，人民以中国为最众，则中国之希望，直为全亚之希望；中国之前途，直为全亚之前途。诸君！中国之前途，关系一洲之前途，则中国之前途真重要，比何国都重要！（鼓掌）

试论中国之前途：

一、政治之前途。中国海禁未开之前，以国家为天下，复羁绊于帝制之下，素无国家思想。互市以来，爱国之心，油然而生。海内志士之奔走号呼，以捍国御侮为己任者，前仆后起，愈接愈厉。故能推翻专制，建设共和，脱去老大病夫之丑名，一跃而为维新之民国。盖有爱国之心，乃有爱国之行。有今日之爱国，乃有将来之富强，爱国为富强之预兆，富强乃爱国之效果。昔之以老大见称者，如埃及，如巴比伦，今尽沦于乌有，仅留历史上之名词。而中国独以古国存留于世，其前途真未可限量。美有大民国，曰合众。其国民实望贵国前途远大，俾得相与携手于太平洋两岸也！（鼓掌）

二、智育之前途。中国知识之进步，大有一日千丈之势。学校林立，学子殷勤，俱能专心新学，取人之长，补己之短。将来学术之进步，必足以左右世界！（鼓掌）

三、工商之前途。中国以农立国，四千余年于兹矣。今已由农而渐入工商，吾游汉口，参观兵工厂，其规模既壮观瞻，而所出钢铁，南至广东，北至天津，皆仰给于此。吾美某富商对某友曰："君愿代鄙人创一铁厂于太平洋岸否？"友答曰："他事无不应，此职不敢承受。盖中国在我对岸，铁矿既丰，煤产又富，加之人众佣廉，将来一经开采，吾美实难与抗。故不如勿开之为愈也。"此可见天然物产，中国有专富焉！以商业而论，印度每年贸易增至5%，中国每年则增至6%。循此递增，吾必其将来之足以富国，吾必其将来之足以富民！（鼓掌）

四、社会之前途。中国古俗重男轻女，今则男子有教育，女子亦稍有教育，实为男女平权之始。至于个人问题，其先不过随社会之调度，今则自由平等之权，虽政府亦不能剥夺之。他若孩童教育，以及安置贫民之事，亦俱已有人极力提倡。将来人道必由此昌明，世道必由此郅治！（鼓掌）

五、宗教之前途。向者华人信仰，大都不得其正。自耶道[3]入关，教堂棋布，教徒叠兴，始渐入于正途。德儒康德[4]曰："世运进化，非由学术，乃在宗教。"天人之道愈明，则中国前途必愈益进化。

然此至五者，不过中国将来之前途。能达其目的，则富而强以久存于世；不能达其目的，则贫而弱以终至于亡。存亡一发，现在之谓也。故现在者，中国最危急之秋也。其富其贫，其强其弱，其存其亡，其荣其辱，胥于是时定之。英人能救中国之危急乎？不能！美人能救中国之危急乎？不能！能救中国之危急者，中国人耳！诸君耳！（鼓掌）诸君欲中国富乎？抑欲中国贫乎？欲中国强乎？抑欲中国弱乎？欲中国存乎？抑欲中国亡乎？欲中国有荣乎？抑欲中国受辱乎？中国命运之长短在乎汝，在乎汝少年，尤在乎汝少年之学生！（鼓掌）法国革命之时，有人曰："幸福哉，少年！"少年有幸福，以其年富力强，足胜远道之重任耳！中国有极大之责任，将加之汝身。汝能胜其任乎？汝愿负其任乎？愿负责任，斯胜责任矣！诸君对于中国须负之责任，有问题五，能解决此五问题，而后中国乃有以上五项之前途，而后诸君对于国家之责始尽。试言之：

一曰国家统一。天下事物，合则力强，分则力弱；合则足以捍国御侮，分则适以自招灭亡。中国五族[⑤]宜统一，南北宜统一，行省宜统一，形式宜统一，精神宜统一，民力宜统一，民心尤宜统一。昔希腊南北列邦，始也相忌，继也相侵，终以势孤力弱而俱伤。罗马初建，威权横行天下，非不赫耀一世，惜日后权贵自相倾轧。自相瓦解，故终至于灭亡。波兰之始，亦既四方无事，迨至南北自不相能，而后乃有俄、普、奥三国之垂涎，而后乃有瓜分之祸。舍兹不论，日耳曼列邦分立之时，内祸频兴，外侮叠至，几不保其坵墟。联邦以后，即一跃而为世界之强国。吾美未合众以前，小邦林立，意见争持，烽火时举，与英有衅，与法有怨，内无法家拂士，外无同盟友邦，存亡一发。迨华盛顿联合各邦，驱逐仇敌，终建极稳固之民国。美国、德国能以统一而强，中国何不能以统一而强？盖合则可以称雄于天下，分则可以剖割于列强。诸君欲分乎？抑欲合乎？欲称雄乎？抑欲雌伏乎？欲称雄不欲雌伏，则非合力不可，非统一不可！（鼓掌）

二曰实行爱国。心思爱国，未可也；口言爱国，未可也；纸谈爱国，未可也。必实行爱国，而后谓之爱国，而后谓之真爱国。真爱国者，常使国家循理而行，勿使国家陷于非义。美将某曰："不问吾国有理无理，吾惟左袒之而已。"此非爱国之正也，吾不欲诸君若是之爱国也。马志尼[⑥]曰："爱汝祖国，荣汝祖国，忠汝祖国，勿污汝祖国。"爱国易，爱国而能不污国则难。爱国而能不污国，始可谓之爱国，始可谓之真爱国。上帝命中华四万万国民，生于此土。赐以山林、川泽、草木、鸟兽，使之居于斯，衣食于斯，繁息于斯。诸君宜如何爱之、荣之、忠之，并有以不污此大好河山也？诸君，诸君！外人垂涎中土，外人之罪也。诸君不能爱之、荣之、忠之，甚且污之以启人之侵凌，则诸君不得逃其咎矣！诸君欲爱祖国否耶？欲荣祖国否耶？欲忠祖国

否耶？欲荣祖国，欲爱祖国，欲忠祖国，必自不玷辱祖国始。(鼓掌)

三曰为社会服役。为社会兴利，是为积极之服役；为社会除害，是为消极之服役。二者并行，而后社会乃有进步，而后社会乃日趋于上流。就中国今日社会之情形而论，冻馁载道，流亡充途，老弱转乎沟洫，病夫呻吟床褥，此皆诸君服役之机会。彼等皆诸君之同胞，贫者宜助之，弱者宜济之，倾者宜扶之，病者宜医之，老者宜恤之，危者宜安之，愚者宜教育之，不肖者宜匡正之，此诸君之责也。诸君既生于中国社会，是宜为中国社会戮力，是宜为中国社会服役。以开通民智而言，日本大限伯之义务校，有生徒九百人。若无此义务校，则兹九百人终无机会读书。印度亦多有人，尽纯粹义务，设日夜学校，以开通民智。中国亦间有之，然多多益善。诸君须一往直前，坚忍持久。必达人人识字、人人通理之目的而后已。印度学生闲时，常往村落，对农人演说。诸君暑假、年假亦可如此演说。俾不识字之农夫可稍闻大道。再，我辈见贫苦之人，当存矜怜心，勿存轻忽心。北京、天津等处，有学生专在穷困中调查情形，并研究拯之之法。吾甚望各处，皆闻风兴起焉！以除害而言，则鸦片流毒既久，害人亦最多。中国今日亦竭力禁止，然须绝其根株，勿使余蘖复生。鸦片而外，其害人最大者，莫如洋酒。诸君宜极力节制，勿饮酒，斯酒不来矣。昔英强美买酒，美人投之海中。中国亦须如此对将害人之洋酒。（鼓掌）不宁惟是，贪也，博也，皆害社会于无形者也。吾侪既以服役社会为己任，则当举一切贪、博之事芟荑蕴崇之，而后始谓之服役；始谓之戮力服役。（鼓掌）吾美百年前，凡中国社会所显之情形，莫不全具。其后青年努力抵制，复有罗斯福[7]之雷厉风行，社会始渐臻良善。此可见为社会兴利除弊，无往不在青年。中国社会之希望，中国社会之能改良兴否，是在中国之青年，是在诸君，是在诸君之愿否服役！（鼓掌）

四曰热心道德。语云：“得道者昌，失道者亡。”埃及淫著于碑，罗马淫不为耻，故亡。前兹土耳其兵，号称无敌兵，何以巴尔干战起，即一败涂地乎？曰：惟淫故。近世士兵，多数淫乱无度，淫则性懒，淫则心歧，淫则胆怯，淫则身弱。安有性懒、心歧、胆怯、身弱之兵，战而不败者乎？便加悯曰：国家之立，不在府库，不在物产，而在人格。诸君试一思之。若只有法律，而法官品格不端，徇私妄断，则法律有何益乎？只有矿产，若矿师秉心不正，蠹公私己，则矿产有何用乎？黄河溃堤，损失最巨，而堤工故不坚筑，望其常溃，俾可以饱充囊橐，以致生民漂溺，兆金枉费，殊堪痛也。故中国不患黄河，不患溃堤，所患者，自私自利无心肝之贪官耳。（鼓掌）襄河有一次将溃，察觉者电报通知，乃电生昼寝，致误事机。冲坏船二千艘，使电生不寝，何由此损失？故中国不患襄河，所患者自暴自弃，不尽职之败类耳。（鼓掌）罗斯福曰："有知无德之人，为害甚于愚夫。"吾闻赈济水灾，有人用药毒害饥民，从中渔利。此无他，有小聪明而无道德耳。吾在日本演说清政府腐败时，有汉人某鼓掌甚热。今某亦以革命功置身政界。吾闻其所行，大反向昔。贪贿荒淫，无所不至。此种人有手无心，只知说人，不知正己，于中国无益，于中国有损。吞款即是吞国，荒淫即是荒国，中国尚能容之乎？（鼓掌）然诸君亦将来之官也。今日在此鼓掌，他日切不可自蹈于非义。因诸君之前途，与中国至有关系。须有远大之前途，须有道德之前途。孟子曰："国必自伐，而后人伐之。"若中国人人热心道德，人人品格端正，则举天下兵，莫能与敌矣。岂不壮哉，岂不壮哉！（鼓掌）

五曰信仰真诚之宗教。讲求物质不信真理者，国恒亡。日本此风最盛，是自取衰弱。中国不可则而效之。欲中国富强，当遵从圣贤之言，小心翼翼以服事上帝。华盛顿[⑧]临殁之遗训曰："吾美欲固邦基，第一须同心戮力；第二须普及教育；第三须以宗教立国。"美新总统所著之《国家泛论》亦曰："法律、风俗、文化，皆系于宗教。"可见宗教为立国之必要。孟子曰："顺天者存，逆天者亡。”世安有离弃真诚宗教而能自存者哉？中国可以鉴矣。

曰国家统一，曰实行爱国，曰为社会服役，曰热心道德，曰信仰真诚之宗教，中国转弱为强之五大关键也。中国将来前途之五大问题也，能解决之，则富而强；不能解决之，则贫而弱。谁能解决之？非英人也，非美人也。能解决之者，中国人耳！诸君耳！诸君而欲解决此五问题，不可不效法马志尼，不可不效法加富尔⑨，不可不效法哥利波特⑩。兹三人者，意大利之三杰也。马为书生，以为欲革命不可无气魄，不可无见识，不可无学问，尤不可无道德。遂努力自修，组织少年意大利。意大利之成功，实赖其学识。加为贵族子弟，政治大家，行己无私。革命前后之治内对外，一赖其建设之政策。哥为武将，法人入侵，哥领学生军三千人，与二万法军战，身冒枪林弹雨，口唱忠勇，高歌以固守之。足以损其城垣，乃率军迎战于郊外。誓于师曰：“吾不与汝财货，吾不与汝安乐，吾所与汝者，冻馁死耳。有愿为国冻馁死者，其从吾。”全军感激，力战死伤千人。及夜，复战复败。余二百人，五军围之。哥负创奋臂一挥，二百人步趋冲阵，皆战亡，左右仅余二人。其一即哥妻，被重伤，奄奄一息，寻亦死。哥既葬妻，遂出国门，招募志士，图再举。终为中兴健将。中国欲解决以上五问题，欲达到以上五前途，须人才，须诸君，须诸君有马志尼之学识，须诸君有加富尔之政策，须诸君有哥利波特之勇武。吾知中国有如此之人才，吾知南京有如此之人才，吾知此地即有如此之人才。唉！人才乎，人才乎，人才不出，如苍生何？（先生此时即从袋中取出相片一张，以相片之背，向来宾）吾有相片一张，将示诸君。非华盛顿之相，亦非林肯之相。（先生始以相面示人）此为孙逸仙⑪博士之相。（鼓掌如雷）吾非谓其为完全之人，然以匹夫而推翻四千余年之专制，左右四万万之民心，震动全世界之听闻，实乃不世出之英雄。其始也，无财无产，同志十八人，十七人阵亡，独己得免。亡清令得其首者，受上赏。栖身海外，历尝艰苦。十八年中，惨淡经营。迄今民国成立，夙愿始偿。此为爱国之人，此为救国之人。吾愿中国富强，吾愿中国人人如孙君。人人如孙君，而后五问题乃易于解决，而后此中华五色旗[12]直可大放光彩于世界。（言时先生手持五色旗一面，来宾喝彩如雷）美哉此旗！诸君亦知此旗之意义乎？诸君亦知此旗之所以美乎？试聆吾言：

一、黑为铁色，即铁道罗织国中之意，将使中国交通便利，以促国家统一之进行焉。（鼓掌）

二、白为白玉之白，即人心清白如珪之意，不使国人稍怀污秽玷辱己身，而复以玷辱国家也。（鼓掌）

三、蓝，天色也。在位者，须公平正直，秉天道而行，毋为残暴以虐黎庶。（鼓掌）

（蓝亦水色也。同胞有涸辙者乎？是则吾人所当空西江之水以灌溉之也。译者识）

四、黄为金色。即行敦重，不越道德之范围，如黄金之，见重于世。（鼓掌）

五、红为血色。中华民国既以血造成，亦须以血保之。为国牺牲，为国流血，而后国乃可救。谁为中国牺牲？谁为中国流血？中国人耳！诸君耳！诸君愿否为国牺牲？愿否为国流血？唉，中国之荣辱，中国之贫富，中国之强弱，中国之存亡，是在乎诸君之牺牲，是在乎诸君之流血。唉，中国前途远大，中国前途光荣，吾切望上帝赐福中国，使中国有以达此光荣之目的也。（鼓掌）

## 注释

① 远镜　即望远镜。

② 路德　马丁·路德（Martin Luther，1483—1546），十六世纪德国宗教改革运动的发起人，基督教（新教）路德宗的创始人。

③ 耶道　指耶稣创立的基督教。

④ 康德（Immanuel Kant，1724—1804）德国哲学家，德国古典唯心主义的创始人。

⑤ 五族　指中国境内占人口绝大部分的汉、满、蒙、回、藏五个民族。

⑥ 马志尼（Ginseppe Mazzini，1805—1872）　意大利资产阶级革命家，民族解放运动（复兴运动）中民主共和派领袖。

⑦ 罗斯福　即西奥多·罗斯福（Theodore Roosevelt，1858—1919）。1898年组织志愿骑兵团参加美西战争，1901年当选为副总统。同年，麦金莱总统被刺后，继任总统。

⑧ 华盛顿　乔治·华盛顿（George Washington，1732—1799），美利坚联邦共和国的奠基人，第一任总统。

⑨ 加富尔（Camillo Benso Cavour，1819—1861）撒丁王国首相，意大利王国首相。

⑩ 哥利波特　通译加里波第（Garibaldi Giuseppe 1807—1882），意大利民族运动的著名领袖，杰出的游击战专家。

⑪ 孙逸仙　即孙中山。

⑫ 五色旗　1912年中华民国成立至1927年这一时期所用的国旗。旗上红黄蓝白黑五色横列，代表五族共和。

# 美国大统领罗斯福传*



## 第一章　罗斯福之家世

昔僖伯观孔族，知将必有达人。侯子传子昭，论先推乎相国。盖家庭之化力弥深，亲族之观感尤近。世之成大业、树奇迹，利国福民、流令名于百世者，未必尽因祖德。而家既积善，后人鲜有不昌者也。故传先生，必先叙其家世焉。

先生父籍荷兰（Holland）。一千六百四十九年时，其先祖该马方罗孙福始迁居新大陆。寄庐新阿米斯弟坦（New Amrserdam），今名纽约（New York）。当时为荷兰殖民地，人民践板履，见宽服，吸修管，推风磨，起居清洁，秉性勤敏。荷、纽虽遥间大洋，而风俗之朴实，则侨民与内地无异。致罗族自徙此间，不与他姓通婚姻者，百有余年。因语音不同之故，姓氏屡易。初姓方罗孙福（Van Rosenvelt），旋改罗孙福，寻又改罗撒福(Rosavelt)，迄一千七百五十年，始以罗斯福（Rosevelt）为姓。不但姓易也，名亦渐改焉。罗族先人之取名，均用荷文。如

* 本篇系《罗斯福传》节译。题目在开始发表时为《罗斯福》，其后均为《美国大统领罗斯福传》。原载1913年9月—1914年4月《金陵光》第4卷第4、6、7、8期及第5卷第2期。

尼古拉（Nichlas）、约翰尼斯（Johannes）、雅各百斯（Jacobns）之类是。至美洲宣布独立后，始以英字命名。

初，先世以齐民侨寓马哈大（Manhattan）下游之百特列炮台边。以胼胝[①]为生。寻渐上徙。先祖某见旷地一片，识为要津，即以五百金购之。未几，巷衢蜿蜒，廛肆林峙。昔为荒凉旷地，今则闹热商场，是为罗斯福街。罗氏乃筑室于斯，以宏其家族，以荫其子孙。轮然奂然。未始非某祖先见之明也（美国街市概属方形，先生居罗斯福街之第五十七同。其父之居于第廿同。其祖父之居于方段内）。

然地产既裕，门第亦高，罗族名望日隆，纽约城志载之，不一而足。一千七百五十年，有被称为爱师魁者（Esquire）。一千七百六十年，即有被称为间弟门者（Gentleman）。爱师魁、间弟门者，美人示尊荣之名词，不轻与人者也。其后人，或职自治，或掌法官，或充元老，或任议员，皆代不乏人。惟纽约既为大商埠，罗族概属商人，政治生活非所乐为与闻。故间有一二执政柄者，不过偶然事耳。

罗族既执商务之牛耳，坐拥厚资于兹，稘有半矣。其祖哥方沙罗斯福尤善经营。亿则屡中。承先世之余业，创办银行，运售玻璃，家道益丰。其肄业哥仑比亚（Columbia）大学也，以为学校不足以养育商务之人才，即中道弃学、归而经商，并嘱其子大西呵多（Theodore the Elder）：毋改父道。大西呵多即先生之父也。当任马第连（Maiden Lane）庐斯福公司股东时，自非拉第尔非亚（Philadelphia）送友人某至卓尔基亚（Georgia）完姻，遇马尔撒蒲洛克（Martha Bulloch）女士于途。女士为其友之妻妹，即将来先生之母。倾谈之下，意气莫逆。既敦伉俪之约，遂联南北之姻。

蒲洛克（Bulloch），南美之右族也。其声望之隆，不减北美之罗族。美洲独立，蒲女士之曾祖亚尔其巴蒲洛克（Aihiboldt Bulloch）实为卓尔基亚第一任之都督。其父当墨西哥战时，亦曾任副将，亲冒矢石，尤以勇著。

特罗蒲联姻未久，而惊天动地南北美分立之大战局以开。是时林肯（Lincoln）[②]实统北美。耶弗孙大卫（Jefferson David）[③]实统南美。相持不下。然际此风声鹤唳之秋，最难处而受影响最大者，莫如罗氏家。盖夫则竭忠于北，妻之兄弟则尽瘁于南，各割私谊，以戮力祖邦。知有国而不知有亲。罗蒲之义侠可以见矣。

雅各担威第蒲洛克（James Dunwoody Bulloch）罗夫人之长兄也。前充合众国海军某职，战事开时，适掌保护海商之职。巡驶纽约、纽呵林（New Orleans）之间（纽呵林在南美，纽约在北美）。其所乘舟名：比尼非里。舟主纽约人。当路易西亚那（Louisiana）宣布独立时，蒲队长适抵纽呵林岸。纽呵林都督命其返舟纽约，蒲队长否之。遂为国人所疑，寻思不遵所命，则不足以昭大信而释群疑，即抱爱国热忱，终难展其才猷，于是放棹纽约，归璧原主而南回。

返南后，脱颖欲试。乃亲投耶弗孙大卫，即授南美海军从长之任。奉命赴英购军械，捆载归来，军需以足。复为封港之发始人。其不辱上命，克尽厥职有如此者。

忠勇既显，信任以坚。耶弗孙委以重任，使再赴英国，购置战舰，以为后盾。是时英国为中立条约所拘，不准私售军器，合众政府（北美）复多方挠止，阻其开驶。最后复由华盛顿（北美京城）派员赴英，偿英人金十兆，以为阻止之计。

然蒲队长筹划自如，曾不以难而隳其心，因间而陨其职，终购成战舰六艘，高竖南美国旗，扬帆北驶。不幸两军对垒，该舰击伤甚剧，亚尔巴马舰（Alabama）全艘沉没。迨至战局已息，南北统一，美人以英人违约，控于基尼法（Geneva），判英人赔偿战舰损失金十五兆。

其弟亚尔非司提芬蒲洛克（Irvine Stephens Bulloch）尤英勇。前任南美海军某职，战时实官亚尔巴马舰舵司。当亚尔巴马舰被合众舰职尔撤尔击沉于法兰西海滨时，蒲舰司视死如归，履险如夷。舟虽沦没，犹荷枪击弹，出死力战，毫无惧色，终为英舟援出，得不死。后娶英舟人某之女，报旧德也。

先生曾亟称其舅之战绩曰："牛刚统制（Colonel Newcome）世之勇者也。懦夫闻风，莫不兴起。惟吾舅足以比之。"信哉斯言。

二蒲既为南而力战矣，大西呵多在北，虽不能如蒲之手执刁斗，亲冒矢石，然招兵秣马，接济军饷。则大西多呵所优为其有造于北，实不亚二蒲之在南。忧南北之不能统一也，则征集同志组织同盟，幸达最初之目的。迨战处优胜，无需相助，而大西呵多目击兵士病者病，伤者伤，呻吟荒野，照料无人，而召募之家，孤者孤，寡者寡，哭望天涯，矜恤谁求？慨然忧之，于是发起卫生队，以拯疮痍，劝募慈善资，以纾困穷。兵士无暴露之虞，家人无断炊之叹，大西呵多之功也。

不特此也，观夫两军对垒，兵士汇寄银钱无妥便之方，家因冻馁，赀以浪掷。大西呵多乃条陈利害，令各省政府，如兵士愿将余饷赡养家人，该政府有收管该饷及分发各兵家属之权。既蒙总统之允诺，复得议院之通过，大西呵多乃冒严寒，戴星月，游说纽约各营兵士，将月薪若干，任省会分发家人。统战之始末计之，集欵不下数百万。远戍之家，衣食以足，生命之金，不致虚掷。而战马归来，凯旋男儿得与父母妻孥聚天伦之乐者，非皆大西呵多苦口婆心之所赐耶？

战争已息，和局方开，青年志士之撤伍者，以亿兆计。既事业之难图，复衣食之靡恃，饥鸿遍野，嗷嗷待哺。大西呵多秉己饥己溺之心，划以工代赈之策。特于纽约组织军人工厂，俾得自食其力，以免于死亡。又虑政府剥削其工资也，复立保护战兵会以监察之。

大西呵多之利社会也至，社会之需大西呵多也殷。彼既醉心于慈善之事业，势难分身于商务之经营。虽父有遗命，而其心则为祖若宗历世慈善主义所灌注、所融化，勃然一兴不可遏，不禁为其处世之指导针也。祖充陆军宰人，尽纯粹义务者有年；父逢公益善举，罔不解囊挹注。族人某实建纽约之罗斯福大病院，大西呵多则而扩充之，可谓善于择矣。

罗族支派有二：一曰哈弗（Have），二曰瓦第（Want）。大西呵多虽属哈弗派，常属意于瓦第。其亲亲也，有范文正[④]之遗风焉。其资产之在纽约，虽不足拟于诸大富豪，而一饮一食，固甚裕如。然平生雅不欲聚无益之财，且重讥守财之非道。富人达观，如罗君者世有几人哉？且大西呵多盖所谓："惠人也，惠之外无事业，惠之外无希望，惠之外无愉快。"迹其事实无往而不惠，无时而不惠。苦者乐之，倾者扶之，危者安之，弱者拯之，冻馁者暖饱之。其愉快在是，其希望在是，既其事业亦罔不在是。观其每星期，必用一日以赒济鳏寡孤独茕而无告者，可以信矣。

先生尝谓人曰："吾忆吾父自白兰地来，见市中遗猫一，幼且病。吾父怜之，囊盛以归。"彼固一庄严商人，不以畜而贱之，是其推仁及物欤。

然善举日以众，商业日以释，终且尽弃其锱铢之经营。韶光有暇，乃可以"老吾老，以及人之老；幼吾幼，以及人之幼"。建贫儿教养院于第十八同，每星期晚必探视该院寄宿舍，风雨无间。于是慈声四溢，寻即被举为省立慈善会会正。

西哲曰："天下之最愉快而少抑郁者，厥为吉人。"大西呵多虽与人同忧患，而胸无点尘，乐由心溢，吉人之性然也。泛扁舟于溪间，听鸟啼于深林，运动操场，四马双赛，咸所乐也。先生曰："吾父天下之善人，亦天下之乐人。"信哉。

由政治而言，大西呵多固共和党党员也。虽事事遵循党纲，然党内守旧派之无意识，大西呵多与其子直以风马牛视之不相及焉。哈斯（Hayes）[⑤]总统，因重其行，欲加以大任，举为纽约海关税务司。守旧派知其难制也，授意省议会否认之，事遂寝。

大西呵多去世，不过天命之年。然先生已毕业于哈弗德

(Harvard)大学[6]，身体德性，已由弱而强，一望而知为虎子，此盖大西呵多以人力胜天功也。弥留之际，儿女泣，书雁传来，骑鲸之日，邦人吊幡悬半下，人之云亡，邦国殄瘁，同盟党员乃诔之。其末曰："富者骄损，宴安酖毒，罗居牺牲资财，谢绝宴安，以兴公益，善举而兴邦人士共，可谓普于处已矣。世之富而宴安者，其借鍪而勉旃。"

谨案：昔方域子谓："以孺子之年，而循循然，而庄庄然，逆计其后，可以至于大成者，其有之乎？曰：有之。视其父。然则以孺子之年，且循循然，且庄庄然，逆计其后，可以至于大成者，果有之乎？曰：有之。视其师若友。"先生之父，既以惠名。先生之舅，又以勇著。惠则爱人知己，体天地好生之德，而民受其福，国食其利矣。勇则任重道远，何事不可为？而业成其大、功成其伟矣。天下岂有功伟业大、利国福民而人不归之如蚁之附膻者乎？先生循父之惠，以普度众生为念；师舅之勇，以力行仁义为务。举父与舅之德，备诸一人之身，朝夕而扩充之，旦月而雨露之，则不欲入白宫也，岂可得乎？

## 第二章　童年史

谚曰："幼者壮之母。"壮之成名，于幼是赖。故我家之龙，决之驹齿未零之日。万家活佛，知之击壅出儿之时。少既奇童，壮必英物。吾以叙罗斯福先生之童年史焉。

先生于一千八百五十五年十月二十七日，生于纽约城。名筱西呵多（Theodore the Younger），取其似父也。幼虽慧而实，颠连困苦不可万状。虽生计裕如，不必若华盛顿（Washington）之亲躬旷野；林肯（Lincoln）之跋涉借书，而其资产之充盈，实足为人之毒酖。

耶稣之言曰："富者难入天国。"汉疏广曰："子孙贤而多财，则损其志；愚而多财，则益其过。”盖富，则身广体胖，目空一切，不期骄而骄；山珍海错，呼之立至，不期奢而奢；盈眸皆锦，扑鼻俱香，不期淫而淫；铜山金库，食之不尽，不期佚而佚。是多财，为骄奢淫佚之渐，世安有日，处骄奢淫佚之旋涡中而能超然高举为国戮力者乎？故美国曾未有以富人子而达要津者。先生十二岁时，家医某亦书于案曰：“此子佻达不群，聪颖莫伦，露头角有日，但惜其父之富耳。”彼固逆知富之足以防先生，而孰知先生之出污泥而不滓软。不特此也，先生于骄奢淫佚，则既超然矣；于谦俭勤节，则既服膺矣。而纽约之繁华、壮丽，实为新大陆之伦敦、巴黎。水殿精工、土山华饰，五光十色、满目嚣尘，足以惑人之志也；风俗奢靡、道德污浊，足以损人之德也。故城儿而上达者，千万中不得一焉。而前先生总统美国者，凡二十有四，举皆草泽英雄。彼其钟山川之灵秀，则气概浩然矣；慕松柏之后凋，则节义昭然矣。手执耒耜，则知稼穑之难艰；躬持斧斤，则识藜藿之困苦。见竹之空，而虚其心；闻兰之馨，而礼其行。师鸟之友生，则羊之孝亲；观蜘蛛之结网，而起勤毅；审螳螂之怒臂，而生果敢。志鸿鹄之所志，行大鹏之所行。德性既备于身，善政自施于民，以视先生之朝衣朝冠，坐于涂炭，其难易盖可知矣。然先生卒能尔为尔，我为我，独善其间，既为富人作总统之创见，复为城儿入白宫（White House，美国总统府）之始闻。先生其所谓：冰壶玉尺者非耶！以上二端，既已稍稍言及先生幼时所逢之不利矣。然其最大之敌，最能阻其发展者，厥惟病。先生幼患豚胸症（Pig chested），呼吸壅塞，生机凋敝。斯病之于先生，古巴（Cuba）战争，不足以喻其危；守旧反对，不足以喻其力。自呱呱以迄，弱冠皆为此病所困。然患之既久，抗之亦坚。形躯虽萎瘁，而精神则充。先生之所以能获最后之胜利，亦恃振刷此精神，不甘为病夫，而志在健全耳。

父母惟其疾之忧，乃筑操场于第二十街之庭。使劳筋骨、运血脉，以冀身体之强壮。家人述其升竿之戏，今尚历历在目：始虽未精其技，终则直达其末。要之，先生幼时无论作何运动，恒极激烈，观者莫不危之。其母常曰："不蒙上天眷佑，吾儿之死也久矣。"达兰魁尔地（Tranquillity）距今日呵伊斯第尔海湾（Oyster Bay）罗宅，仅三里。此地林木郁郁，天气阴凉，花嘉鸟好，风景极佳。罗氏之消夏处也。每值炙暑，大西呵多乃携家在此度夏，此数月为先生最乐之时。既一洗城中嚣气，或骑马，或竞走，或款乃摇舟，或逐水游泳，必极乐而反，颇有点也之概。迨天气抑闷、永夜不眠之时，大西呵多乃怀抱此柔弱之子，乘黑夜驱驾荒野五六十里，以吸新鲜空气而益身体。先生之爱林野，固为乐父之所乐，然不仅以为适观娱耳之资料，且作天然科学之研究。见一鸟焉，或听其鸣而科之，或审其羽而类之，或视其所构巢而区别之。每游必与童友数人偕。紫微早放之地，胡桃累结之处，鲦鱼之渊，洗熊之窟，皆彼等寻乐处。彼童友不过藉此以为游玩之一助，而先生固醉翁之意不仅在酒也。

先生幼时雅不欲入校就学，然读书辄朗诵如流，遇不识字必下问，不以难而遗之。其姊常笑谓人曰："吾弟幼时，雏发如丝，衣白衫，披读李佛斯通博士（Dr. Livingstone）之《斐洲[7]游记》，至菜食蚁，忽恍惚不知所云，私度为一种特别蚁，持书徜徉觅人之指教。俄顷，豁然贯通，乃知博士盖指前往之蚁，不觉吔然失笑。"观此则先生之好问可知一斑矣。

身体既弱，学业时阻，以故虽读书而不恋恋于优劣甲乙之较，然其肄业义务学校之成绩，亦非不卓然可观。地理考分九十七，史记九十六；修词学九十八，拼字稍难，均八十六分，亦属优等分数。该校教员告人曰："罗君当时善作文及演说词，绘图尤精妙。"以不能常入校，故将来考入大学之预备，皆延师在家教授。夫身膺伯牛之疾，而学能出类拔萃如此，其天资之聪敏使然也。

一千八百六十九年，父携之欧洲养疴。同舟某为之写真：身修瘦，目光炯炯，两腿如管，盖其时病尚未痊也。后以温暖气候能益肺，乃于一千八百七十三年渡海赴非洲之亚尔基尔斯（Algiers）。顷，其父奉大统领革尔尼第（Pres. Grant）之命，代表美国赴维也纳博览大会（Vienna Exposition）。是行也，先生并其弟以利亚第（Elliott），妹哥利尼（Corime），即今达罗滨松（D. Robinson）之妻，皆与焉。由亚尔基尔斯至德，寓第利斯的（Dresden）某师之宅中。某师为德意志一千八百四十八年革命巨子，因自由而罹缧絏者有年，一千八百七十三年适为众议院议员。识先生虽非彬彬学士，而英气溢于眉宇，逆知其为大有为之儿。于是倾谈之余，道志莫逆，遂结忘年之友。师家某女士尝誓曰："观罗儿常能不学而知，吾决其他日，必为合众之总统。"其在第利斯的也，虽豚喉未愈，难以长谈，然喜读德意志古文，常悉心研究。先生之善操德语，实基于此。留德时，专志研究图画，尤喜天然记载，每见奇石异草，必采之。归当离第利斯的而发瑞士（Switzerland）也，先生满载奇石于身，藉资将来之参考。其母恐敝衣，弃之于途，先生复私拾盛囊中，不遗余力。其天性然也。

先生未入哈弗德大学之前，曾与第利斯的友人书曰："吾行将入哈弗德大学，四年毕业后，始作事业之计划。但彼时之行何事、作何业，今尚不可预知。"夫世事之变迁，桑田沧海难以前知。处今日以担将来之启忧，是犹未抵桥梁而渡者也。先生事今日之所事近矣。然细味此书，先生之言顾行，行顾言，又隐然可睹也。至是先生呼吸渐灵，夙疾已霍。然其所以能战胜此病魔，生死而肉骨者，实赖其精神之健旺与夫身体之勤动二者而已。其自谓云："人谓我为病夫，我不以病夫自居；人谓我必夭折，我不以夭折自期。我志于健全，我勉为健全，我终得健全，夙愿偿矣。我之入哈弗德大学也，凡运动必至，逢体操必临。或赛跑，或角力，或斗拳，靡不竭力为之。虽不能得第一，而受益则莫大。盖吾雅不欲因甲乙之争而过劳身体也。"

## 第三章 入校时代

先生于一千八百七十六年入哈弗德大学。同学一千八百八十八。其在校也，学时则学，息时则息，既得实学，又获休养。以视他童之咬文嚼字，日以考试为目的，与夫优游卒岁，心向鸿鹄之将至者，有天壤之殊焉。以幼年多病之故，性情简俭。其声名财产之在根伯利基（Cambridge）虽盛大，然不喜放浪，且待同学必以礼，曾不恃此自矜而骄人。

哈弗德大学左近各旅馆，学生大半寄宿其中。富家子弟，阮囊充裕，不惮浪掷巨万以求装饰之眩丽者，比比然也。而先生所租之二房，则反以己猎之鸟羽兽革而点缀之。既奇异可目，又俭朴可则，雅非浪荡子所可企及也。

当时士人乘马游猎，相尚成风。先生亦喜之，始虽未善其术，终且疾驰若飞，常以所猎得者，供寓中之饰品。

哈弗德校中著名会社颇多。先生自入校，即入巴斯岭（Porcelain）与亚尔法第尔大斐会（Alpha Delta Bhi，简名亚第会A. D.）为会员。复充饮食促进会秘书。以上诸会，非出类拔萃之学徒，不得入选。而未经选入之学生，复有他会，其范围较广，其入会较易。先生亦与焉。然先生当时入会虽不少，终不若后来之振刷精神、急起直追焉。先生自入名会，根伯利基与波士顿(Boston）人，莫不欢迎，先生虽略与交接，然对于各会之态度，实淡漠无甚趣味。盖自其父筑操场于后庭以来，一则运动日久，习与性成，非体操无以起其兴趣；二则身体虽渐强壮，若运动有间，则恐失已复之健全；三则欲藉体操以增益其力量，而精夫运动之技。故课余之暇，有与比较武力、共同体操者，先生好之若骛。夫心专于此势不暇他顾，无足怪也。是时先生两腿尚未全健。爱创跳绳之术，以发展其筋肉，自兹人相效，家相则，跳绳遂为当时最美之游戏术矣。然先生之绝技，厥为角力运用之巧妙，殆有专门之擅焉。

先生于哈弗德大学之游戏术中最著者，为拳击首之戏。先生当时身重仅百三十磅，身轻若燕，体质又娇瘦，而敢昂步操场以与强有力者敌，见者莫不异之。战斗始起，有二人焉，魁梧其躯，乘先生不备，突然冲来欲击，相距太逼近，眉目常有危险之虞，然先生以其锐敏之臂，力抗之，终能护己而却敌。

一日作拳击首之戏，正在闹战之时，监场员鸣笛令止，先生闻令立垂手休，敌人乘机猛击其鼻，血流沾衣，观者高呼："愚夫、愚夫。"值先生疾趋监场员禀违令而妄击者之时，有声自场众喧哗中颤越而来，曰："勿去，勿去，彼未闻令，彼未闻令。"先生闻而知为误击，立返与该生握手。以致亲恳，场人于是易其轻忽先生之心而为敬爱先生之心焉。兹事凡与罗公同学者，莫不传为美谈。

先生自谓曰："无论何项体操，吾皆不能夺标，但每逢运动，必踊跃先登。与虓将敌，吾不退缩也。且吾运动必择其合吾性情适吾身体者，朝夕而操练之，苟能有裨身体，罔不尽力为之。故由体操而得利益之多，则鲜能与吾匹也。"世有厌学之徒，一入学校，道德不求，其纯科学不求，其通日惟以运动为事，其始非不快愉一时，而终也知识卑下，性情乖谬。先生有鉴于此，标"体操所以操练身体"六字，以为运动之宗旨，故只供适观之运动，如棍球、踢球等，先生均不喜焉。

先生不独勤于运动已也，其对于圣日学课，亦极热心，切磋琢磨，不遗余力。其先祖属荷兰改良教会，先生未入哈弗德之先，在纽约已入该会为教徒。然根伯利基向无该会所设之教堂，聆道无从，无以每星期日则往福音圣日学校习业焉。

大西呵多既以济物之道，朝夕进先生而教之。先生至是已明乎人生、宇宙当以利人为念，不应独善其身，并思所以实行此济物之道，其仁施之在天下者姑勿述。述其一端；某星期日同学某童入校，一目紫且肿。师叩其故，一童以实情对之曰：“恶童某与吾妹邻坐，忽以指痛箝吾妹。吾叱止之，不从。乃助妹与击，因受目伤。”先生闻言，不禁雀跃而言曰：“善者子之行也。”即袖洋一元赠童。但少年之心，莫不乐闻交斗，诸生一见先生是举，同口交赞，以为是公允之模楷。不觉视线同集于先生之身，而忘讲师之哓哓者。自此诸生益佩先生之为人，但该校一般顽固长老师闻之，甚不以为然。先生寻即易校（此校指圣日学校）肄业。

先生寓邻为一马厩。某夕时值深夜，马狂号不已，似受不堪痛楚。邻人闻声起衣往救者，不下六七人，而先生则不待衣衣，早已从二楼穿窗攀梁溜柱而下，以拯此苦畜。邻人至，只见先生已在治马，马已安然如昔。此事乃先生在根伯利基之名迹，不可不知也。

初，先生未入哈弗德大学之先，二舅携之游美尼（Maine），访故友比西蛙（Bill Sewall）。比西蛙彼时躬耕瀑布岛，有巢许之风。先生此行，与其前途，至有关系。因交比氏之故，时与猎徒骑兵伍。古巴战争起，先生所以得立奇勋者，多此辈义侠之力也。

先生自抵此间，起居俭朴，立已恭敬。出则与比氏共游，入则与比氏共宿。乡人称之曰：“罗君直如矢平如衡，凡与交接者，莫不爱慕其为人。”观此可见先生之感人深矣。

先生此时最乐诵者，是为《士子渡渔舟》之文，今达其诣於下：

士子曰：“言者，身之表。言之无文，行而不远。君曾读《文通》乎？”渔父曰：“未也。”曰：“君生已去四之一矣，夫数之不知，何以核计，然则君曾读代数乎？”曰：“未也。”曰：“君生已去其半矣，夫曲直不明，何以度物，然则君曾读形学[⑧]乎？”渔父未及答而大风疾卷，波涛汹涌，舟覆人溺。渔父号谓士子曰：“君能游泳乎？”曰：“不能也。”渔父曰：“惜哉！君生尽于此矣"。

自兹以往，课暇必来瀑布岛一游。盖此地空气新鲜，风景绝佳。来此不独可与比西蛙聚首言欢，亦可以裨益体健焉。廿一岁毕哈弗德大学业。考列第二十二名。与革兰第（Pres. Grant）统领在西方大学毕业等第相仿佛。校中课程，多非所长，行毕业典礼时，仅能以素所研究之天然史鸣。



## 第四章　定入世之方针



先生在校时，对于将来之作何事业，固未尝计及。然志在为一有益社会之人，则持之有素也。平生最恶守财奴，对于国中豪富，诋之不遗余力。其不愿经商之心，固早决矣。

一千八百八十年十月，娶于李女士（Alice Harhaway Lee）既成婚礼，乃东游欧洲，以度蜜月（Honey Moon）游毕返纽约，充监狱改良会干事，同时兼任慈善会职务。既思徒守父道，不能自树，终鲜进步，故一切均本己意，因时而损益之。

当时先生不喜握管，故不欲作笔耕之生活。虽历任哈弗德学报主笔，然罕有表见。惟喜研究战史，偶读一千八百十二年英美海战史，见其疵谬丛脞，难以征信，即食不暇饱，居不暇安，朝夕在哈弗德藏书楼中，搜罗战绩，广集事实，另行妥为编辑，期于可作信史之用。毕业后一载告竣。材料宏富，全书二帙。命名：《一千八百十二年之海战史》。英美人士莫不叹为奇才。然此书不过先生偶然触机而作，非可以其概趋向也。

先生入学之时，初游美尼之日，于学问中，最喜考察天然史。故在呵伊斯海湾，则研究禽兽花木；在哈弗德，则侧重天然科学。前章已略及之。然于性情相近之中，不觉即有一天然科学教授之希望，存于心内矣。

先生在校，不独以所获鸟点缀宿舍，足以显其猎技之精，复乐玩水栖之鳞介动物。某日一大龟自先生宿舍爬出，欲赴浴室取饮，邻舍同学见之，莫不受惊。

此外复有一事，足征其所好。某日自波士顿乘城车归，随带龙虾多头，以供科学之试验。不慎逸袋出，向坐客爬，同座皆骇之若狂。以上种种事实，与夫毕业试论以天然史为题，皆足证先生入校之始末，无时或离天然科学。习与性成，势难舍此他图。其不终身于天然科学教授者几希，而孰知事有大谬不然者。

志向之高下，视乎精神之充虚。精神之充虚，视乎身体之强弱，故先生当身体未健之时，幼则不喜入学。长则志于教授。迄乎始以荒野时，游而胸襟旷达，继以体操日练，而血气以刚，终则身体达于健全，精神日以充，志向因以高，始不屑于教习之生活，而欲求活泼有为之职业，以从事焉。比西蛙尝劝入政界。先生然其言。答以倘能染指其中，是亦甚善。噫！政界汪洋万顷，不意先生方针一改，自兹即乘风破浪其间也。

先生尝曰："生计不足，其责在家。家有余蓄，其责在国。日以累积金钱为事，是为无耻。今而后吾将以义务之道，大声疾呼于富人之前矣。"然欲正人，必先正己；欲人为国牺牲，必先以身作则。先生之入政界，实此数语有以促使之也。自兹政界一举一动，有友人在内，必与联络，藉以增长法律之知识。虽用意难以推其所在，然亦足征其宗旨之一斑。旋入哥伦比亚大学习法律，同时又在柏舅处研究。当教习演讲时，不论何科，莫不倾心而听。疑则置问，同学某尝登英文某报，略谓："罗君于教习演讲时，常求赘解，足见其天资迟钝。"殊不知，知之为知之，不知为不知。先生之所短，正先生之所长也。

先生于法律知识，进步一日千里。政界之趣味，复日益浓厚。将来之翻云政海，固已决于此矣。然欲入政界，必从乡镇着手。盖在乡，始则亲友扶助之，继而学优亲友又从而促进之、维持之，终乃可以迎刃而进。故著名政客，鲜不发轫于乡镇。而纽约城，幅员如此其大，人民如此其众，先生以一书生，乃欲染指其中，不其难乎？故先生初入政界，遭遇甚不利焉。

先生之祖若父，既累世经商，结交皆商人。彼辈除选举时投一票外，毫不与闻国事。辅助无人，而政客之集所，非旅馆，即酒肆。选举及各项政权，莫不操纵于波士（Boss 守旧政客）之手。彼等既否认其父海关监督之委任，又何能收纳先生而为其同志乎？故第一次入会，即有四分之三票表不同意。

然先生自受学校教育及游历欧斐，不觉自信以坚，力行以勇，曾不因小有困难，而隳其心；稍逢失败，而丧其志。反以困难、失败而愈激愈厉。故法校毕业后一年，终跃入政界。一日，赴哈弗德午宴。某师告以毕业某生事曰："吾问该生曰：'君受文明教育，将来作何事业，可得闻乎？'讵该生答曰：'师亦知世事于吾无一足为也'。"先生闻言，不禁奋身拍案而言曰："该生是应受夏楚⑨者。"盖先生惟知天下无事不可为，惟力行而后始可以为。本此以行。故虽外有守旧之反对，内无亲友之扶助，终能达其入政界之目的也。

然先生之入政界，非若富家翁同集一室，哓哓然曰："此宜改良，彼宜兴设。一若国事，为有形之物质，可以招之即来。稍作谈判，即哄然而散。以为能有是是亦足矣。殊不知言之而不能行，行之而不能力，虽厕身政界，究有何裨益哉！先生则反是，目睹百凡待改，慨然忧之，凡事必身任其难，力图完善，未尝厚责于人。

## 注释

① 胼胝　俗称"老茧"。这里以此泛指从事体力劳动。

② 林肯（Abraham Lincoln，1809—1865）　美国总统（1861—1865）。共和党人。任内颁布了著名的《解放黑奴宣言》。

③ 耶弗孙大卫　美国南北战争时期"南方联盟"的领导人。

④ 范文正　即范仲淹（989—1052），字希文，谥文正。苏州吴县（今属

江苏）人。北宋政治家、文学家。

⑤ 哈斯　通译哈里森（Benjamin Harrison，1833—1901），美国总统(1889—1893)。共和党人。

⑥ 哈弗德大学　通译哈佛大学。

⑦ 斐洲　通译非洲。

⑧ 形学　即几何学。

⑨ 夏楚　夏即榣（山楸），意指棍棒；楚即荆，意指荆条。夏、楚均为中国古代扑责之具。一般作为肉体惩罚的代名词。

# 未来之中国*

主席先生，外县与本城之来宾，以及各位豪士、各位女士等：

鄙人今得于偌大华屋之下，与诸位相谈一切，欣幸奚似。鄙人虽一生客，但中美邦交，素称浓厚。我为友邦公民之一分子，故敢于诸位之前，祷祝未来之中国，成为一世界上最强大最庄严灿烂之中华民国，并希望其国民道德高尚，智识日进。中国与美国，实太平洋沿岸东西遥对之两大民主国，当互相联络，维持共和。且中美两国之政府，均为其公民（of the people，by the people and for the people）而设。美总统林肯（Lincoln）氏，有一格言曾为威尔逊（Wilson）氏所演绎。其言曰：民主政体，可维世界和平。故吾侪天职，当提倡民气，联络世界各国，拥护共和。言此诚然。

在中国五千年之历史中，曾经多少利害关头，欲博一民主国，迄未成立。至一九一一年，始得推翻专制，建立共和，为中国历史上第一之破天荒。以中国历史考之，中国人民，性喜和平，与美人等。但欧战开始，震荡全球，使和平之人，亦与协约国联合，戎装持枪，对彼宣战，遽败欧洲穷兵黩武之民族。自是以后，中国在万国和议委员会席上，发表言论，且将攫得一切主

---

* 本篇系狄雷（J. Q. Dea Ley）博士的演讲，由陶行知口译，王玉章记录。原文无标点。原载1921年5月1日《时事新报·学灯》。

要权利。即昔日丧弃之利益，不久即将恢复。而日后内政刷新，商务日旺，前程浩大，未可限量。中国、美国，历史相仿。今之中国与百有五十年前之美国，情况略同。其时美国正受制于专制之下，然不旋踵，竟脱专制政体之压迫，创立共和。当是时，欧洲各强，见美国土肥产丰，屡欲侵占之，或设一领土之领事官，以制裁之。美国势孤力弱，不能与彼抵抗。一八二三年，美国门罗政策（Monroe Policy）渐渐发展，并警告欧洲各邦。所谓门罗政策者，即云美洲为美洲人之美洲，美洲内政，无论何地，不得为欧民或其他民族所占有。英国知不可违，首先赞成，欧洲列强和之，此政策始告厥成。一九〇〇年，中国义和团（Boxer Uprising）爆发，各国联军，集中中国。美国约翰赫（John Hay）即主张此政策布行中国。今中国内部，势力渐大，国民有自由之资格与热心。爱国之徒，亦日增一日。如敢效美国前例，亦振臂一呼，谓亚洲乃亚洲人之亚洲，无论何国，不得干预。美国人当本约翰赫之意，极力襄助。

一七七六年，美国始创民主国，但黑奴未放，女子无自由权，有选举权之公民，亦寥寥无几。教育尚未普及。例以民主国法度，大相悖逆。后稍觉悟，改换方针，故百五十年以来，即从教育上建设共和。教育普及，迷信渐消，将一切阶级制度，净尽铲除。又复极力推广选举权，直至近今。调查昔日之奴仆，平均计之，约半数有选举权，但百年之前，二十五人中，竟无一人有选举权者。不知中国人亦欲照此历程进行否？

美国今时宪法所规定，不论男女，至成年时期，即有选举权。但选举权落于无识人之手，甚属危险。因彼把持权利，易为纳贿领袖故也。要之：选举权为共和国家之基础，无选举则不足以称为共和国家。故欲保障共和，首先保障选举。欲维选举之善果，当以提倡教育为先。美国人有鉴于此，无论男女以及小孩，当受相当之教育。昔时之教育，甚为简单，仅仅使人民略识数字，摹习字形；教授数学，亦不过练习一二算法，只求其足够社会与家庭日用而已。欧战以后，精神改换，方针渐变，有职业教育、科学教育、社会教育种种之提倡。以学制方面而言，则下自初等教育、中等教育，以迄高等学校、大学院、研究院而止。以学费而言，则无论男女，凡青年求学之人，免缴费者甚多，己惟具一种有用之干才可也。教育范围，渐次扩大，教育价值，亦逐渐增加，故政府之投资于教育中者，为数亦益巨。而对于政治问题、社会需要，均可以科学方法补充之。计其所得胜于所失，国家受益，岂浅鲜哉。因此教育普遍、知识推广之结果，不但物质上有所影响，即文化上亦有递变。人民居于此类欣荣之社会中，其兴趣当复不浅。

美国训授教育，创办学校兢兢恐惧，惟恐陶铸学生成为呆板无生气之人才，而有妨自由。故美国学校，除政府出费创办外，有自由捐款之学校、私立学校以及各种教会学校，必得互相争善，互相标榜，使教学双方共趋高尚之目的。若私立学校，稍受政府补助费则毗连牵制，于教学增进之一途大有窒碍，且甚危险。故私立学校而有政府补助者，其危机约有二：

（一）政治与宗教之性质不同。若政教合一，教主之所欲，即君主之所为。互相调和，则彼此无竞争之观念。其所训导之学生，亦无进取之欲望。且美国法律，特定政治与宗教，永不契合，强使之合一，以为违法云。

（二）照教育进步之程序而言，一国之教育决无统一之理由，若强使之统一，则妨害个人之天才与自由。盖各地有各地之境况，各校有各校之特长，各人有各人之干能。办教育者当按其风土情形，须其自然固有之特质，发挥而广大之，斯为最高无上之教育。若以稍助资斧，而统一教育，其戕贼个性之发展也滋甚。

在美国市镇上，无统一教育之办法。以其遏抑个性摧残自由故也。大凡良好教育，当用特别之教育方法，新异活泼之教材。使一般公民于发生战争时外，得以有评论政府之自由权，并使彼辈有个性发展之机会，养成创造力，发挥新智识。故出版自由、言论自由，尤为当务之急。年来美国人民，对于国内一般有妨害言论自由出版自由之恶徒，辄鸣鼓而攻之。固然言论与出版自由，往往有不合理或无意识之言论发见。但互相讨论研究，亦可使无意识之言论，渐渐合轨。若其遏制之，则防民之口，甚于防川，久壅必溃，殃祸弥穷。且共和国家，人民自由讨论问题、自由印刷出版，已为固有之职分。

中国人是否与美国采用同样政策培养、教育，造就人才？偌大巨款，必施之适当而后可。共和国家当轴之主张，宜明白宣布，使各人有研究讨论之余地。其所主张与本国之民性环境相符合。则毅然行之可也。若稍窒碍，则必不施行。中国自革新以来，不但为民主政体（Democracy），且是民主国（Republic）。而民主国家与民主政体之国家，二者究何区别。大凡民主政体国家之意义，即云此一国家，乃人民之国家。民主国之意义，即代替人民造就幸福之国家。故民主国家，未必即民主政体之国家。（如古代罗马国，名为民主国，而罗马全土，究非罗马人民所公有，仅为一二霸主或贵族操纵而已。）中国即为纯粹之民主政体之民主国，则现时之社会学家、法律学家，当为全国之男女以及孩提之童，谋有完全之幸福。且于彼辈之社会生活、家庭生活上，当有增进之乐趣。惟科学一道，却可增进人类之乐趣。譬诸眼瞎耳聋之人，固受黑暗寂寞之苦痛，科学家能将其恶劣性质，身体苦痛，而代以欣荣快乐之事。故民主国当与科学有密切之关系。

居二十世纪之世界，一国国民，不知不识，甚为危险。缘以万恶之中，无识为首，祸福无门，惟人自趋。此言虽俚，确是科学之教训。中国山藏甚富，油煤金银各矿，比比皆是。若以科学之法则，掘山开矿，则利源深长，财用丰足。要之：科学应用范围颇广，若以之治理百事，则鲜有不奏效者。譬以科学方法，增加食物或制造物品，以代地产，则虽遇水旱凶荒，而我国国民，终不之惧。若以研究医药，则已病之人可致速愈；无疾之人，可先预防。以之研究卫生术，则卫生之道，可以时时促进，而通都大邑，以及灿烂光明之市场中，免有不洁之病源发生。以之经营银行税利，则一国之经济，自能宽裕，而利权不致外溢，亦不至为资本家所垄断。以之研究工业，则可知工人之场所如何改良，工匠之乐趣如何增进，其闲暇无事之秋当如何消遣时刻，不致歧途出轨,演成种种不道德之事实。以之训练小孩,可养成最好之习惯,使入善途。由此观之,普通科学学术之演讲。当不可一日无。

迩来美洲各市场，颇注意小孩之幸福。大凡一国之小孩，不能得其幸福，则一国之太平亦无希望。故小孩饮食之适宜，以及卫生、光线、训练等诸节，尤为料理小孩者所当研究。中国人素爱小孩，苟能教养得宜，训练有法，必成为健全之小孩，道德高尚、心灵玲珑之小孩。共和国家，各个男子固当享受应有之权利，而女子亦当享受国民应有之权利。不惟女子为然，即孩童亦当享受其固有之权利。现时文化增高，民智日进，男子为己之权利而奋斗，女子亦为己之权利而奋斗。孩童能力薄弱，应享权利。全凭前辈人之智力与科学智识为之保障云尔。往时世界各国之定论，佥以为男优而女劣，男智而女拙，天经地义，牢不可破。当美洲民主国告成时，一班守旧家，尚坚持此说。但千言万语总不能得一确证以缘其说。年复一年，新陈代谢，科学昌明，迷说破除。女子即欲收回其权利，拟与男子同享平等之福。又历许久年所，彼辈竟自决婚姻问题、家庭治理权以及小孩之保护权。即与男子平等肩任，而不能男子独断独行，如往昔之妇女然。往时美国妇人之崇拜神道，必与其丈夫同。即有不同，亦曾经丈夫之替许，而后可崇神拜像。至家庭如何处置、小孩如何教养，一听其丈夫所为，妇女不必过问。中人之家，为父母者，往往重视男童，蔑视女孩。男童有读书求识之机会，女孩则不能享受此项权利。今世民治主义之声浪日增一日，兄弟姊妹当同一款待。兄弟欲上学读书，姊妹亦当上学读书。如资操高洁，不愿出嫁，为父母者，尤当听其选习职业，谋所以生存之道。至男优女劣之说，早经打破。在欧战期中，男子戎装出征，女子主持家政，教养儿童，井然有条不紊，已可证男优女劣之不可信。而古人之言有所偏也。

在民主国家中，上述之权利尤当急急交付于女子，女子亦当以相当之义务帮助男子。则一国之中，或男或女，共同负责，而国家不兴隆者未之有也。一国之女子，无论为人之妻、为人之女或为一家之主妇，对于卫生术、选举权、公民普通之智识以及一切公民应有机关之意义，当明晰了解，以重负公民之资格。女子与男子天赋既同，则有一切权利，义务亦当相同。今中国若能革除旧弊，提倡女权，最后之结果必能完善。大凡女子之对于国，对于家，对于社会，均有甚大之贡献。国家能受其贡献，使与男子平列负责，方确成为真正之民主国。美国女子，由普通程序达到现时之状况。未识中国女界是如斯之进行否？

中国土地肥美，利源丰富。矿产之中，颜料与金属尤为繁多。且天气温和，河流交错，海岸蜿蜒曲折，几为亚洲冠。凡此者，均为他日国家发展之资料。中国户口稠密，平均计之，约占全世界四分之一。人民耐劳而性喜和平，国家若能利用科学方法发展民性，则可建一最高尚最优秀之民主国于世界上。参照历史而言，人民血统数千年如一贯。孔子之伦理、教学，系历史之远源。艺术、道德之进步，固于过去时代，甚为伟大，且为将来民主国之保障，正是前程远大，不可测臆。

美国在五十年之前，曾亦经受许多挫折，若非华盛顿（Washington）、赫密尔顿（Hamilton）、极富尔逊（Jefferson）、麦迪逊（Madison）等出而排难解纷，早为欧洲之属土矣。今中国亦当有此种领袖，支持国运，谋全国统一，并研究国家制度与公共责任。于是提倡农工商各项以奠国基，又从而治理社会、教育、平民政治、普通法律等，增进国民之兴趣与幸福，操纵国运，一扫陈腐。要之：国家领袖不知不识最为危险。故一国领袖，当受高等教育之人充之。美国近二十年来，无论男女，有高等大学之智识，方能共负国家之责任。故谓新时代中新人物可充国家之领袖。托留琴（Trojim）之大英豪吼克脱儿（Hictor）祷上帝之言曰，此孩童当较彼父为伟大（The boy might be a greater man than his father.）。能如此者，则中国之隆计日可待。按世界公例，文化有进而无退，则后代之道德、教育、实业、社会、国家等等当较前人为胜。

鄙人有幸，得逢贵处学术讲演会。今日确又为公用演讲厅落成之日[①]，此事之重大迴非寻常可比，且此厅建于富有历史之古城中，尤为千载一刻之胜举。鄙人躬逢其盛，真不可多得。满座之中有学生，有教员，有大人先伟，有农工商各界。默想此会，非寻常家庭之叙，实乃公民之叙会也。此为公用演讲厅，此后公民之集会，讨论公共问题之声浪当充满此室。彼生之大科学家，将于此讲台上讨论各种普通科学问题，政治家将于此讨论各种政治问题。教育家将于此宣讲各种教育状况，社会政治学家亦将于此发表社会政治之研究。即女界对于将来婚姻自由问题、选举平等问题以及其他各种权利，亦将于此发表其意见。且公民之公共问题事前之准备，将无一不在此室中公共讨论之。

昔美国波斯顿（Boston）[②]地方有一讲演厅。人民于该处辄发表公共意见，即称之为自由发祥地（The Cradle of Liberty）。今诸位公民慷慨捐助巨款构成斯室，亦当称为南京自由发祥地（The Nanking Cradle of Liberty）。举凡法律、公道、仁爱、命令、权利，将无一不在斯发表。询为发展公民自由之中心，作为公共精神上之要用。然则此厅存在一日，即中国国家富强一日，前途远大一日。敬此顺祝。

## 注释

① 指南京市公共讲演厅。

② 波斯顿　通译波士顿。

# 孟禄在苏州第二女子师范的讲演*

教育界诸君！昨天我到了苏州，受到很大的感触，就是教育界的表示，像教育的问题、方法、进步、势力等，很是热心奋发的，使我十分愉快。

今天的相聚一堂，我都称他是教育界，我还称他是研究教育的同志，因为诸君，或是教员，或是做预备教师的男女师范生。

我们都可称是同学——小孩子是一年一年的体力增大，学问年年增高。教育上也要随他变动，去改革他的陈腐，学生是学，教员也要天天的热心去学，好使学生和教师都生出兴味来。我是研究教育史的，对于日新变动的教育继续不断的学着，所以我也是一个学生。

教育的变化是很大的，也是很迟缓的，所以各国谋着教育的革新，都是经过了几十年。现在中国要几年内，有多大的发展，实在使我在教育史上，生出增大的兴趣，因为无论那一国，都是有几十年的经过。中国要在短时内去研究，所以他的问题很复杂，因此可引起研究的兴味。

现在拿新旧教育去比较一下，不论在什么一点，总有不同的。以前的教育，是注意人才，是给少数优秀分子的教育。在全

* 本篇讲演地点苏州第二女子师范，时间1921年10月22日夜，口译陶行知，记录潘连奎，蒋清涛。原载1921年11月1日《吴县教育月刊》第一卷第二号。

国人中间，受到教育的，不过很少数的人。其他，工人、农人……的子弟，不过在自己的田野间家庭里……去接受他的教育，但现在的教育是普遍的。人才教育的所以发生，其中有两个原因：

（1）国家要几个人才做治人的阶级，所以要用特别的教育，使少数优秀分子，能特别的发展，治理国家。

（2）平民不能享到教育，聪明的也不能享到教育，好把国家没有人来不信仰他，贵族没有人来捣乱他。贵族的人才教育，就是贵族可永远笼络，国家可永久维持现状。

旧教育的缺点，就是不过选了几个人才，去特别的教育他。像中国的科举、秀才、中举……一步一步的紧住，把优秀的选了几个，淘汰了几个，这就是人才教育。欧美的人才教育，与中国不同，中国是选的读书人，而中世纪的欧洲和埃及，选的是牧师，神父，所以现在美国，还有教会所办的教育事业。大概教会里的人，还有些心灵的修养，也不必去拒绝。中国和欧美的人才教育，其所用的方法格式，虽是不同，但是目的总是一样。

再讲第二，就是维持社会现状，把现在的社会，保持以前一切规模，使他永远如是。要达到这个目的，非教育最少数人，来照顾旧时社会的制度、组织……和信仰现社会的文化。使社会去操纵个人，使得社会的轨道永远不生变化。这种教育的结果，是使社会成为不动的，不变化的，现在的教育是动的、变化的。——在各国的旧教育上都是如此，在中国更可特别看出。

新教育和旧教育，总是立在反对地位，不论英国，法国……新教育就是注重人民的全体，使平民都得到应有的知识，不是专在少数优秀分子身上。所以可说新教育注重的第一点，是Democracy的教育。

倘使要讲什么Democracy教育，须要发展实业，使人民生活安乐，有空余的时候，经济上也不生什么恐慌，让他的子弟来受教育。所以实业发展，实在是普及教育一件很大的帮助。这种运动在美国已有百多年，英国五六十年，德国……无论什么国，都是在19世纪内的事业。中国现在虽是还不能完全提出来谈，也是当今的一大要点，还可说旧日不变化的教育，完全选了少数优秀分子，去看管文化；新的是进化，向前的，变化的，社会也随之而变化、所以静的教育，是容易办的，动的教育，是难办的，不过我们不能舍难而就易。好像你坐在椅子上，尽可以坐来长久；倘坐在自动车上两个轮子是动的，不小心，就要坐不住，使你坐在上面，总要小心谨慎的随着动，因此新教育是很复杂而难办的。不过人类为随着进化，不能不从困难中做去，并且为着全体人民得到并驾齐驱，也是不能不从困难中做去。中国的扶东倒西的教育，那不是现在站在正轨上走去的教育。

方才所说的德谟克拉西的精神，可使教育进步，但是教育的普及，除了德谟克拉西主义，还要靠着科学。科学的进步，于教育上有什么关系呢？

（1）科学上发明蒸汽机，什么轮船、火车，不是专门去给少数人享福，是要全人类能够享受，所以科学的发明，是给全人类享幸福，可使我们为着全体两字上去做。

（2）科学的发明，可给我们一个公开研究的态度和精神。从科学发明以后，我们遇到一个问题，必详细的去求真理，这不是少数人可独断的，简直无论什么国的人，都有审察的机会。像用这几百年的煤油灯，从电灯发明以后，我们就要去把这两样来详细的考究一下，然后我们来使用便利的电灯。所以德谟克拉西精神之外，第二点就是科学来做我们新教育的进步。

除了德谟克拉西和科学之外，还有实业的发达，也可使新教育进步。因为人民的经济丰富，国家的财力宽裕，就有普及教育的设施。并且他们有了财力，肉体所需要之外，再要去增加精神方面的需要，那末，一般人民的子弟都要向学，所以教育的普及，也是自然的趋势；——这就是能力增加，需要也随着而增加的道理。并且他们的环境变了，自己的需要也要改变，普及教育，教育革新，不过都是适应这种需要罢了。所以德谟克拉西主义和科学之外，第三点就是拿实业来做促进我们新教育进步的原动力。

第四点就是国家主义，因为国强须要民强，国富须要民富，要去发展，不得不靠教育。因为要国家好，须要政治好，怎样叫做好政治呢?

(1) 人民花着最少的钱，最轻的力，去得很大的幸福。

(2) 政府里的人，都要诚实无欺，为公从事。

要想有这样的好政治，须要有新教育的设施。国家要望强盛，须要教育和人比得上，譬如四个人聚在一处，三个都是衣冠楚楚，却是一个好像乞丐儿，他怎样能站在一处呢？所以各国都要把教育来革新，改变，来做国家发展的基本。所以第四点的国家主义，也是一种原动力可促进新教育的进步。

我上面的四点，是新教育所以发生的原因，也是说新教育的四大势力：

(一) 德谟克拉西主义的提倡，

(二) 科学的发明，

(三) 实业的发达，

(四) 国家主义的盛行。

这四大势力，在外国已有百年的成绩，而中国刚才发生，像国家主义的一个问题，各国已过了四五百年，应付，后来仍旧不能免掉一场欧战的大难。德谟克拉西的运动，在美国有百年以外，现还不过比较的进步；实业的工业革命，已有一百五十多年，但是工人的幸福问题，还没有解决。科学已有四五百年的历史，尚须急待改进，现在中国，要在二三十年内的时间，应付人家四百年五百年的问题，那实在是很难的。因为他困难、复杂，所以我们先研究他，很有兴趣。并且我们美国人很愿尽力，做友谊的帮助。

上面所讲的，不过是引论，现在总结一下，就是上面四个势力，在组织上，教材上，教法上，有怎样影响，我们应该怎样应用？可惜时间太匆促，不过提出几个问题，来供诸位的参考！

（一）组织

（甲）中国要办普及教育，先要注意到数量问题，先求量好，然后再讲到数，可先划了一个小区域，来做开始的第一步。宁使在起始时，先求地域小而成绩好，不必地域广而成绩坏。

（乙）地方上教育，要从地方上人去担负教育经费，还有参考与讨论的权，让一般人都来思考注意。现在附加税里面几分之几，就是去办教育的，不过他们还没有知道。我们希望有一种新的教育税，去做本地的教育经费，使教育进步，并且让他们有参与权，可使他注意，那未地方教育可以有些发展了。中国现在最缺乏的一点，就是地方教育的组织。

（二）课程

（甲）要定学校里的课程，我们应该知道社会的需要是什么？我们所定的课程，一面要以现在社会环境里的问题，做我们的课程，可以得到社会来供给我们的材料；一面应该在社会生活中有实用，能用他来改进社会。并且要去同社会接触，造成社会化的学校，不但这样，还要使学生明瞭一切，以后可以应用。总之，非但养成社会化的学校，还要养成学校化的社会。

（乙）在第一点是制裁社会，第二点，就是要制裁天演环境。我们看到了电灯，我们应该明白他内部一切构造，功用，不单去默记些名词定义，还应该训练学生，使他能够使用电灯。读植物学，知道了生长怎样……应该使他怎样制驭花种，在红花和黄花里面，可生红黄相间的花，或是更黄更红的花。

（三）教学法

对于教学法上发生的问题，最要紧的就是知识须从经验中来才能称为真知识。像小孩子的说话，是无论什么国，总是都能够说的，他不过说出本国的话——常接触的——就是从经验中来。倘若学生研究学问，能注重在经验上，那就是有生气的，活泼泼的，有用的。我参观了此地的小学，见他们的教学法，都领学生自己去参与种种作业，教师不过或者是同他们共同work，或者是随旁领着，我觉得现在的小学的教学法，注意到这个问题，实在是中国的生机。不过不要专在几个少数的学校里，想法去推广传播才好。

今天讲话的时间颇长，实在是抱歉！我参观两个师范，两个附属小学，见他们学生参与动作发表的机会很多，这一种方法，应该还要去求进步。各国的学校，还是在向上进行，注意养成自动的创造，确是培养他的人格，和造就学生的正当有效的进行，继续下去，顾得更妙的方法。今天能够来参观两校，同相聚一堂的机会，谢谢！

# 孟禄博士在南京讨论会中之谈话*

今日得与教育行政人员、教育界领袖，聚晤一堂，甚觉愉快。现在世界教育有大变化，中国对于教育，亦思有以改革之。近四五百年，自欧洲战争后，欧洲各国直接受其影响，如加拿大、墨西哥，均思有以改革之。其大旨颇与中国相仿佛。惟现在教育新趋势，有不得不改革者，归纳之有二端：

一、欧洲战争。破坏前人所铸成之文化，教育应思所以修正之，不使毁弃。

二、社会制度。在欧战前或欧战后，均有许多弊端，教育亦然；教育应改良此种弊端。

各国改变教育之趋势，往往相同，甚可奇异也。惟教育制度甚不同，如德、美之教育制度，立对峙之地位。余曾游历德意志诸国，与彼国教育当局谈，觉趋势相仿佛。且同一事实，如欧洲大陆各国，若德、若奥、若奥斯马加。教育制度则有两种：

1. 凡平民受过初等教育者，每不思上进。

2. 贵族教育，当未受小学、中学教育时，即分别一己，自问为平民乎？为贵族乎？决定之后，永不能逾轨。换言之，平民不

* 本篇系孟禄博士1921年10月17日在南京教育界人士二百余人讨论会上的讲话和答问，由陶行知口译。会议主席：郭秉文。记录：卫士生。原载1922年3月《教育汇刊》第3集。

能变贵族，贵族不能变平民，此之谓双轨制。美国则行单轨制，一线上行，有知识有能力者，即有机会上进。此欧美教育制度不同之点也。

上列两种制度，适合各该国社会情形，颇有牢不可破之势；倘欲改变之，觉有不可能者。而此两极端，思如何以趋于中道？此现今教育之新趋势也。在德国，奥斯马加、普鲁士、撒格逊民等，对教育有一种革命，即从双轨制到单轨制，而有共同学校出焉。在中等学校与小学校各六年制。美国变化初等教育为六三三制，此与德国六六制大致相同。教育变化共和试验已一百年，教育是为共和政治之工具。百年中之历史理想，日渐统一，有如共同经验发生共同理想者，此种教育趋势之所在，吾人亦可得而知焉。第二种趋势，在东亚各国，如缅甸、俄罗斯、安南[1]，其文化以受各种影响而不能进步，应以教育作工具，而提高文化，此亦最近趋势也。此种趋势，在中国教育中，或相交，或集中而来；同时影响教育社会，教育应用选择方法，以妥当解决之，使中国数千年来之文化，用教育以促进之。至教育与政治有密切关系，教育与政治，对于国家亦有同等关系；故教育应思所以谋解决国家问题之方法。美国有格言云："国家顾全疆土，应先预备教育，度量国家之文化，先度量其人民教育程度如何。"足见从前训练，不复足以行于国中，当取新趋势、新思想以适合于新环境、新潮流。又有一格言云："在变化进步中有变化进步之教育，社会变化进步，即教育变化进步。"故对教育，应时刻用心思研究之，如何有新观念及新方法以适用于社会。

不期今日与诸君谈如许言语，但予来此宗旨须请诸君了解者：予各处调查教育，将在广东全国教育会议诸领袖接谈后，复回北京，作总讨论之，以讨论改良教育问题。故此时须先得各地统计报告之种种材料，但此乃死而不活动的，不无缺憾处。故愿与诸位领袖晤谈，期诸君对于身受种种不妥当的，须去除或保存的，以及行政、地方行政与中央行政有关系的教学法、课程编制、教育精神等，提出讨论，以供参考焉[②]。

问：江苏省义务教育限八年前促成，进行方法，计分二种：① 劝导方法；② 惩罚方法。但劝导方法，仍无效果。究竟各国制度如何，先劝导，后惩罚；先惩罚，后劝导；抑劝导、惩罚同时并行？请指教之。

孟禄博士答：此问题须先视国家政体之如何？例如德国专制政体，儿童求学，纯用法律强迫之，罪其父母，或罚其老板。在美国则不同，美国共和政体，素重自由，故先用劝导，后用惩罚。支配其教育经费高低不同，根据其进学校学生之数目多少，多一学生，多一点经费，经费之多少，以进学校学生之人数为标准，且有以进学校月日先后以支配之者。此奖励学生求学绝好之方法。各州中有偏于工业方面，有偏于农业方面。其偏重工业各州，学生入学尚多；惟偏重农业各州，义务教育颇非易易，故不得已用强迫制，但最初一步，仍用劝导方法耳。

问：义务教育在苏省提议已久，此后拟在四年内办全，但照中国财力，即四年亦甚困难；在此经济困难时期中，拟用半日学校、夜学校等等以替代义务教育。此法适当否？

孟禄博士答：先视强迫之年限若干，大概欧美各国儿童过十四岁，即为超过强迫时期。而十四岁以内，得到相当国民之教育与否不问也。最近新趋势，十四岁后，尚须加工业教育或职业教育，每隔一星期、隔一天或隔几点钟不等，使经过强迫期限后，尚能得中等教育焉。至夜学校或通俗学校，能否替代强迫所入之学校者，此影响于父母者小，而影响于国家经济者大。如何可得经费以普及教育？及如何可以普及教育？在华期短，此时尚无把握。

惟欲普及教育普通应有三种条件：① 良政府；② 有极好税则，即教育税根据财产或根据营业以征收之；③ 地方组织完美，给以施用之权力，使知责任所在，自己事非中央政府事。故组织之不必过大，过大则鞭长莫及；亦不必过小，过小则不能完善也。至于能达到此种目的，另一问题。

问：学制问题，近来闹得很厉害，中学有改为选科制者，颇觉不经济，究竟对于选科制利弊如何？

孟禄博士答：中学有分科选科制度，在德国则有分校制度，另立专门某种科目学校。美国倾向分科制，尚有分组者，如欲学商，则进商组，学工则进工组等等。惟选科当注意者：

1. 学生毫无经验，选科必感无把握之困难，或有择易舍难之弊。

2. 教育行政人员，自己能力不足，不能指导学生及不能分配功课，或因行政便利，不能定学生确实所欲选读之功课。

3. 美国学生统计之，能始终读毕某科所欲学者，占百分之七十五，故选科能维持学生始终贯彻之能力。三十年前，美国学生选课者二十五万多，现则增至二百余万。此足以证明选课之效果。

问：初级师范学生有出而即为小学教师者，是否宜于分科？分科制对于将来服务时有感困难处又如何？

孟禄博士答：甫来中国，尚未明了师范学校所授课程，俟参观明了后，再答复之。惟据美国学校所得之经验言之，师范课程悉根据中学所授者，不过更加教育学一门，此外则视社会或学校之需要，得临时加添之。

问：师范生例应寄宿学校中，其膳宿由公费津贴之，但义务教育扩充后，师范生势必增加，对于国家财力当然感受困难。鄙意以为改师范生为走读，未知妥否？

孟禄博士答：英美各国养成教员学校，大概学生自己担负经费，国家不负此责，且甚有自出学费者，学校为备宿舍，但须由学生自己纳费。日本及中国，师范生如为教官，不纳费用，较英美各国为优待。对此问题，余尚无把握，不过以为宜竭力维持优待师范生办法，俟兴盛之都会，见投考之师范生日多，人民颇乐为教育服务时，始酌量收费[③]。

师范生寄宿校中，对于环境、陶冶、训练与教学同为重要，故觉此实师范生寄宿之优点。惟至教员缺少，对于社会有能力，使国民愿受师范教育，即自备费用。亦多愿学师范时，方能豁免公费之优待，否则吾人应竭力维持④。

## 注释

① 安南　越南的旧称。

② 孟禄的演说至此结束。会议主席郭秉文起立说："诸君有疑难问题，尽可发问。问题请由徐则陵先生翻译，答语则请由陶行知先生翻译。"

③ 此时郭秉文插话说："孟禄博士欲多得困难问题，备录之，俟将来正式答复，故此时为时局促，诸君中不妨尽量发问，提出来，暂不希望答复。"

④ 孟禄答问完后，与会者又提出问题若干，孟禄博士均一一载入记事册中。

# 共和与教育 *



鄙人自到沪后，承亲友欢迎，极为感激。今日又承省教育会招请演讲，到者都系青年男女学生及教育界领袖人物，深以为幸。今日中国之各问题极复杂，并经过许多变迁，与欧洲百年前经过之情形略似。考泰西[①]各国社会状况之变迁，约分数时代：（一）工业改革时代，（二）社会改革时代，（三）文学改革时代，（四）宗教与各方面之改革时代。一时期有一时期之变迁与改革。而中国则不然，这许多事情同在一时期发现。吾以为诸问题仅得以教育解决之。鄙人第一次到华在八年前，见一书，名《变化之中国》，颇令余注意。现在系余第二次到华，有数点感触，即中国正在变化期中耶？抑或已经变化耶？然不论中国为正在或已经变化，而在教育基本之眼光观之，则中国教育情形与世界相同，已有莫大之变迁矣。各国教育之变迁，可得而言之，若英，若美，若墨西哥，若日本，各国教育莫不有变迁。我不能谓中国今日之教育问题，即得适当之解决，但愿助以解决之。今日有一须与诸君讨论之问题，我不敢说此问题即可就此解决，一方面亦不欲解决此问题，盖仅欲使诸君对此问题有清晰与正确之观念而已。从历史上观之，从来支配教育之势力不外个人与社会。

* 本篇系美国教育家孟禄博士1921年9月7日在江苏省教育会的专题演讲，由陶行知口译。原载1922年4月《新教育》第4卷第4期。

分析起来，约有四端：（一）知识与科学，（二）工业与经济，（三）宗教，（四）社会与国家。今日所欲讲者即为社会与国家如何支配教育而立论也。近二百或二百五十年来，有支配教育之两种学理，即上所述之国家主义与共和主义是也。此二主义常暗相争竞，然其发生，各有特殊地点。德国教育制采取国家主义，以操纵为宗旨。美国则于教育上之教材学理，皆采共和主义。

弟不知中国将采何种主义之教育制。换言之，即中国是否将向平民的自由的路进行？抑向军国主义的专制的路走去？

教育与政治有密切之关系。欧战后，大有变迁，战前一般人莫不料国际感情将渐趋大同，顾观诸事实，则不特不趋不同，反更趋于国家主义之一途。又如拿破仑未战以前，似有趋向大同之势。迨拿氏败而国家主义之观念益深。（中略）

教育有制造国家观念及一切文化的力量，如德日二国，明明以教育养成共同习惯。德国学校专以养成国民信仰皇帝为心；日本亦然，教导学生信仰天皇是万世一系的。可知此等国家明以教育为建造国民性之工具。德帝国发生于五十年前，一般国民均抬高德皇，视为神圣不可侵犯，这种国民性大半由教育造成。欧战既起，即令国民全体从军，此即所谓国家主义之教育制也。今中国正当改革教育之际，对于国家主义与共和主义之教育制，不可不加以选择。然敝人非述二者之孰优孰劣，仅解释二者之不同点而已。如美国采取共和主义，而德国前此则采取国家主义。二者性质各异，各有优劣。目下美国方面，均思如何利用国家主义，以补共和主义之不足，盖为此也。

欧洲大陆为采用独裁制之国家主义之代表者。申言之，即欲以政府之意志，而造成国民性，使国民一如机器，专供其利用指挥。所有学校之课程教法，均属一致，教员学生无置喙余地。美国则为共和主义之代表者，主张各个人须自由发展其个性，所采制度，县乡各异。盖美国教育乃个人的自由的，而非独裁的。

以上所述，可知德日乃代表国家主义，而英美则代表共和主义。今中国教育正当改革之际，须审慎选择，采取那与国家进步有关系者而实行之。

今请分别言之。第一点为学校之系统。欧洲大陆，以德为代表，德国从前学校系统乃双轨制。学校分二种：一种小学校乃为平民而设，只须教以极普通之学识，使其成一平民而止，无升入中学大学之机会；一种为造成领袖人才而设，进此种学校后，可再升入中学大学。故人当年幼之时，即须慎为选择孰舍孰从。一不慎，即终生成一平民，不能再入大学。故德国教育又可称为阶级制的教育，其教育制度不啻有二轨，划分国民何者为人才，何者为平民。美国则否，小学毕业后，即自由升学，并无限制，此即单轨制共和主义之学制也。中国亦采此制，诚幸事也。

第二点，教育行政，代表统一制者如法兰西。百余年前，法教育部某总长看他的钟表说："我于此一小时内，可知全国小学校所上之功课。"盖学校一切权力管理均由中央政府支配者也。美国则代表采不统一制者，中央政府权力甚小，权多操于各地方，美国学校教员亦均有自动之机会。

学校教材与制度业已约述。今更请进而述教学法。教学法各国颇不一致，如欧洲大陆，战前所用方法（现在改良亦未可知），每日教员上课有一种教材，先将一字一句为各生详解。次日即令背诵，故学生所得教材乃来自教员，而教员则得自政府者。美国则不然，教科书与参考书种类繁多，各地各校并不一致采用，亦不一字一句的解释。如有问题，各生可至图书馆搜寻，故所发意见，各有贡献，而对于一种问题，均有详切之研究。以上二种教育法完全不同。后者学者有选择之机会，并可得思想之训练。至于德育方面，在独裁主义之下之宗旨，专以养成一种服从心。然在共和主义之下则不然，其宗旨在养成独立与彼此有一种同情互助的志愿。

近年来日本赴美考察教育团有一问题，即战前日本对于美国所采的共和教育制有所怀疑。他们以为美国欲国民自由独立，如何可使国民为国牺牲？彼辈每至一处考察，必询欧战时美国用何方法使国民服役战事，盖此问题实日本教育考察团所最关心者。

敝人现有一诚恳之言奉告。今当中国新教育兴起之际，我人抱无限希望。新教育固须将外国新知识灌入本国，然亦不可推翻旧文化，务将固有文化扩大之。中国向以家长为中心，子弟愿为家庭牺牲，家长愿为子弟牺牲。

今望发展此种优点以对国家。简言之，即欲求旧文化有新功用也。诸君，我在美国，闻中国有学生运动，欣愉之至。

鄙人最后又有二言为赠：（一）愿有团结力与互助精神；（二）愿为国牺牲，为群牺牲。

**注释**

① 泰西　当时对西方国家的统称，一般指欧美。

# 孟禄博士与苏州教育界之谈话*

今日承蒙诸位教育家欢迎，非常感谢！现把这欢迎分析起来，可分三层：第一是诸位先生对于吾个人的欢迎；第二，诸位是教育界人，吾也是教育界人，那么今天的欢迎，是有同事的关系；第三，中美两国，素称友谊之邦，今天欢迎，当然也有国际的关系。所以吾今天受此盛大欢迎之后，除了吾个人感谢之外，还要代表美国的教育界和国民，来感谢诸位先生的盛意。吾到中国以后就有三种感想发生：第一，中国欢迎外人，至优且渥，不但苏州如是，无论何处，如北京、保定、太原、南京，都是受着同一之优待。扩而充之，即可知能欢迎世界之文化与思想；第二，中国办教育者，都能以教育为专门事业，十分热心；第三，中国近年来变迁极速，此种变迁，是有向前的进取。但是欢迎世界的文化思想，必定要有辨别的能力，因为世界上的文化思想，有优有劣，吾们应该详细辨别，取其优者而去其劣者。然欲养成此辨别能力，则唯教育是尚。盖有了教育，就能指导其如何辨别，既采取以后，又须赖教育的力量，使之普及，所以教育之功用极大！

一师[1]代表——中国现在需要何种教育？

---

* 本篇系孟禄博士1921年10月21日，在苏州教育界同人宴会上的讲话和答问，由陶行知口译。记录者：朱麟。原载1922年4月《新教育》第4卷第4期。

孟——此题关系全国，须调查告竣后，方可决定，此时只得从缓答复。

一师代表——如何可使学生专心学习？

孟——学潮[2]问题，为美国所无，因为美国学校，都能够用学问来管束学生。近年来中国学校，迭次发生学潮，救济之法，应该改革教育的方法，务使学生精神，均能缩归于功课之内。若体育、美术等科，均可管束学生之精神，使无越规举动。至于公民陶冶，也很重要，盖有公民之资格，则学生运动，自能切中。

一师代表——学生服务，欲求其有永久之热忱，有何方法？

孟——中国情形，余尚未十分了解。在北京之时，有许多学生以干涉学校行政废止考试等事来问，足见中国学生之能自动。此种自动，欲使之具有良好之精神，养成永久之习惯，则必须有良好之组织。美国学校，上课之外，注重体育，如足球、篮球以及其他团体游戏等，此皆所以养成其同作业之习惯，又有缔结兄弟之风气。譬如有几个程度相等的学生，他们就结为兄弟，成一小团体，自己管束，不过结合的人数很多，不像中国人的桃园结义只限于两三个人。现在中国的少年中国学会[3]就是如此。又如组织学校市、学校省、学校国等，模仿地方制度，以养成其有公民之资格。不过此种组织多行之于中学小学，大学却是无此组织。以上三种方法，均可作为解决这个问题的参考。除此之外，还有一件很紧要的事情，就是引起学生的兴味，怎样去引起呢？第一，对于学生自身，要会有极大的幸福；第二，所有的事情，要适合学生的需要，那么他的热忱，自然可以永久保持而不衰。

一师代表——如何养成学生自治的能力？

孟——养成学生自治的能力，各国略有不同，兹分言之：

（甲）英国　老班生管理新班生，仿佛是个学监，学校中一切管理的责任，校长都付之学生，不过不是职员。

（乙）德国　中等学校以下之学生，大都没有自由；大学学生，完全能够自由。这是欧战以前的情形，战后未详。

（丙）法国　与德国相同。

（丁）美国　考试时由学生自己管束，若有偷看等弊，均由学生告发，先生不加监视。校中有学生会议，会议时，各班学生，都有代表出席，譬如地方上有集合团体，各校亦都公举代表出席，不过学生会议之范围，有下列两项的规定：

（一）关于各人行为的优劣，由学生自行办理；至于重大的事情，统归教务处办。

（二）对于校务应兴应革，学生只有提议权。除此之外，关于自治团体之组织，亦甚重要。凡此种种，皆养成学生自己能有系统。

职业中学代表——按能力编制，倘使学生数少，如何解决？

孟——此种困难，大的小的学校，都是没有的。因为大的学校级数很多，升降容易，不生什么困难；在小的学校，先生可多费一些精神，去和劣等生补习。最感受这种困难的，就是在不大不小的学校。美国各校，都无此种困难之感受，因为学生数多，下愚又很少，至于解决这个问题的方法，吾想有三种：

（A）应该先去测量学生的智慧。④

（B）将校中许多课程，分为选修科、必修科。有几种基础的课程，可算他是必修科，其余是选修科。必修科是个个人必须学习的，选修科可以不定：年龄大智慧高的学生可以多修一些，年龄小智慧低的学生可以少修一些。

（C）学生留升，每年可分二期或四期，不过此种办法，仍旧只得行于较大的学校。

一师小⑤提出：

（一）学生因染环境的势力，不能养成清洁的习惯，应用何法以救之？

（二）中国人的旧道德，应否发挥？

（三）歌谣谚语，宜否用做教材？并且怎样收集？

（四）苏州人的柔弱天性，应否保存？

二女师小⑥提出：

（一）学校怎样可以和社会接近？

（二）儿童课外读物很少，怎样采取？

（三）学校中训练的良好习惯，往往抵不住社会势力，应用何法以救之。

（四）怎样可以养成学生的创造力？⑦

**注 释**

① 一师　指当时设立在苏州的江苏省立第一师范学校。

② 学潮　指“五四”运动前后我国爆发的历次学生运动。

③ 少年中国学会　“五四”时期有影响的青年团体。1917年7月，由李大钊、王光祈等创立于北京。

④ 即进行智力测验。

⑤ 一师小　指当时江苏省立第一师范学校附属小学。

⑥ 二女师小　指当时江苏省立第二女子师范学校附属小学。

⑦ 上列八个问题，由于时间关系未及答复。孟禄博士记录了这些问题，俟有机会另行作答。

# 旧教育与新教育的差异 *



今天在这里和诸君共聚一堂，何等愉快！在坐诸君，多是男女两师范的学生和教师。学生是求学的，教师是指导的。但是现在的学生，就是将来的教师，到了做教师的时候，仍要不绝的研究，则研究的同志，一年增多一年，学问上的贡献，也一年进步一年。假使做了教师即不去研究，非但所讲授的资料，都是陈腐的不变的无趣的，就是做学生的对于求学也觉得无甚兴味了。所以研究的事情，不论做教师做学生，都不能少的。我是研究的一分子，亦是一个学生。默察中国近几年来教育上发生种种变化，在外国几十年来办成的，在中国要于数年里面就要办成，岂不是研究教育的一件快事么？现在先说旧教育与新教育不同之点：旧教育在中国、美国、英国、法国、及其他任何国，总有一个共同目的。共同目的为何？就是注重造就人才的、注重少数人的、专门为几个领袖的所受的教育；其余普通一般人，受不着相当的教育，没有发展才能的机会。做农的世世做农，经商的世世经商，作工的世世作工，绝无发展天能的余地。所以这种人才教育，完全是少数人的特别教育，完全把平民的才能埋没，使他们的天资蒙蔽，不致起来反对、扰乱、变动。以前无论何国都有这点现

* 本篇系孟禄博士1921年10月22日在江苏省立第一师范学校的专题演讲，由陶行知口译。记录者：瞿雪野。原载1922年4月《新教育》第4卷第4期。

象，而尤以中国的科举最显明。一套一套的，由秀才到举人，到进士，点翰林，中状元，把他的聪明智慧，全用在文章上面，中国就把这少数领袖的人才，取出来当国家的重事。欧美的旧教育，不但要读书，如埃及及中世纪各国，还注意宗教。像牧师、神父等。凡是读书人，都在他们手中；所有的人才，都归宗教操纵；领袖社会的人，都从宗教中选出。美国现在的教育，由教会办的很多，就是以前宗教士培养宗教人才的特征！兹将旧教育结束起来得二点：

一、旧教育注意少数领袖人才，不顾平民的智识开通与否，也不顾平民的教育普及与否。

二、旧教育是要使社会不进化、不动的、不改变，以前怎样，现在也该怎样，日后亦希望怎样。他非特教训几个领袖，并且蒙蔽新动机；使社会专在那旧轨上走去。这种情形，在中国特别显明。

至于新教育和旧教育，完全立在反对地位，第一种革新的原动力，就是德谟克拉西的精神。旧教育是少数人的教育，新教育是人民公共的，个个有相当的机会，发展他们各个的道德、技能、学识，所以新教育的真精神，是德谟克拉西主义。德谟克拉西要求普通人民都得相当的教育，这是中国当今之急务！旧教育是选了几个领袖，保管固有的文化；新教育是动的，进化的，向前进的，向上进的。但是办静的旧教育易，办动的新教育难。譬如我们坐在椅上，是静的，不动的，虽然坐了一年、十年、百年，不致跌倒；新教育犹之坐在自由车[①]上，车轮是转的，如不留意必致跌倒！现在的社会，是坐在自由车上的，不是坐在椅上的。坐椅易，坐自由车难。故新教育很难办，并且颇复杂，因为要使个个人享受相当教育的幸福，可以与社会并驾齐驱。谚曰："扶得东来西又倒。"所以我们坐在自由车的社会上，必须脚踏稳固，使自由车依势转动得当，就能为社会同时进化了。这是德谟克拉西精神要教育不得不动，不得不变化。

第二种革新的原动力就是科学。如电灯、汽油灯、火车、电报……此种东西由少数人发明，给多数人享幸福。这种幸福如何可享，也是要受教育的。

对于科学要有研究的精神，我们遇了一件事，必须审慎考察，来判断他的真相。十九世纪至二十世纪科学昌明了，非但知道使用他，并且要知其所以然，不是以前闭关自守不教平民的。人人都有审考的机会。以这样他们的脑筋里面，就起了变化，用惯电灯、汽油灯，再去用豆油灯、火油灯遂觉得不便，那么豆油灯、火油灯，便难于存在了；他们都知道电灯、汽油灯……之理，此即变化之原动力。故科学的发达使得教育，不得不动，不得不变化。

第三种革新的原动力就是实业的振兴。实业振兴以后，则人民的生计好了，就想上学，他们在肉体以外，还要求精神上能力的增加、精神上能力的培养。环境既然变化，则所需的教育亦起变化。故实业振兴了，教育也不得不动，不得不变化。

第四种革新的原动力就是政治。政治怎样才能好呢？有两要素：

一、效率的行政：就是要拿最少的力量和金钱，做出最大最有益的效果、事业。

二、高尚的行政：政治里的人，个个廉洁，不私不利，涓滴归公。

能如上面所说的两要素，政治自好，而好的实业教育亦因而出来。现在各国的政治大多是好的，中国则不然。譬如在一个会场中间，人人的衣服非常华丽，惟我的不好，破碎、龌龊，自己就觉得惭愧，站不住脚了。中国政治的不好，亦是这样。然而做国民的不可听政治的不好，必须要使他变好，然后自然可得到真正的自由幸福了。

上面四种，别国在数百年中办成的，而中国要以二三十年的工夫应付，所以很难。国家主义在四百年前开始应付，到底得到欧战的结果！共和主义在美国一百年前我们已经开始应付，在中国要于二三十年内就要办成；实业在欧洲一百五十年前就开始应付的，现在工业问题还待人民自己来解决，在中国又要于二三十年就要办成；科学在欧洲四百年前，就开始应付了，中国也要在二三十年就要办成。所以四百年来的国家主义，一百年来的共和国，一百五十年来的工业革命，四百年来的科学问题，在中国对于这种很复杂很难的问题，一概要于二三十年内应付，岂不是很有兴味的。美国对于中国的教育，当竭力相助！

我们再谈新教育怎样应用出来。

一、组织问题

甲、普及教育使人民公共得到求学的机会，必须注意小区域的好，不要起始就希望达到目的，故当按部就班的进行。与其范围大而不好，孰若范围小而好呢？

乙、要普及教育，当使人民自己管理教育费，因为经费从地方上抽出来的，对于他们很关痛痒；普通附加税拿来做教育经费，人民大多不知道他的用途。如特别征收教育税作教育经费，请人民自己管理，他们一定很乐愿。中国教育就少这点地方教育的组织！

二、课程问题

甲、现在的课程如地理、历史、数学等，教材组织不过一个大纲，课程须包含社会上所必需的，也是社会上能供给的。学生在上课的时候，要记念社会上的情形，要与社会联络，不致隔膜；学校所教的，也即社会上所需的。不但是要社会化，并且使学生的脑海里有社会的观念，将来当尽力于社会，使社会刻刻进化，这就是化社会了。

乙、课程并且要包含天然环境，使学生能做他们的主宰。读电学明电之理，就要来使用他。譬如花要他不红不白，即当用我的才力，去选择种子，如何可以不红不白，如何可以比别株美丽，使花听我的命令，这亦是课程中应包含的要素。

三、教学问题

甲、一切事业，从经验中得来以后，自然明了。天赋我以智力，我就要想怎样来用他。比如说话，常在那国，即能操那国的语言，此即从经验中得来，能以学问必须从做事上磨练出来的，方为实在的、具体的、有生气的、有实用的教学。我到中国参观各师范、各高小和国民学校，大多注意学生的自动和发展各个的才能。做教员的不过处于指导地位，使学生从头至尾的去研究。我参观以来，非常满意。但是教育问题是无止境，还当继续的进行，若大家都有百折不回的精神，那么这许多的问题自有相当的解决！

## 注释

① 自由车　即自行车。

# 学理与应用*

诸位同学：

我来中国参观学校，研究教育，并考察中国之情形，故与诸君同为学生。我在美国任哥伦比亚大学师范院事[①]，因同时与中国学生晤谈讨论，故我与诸君实为真正之同学。且我对于中国教育，及其将来之事业，甚为关心；而诸君将来出其所学以兴办社会之事业，与中国将来之事业，有极大之关系；故愿与诸君研究中国之教育。

科学非尚空谈，而重应用，即将原理应用于事业是也。

今日参观工业学校，其中工专以及甲乙两种讲习所[②]合设一处。见许多学生，均忙碌于工作，将科学之原理，应用于事实：原理与事实熔为一炉，一变曩昔之习惯。原来知识学问不仅不在教科书上，亦不在多做几篇文字，必须将知识施之于有用之地而后可。无论何处，不讲真正之学问则已，欲讲真正之学问，则必须将原理变成事实，此乃教育上最大之原则也。新近又参观两个高等专门[③]，而得两种教训：第一，在一个工科大学，参观其中设备完全，一机器架一石及木上，加压力，此即试验石与木能有几许能力，以受此压力也。吾人之建筑一室，非有木与石即能砌

* 本篇系孟禄博士1921年11月23日在浙江省教育会的专题演讲，由陶行知口译。记录者：朱恬生、李绍光。原载1922年4月《新教育》第4卷第4期。

成也，必审木石之多寡，并择其适宜者而用之；否则压力与受压之间不得其平，则其室必倒矣。我欲讲科学之实，试而举建筑房屋以为例者，诚以建筑房屋必须将材料一一加以选择，孰为适用，孰不适用。建国亦然。欲改造中国，所需材料，何种适用，何种不适用，即不能不加以选择。中国现有两种文化：一为旧有之文化，一为新来之文化。现在既有此两种文化，则欲改造中国，而建设新中国，以何者为适宜于中国，是为一大问题。工程师对于材料之使用，孰者宜为梁，孰者宜为柱，必视其能力而支配之，有志建设新中国者，亦当有如此态度也。办教育论及中等以上之学校有选择之性质，即择其品优、体健而聪颖者，施以相当之教育，俾能胜改造社会之任，以有用之金钱造成优秀之人才，为中国之栋梁。

我前往参观第二个大学时，有一工程师为我之同事，彼谓现在工程上之最大问题，即为使人造之材料，能胜于天然者，且能坚硬而适于用，例如水门汀④，由种种物质融和之，使其由涣散而成为团结之整体。筑室建国，其理正复相同。我今日之所欲讲者，即为最后之一点，即社会如何能团结而为一整体是也。如何能团结社会，此即为教育上之一重要问题。中国立国，已数千年，而能团结至今以立足于世，即足以证明中国实具有一种团结之能力，然至今日各方之压力交加，故压力较从前为大，因之从前之团结力，有不能胜任之趋势，故必须有一种新团结力，以应付此压力。此团结力为何？即新教育是也。现在中国有数种新压力能使中国分裂：其一为工业主义，使女子离开家庭各往工厂从事工作，而家庭制度因呈破坏之象；其二为政治趋势，使中国南北分裂⑤，而有涣散之势，又因感受德谟克拉西⑥之潮流，而欲打破集中主义；其三为理性主义，因人生观之改变，致对于旧有之文化及制度习惯无不怀疑，渐成四分五裂之象。中国处此种情形之下，如欲免于危险，非筹所以应付之方法不可。今日参观工业学校，彼等能以科学之方法，应付工业之问题。见有颜料从前无甚充分用途，而外国又秘不传布，旧法又不适用，故只能自用科学之方法，以制造一种颜料，既可不致褪色，且甚美观；又如纺织工业，欲与外国竞争，必须应用科学之原理，从原理以得应用，复由应用而得原理。工业能使社会分裂，而科学实能团结之。进言之，改良纺织，须需机器，使用机器，须需煤铁。有铁而后能造机器，燃煤而后机器能显其力，故必须研究开矿之法。又欲将他处之煤铁输运于杭，必需铁路，管理铁路，则非应用物理、化学，算学不可。中国今日欲开实业，厥有两途：（一）使外人筑路开矿，然仍实不可恃，盖铁路一日在人手，则一日不能自由也。（二）自行研究科学，应用其方法，以开发天然之富源，然后权在己手，而能充分自由。故欲自由，须研究科学；然此之所谓科学，非纸上口头之科学，乃有实用之科学也。科学不仅能操纵天然，而当外侮之来，亦可用科学之法以抵御之。论者谓欧战为科学之战争，数百万兵士之后，随有十倍之科学家为之制造杀人之利器，实较总司令为利害。故欲御外侮，须具利器；欲制利器，须究科学。科学精而后可以无惧乎外侮之侵入也。以言教育，内部亦发生种种问题，有时科学与宗教冲突，有时文学与科学冲突，故如何能团结教育本身，即何种教育具有此种团结之能力，实为一大问题。我以为其道即在原理应用而已：能应用者，即为真知识，否则必非真知识也。知识之真否，可由实验而知之也。

惟教育偏重原理，固易分散；而偏重经验，亦易分散。

故当以原理指导经验，以经验发挥原理，原理与经验联结，方为有用之真知识，方能应用于行为上。此乃教育之目的，亦如此方能谓为有团结能力之教育也。

欧美各国，极讲效率，以最小之时间，得最大之效果。

有效力，有结果者，即为真正之教育。吾人之讲教育，应当讲内力充满、有充分实力之教育也。中国与美国不同。必谓美国前进，中国退后，亦不尽然，盖因确有不同之点也。例如美人之读书，自左而右，而中国则自右而左；美人见客必脱帽，而中国则否[⑦]；中国称王先生，而美国则称密司忒王。教育方法亦有不同之处，中国之教育，不以学生之质问为然，而美则否，以使学生练习机会之多寡判断教育之优劣，能使学生有充分讨论、参与之机会，方为良教师。故教育当留适当之时间，以为学生讨论参与之地步也。学校之目的何在？教育之目的何在？此则须视其国体而定。中国既为共和国，则当施共和国之教育，其要素有二：（一）为独创的能力，能以自动之精神，自己研究，自己判断，而自用方法以达一定之目的；（二）效率，以少数之金钱、时间、精神，而得多数之效力。有此两种要素，方合共和之精神。在学校与学生以自动之机会，独创之能力，则卒业后其创造力、判断力自能充足，即此共和教育之目的也。美国有一牧场故事：场内有三猪，大小相同，种子复同，甲吃何物，如何清洁，栏大若干，均如式布置；乙亦如前，食住皆同，惟混一种之豆放于稻草上，能觅得则始得食；丙亦同，惟少与之食料，栏中有一穴，使能出外栏，外有豆，能出穴始得食。结果甲重百磅，不抵所费；乙重两百磅，适相抵；丙则五百磅，除养甲乙丙三猪资本之外，尚有盈余。学生诸君：欲为甲乎？为乙乎？抑欲为丙乎？自觅物以食，能利用环境以得生活，是乃我之所希望于诸君者也。

## 注释

① 当时孟禄任哥伦比亚大学师范院教务长。

② 工专　工业专门学校的简称。甲乙两种讲习所，指附设于甲、乙两种实业学校内的讲习所。甲种实业学校为省立，学程4年（预科1年），入学资格须在14岁以上，具有高小毕业程度者；乙种实业学校为县立，多以3年毕业，入学资格须年在12岁以上，有初小毕业学历。

③ 高等专门　高等专门学校的简称。

④ 水门汀　即混凝土。

⑤ 南北分裂　当时的中国有两个政府：北方的北洋军阀政府和南方孙中山领导的广东革命政府。

⑥ 德谟克拉西　英语democracy（民主）的音译。

⑦ 记者在此句后有按语曰："近年国人见客亦多行脱帽礼矣，博士盖据曩昔之情形而言。"

# 孟禄博士与无锡教育界谈话*



今天时间很匆促，不能和诸君作长时间的讨论，很为抱歉。但是得到贵地参观教育，非常荣幸。贵地工商业的发地，早已闻名；今来锡参观，真是名不虚传了。工商业和教育的关系，很是密切。那最紧要的有两种：一种是效率，一种是实用。大概工商业发达的地方，常常能够促教育效率的时时增进和教育方法的处处实用。贵地的教育照现状再求改进，一定可以成为全中国的模范。诸君可以勉力求用力少、收效绝大的方法，去贡献全国，指导全国。今中国各地的教育，各有各的特长。有以设备见称的。有以教学著名的。不过都是分散各地，没有齐集许多好的地方在一处。这是我很为贵国惋惜的。

效率的表现，可在学校行政、学校设备和教育方法等看出。贵地无锡市立第一国民学校，学童很多，经费又省，算得是好学校了！因为他处每一个学生的费，从数元至四十元不等，大多因陋就简。锡市一校每一个学生的费只有五元，这是学校行政显在效率的特征。再有贵地师范和附属小学的教育方法同精神，也能令人满意。参观各地教育以后，普通有两件事体可以令人注意的：一、公共教育终要有公共机关的管理。现在中国私立学校，

* 本篇系孟禄博士1921年11月25日对无锡全城各校校长和教员的讲话，由陶行知口译，记录者：秦凤翔，原载1922年4月《新教育》第4卷第4期。

大多比公立学校的成绩好。这个实在是公立学校教员的重大责任。总该把公立学校的成绩办到斐然可观，去促公家的注意才好。二、家庭的信仰私塾，比公立学校来得深。好像南京、广州等地方学校的学生数，统合中学、小学，还不及私塾那样多。可见公立学校，还没有令人完全信仰。这个也是公立学校教员的责任，总该把学生的程度教到优良，使得私塾受天然之淘汰才好。

学校效率，一定要和社会的需要联络。中国的中学校，大多不能够和社会的需要，因为只有书本上面的知识，没有把原理应用。差不多全是书本的教育。假使还不想法研究去实践怎样的应用，恐怕用的金钱尽付流水了。又像中学教育的科学教学，拿参观到的说起来，只有三四处，正是依适当的轨道进行，其余就差不多没有注意这一点的了。然而中学教育的精髓，全在科学。做教员的，应该养成学生做天然的主人翁，能够去利用他去控御他。并且种种政治、水利、医学、工业，没有不依科学的方法去解决。没有科学的方法，只可拿不了了之；再不然，请外国人来办理。中国要有独立的国家，当然要有科学的精神。他的基础，全在中学时代培养的。现在中国中学，还没有着手这一点。真是可怕！

今天因为时间匆促，不能把特长的地方多谈；不过指出缺点的大概，希望逐渐改良进步。贵地既然是工商业发达的地方，教育能够利用这个机会去发展教育，去促进教育，这是我更加盼望的。

# “德谟克拉西”的教育*

各省教育代表，与广州教职员诸位先生——今日我得与诸位讨论这至重大的“德谟克拉西”的教育问题，我觉得非常愉快，非常荣幸。现在的世界，是民治潮流澎湃的世界，我们教育上唯一的大问题，即共和主义或民治主义，在教育上应如何应用，如何培植？换言之，即我们应采何种的教育方法，以达民治之目的。美国采收各国教育的制度，试验至一百余年，于各种教育制度的利害得失，都有比他国较多的经验，现在即谈美国教育以作参考。

民治主义之在美国，比较的发展甚慢，经过许久时间，才有今日的实现。这是因为美国人民，是盎格鲁-撒克逊民族，与英国人民同种。这个民族以质实稳健称于世界，不轻举妄动，不求近功，所以对民治主义试验研究培植，发展虽慢，而根柢则深。民治主义是代表盎格鲁-撒克逊民族的精神，内中包含两个要素：（一）重视个人人格。（二）政治予个人以特权。美国在此二要素的基址上，经若干年的试验与培植，始造成今日统一的民治国。故在企达民治主义目标之时，必先培植民治主义之根本，或民族之精神。

* 本篇系孟禄博士1921年10月31日在广州全国教育联合会上的演讲记录，演讲时由陶行知口译。本篇原载1923年8月《中国教育一瞥录》。

美国人应用民治主义于教育，倒过来说，即是应用教育以达民治主义，使教育为达民治主义的过程，即所谓民治的教育。今天我有三点提出：（一）民治教育，对于教育制度或组织上的要求。（二）教授与材料（即科目），对于民治主义的适应。（三）适于培植民治国民的教学法。现在先讨论民治对教育制度上之要求。

民治主义对于教育制度有二大要求，第一地方与个人要负担开办与维持教育的责任。即要有经费上的负担。第二地方与个人，要负责任管理监督学校。这两样是民治主义的教育的根本要事。美国的教育，就是这样成功。因为美国人的精神，大部分是英国人传来。所以美国人的背景有二：（一）英国人个人主义的精神，即自己管理自己，治化自己，不受他人之干涉。（二）英国的教育，到1895年才由教会手内收回，所以发展不快。美国自始即由地方人民自办，各尽所能，所以发达较速。现拿教育费一端说，取德英美比较言之。普鲁士在欧战前，政府担任地方教育经费，支持国家教育必要的费用。如教员之薪水，余任地方负担。在英国则与德国相反，凡不可少的教育，则责成地方自办。中央政府，看有应办的教育，则提倡之，补助之，办理进行之责，则交之地方。在美国与德国既完全相反，与英亦不相同。办理教育之责，完全交之地方。凡地方太贫或以其他原因不办的，政府则司分配教育费之劳，或稍与以相当的补助。但要求补助费的地方，所办的教育，必合政府规定的标准。于是政府有指导教育之权，使各地方教育，齐向一个完善的标准进行。但补助是从旁帮忙。教育经费之大部分，仍是地方负责。

中国有22省，美国则有48州，各州办教育之历史，有百余年者，有年限很少者。到现在各州有一个公共的趋势，即：（一）地方担负教育经费，负管理监督进行之责任。（二）中央教育费，多用在增多教员薪水，地方费则用以设备。（三）中央教育费之给与，有一定之标准。凡欲得中央补助费之地方，如于教员之资格，课程，与卫生之情形，皆须合乎规定之标准，而后始可得省库或国库之补助。相因而生的困难问题，即须根据何样标准以支配此项经费。从前的办法，是由什么地方来的经费，仍还以补助什么地方。结果贫的地方得的少，富的地方得的多。富的地方愈有钱办学，贫的地方愈无钱办学。或以地方的人口数，学校数，学龄儿童数为标准，以支配经费。试验结果，即觉有不妥的地方。最后乃根据每日学生平均出席数目以支配经费。再后又以地方实地的需要，为支配全局教育费之标准。贫的区域地方款少，得补助费多。富的区域地方款多，得补助费少。美国各州教育费，有百分之五十留存以作此用，为调剂贫富区域，使贫的地方教育，与富的地方教育，办的一样好。近今美国国会通过一案，以一百兆金元补助各省教育，以同化人民。使各州教育费无不足之患。这个问题，在现今的中国，尚不易发生。必有普及的教育税，才有这问题发生。中国若想振兴教育，非有普及的教育税不可，这是第一需要之点。

第二需要之点，即办学监督之权，应当多给地方。即渐减中央的权，分给各省，将来省再分给县，县再分给区，由上贯下，不久定有好效果发生。山西地方，村长村副，有办学之权，于是小学校竟达到三万五千之多，大有普及之势。法国制度，中央集权，凡拉丁民族，其制度多半如此。中央有教育局，地方人民有权不多。惟法国的情势与其他拉丁共和国的情势，比中国与美国，皆有不同。地面小，人口少，集权甚易。若夫中国与美国，地大物博，集权便有运用不灵之弊。这是分权第一个好处。第二地方分权，能使课程适应本地社会之需要。如本地工业发达，教材便可注重工业材料，农业发达，便可注重农业材料。又地方入籍的外国人多，便可注重同化外人的教育材料。第三地方管理教育，能把教育推广，使教育不止普及青少年人，且及于一般的社会，使一般成人，皆得有进步的机会。以农业试验场为例，如中国的山西。其农业试验场，专有人管理与乡村农民联络，与农人以紧要的农业上的知识。美国的办法，比中国更切实，更有效。各州除农业学校外，复有专人司以种种农业知识授给农人。又各州的乡村，复设有女子巡行教员，专管到各家庭内教授主妇怎样调制牛奶，怎样烹饪食物，与夫怎样讲求卫生等等家事。复有专设保姆于乡村的，担任指导卫生与育儿之事。凡此皆为使教育普及一般社会，切合地方需要。在爱欧瓦州（Iowa）有保姆教儿童选子择种等事。如养鸡仔一事，教儿童使知何种鸡产卵多，何种鸡产卵少；能产卵多的鸡，则留下喂养，不能的则杀而食之。

以上是讲民治主义教育的管理，现在讲施行民治教育的方法。民治的潮流，对于教育的方法有两个影响，第一学生学习的时候，须学生亲身参与学习的手续，即不要教师一人活动，要学生人人参加活动。无论何种知识技能，要学生自动的受领，不要被动的受领。因为若不使学生自动的参加活动教授不会有效。第二是心理上的影响，即参加活动，是人心理上的天然要求。凡事亲身实行后，才会得到真正的知识技能，这是近今发现的心理原则。中国的教育方法，须大大的改良。拿欧美两处教学法与中国比，在欧洲如德国，其中学以前的教学法，是教员上堂之后，完全讲授；次日上堂，教员则就前日所讲授的发为种种问题，使学生回答，务令学生完完全全的了解。美国则不然，由教师给学生以材料与书籍，使学生就题目自己预备，次日上堂教师则问以所得的是什么东西。日本人的教育方法，是取法德国。中国复又取法日本。但据我所知，现在欧洲与日本的教学法，已有许多改良之处。而中国还是墨守旧法。最不合理的，是欧洲的教学法本分为两部：第一日完全讲授，第二日则彻底发问与批评。中国间接采取欧洲之方法，只取其前半，而丢其后半，完全把教材由儿童的耳朵输进去。能否由儿童的口，或别的活动中返回来，则不复过问。日本的教学方法，我八年前考察一次，到近来我没有考察。但过日本时与其教育者谈话，知其教学方法一项，虽未完全脱离旧法，已大改良了。所以中国的教学方法，要大大的改良。

教法改良，则学生学习才有兴味，精神有地容纳，自可免逸出轨外。改良的关键就是令学生参加活动。例如教授国语，应令学生常常的听，常常的说，而后才可练习纯熟，变为日用的语言，中国的国语，才会有统一的一日。又如教授科学，目的并不在学习一些教科书，在得到实用的艺能。欲得实用的艺能，必令学 生亲身参加实际的活动，如学电，于电线如何结接，电流如何传导，皆非令学生亲手试验作去不成。又如学驾驶汽车，不止要学知其理，还要坏了时候知道如何修理。科学的功用，不只是知，顶要紧的是行，是学得一种力量去驾驶天然力以为人用。中国现在的科学教授法，乃是令学生学书学国文，哪够的上科学的教授。

再者学校对于学生，往往取许多天资不同的儿童合一炉而治之，不知个人有个人的特性。宜于甲的教育，不必合于乙。民治主义的教育，要在机会公平，使无论何人皆得顺其天然能力发展。换言之，个性差异，教育便不能不随之差异。即所谓适应个性的教育。施行之法，（一）设立多种学校。（二）一校之内，设立多科。采并行科（Parallel Course）或选科（Elective Course）制。总之个人需要，应当重视。我们试取多人考验之，便可得一个钟形的智慧曲线。由下愚以至上智，以渐高，以渐低，两端相差甚远。上智应得上智的教育，下愚应得下愚的教育，不能勉强纳于一处。又如人身体高低，很高与很低者为数皆不多，以不高不低者占多数。也适成为一钟形曲线。倘合高材与低能于一地教育之。如同使跑快慢不同的人合为三足赛跑，跑快的人有慢者累赘，不能尽量前跑，跑慢的人有跑快者向前拖曳，其苦非可言状，终归非二人皆倒，俱无成功不可。现在中国的学制，定为国民四年，高小三年，只可为中材生的教育。共合七年的学科，若以高材生学习，三四年可了。若以低能生学之，非八九年或十一二年不能了。所以学校的编级与支配功课，不能按之年龄办理。人之年岁，有年龄（Chronological age）、智龄（Intellectual age）

与体龄（Physical age）之别。编级支配功课，应完全以智龄为准。所以我对教员有两种疑问：（一）我问你的班里有多少人及格、有多少人不及格？答的人每说都及格或都不及格。从钟形曲线上说，可知道他所施的教育必有毛病，绝不会那样一律。因为功课适合于中等生的，高等生必超过之，低等生必赶不及。这是一定的道理。（二）你看出你班里的学生，是大者聪明，还是小者聪明？据现在用科学方法的考察，知小者往往比大者聪明。因为小者，其智龄高出于年龄，是天生聪明的。大者的年龄高出于智龄，是天生愚笨的。学校对于天才与下愚的儿童，应为备特种班次。教育制度中，更应为是种儿童设特种学校，使天才与下愚，各得受其应受的教育。美国现在对于低能生，已设有特种学级容纳之。惟对于天才生尚没有相当的方法。欧洲各国从来国体多为君主，素重视人材教育。所以凡天才优越的学生，莫不受特种教育。共和国家，重在国民教育，所以特重中材。其实领袖教育也极要紧。民治主义的精义，即在一切人无论上智下愚，皆要得充分发展的机会。

今天我这个题目太大，只能取其中一二要点说出现在我归结我的话，第一应令学生参加学习活动，使理想成为行为。第二要设法使各个人皆受适当的教育。天才与下愚，各得充分的机会发展。第三要有一定教育旨趣，使学生活动到社会活动，有密切的联络。令学生的动作有目标，有效果，则学生学得所用。这项在教育方法上最为紧要。以上之事是顶要紧的，这不过是片断的研究，于民治主义的精义，未能完全发挥。故我极愿与中国教育者接洽，并考查中国学校之情形，以便更有切实的研究。今日深谢大家的盛意。

# 一八六二年之白宫厨房*



近来在旧书摊上，买了一本书，叫做*Heart Throbs*感动人心的小品文。这是国民杂志的征文选集，从五万人的投稿中选出的四百零四篇散文、诗歌，反映着二十世纪初年美国人心爱的文章。我看到《一八六二年之白宫[①]厨房》，心里也受了一些感动。这是林肯先生初任总统时白宫前之一幕，幕中人之苦孩子是和中国的苦孩子有点相同。我在一个睡不着觉的深夜里把它翻译好了。倘使读者之中能出几个乃至无数个大德少爷，我便喜出望外了。

大德少爷（Master Tad）把街上的穷苦龌龊饥饿的流浪儿带进白宫（White House），向厨房里来要饭吃。管事先生和大司务都责备他，最后彼得说必须报告林肯夫人知道。

大德大不高兴，自己跑上楼去看母亲。母亲不在，就到处去找他的事忙的父亲。

同时，他要所救济的小孩子等候在下门口，彼得绝对不让他们进门。

怒气冲冲的大德看见父亲低着头，眼睛望着地，同西瓦尔德（Mr. Sewald）先生谈得起劲，正从草地上走过，往国

* 本篇原载1942年3月《战时教育》第6卷第10、11、12合期，作者文末尾注1941年10月19日译自Heart Throbs。

务院去。他立时放声喊叫："父亲！父亲！我不能把那些又冻又饿的苦小孩，在我认为需要的无论什么时候，带到家里来吗？这不是我们的厨房吗？"

这时他的父亲停住了，听取这直爽的请愿。大德拉着父亲的手。

"你说，我不能给他们一顿好饭吃吗？他们饿得像熊一样，而且有两个是兵士的孩子！父亲，如果彼得不把昨晚剩下的鸡、肉、饼和一切的东西弄出来给他们吃，我就要立刻把他们辞退。你说，我不可以这样干吗？父亲，这不是我们的厨房吗？"

西瓦尔德国务卿笑得不止，林肯先生回头向他一望。"西瓦尔德，请你指教。这事要借重外交方法。"

西瓦尔德先生拍拍大德的肩膀说，他必须留神不要把政府弄亏空了。总统把大德的棕色小手拿在他的大手里，笑着吩咐他跑回家去招待小客人吃饭。"你告诉彼得，你是服从圣经把瞎子和残废人带进来，他也必须做一个比现在更好的基督教徒。"

不到一个钟头，西瓦尔德说，当他们经过草地去赴国务会议的时候，至少有十个小孩子和大德坐在下层阶台上剥硬壳果子吃。享受他们的盛宴。

林肯说："这厨房是我们的。"

## 注释

① 白宫　美国总统的官邸，是一座白色二层楼房。通常作为美国政府之代称。

# 手*

从多方面看来，代表触觉之手，在各种感觉器官中，要算最奇妙的了。别的感觉的器官是被动的，唯独触觉的器官是处在主动的地位。眼睛、耳朵、鼻子都是门户开放：光、声、香随便进来。我们不得不看，不得不听，不得不嗅，但是手对于所触的东西，会加以选择的，高兴触则触它。

凡是它所憎恶的东西，它会把它们推开；它所喜欢的东西，它才招之而来。不像那眼睛，必须瞪着恐怖的景象而不能移动；也不像那耳朵，必须倾听邪的杂声而不能逃避；也不像那鼻子，在可恶的气味中而不能自卫。

不但如此，手不仅无顾自的需要，而且当别的感觉器官失了效能的时候，会代替它们负起责任来。瞎子过街，手是成了眼睛，陪着他，并且平平安安的引导他摸黑路。手代他看朋友的面貌，使他知道朋友们以和颜悦色活着。手代他读书，并用它的默读使他的漫漫长夜活泼的过去。

它甘心情愿为聋子服务，当舌头不能说话，耳朵失效，手指可以流利的对眼睛谈心，并且可以代替耳官效劳，听人讲话。

而且别的感觉的器官即使是尽善尽美了，也要感谢手的帮忙，使它们的力量发扬光大。手依照眼睛的模型，为眼睛造成一

* 本篇原载1945年1月《民主教育》第3期。

架千里镜，使它可以观察星象；再依据一个稍微不同的计划，为眼睛造成一架显微镜，把它介绍到另一奇异的新世界里去。

手也为耳朵造乐器放大器，使它受这些器具的教育，使它听他们所发的声音，直到它的能力训练成功。手为鼻子采它所想嗅的香花，并且为他蒸馏它所爱用的香水。至于谈到舌头，假使没有手的帮忙，它那五味之王也只退位了。总之，触觉器官是它的姊妹器官之公仆，并不是玩弄字眼，它简直是它们大家的助手。

如果手是这样的慷慨的为我们的身体服务，他同样而毫不减少的对于我们的天才与聪明、勇敢与爱情、意志与权力尽了力，使它们发挥出去。

放一把剑在手里，他会为人战斗；放一把犁在手里，它会为人耕地；放一架琴在手里，它会为人弹；放一支铅笔在手里，它会为人画画；放一支钢笔在手里，它会为人说话，为人申诉，为人祈祷。

它有什么不愿做？它有什么不曾做？一部蒸汽机，不过是一只更大的手，是人的小手做成来扩大它的权力。电报不过是为那小手用以写字造成的长笔。我们用来这样有效的屠杀兄弟们的大炮和武器，不过是该因的手段放大、加强、流血更多而已。

而且，什么是一条船、一条铁路、一座灯塔，或者一座皇宫，的确，什么是整个的都市，整个大陆的都市，全地球所有的都市，还不止，乃至地球本身，只是人改变了它的地方，那人类便像一个巨人，所以也有执行它的意志的那只巨手的功绩。

当我想到人的手所做的一切，从夏娃伸出她的做错事的手去摘那禁吃的水果之日，一直到救世主的戳穿的手被钉在预言可耻之树上的黑暗之时，并想到人的手以后所做的一切好事、坏事，我拿起我的手望望，不禁令人惊讶：这是行善如何好的工具呀！又是作恶如何坏的工具呀！整天的永不止息。

没有一个工具非手所运用，而且在工作的时候，绝对不会连一个工具也没有。我们把“手艺人”或手工人这个名词用于较为劳苦之行业，这个限制是不智的：这名词是属于一切忠诚实干的男人女人，而且是每一个人所应求得的封号。

为皇后之手有王杖，为士兵之手有剑，为木匠之手有锯，为铁匠之手有锤，为农夫之手有犁，为矿工之手有铲，船人之手有桨，为画家之手有画笔，为雕塑家之手有凿，为诗人之手有钢笔，为妇人之手有针。

如果没有一样工具适合我们用，那么犯人的锁链会套上大腕，而镣铐会加上我们手上了。凡是愿意做工的人，不论男女，都有一种工具可以学会，人生有一条共同的使命：

“无论你的手找到什么工作，你得尽力去做。”

# 学习怎样运用自由 *

阿里奥斯多说及一个好听的故事：一个仙人，依着她的奇妙的本性所规定，在一定的气候来到时，她会被处罚而变成一条可恶的毒蛇。在她变形的时候，如果有人伤害她，那个人便永远不能享受她所给的幸福。但是如果有人不嫌她的丑恶，怜悯她、保护她，那么，等到她现出美丽天仙的原形的时候，那个人会得到她的保佑：有求必应，经营必富，恋爱必乐，战斗必胜。

这样的仙人便是自由神。有时她好比是一条可恶的爬虫，匍匐而行，丝丝作响，遇着阻碍她的人便咬。有人讨厌她而想冒险去打死她，就该倒霉。有人看见她的卑贱可怕而敢于迎接她，就算有福，到后来，在她美丽而光荣之时节，终究会得到赏赐。

新获自由，难免有流弊，医治之道，只有一样药，这药还是自由。当一个犯人初出监牢，他受不起白天之光芒。他不能辨别颜色，不能认识面目。办法不是把他送回监牢，而是令他惯看阳光。

久经奴役之民族，势成半盲，忽见真理与自由难免眩迷。但

* 陶行知在本篇译著文前，对英文原文作者马可里作简介如下：
马可里（Thomas Babington Macaulay）生于1800年，死于1859年，是英国的散文家、演说家和史学家。他所著之英国史是一部大的著作。这篇短文虽是在一百年前写的，但对于现代中国的读者还有一些益处，特别是对于相信民主而不知如何下手，以致成为等待主义者尤其要看最后三段。
原载1945年10月6日《民主·星期刊》第2期。

只须让他们面对着看看，不久就惯了。几年之中，他们学会讲理。舆论之。极端的沸腾趋于平息。敌对的理论互相纠正。真理之碎片终止冲突，而开始合为一体。最后公道与秩序之系统乃从纷乱中出现。

当代的政客，自以为是的说：人民若不会使用自由就不应让他们自由。这句格言只是为传说中的一愚人说法，他立志若不学会游泳决不下水。如果有人要想在奴隶的生活中学得尽善尽美，等待着自由之来到，那真正只好让他们永远的等待吧。

# 林肯凯梯司堡演词

八十七年前，我们的祖先在这大陆上，产生了一个新民族，怀胎在“自由”里而献身于“万民平等”之主张。现在我们参加在一个大规模的内战里面，要试验这民族，或这样怀胎，这样献身的任何民族是否能够长存。在这战争之大战场上我们接触了，我们到这里来，对于那些为争取民族生存而牺牲生命的战士，要奉献战场一部分之地，作他们安息之所。这样干是完全适宜的，我们应该这样干。但从更广大的意义看，我们不能再奉献地，不能再使它更神圣，不能使它更光荣。在这里奋斗的勇士，活着的和已死的，已经把它化为神圣之地，超出我们薄弱的力量，企图有所增减。我们在这里所说的话，世人对之，将很少留意，也不会记得很久，但是对于他们所立的功绩，将永远不会忘掉。在此地战死之烈士已创立了高贵之基业，我们活着的人的本分，倒是要把我们自己奉献于他们未完成之工作。在这里的我们的本分倒是要把自己献于留在我们面前的伟大的工作——光荣的烈士曾为共同主张尽了全忠。让我们从烈士们的榜样中，取得继长增高的力量，以尽忠于同一的主张——让我们在这里立下最高的决心使烈士之死不是白白的牺牲——让这个民族，在上帝爱护之下，得着自由之新生——让这人民所有，人民所治，人民所享之政治不会从地面上消失掉。

## 注释

① 林肯（Abraham Lincoln，1809—1865） 美国第十六任总统。

凯梯司堡，亦译葛梯斯堡，在美国宾夕法尼亚州南部阿勒格尼山东麓。1863年7月1日至3日，此地曾发生美国南北战争中著名的“凯梯司堡战役”。